David Ragan

a native of Jackson, Tennessee, and for several years a resident of Hollywood, began writing about screen personalities for national periodicals while still in his teens. Working exclusively in the show-business field, he started his career in magazine publishing as managing editor of *Tele-Views*, a Los Angeles–based television monthly. Later in New York, he was editorial director of entertainment magazines both at Macfadden and Warner Communications, where he also created and served as publisher of *Movie Digest* and *Words and Music*. In addition to editing and writing for magazines, he is the author of numerous books about film personnel. Among them are *Who's Who in Hollywood 1900–1976*, a critically acclaimed one-volume encyclopedia on motion picture actors and actresses, and a recent biography of actor Mel Gibson. He lives in New York City with his wife, Claire, and children, David Nathaniel, Sarah, and Jennifer.

DAVID
RAGAN

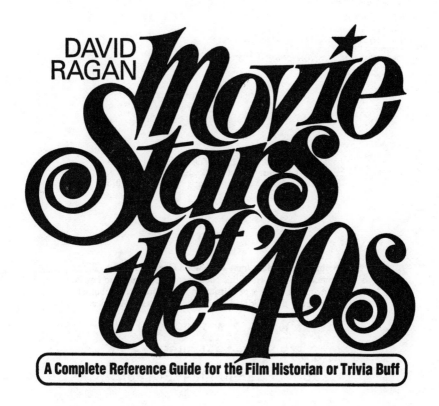

Movie Stars of the '40s

A Complete Reference Guide for the Film Historian or Trivia Buff

A SPECTRUM BOOK

Prentice-Hall, Inc., Englewood Cliffs, New Jersey 07632

Library of Congress Cataloging in Publication Data

Ragan, David.
  Movie stars of the '40s.

  "A Spectrum Book."
  Includes index.
  1. Moving-picture actors and actresses—Biography—
Dictionaries.   I. Title.
PN1998.A2R293 1985   791.43′028′0922   85-6260
ISBN 0-13-604992-3
ISBN 0-13-604984-2 (pbk.)

This book is available at a special discount when ordered in
bulk quantities. Contact Prentice-Hall, Inc., General
Publishing Division, Special Sales, Englewood Cliffs, N.J. 07632.

10   9   8   7   6   5   4   3   2   1

ISBN 0-13-604992-3

ISBN 0-13-604984-2 {PBK.}

Editorial/production supervision
and book design by Eric Newman
Cover design by Hal Siegel
Cover illustration by Debi Hoeffner
Manufacturing buyer: Carol Bystrom

Prentice-Hall International (UK) Limited, *London*
Prentice-Hall of Australia Pty. Limited, *Sydney*
Prentice-Hall Canada Inc., *Toronto*
Prentice-Hall Hispanoamericana, S.A., *Mexico*
Prentice-Hall of India Private Limited, *New Delhi*
Prentice-Hall of Japan, Inc., *Tokyo*
Prentice-Hall of Southeast Asia Pte. Ltd., *Singapore*
Whitehall Books Limited, *Wellington, New Zealand*
Editora Prentice-Hall do Brasil Ltda., *Rio de Janeiro*

This is for
Fredda Dudley Balling

PREFACE

Hollywood's "Golden Age," beginning in the late '30s, flowered and flourished in the '40s as one fondly recalled film followed another in the nation's movie houses, adding up, finally, to a cornucopia of classics.

No decade before or since produced such an array of cinematic riches. Every moviegoer has his or her own favorites of the time. But no list of highlights of the decade would be complete without *Rebecca, How Green Was My Valley, Kings Row, Going My Way, Mrs. Miniver, Laura, National Velvet, Gaslight, Anchors Aweigh, Now, Voyager, State Fair, Notorious, The Lost Weekend, Kiss of Death, The Postman Always Rings Twice, The Yearling, Johnny Belinda, Gentleman's Agreement, The Jolson Story, Intruder in the Dust, Red River*. The list seems endless.

Players, one or several, from each of the movies mentioned above (and many more) are to be found within these pages. In fact, it would be difficult to name any picture of importance released between 1940 and 1949 that is not represented here, either by its stars or principal character actors. Included, too, are many players who worked mainly in B's, Westerns, or serials.

Casablanca, a greatly treasured landmark film of the '40s, offers an example of how performers were selected to appear in the volume. Included herein are profiles of the film's stars, Humphrey Bogart, Ingrid Bergman, and Paul Henreid, as they each reached a personal peak of popularity in the 1940s. Also to found here, since they are most closely identified with this particular Hollywood era, are various supporting players who lent distinction to *Casablanca:* Conrad Veidt, S. Z. Sakall, Leonid Kinskey, Helmut Dantine, and Sydney Greenstreet. Claude Rains and Peter Lorre, on the other hand, both appear in *Movie Stars of the '30s,* as that was the decade in which they first firmly established their reputations in Hollywood, even though they, too, only added to their laurels in the '40s.

In choosing the players to appear in this volume, or some other in the series, the decision has rested on the answers to a three-pronged question: When were they first famous, most active, and/or most popular?

I can only hope that the selections made will be pleasing to most readers.

MOVIE STARS
OF THE '40s

Abbott & Costello

Bud Abbott (b. William Alexander Abbott, Oct. 2, 1895, Asbury Park, N.J.; d. April 24, 1974) and **Lou Costello** (b. Louis Francis Cristillo, March 6, 1906, Paterson, N.J.; d. March 3, 1959) "Who's on First?" was the most famous routine of Universal's great comedy team, and in 1942 they were #1 of the Box-Office Top Ten; also ranked high on that golden roster in '41, '43, '44, and '48 through '51; had long been partners when, in 1940, they made their first movie, *One Night in the Tropics,* as comic support to stars Allan Jones and Nancy Kelly; stealing the picture, they starred in their second, *Buck Privates,* a huge success; in the 36 hits that followed, their laugh-getting pattern seldom varied—they'd always get into trouble and then just barely get out, with thin, sharp-featured wise guy Abbott playing it straight and roly-poly, squeaky-voiced Costello taking the falls; traveled quite different routes before teaming up; Abbott was born in a Barnum & Bailey Circus tent, his father being an advance man and his mother a bareback rider; quit school at 15 and, after trying sign painting, became a box-office cashier in a Brooklyn burlesque theater, a post he held for 13 years; eventually operated six burlesque houses of his own; high-school graduate Costello, a whiz at basketball, was New Jersey's foul-shot champion for three consecutive years; was the son of an Irish mother and an Italian immigrant father who became a successful

1

life insurance salesman; stagestruck, he clerked for a while in a hat store, then, at 20, hitchhiked to Hollywood, arriving with 65¢ in his jeans; for two years at MGM he worked as an extra and stunt man; in his final stunt he doubled for Dolores Del Rio in *The Trail of '98*, taking a dive from a two-story Klondike gambling joint—which landed him in a hospital; recovered, he went back East and became a burlesque comic at Minsky's with straight man Joe Lyons; met and teamed up with Abbott at Chicago's Oriental Theater in '36; next came vaudeville, radio (Kate Smith's show, on which they became regulars), Broadway (*Streets of Paris*), and Hollywood; their partnership was often stormy—Abbott had an argumentative streak, Costello was stubborn, and each resented being mistaken for the other; off screen, one would try to top the other: Abbott bought a house, Costello got a larger one; Abbott built a swimming pool, Costello had one installed exactly one foot longer and one foot wider; suddenly wealthy, they lived like rajahs (Abbott's 17-room mansion, for example, had a ten-car garage filled with Cadillacs); after they broke up the act in '57, Costello sued Abbott for almost a quarter-million that he claimed was owed him from their TV series; Costello died (in financial trouble) before the suit was settled; upon retirement, Abbott thought he was fixed for life, but the IRS wiped him out with a bill for $750,000 in back taxes; in his last years, he and his wife were getting by, mainly, on joint Social Security checks of about $180 a month.

MOVIE HIGHLIGHTS: *In the Navy, Hold That Ghost, Keep 'em Flying, Rio Rita, Pardon My Sarong, It Ain't Hay, Who Done It?, Lost in a Harem, Hit the Ice, In Society, The Naughty '90s, Abbott and Costello in Hollywood, Rookies Come Home, Mexican Hayride, The Noose Hangs High, Africa Screams, Abbott and Costello Meet the Invisible Man, Lost in Alaska.*

Brian Aherne

(b. William Brian de Lacy Aherne, May 2, 1902, Norton, Worcestershire, England) Handsome blond leading man, with moustache and abundant charm, who published his autobiography, *A Proper Job*, in '69 and humorously explained its title this way: "I have never advertised in trade papers, as many actors do. But if I did, I suppose my ad would read: '(William) Brian de Lacy Aherne, professionally known as Brian Aherne, having signally failed to find a proper job in life, is still available in show business. Not arrogant or difficult any more. Has wardrobe. Will travel' "; "a proper job," though, he has always done on screen, as could be attested to by his famous leading ladies

(Hepburn, Colbert, Davis et al.) and by his nomination for the Best Supporting Oscar for *Juarez*; the son of a prosperous architect, he was trained for the stage as a child, making his debut at 9 at London's Garrick Theater; growing up to be a matinee idol, dashing and polished, he fulfilled his youthful dream "to know great men and beautiful women, to experience a grand passion, to walk on top of the world and experience it all"; made his screen debut in *The Squire of Long Hadley*, a British silent, and "hated the work," noting, "Makeup in those days was sticks of #5 Leichner greasepaint and heavy lipstick, which we applied so thickly that we looked like clowns and could scarcely move a muscle of our faces"; Broadway audiences saw him first in '27 in *The Silver Cord*, but it was being Katharine Cornell's leading man in *The Barretts of Wimpole Street* in '31 that made Hollywood snap him up; began opposite Dietrich in *The Song of Songs*; far better opportunities awaited him in the '40s when, with easy assurance, he alternated between serious films like *My Son, My Son* and wacky comedies such as *My Sister Eileen*; first wife Joan Fontaine (1939–43) was not entirely kind to him in her autobiography, *No Bed of Roses*; married to Eleanor Labrot since '46, he now lives in a chateau in Vevey, Switzerland.

MOVIE HIGHLIGHTS: *Strange Interlude, The Fountain, What Every Woman Knows, Beloved Enemy, Sylvia Scarlet, Vigil in the Night, The Lady in Question, Smilin' Through, Hired Wife, Skylark, A Night to Remember, What a Woman!, Forever and a Day, First Comes Courage, The Locket, Green Dolphin Street, Titanic, The Swan.*

Louise Allbritton

(b. Beulah Louise Allbritton, July 3, 1920, Oklahoma City, Okla.; d. Feb. 16, 1979) Brilliant at screwball comedy, this beautiful, sophisticated blonde gave promise of becoming the "new" Lombard; after '46, though, when she married CBS foreign correspondent Charles Collingwood, career took a backseat to her private life; grew up—and grew tall (5'9")—on a 100,000-acre ranch near Wichita Falls, Texas, the transportation lines of which her father owned; began acting in high school, continued for two years at the University of Oklahoma, then spent four years training at the Pasadena Playhouse in California; once played the lead there in *Kiss the Boys Goodbye*, when the show's star became ill, with only two rehearsals; rejected numerous "starlet" contracts; finally felt she was ready for Hollywood after Playhouse director Gilmor Brown showcased her versatility by staging a series of plays just for her:

The Little Foxes, Dinner at Eight, The Merchant of Venice; accepting an offer from Universal, she surely would have been better served at a more prestigious lot; studio consistently gave her starring parts in Bs and second leads in big-budget films; brainy and voluble, she battled for better roles, with scant success ("We call Louise 'The Crocodile,' " a studio topper once said, "because she sheds such huge tears when she fails to get a part she wants"); recalls a friend: "Off the screen, she was wacky and totally delightful, strictly an all-or-nothing girl. When she bought clothes, she went mad. And when she lost her temper, which was often, it was with such force that bystanders would be shocked silent"; after her Hollywood years she starred on Broadway in *The Seven Year Itch* and on TV in "Stage Door," a short-lived series; financially well off, she and her husband, who did not have children, had residences in London, Manhattan, Fire Island, and Puerta Vallarta.

MOVIE HIGHLIGHTS: *Parachute Nurse, Who Done It?, It Comes Up Love, Fired Wife, Pittsburgh, Follow the Boys, Her Primitive Man, This Is the Life, San Diego, I Love You, Bowery to Broadway, That Night with You, The Men in Her Diary, Tangier, The Egg and I, Sitting Pretty, Walk a Crooked Mile, An Innocent Affair.*

June Allyson

(b. Ella Geisman, Oct. 7, 1917, Bronx, N.Y.) Perky in her Peter Pan collars, with her bouncy blonde pageboy hairdo, the petite, husky-voiced star smiled sunnily through glycerine tears in many World War II movies and made a lot of people happy, including MGM accountants and stockholders; studio publicists may be consigned to a collective hell for lies they peddled to fans back then; in '44, when she was wildly popular, they claimed she was 20; they said her real name was "Jan Allyson" and she was the daughter of "comfortable but far from wealthy" parents—"Arthur and Clare Allyson"—of posh Westchester County, N.Y.; the truth: she was born in near-poverty in the Bronx and her parents were Robert (janitor of the building in which she was born) and Clara Geisman; June was six months old when her father deserted the family; her mother then slaved in a print shop for $20 a week; of the "cold, dreary railroad flat" in which she grew up, the star later recalled that it had no bath and "we heated water on a coal stove and bathed in a washtub. We never had enough coal, so in the winter I used to go along Third Avenue collecting wood—boxes and crates from grocery and delicatessen stores"; determined to have a better life, she seized upon dancing as her escape route; memorized Ginger

Rogers' dance steps from movies, entered amateur nights, graduated to dancing in the chorus at the Copacabana and on Broadway (*Sing Out the News*), made her movie debut at 20 in a two-reel musical short (*Swing for Sale*), understudied star Betty Hutton on stage in *Panama Hattie*; a lead in 1941's *Best Foot Forward* took her to Hollywood, where she repeated the starmaking role in the movie; was wed to Dick Powell for almost 18 years, until his death in '63; they adopted a daughter, Pam, and had a son, Richard Keith (made her a grandmother when his son was born in '84); next was twice married to and divorced from barber Glenn Maxwell; married Dr. David Prince Ashrow in '76.

MOVIE HIGHLIGHTS: *Girl Crazy, Two Girls and a Sailor, Meet the People, Music for Millions, Her Highness and the Bellboy, The Sailor Takes a Wife, The Secret Heart, Two Sisters from Boston, Till the Clouds Roll By, High Barbaree, Good News, Words and Music, Little Women, The Stratton Story, The Glenn Miller Story, Executive Suite, Strategic Air Command, The Shrike, The McConnell Story, The Opposite Sex.*

The Andrews Sisters

Patti (b. Patricia Andrews, Feb. 16, 1920, Minneapolis, Minn., as were the others); **Maxene** (b. Maxene Andrews, Jan. 3, 1918); **La Verne** (b. La Verne Andrews, July 6, 1915; d. May 8, 1967) One hit song recorded in 1937, "Bei Mir Bist Du Schön" ("Means That You're Grand"), made the harmonizing trio famous; was the flip side of their second release under a Decca contract paying a flat $50 per record; stayed with Decca 16 years, recorded 400 songs, sold 75 million records (19 gold ones), and finally made a mint; their follow-up hits, "Hold Tight" and "Well, All Right," made them the darlings of the jitterbugs, and their rollicking "Beer Barrel Polka" catapulted them into movies, where they boogie-woogied for Universal through all the war years; first flick: *Argentine Nights* ('40) with the zany Ritz Brothers; were the most successful singing group of the time, in all media; biggest disc hit of all: "Rum and Coca-Cola"; as devised at the start, their act had a set pattern: blonde fireball Patti (the only one who couldn't sing harmony) was in the middle, the "star," doing the intros, solos, cracking wise, and flanked by brunette Maxene and red-haired La Verne; the novelty was that, instead of standing rooted as other trios did, they moved—wildly; influenced by the Boswell Sisters on radio, these three, who were of Greek–Norwegian descent, began singing together as children; none of them could ever read music; got their show-biz start in a cross-country tour with Larry Rich's kiddie revue, making their professional debut with it in Atlanta; soon branched out on their own and found it rough going; auditioned for and were turned down by Paul Whiteman, Fred Waring, and Rudy Vallee; once their luck changed they sang with many big bands (the Dorseys, Gene Krupa, Harry James, etc.); a Hollywood reporter interviewing them in '40 found Patti "strictly a madcap," Maxene to have "good hard common sense," and La Verne to be "the balance wheel"; Maxene, their business manager, has also described herself as "the most ambitious" one; privately, they were not always in tune; Patti, after divorcing Marty Melcher (who next wed Doris Day), has been married since '51 to Wally Wechsler, once the group's pianist-conductor, who became her manager ("He was never fond of me or La Verne," Maxene has said); Maxene married the trio's manager, Lou Levy, in '41, had two children (Aleda and Peter), and divorced him in '50; La Verne was married from '48 on to Louis A. Rogers; personal problems eventually caused the sisters to be "at each others' throats most of the time" (in Patti's words); breaking up in '53, they reunited in '56 and worked together until La Verne died of cancer; in '74, Patti and Maxene teamed up to star in a hit Broadway musical, *Over Here*, amid rumors of a bitter backstage feud; years later, Patti was quoted by a New York reporter as saying: "Maxene and I will never get back together again"; said Maxene about the same time: "She's my kid sister and from the bottom of my heart I love her" but when "I tried to patch things up . . . she hung up on me."

MOVIE HIGHLIGHTS: *Buck Privates, Hold That Ghost, In the Navy, What's Cookin'?, Private Buckaroo, Give Out, Sisters, How's about It?, Always a Bridesmaid, Swingtime Johnny, Moonlight and Cactus, Hollywood Canteen, Her Lucky Night, Road to Rio.*

Dana Andrews

(b. Carver Dana Andrews, Jan. 1, 1912, Dont, Miss.) *Laura* ('44), of the dozens in which he's starred, remains the movie that fans most readily recall; his "lucky" film, in which he was the young detective haunted by the face of Gene Tierney, turned the tide, making him a ranking romantic lead; earlier, with Goldwyn and 20th Century–Fox sharing his contract, he said, "I'm a stepchild at both studios. At 20th I'm the guy who always loses the girl to Tyrone Power. At Goldwyn I'm the guy who loses the girl to everybody—even Danny Kaye"; the oddity is that he became an actor at all; was one of nine children (a younger brother being Steve Forrest, who followed him to the screen) of a Baptist minister who preached against movies as being "sinful"; grew up, as his father answered the call to various pulpits, in parish houses in Louisville, Ky., and all over Texas (Waelder, San Antonio, Uvalde, and, most lastingly, Huntsville); put himself through three years at Sam Houston College (got the acting bug there) and, after working as an oil company accountant, hitched a ride to Hollywood with $10 in his pocket to become either an opera singer or a movie actor; finding no takers for his unproven talents, he drove a school bus, dug ditches, pumped gas; also married a young California girl, Janet Murray, who died soon after the birth of a son, David (now also deceased); finally found a patron who backed him, paying his tuition and giving him a weekly salary, while studying at the Pasadena Playhouse in exchange for a percentage of his earnings as an actor; in '39 married Playhouse leading lady Mary Todd, by whom he has three children, Kathryn, Stephen, and Susan; making his movie debut in '40 in *Lucky Cisco Kid*, he soon got rich—but richer still in recent years in real estate after taking a course at UCLA night school.

MOVIE HIGHLIGHTS: *The Westerner, Kit Carson, Tobacco Road, Swamp Water, Ball of Fire, The Ox-Bow Incident, Crash Dive, The North Star, The Purple Heart, Up in Arms, Fallen Angel, A Walk in the Sun, State Fair, The Best Years of Our Lives, Canyon Passage, Boomerang, Daisy Kenyon, My Foolish Heart, The Iron Curtain, Elephant Walk, Strange Lady in Town, In Harm's Way, Battle of the Bulge, Airport '75.*

Eve Arden

(b. Eunice Quedens, April 30, 1912, Mill Valley, Calif.) It's not for nothing that she's been called the "queen of the caustic crack," for a drop of Arden acid has often been enough to save the most dismal of films; became a comedienne because she regarded herself as the "ugly duckling" daughter of a onetime stage actress (turned milliner when deserted by her husband) whose reputation was that of a great beauty; began on the stage in the early '30s with the Henry Duffy Players' summer stock troupe in San Francisco; with three other aspiring comics (the Bandbox Repertory Theater), she next played the "hotel lobby circuit" from Palm Springs to Santa Barbara; in a musical, *Lo and Behold*, at the Pasadena Playhouse, she attracted the attention of producer Lee Schubert, who featured her in comedy sketches on Broadway in the *Ziegfeld Follies* (both the '34 and '36 editions); her debut movie, *Oh, Doctor*

('37), with Edward Everett Horton, did little for her; her second, *Stage Door*, did everything (remember the live cat she wore for a fur?); her role as a theatrical hopeful was mainly written during shooting, and what started out as a minor role wound up as a major showcase for her droll, wisecracking talents; Broadway claimed her then for two more musical clicks (*Very Warm for May* and *Let's Face It*, the latter with Danny Kaye) before she returned to Hollywood to corner the market as the staunch, fast-talking best friend of every top femme star; one such role, with Joan Crawford in *Mildred Pierce*, rated her an Oscar nomination as Best Support; claims to have seen only "about six" of the 70-plus movies she's done; television made her a star in her own right in the long-running "Our Miss Brooks" (also a radio hit), which brought her an Emmy, and "The Mothers-in-Law"; first wed to agent Ned Bergen (1939–47), she was subsequently married to actor Brooks West, with whom she often appeared on stage, from '51 until his death in '84; four children: Liza, Connie, Duncan, and Douglas; being funny pays—is the owner of Polynesian Gardens (600 condominiums) in Plantation, Fla.

MOVIE HIGHLIGHTS: *Cocoanut Grove, A Letter of Introduction, At the Circus, No, No, Nanette, Comrade X, Whistling in the Dark, Ziegfeld Girl, Manpower, She Knew All the Answers, Hit Parade of 1943, Cover Girl, The Doughgirls, Night and Day, The Kid from Brooklyn, My Reputation, The Unfaithful, One Touch of Venus, Voice of the Turtle, Tea for Two, Goodbye My Fancy, The Dark at the Top of the Stairs, Grease.*

Edward Arnold

(b. Guenther Schneider, Feb. 18, 1890, New York, N.Y.; d. April 26, 1956) Character star of commanding size and voice who could be Machiavellian (political boss in *Mr. Smith Goes to Washington*), majestic (Daniel Webster in *The Devil and Daniel Webster*), or a man of mischief and mirth (highroller Jim Fiske in *Toast of New York*); first a stage leading man, he opted for character parts when 27 and had years of roles—small and large—on Broadway before becoming a hit in Hollywood, at 42, in *Rasputin and the Empress*; said then: "No one who works faithfully and hard, without tangible reward, should ever lose hope, for success does come to middle-age—and when it comes late, it's best"; *Diamond Jim* ('35), a great early triumph in which he played the flamboyant millionaire who drank splits of champagne for breakfast and wore Shepheards plaid suits and diamond rings on thick and lavish hands, was irony in the extreme; born on New York's Lower East Side, he was a child of the tenements and poverty; "I had no advantages, no education," he said. "I had to stop school in the sixth grade. My father was sent to an invalid home when I was eight and my mother died when I was ten. After that, I had to work for my living"; was a bellhop, a package deliverer for a butcher, an errand boy for a jeweler and, at 14, oiled engines in the basement of Columbia University; an appearance in a settlement house production of *The Merchant of Venice*, firing his ambition to act, led to stock experience and a career on stage; an early marriage, ending in divorce, left him with three children (Betty, Dorothy Jane, William) to rear alone until he married singer Olive Emerson in '29; divorced in '48, he was wed to Cleo McClain from '51 on; wealth did not ease his fear of poverty—in '38, when famous and earning thousands weekly, he lived in a house he rented for $100 a month.

MOVIE HIGHLIGHTS: *The White Sister, Three on a Match, I'm No Angel, Madame Spy, The President Vanishes, Cardinal Richelieu, Meet Nero Wolfe, Come and Get It, You Can't Take It with You, Idiot's Delight, Lillian Russell, Johnny Apollo, Meet John Doe, Nothing But the Truth, Johnny Eager, Design for Scandal, Kismet, Janie, Mrs. Parkington, Dear Ruth, The Hucksters, Command Decision, Take Me Out to the Ball Game, Annie Get Your Gun.*

Lauren Bacall

(b. Betty Jean Perske, Sept. 16, 1924, New York, N.Y.) Cucumber-cool, she looked slant-wise at Bogart through sea-green eyes and, in that trombone voice, growled: "You don't have to do anything. Not a thing. . . . Oh, maybe, just whistle"; the year was 1944, she was 20, the movie was *To Have and Have Not*, and a screen legend was in the making—but, it must be admitted, she never again had a role that quite equalled it; later blamed both herself and studio boss Jack Warner, who "convinced me very early that I was no good, worthless, rotten to the core. He was terrific at that. I learned one thing from him: to keep myself covered at all times"; director Howard Hawks discovered her in a fashion ad in *Harper's Bazaar*; intrigued by her looks, he asked a secretary to check out her background, but this woman misunderstood and, by mistake, brought her to Hollywood; upon her arrival, Hawks has said, she talked in a "little high nasal voice"; following his suggestion to get the bass tones that made her instantly famous, she drove to a quiet spot in the Hollywood hills "and proceeded to read *The Robe* aloud, keeping my voice lower and louder than normal"; her characteristic insolence-with-a-grin was also Hawks' creation, and he once admitted it was patented after Dietrich; screen surname came from her mother; after divorcing her husband, the mother took the name "Bacal," the Russian version of her German–Jewish maiden name, Weinstein; in both languages, it translates "wine glass"; falling in love with co-star Bogart, the actress was married to him in '45, bore him a son and daughter, Stephen and Leslie, and was widowed in '57; has said: "What I learned about acting, I learned from him. I learned from a master, and that, God knows, has stood me in very good stead"; following Bogart's death, she turned her attention to Broadway; becoming a major stage star in *Goodbye, Charlie*, she followed it with other smash hits, including the musical *Applause*; her marriage to Jason Robards in '61 ended in divorce in '69; one son: Sam Prideaux; published her autobiography, *Lauren Bacall by Myself*, in '79.

MOVIE HIGHLIGHTS: *Confidential Agent, The Big Sleep, Two Guys from Milwaukee, Dark Passage, Key Largo, Young Man with a Horn, Bright Leaf, How to Marry a Millionaire, Woman's World, The Cobweb, Written on the Wind, Designing Woman, Gift of Love, The Moving Target, Harper, Murder on the Orient Express, The Shootist, The Fan.*

Lucille Ball

(b. Lucille Desiree Ball, Aug. 6, 1911, Wyandotte, Mich.) In 1940, when still a blonde and a contract player there, RKO cast her in a minor musical, *Too Many Girls*, opposite a bongo-playing Cuban named Desi Arnaz; no one could have predicted that they would marry, have two children (Lucie Desiree and Desi IV), and one day not only co-star in the most acclaimed comedy series in television history ("I Love Lucy") but also buy the studio and rename it Desilu; the daughter of an electrical linesman for Anaconda Copper Co. who died when she was 4, she was brought up by her mother in Celoron, N.Y.; school pals still living there recall her as a "pacesetter" who "stood out like a diamond in a plain setting," was "movie-crazy—saw six pictures every week," and was "dying to get into show business from the time she was a kid"; headed for New York City at 19 when laid off from her first job—elevator operator at Lerner's dress shop in Jamestown; worked as a model at Hattie Carnegie's fashion salon and for commercial photographers; next danced in the chorus in Schubert musicals and then, personally chosen by Busby Berkeley, was taken to Hollywood in '33 to be one of 12 "Goldwyn Girls" in

Eddie Cantor's *Roman Scandals*; dance director LeRoy Prinz, who used her in later musicals, once recalled: "She was so skinny we had to put her in the back row of the chorus, although she had a lovely face"; did extra work and many bit roles before finally getting her name on the screen, at the bottom of the list, when playing a nurse in 1935's *Carnival*—her 15th film; at RKO from '35 to '42, she got her first lead, as comedian Joe Penner's wife, in 1938's *Go Chase Yourself*; signing her to a contract in '43, MGM gave her the glamour treatment, dyed her hair red, starred her in *Du Barry Was a Lady*, a Technicolor musical (her first such), and publicized her as the "new" Harlow; did not, of course, become that—only one of the great comediennes of all time, in movies, on Broadway *(Wildcat)*, radio, and TV; divorced Desi Arnaz in '60 and has been married to comedian Gary Morton since '61.

MOVIE HIGHLIGHTS: *Roberta, Follow the Fleet, Stage Door, Affairs of Annabel, Room Service, Five Came Back, Dance, Girl, Dance, The Big Street, Best Foot Forward, Without Love, Easy to Wed, Ziegfeld Follies, The Dark Corner, Lover Come Back, Lured, The Fuller Brush Man, Sorrowful Jones, Fancy Pants, The Long, Long Trailer, Forever Darling, The Facts of Life, Yours, Mine and Ours, Mame.*

Lynn Bari

(b. Marjorie Schuyler Bitzer, Dec. 18, 1915, Roanoke, Va.) Brunette star with a cello voice, great legs, and a dynamite style of acting who in the late '30s inherited Claire Trevor's mantle at 20th Century–Fox as "Queen of the Bs"; arrived in Hollywood in her teens from Boston, where she grew up, with her mother and brother; oddly, though she had never danced, she broke into movies as a showgirl in Crawford's *Dancing Lady* in '33; was a chorine in others *(Meet the Baron, Coming Out Party)* before she was signed in '34 to a contract at Fox, where she remained for 12 years; played small parts in many films, including *Pigskin Parade*, featuring a kid named Judy Garland who, years later, would cause her great distress; headed into the homestretch in '38, playing the romantic lead in *Mr. Moto's Gamble*; was termed at one time a young woman "of Dresden and steel," and both elements were in evidence in her screen performances as well as her private life; has been married and divorced three times; was first married in '38 to agent Walter Kane, on the spur of the moment between the main course and dessert at Hollywood's then chic Lamaze restaurant; had dashed out and found a judge—a traffic court judge—to perform the ceremony; in her words, it was "a very tempestuous marriage"; the day after divorcing him in '43, was married to test pilot Sid Luft; had a son, John, before they divorced in '50; Luft soon became Judy Garland's husband and the two of them sued and won custody of the boy—a court decision reversed later by another judge; was next married for 17 years (1955–72) to Dr. Nathan Rickles, a Beverly Hills psychiatrist, for whom, after essentially giving up her movie work, she acted as secretary and nurse; resumed her career then on the stage, touring in *The Gingerbread Lady*; one major critic, hailing her as "a terrific actress," added, "No one could question that after having seen her so dominate the stage, giving so much power, poignancy and biting comic emphasis to the role"; clearly, during her self-imposed absence from acting, nothing had changed.

MOVIE HIGHLIGHTS: *Elsa Maxwell's Hotel for Women, City of Chance, Return of the Cisco Kid, Lillian Russell, Free, Blonde and 21, Charter Pilot, Kit Carson, Sleepers West, Blood and Sand, The Perfect Snob, Sun Valley Serenade, The Magnificent Dope, The Falcon Takes Over, Secret Agent of Japan, Orchestra Wives, Hello, Frisco, Hello, The Bridge of San Luis Rey, Captain Eddie, Home Sweet Homicide, I'd Climb the Highest Mountain.*

Ethel Barrymore

(b. Ethel Mae Barrymore, Aug. 15, 1879, Philadelphia, Pa.; d. June 18, 1958) For many decades one of the stage "greats," with that steadfast gaze and magnificent voice, she starred in 15 silents (*The Nightingale, An American Widow*, etc., including *The Awakening of Helena Ritchie*, her personal favorite), between '14 and '19; made her talkie debut with brothers John and Lionel in 1932's *Rasputin and the Empress* and, unhappy with the result, did not return to the screen until '44; came into her glory then as an incomparable character star when she played Cary Grant's Cockney mother, and won a Best Supporting Oscar, in *None But the Lonely Heart*; snagged other Academy Award nominations for *The Spiral Staircase, The Paradine Case*, and *Pinky*; was 16 and studying music at the Covent of Notre Dame in Philadelphia when her grandmother, Louisa Lane, matriarch of the Barrymore clan and manager of a touring stock company, ordered her to report to Montreal to replace another actress as Julia in *The Rivals*; the die was cast; making her London stage debut in 1899, she was ardently wooed by such dashing young bluebloods of the time as the Earl of Ava, the Duke of Manchester, and Winston Churchill (who remained her lifelong friend); a star of the first magnitude after appearing on Broadway in 1901 in *Captain Jinks*, she was the rage of the era, widely imitated and heralded as the most beautiful woman in America; at 30, she was married (for the one and only time) to Russell Griswold Colt, son of the president of the United States Rubber Co.; had three children—Samuel, Ethel, and John—before divorcing Colt in '23; among her many great stage successes: *Alice Sit-by-the-Fire*, *Declasse*, *Mid-Channel*, *White Oaks*, *The Corn Is Green*, and *The Twelve-Pound Look*, which James M. Barrie wrote especially for her; perhaps the most surprising thing about her was her ardent interest in prizefighting—never missed a Joe Louis or Henry Armstrong fight, and her hobby was collecting boxing prints.

MOVIE HIGHLIGHTS: *The Farmer's Daughter, Moss Rose, Night Song, Portrait of Jennie, Moonrise, The Great Sinner, The Red Danube, That Midnight Kiss, Kind Lady, The Secret of Convict Lake, Just for You, Deadline U.S.A., It's a Big Country, The Story of Three Loves, Main Street to Broadway, Young at Heart, Johnny Trouble.*

Anne Baxter

(b. Anne Baxter, May 7, 1923, Michigan City, Ind.) Hers has been a riches-to-riches success story, for she was the daughter (only child) of a high-ranking executive of Seagram Distillers and, on her mother's side, the granddaughter of Frank Lloyd Wright, dean of American architects; growing up in the poshest of New York suburbs, she saw Helen Hayes in a play and decided at 10 to become an actress; while attending private schools, she studied at Theodora Irvine's School of the Theater and with Madame Maria Ouspenskaya; made her Broadway debut at 13 in *Seen but Not Heard*, following that up at 15 with *There's Always a Breeze* and *Madame Capet*; at 16 tested for the starring role in *Rebecca*, which Fontaine got; an exceptionally good test, it won her a contract at 20th Century–Fox; remained there for 13 years, winning a Best Supporting Oscar for *The Razor's Edge* and a Best Actress nomination as the insidious Eve Harrington in *All About Eve*; an oddity: In '71 she succeeded Lauren Bacall in *Applause*, the Broadway musical based on *All About Eve*, and found herself playing the Bette Davis role; also, in '83, when illness forced Davis to relinquish the lead in the TV series "Hotel," Baxter was called in to replace her; made her screen debut in '40, on loan-out to MGM, as the ingenue lead in Wallace Beery's *Twenty Mule Team*; when she graduated from Los Angeles High in '41, she had already played major roles in four films; met her first husband, late actor John Hodiak, when they co-starred in *Sunday Dinner for a Soldier*; married in '46, they had a daughter

(Katrina), then divorced in '53; between '60 and '68 was married to young millionaire Randolph Galt, by whom she has two daughters (Maginel and Melissa), and lived the first three of those years as the wife of an American sheep rancher in the Australian bush; published a best seller, *Intermission* ('76), about that experience; at 53 was married to David Klee, a Wall Street financier much older than she, who died before their first anniversary.

MOVIE HIGHLIGHTS: *The Great Profile, Charley's Aunt, Swamp Water, The Magnificent Ambersons, The Pied Piper, Five Graves to Cairo, Crash Dive, The North Star, The Sullivans, The Eve of St. Mark, Guest in the House, A Royal Scandal, Angel on My Shoulder, The Luck of the Irish, Yellow Sky, I Confess, Blue Gardenia, The Ten Commandments, Summer of the 17th Doll, The Late Liz.*

William Bendix

(b. William Bendix, Jan. 14, 1906, New York, N.Y.; d. Dec. 14, 1964) Paramount's all-purpose star, with a meat-grinder face, gravel in his voice, an accent strictly from Thoid Avenoo, and brute charm; could be lovable *(The Babe Ruth Story)* or loathsome (the white-suited hood in *The Dark Corner*), and many Alan Ladd movies *(The Blue Dahlia, Two Years Before the Mast, The Glass Key,* etc.) would have been less without him; the son of an Irish-musician father, who hoped he would be a violinist, this onetime bat boy for the New York Giants was more eager for a career in baseball; lasting only a few months as a rookie with this team in spring training in Texas, he then married his childhood sweetheart, Therese, in '28 and settled in Orange, N.J., where he worked as a grocery clerk; when the Depression wiped out that job, he dreamed up an imaginary theatrical background and was accepted as an actor by the New Jersey Federal Theater, a WPA project; two years' experience there gave him the courage to try Broadway where, after six succes-sive flops, he wound up in a hit—William Saroyan's *The Time of Your Life*, playing Krupp, the philosophical and gabby cop; the performance rated him a one-picture deal at MGM as the tavern keeper in a Tracy–Hepburn comedy, *Woman of the Year* ('42); overnight fame, and a Best Supporting Oscar nomi-nation, came later that year at Paramount (where he stayed a decade) with *Wake Island*, in which he played the heroic Aloysius "Smacksie" Randall from Brooklyn; was his fourth movie and the first of his several in military garb; fans may have wondered why he didn't actually serve in WWII, and he never explained—the fact is that he suffered from chronic asthma and, despite

14

repeated attempts to enlist, no service would take him; was greatly popular on radio and TV in "The Life of Riley."

MOVIE HIGHLIGHTS: *China, Guadalcanal Diary, The Crystal Ball, Hostages, The Hairy Ape, Lifeboat, Abroad with Two Yanks, Greenwich Village, A Bell for Adano, Sentimental Journey, Blaze of Noon, Calcutta, Variety Girl, Race Street, The Time of Your Life, A Connecticut Yankee in King Arthur's Court, Kill the Umpire, Detective Story, Battle Stations.*

Ingrid Bergman

(b. Ingrid Bergman, Aug. 29, 1915, Stockholm, Sweden; d. Aug. 29, 1982) Sweden's illustrious gift to Hollywood, she was the most idolized woman on Hollywood screens in the '40s and, arguably, the most versatile; for a fact, she never gave a similar performance in any two films; became the first star to win two Best Actress Oscars *(Gaslight, Anastasia)* and one as Best Support *(Murder on the Orient Express)*; in the '40s was also nominated as Best Actress for *For Whom the Bell Tolls, The Bells of St. Mary's*, and *Joan of Arc*—and there was yet another nomination for her final feature film, 1978's *Autumn Sonata*; for a while, of course, she was filmdom's most "notorious" femme, when she left her husband (Dr. Peter Lindstrom) and daughter (Pia) behind in Hollywood and went off to Italy to make *Stromboli* for director Roberto Rossellini, by whom she soon became pregnant out-of-wedlock; that international *cause célèbre* was to die a natural death six years later, after she married Rossellini, bore him three children (Robertino, Isabella, Isotta Ingrid), starred in several failed films for him in Europe, divorced him, and made a triumphant "comeback" in *Anastasia*; never again would she be among the Box-Office Top Ten, as she had been earlier (1946–48), but there would be many glorious performances to remind audiences of what they'd missed in the years she was *persona non grata*; David O. Selznick saw her in a Swedish film, *Intermezzo* (one of several in which she starred after making her debut in '34), and sent an emissary to Sweden to secure rights to the story and with orders to "not come home without a contract with Miss Bergman"; the "exciting beauty and fresh purity" perceived by this genius producer was amply in evidence in the '39 English-language remake of *Intermezzo*; these characteristics, coupled with an inner radiance and a gigantic talent, made her an immediate, much-loved star, and in time, an immortal one.

MOVIE HIGHLIGHTS: *Adam Had Four Sons, Rage in Heaven, Dr. Jekyll and Mr. Hyde, Casablanca, Spellbound, Saratoga Trunk, Notorious, Arch of*

Triumph, Under Capricorn, Europa, Elena et les Hommes, Indiscreet, Inn of the Sixth Happiness, Goodbye Again, The Visit, The Yellow Rolls-Royce, A Walk in the Spring Rain, Cactus Flower, A Matter of Time.

Turhan Bey

(b. Turhan Selahettin Schultavy, March 30, 1920, Vienna, Austria) At Universal during the war years he was the poor man's Valentino, figuring in the dreams of millions of young women who rained a deluge of fan mail on him; fit the "great lover" image well—having sideburns, a fine physique (6'2"), challenging slanted black eyes, and a smoothly accented voice of deep timbre; but poor he was not; was born an aristocrat and cradled in the lap of Continental luxury; his Turkish father was a diplomat with his country's embassy in Vienna, where the actor's mother, of a wealthy Czech family, was reared (at war's end, she learned that, while factories she owned in Czechoslovakia were destroyed, her theaters in Austria had continued to operate and deposit profits in the Bank of England); his earliest occupation was that of test driver of European racing cars; came to America, with a letter of introduction to movie director Arthur Lubin, with his mother (separated from her husband) and grandmother just before Hitler took over Austria; attended Ben Bard's Drama School in Hollywood, mainly to learn to speak English; won a Warners contract when in a play there, made his debut in '41 as a villain in Flynn's *Footsteps in the Dark*; studio changed his name to Bey, which, in Turkey, would be rather like calling Sir John Gielgud "John Gielgud Sir"; transferred to Universal and was soon starring in Technicolor sex-and-sand epics, sharing silken desert tents with equally exotic Maria Montez; shared off-screen love scenes with Susannah Foster, Rose Hobart, and Lana Turner (her ex, Steve Crane, brawled with him once over her affections—and lost); what few fans recall is that early on he played "heavies" in two Universal serials: *Junior G-Men of the Air* and *Adventures of Smilin' Jack*; in '44, at the height of his fame, made two interesting predictions about himself—first, that he would not marry, and then, that Hollywood wouldn't want him when the established stars returned from the war; both came true; returned to Vienna, where he owns a travel agency (Glamour Travel) and, reportedly, is now "a heavyset man, quite bald, and very rich."

MOVIE HIGHLIGHTS: *The Gay Falcon, Drums of the Congo, Arabian Nights, Danger in the Pacific, The Mummy's Tomb, White Savage, Dragon Seed, Bowery to Broadway, The Climax, Sudan, Ali Baba and the Forty*

Thieves, Frisco Sal, A Night in Paradise, Out of the Blue, Adventures of Casanova, Prisoners of the Casbah.

Vivian Blaine

(b. Vivian Stapleton, Nov. 21, 1921, Newark, N.J.) In long-ago Hollywood, glamour girls were given catchy nicknames, so 20th Century–Fox lost no time in dubbing its tuneful recruit from swing bands and nightclubs "The Cherry Blonde"; had always been blonde—the reddish tint came from the Fox dye pots; was groomed in small parts in comedies (*Girl Trouble* with Don Ameche, etc.) for two years before being starred in '44 (again with Ameche) in a Technicolor musical, *Greenwich Village*; got her break because both stars announced earlier for the role, Alice Faye and Betty Grable, became pregnant; went into show business reluctantly, she has said, and only at the behest of her CPA father, a "frustrated actor"; started with an agent, Manny Frank, whose first order was "go on a diet," which she did, dropping 50 pounds, trimming down to an even 100; was wed to Frank from '45 until they divorced in '56; was later divorced (in '61) from Universal Pictures exec Milton Rackmil after a two-year marriage; in '73 married a New York garment manufacturer–turned–theatrical manager, Stuart Clark; winding up her studio contract in '46, after five years, and leaving California, she said, "I wasn't happy in Hollywood; I was a kid and I really didn't want to be there. I had no training and no preparation for the whole thing; I was a star but not an actress"; admits that, professionally, the next few years were rough—took any kind of booking (TV variety shows, clubs, touring musicals); became part of Broadway history in '50 by scoring brilliantly as Adelaide in *Guys and Dolls*, finally repeating the role opposite Sinatra in the movie; many other Broadway musicals followed; tackling the stage, she invested all her movie earnings—a half-million—in a 150-unit apartment house in Manhattan, which she sold years later—for $7 million; in the autumn of '84, she welcomed an army of movie-TV-stage celebrity friends at the opening of an elegant New York supper club, Vivian Blaine's Park 10, of which she was a part-owner; before Christmas, though, she and her partners had a "difference of opinion," and she withdrew from the enterprise.

MOVIE HIGHLIGHTS: *It Happened in Flatbush, He Hired the Boss, Jitterbugs, Nob Hill, Something for the Boys, State Fair, If I'm Lucky, Doll Face, Come Back to Me, Three Little Girls in Blue, Skirts Ahoy!, Public Pigeon No. 1.*

Janet Blair

(b. Martha Janet Lafferty, April 23, 1921, Altoona, Pa.) For eight years (1941–48), Columbia comedies and musicals were better for having his vivacious, fresh-faced redhead in them; borrowed her professional surname from her father, Fred Blair Lafferty, and inherited her musical talents, which surfaced early, from her pianist-organist mother, Florence; at 16 went directly from singing in the choir in her hometown's Lutheran Church to being the soloist with the Hal Kemp band, getting the job through the influence of a family friend, Kemp's business manager; began in movies at 20, and at $70 a week, as a campus cutie in *Blondie Goes to College*; at the end of her contract was still one of the studio's lowest-salaried stars, earning a weekly wage of $750; became a star when cast in the title role in *My Sister Eileen* ('42) with Rosalind Russell; Russell later recalled that Janet "started out trying to upstage me. She was new and nervous . . . so I invited her into my dressing room and delivered a short speech about the inadvisability of the course she'd embarked on"; the older actress also gave her tips—which worked—on ways to make selfish sister Eileen a girl audiences would still find adorable; married musician Lou Busch in '43, divorced him in '50; began a new career that year on the musical stage, starring in the national company of *South Pacific* and playing Nellie Forbush in 1,673 consecutive performances; from '52 to '72, she had with theatrical director Nick Mayo what was regarded as one of Hollywood's happiest marriages; had her first child, Amanda, when almost 38, and a son, Andrew, two years later; with the children present, she and Mayo repeated their vows on their 11th anniversary, in the same small church in San Francisco and before the same minister; their breakup in '72 shocked many, including, the star has said, herself; longtime fans were equally astonished to see her (still beautiful) starring, in '69, in Disney's *The One and Only, Genuine, Original Family Band*, playing the mother of eight; in the early '70s co-starred with Henry Fonda in the TV series "The Smith Family."

MOVIE HIGHLIGHTS: *Three Girls About Town, Two Yanks in Trinidad, Something to Shout About, Once Upon a Time, Tonight and Every Night, Gallant Journey, Tars and Spars, The Fabulous Dorseys, The Black Arrow, I Love Trouble, The Fuller Brush Man, Boys' Night Out, Burn, Witch, Burn.*

Ann Blyth

(b. Ann Marie Blyth, Aug. 16, 1928, Mount Kisco, N.Y.) A tiny (5'2") porcelain doll with China-blue eyes and a mouthful of dazzling white teeth, she had, between '44 and '57, what essentially were three separate careers; first was a teen-ager bopping about in low-budget Universal musicals with Donald O'Connor and Peggy Ryan; next was in heavy dramas, one of them, *Mildred Pierce*, playing Joan Crawford's snobbish, amoral daughter Veda and winning a Best Supporting Oscar nomination; finally at MGM, her dark tresses dyed Technicolor red, she blazed forth as the radiant star of absolutely Grade-A musicals (*The Student Prince*, etc.); father deserted her Dublin-born mother when Ann and sister Dorothy were small; made her professional debut at 5, singing and reciting on "Madge Tucker's Children's Hour" on radio station WJZ in Manhattan; was kept busy as a dramatic actress on radio while attending St. Patrick's grammar school and, later, the Professional Children's School; also sang for three seasons with the San Carlo Opera Company; at 13 was playing Paul Lukas' daughter on Broadway in *Watch on the Rhine*; mother died shortly before Ann landed her movie contract at 15, leaving her to be reared by her Aunt Casey and Uncle Pat; suffered a broken back in a tobogganning accident when 17; though it was feared she'd never walk again, she staged a complete recovery, after spending eight months in a plaster cast and wearing a steel brace for another six; in '53, with Elizabeth Taylor, Joan Leslie, and Jane Withers as bridesmaids, the staunchly Catholic star was married, in an elaborate (600 invited guests) ceremony, to an obstetrician, Dr. James McNulty (brother of singer Dennis Day); five children: Timothy, Maureen, Kathleen, Terence, and Eileen; left the screen after starring in *The Helen Morgan Story*; continued to star in summer stock musicals (*The Sound of Music*, *Show Boat*, etc.); in '73 she and her husband were invested with the rank of Lady and Knight of the Holy Sepulchre by Cardinal Cooke at his residence in New York City.

MOVIE HIGHLIGHTS: *Chip off the Old Block, The Merry Monahans, Babes on Swing Street, Swell Guy, Brute Force, Killer McCoy, A Woman's Vengeance, Another Part of the Forest, Mr. Peabody and the Mermaid, Red Canyon, Top o' the Morning, Once More My Darling, The Great Caruso, Our Very Own, Thunder on the Hill, All the Brothers Were Valiant, Rose Marie, Kismet, The King's Thief, Slander, The Buster Keaton Story.*

Humphrey Bogart

(b. Humphrey De Forest Bogart, Dec. 25, 1899, New York, N.Y.; d. Jan. 14, 1957) Warners' irreplaceable tough-tender guy who played major roles for more than a decade before *High Sierra* (a George Raft reject) and *The Maltese Falcon* made him a ranking favorite in '41; was in the Box-Office Top Ten each year between '43 and '49 and again in '55; nominated for a Best Actor Oscar for *Casablanca* ('43) and *The Caine Mutiny* ('54), he snagged his Academy Award in '51 for *The African Queen*; the son of a wealthy New York City surgeon and famed magazine illustrator Maud Humphrey, he was educated at exclusive schools—Trinity and Andover, where he was expelled after two years (was caught dunking a young professor he disliked); spent two years in the Navy in WWI, worked briefly at the brokerage firm of S. W. Strauss & Co. on Wall Street, then went into the theater ("so I could sleep late"); was first an office boy and then a stage manager for William A. Brady before the producer gave him a small role—at 21—in *The Ruined Lady*; said critic Alexander Woollcott of one early Bogart performance: "The young man who embodies the sprig is what is usually and mercifully described as inadequate"; lifelong pattern of falling in love with and marrying actresses with whom he worked began early; was married to Helen Mencken (1926–28), with whom he appeared on stage in *Drifting*, Mary Phillips (1928–37), his stage leading lady in *Nerves*, Mayo Methot (1938–45), who acted with him in the movie *Marked Woman*, and Lauren Bacall (from '45 on), who was introduced in his *To Have and Have Not*; first on screen in Victor McLaglen's *The Devil with Women* ('30), he continued to alternate between movies and Broadway until he scored a major success as killer Duke Mantee on stage in *The Petrified Forest*; got the same part in the movie only because star Leslie Howard refused to appear in it unless Bogart also was signed; *The Harder They Fall* ('56), his 75th film, was his swan song; essence of his screen persona was well put by Raymond Chandler, who once said the star could "be tough *without* a gun; also he has a sense of humor that contains that grating undertone of contempt."

MOVIE HIGHLIGHTS: *Up the River, Three on a Match, China Clipper, Dead End, Kid Galahad, San Quentin, The Black Legion, Angels with Dirty Faces, The Roaring Twenties, Dark Victory, They Drive by Night, Across the Pacific, Action in the North Atlantic, Sahara, Passage to Marseille, Conflict, The Big Sleep, The Two Mrs. Carrolls, Dead Reckoning, Dark Passage, The Treasure of the Sierra Madre, Key Largo, In a Lonely Place, Chain Lightning, Beat the Devil, The Desperate Hours.*

Eddie Bracken

(b. Edward Vincent Bracken, Feb. 7, 1915, Astoria, N.Y.) Of all the comedies in which he starred at Paramount in the '40s, he recalls only two with any affection—*Hail the Conquering Hero* and *The Miracle of Morgan's Creek*, both of course, written and directed by the incomparable Preston Sturges; was typecast as the naïve schnook who always took no for an answer and as WWII's favorite 4-F; born to a father who was a foreman at the East River Gas Co. and a mother who was a saleswoman at Con Edison, he got his picture in the papers first by winning a Most Beautiful Baby contest; a boy singer in vaudeville, he began working in movies in the '20s in "The Kiddie Troupers," a series of comedy shorts on the order of "Our Gang," made in New York; attended the Professional Children's School and made his Broadway debut at 15, playing a Western Union messenger in *The Man on Stilts*; was in many other plays of the '30s—33 fast flops, he has said; finally achieved stardom as Henry Aldrich (with Van Johnson as his understudy) in *What a Life*; the young leading lady in this, Connie Nickerson, became his one and only wife in '39; married on a Monday because, he said, he wanted "to start the week right"; five children: Judith, Caroline, Michael, Susan, and David (and, at last count, seven grandchildren); the musical comedy *Two Many Girls*, in which he introduced "I Didn't Know What Time It Was," took him to Hollywood; repeated his role in the movie in '40 (and introduced Lucille Ball to his stage pal Desi Arnaz); began his seven-year stint at Paramount the following year; free-lanced awhile, then left the screen in '53 after *A Slight Case of Larceny*, preferring to work on the stage; has had many long-run hits, including *Hello, Dolly!*, which rated him a Tony nomination; in '82 was able to boast with pride of having achieved his 10,000th performance on the legitimate stage.

MOVIE HIGHLIGHTS: *Life with Henry, Reach for the Sun, Caught in the Draft, The Fleet's In, Sweater Girl, Star Spangled Rhythm, Happy Go Lucky, Rainbow Island, Bring on the Girls, Hold That Blonde, Ladies' Man, Out of This World, The Girl from Jones Beach, Summer Stock, Two Tickets to Broadway, About Face, We're Not Married.*

George Brent

(b. George Brent Nolan, March 15, 1904, Shannonbridge, Ireland; d. May 26, 1979) Bette Davis, whose leading man he often was, has gone on record as saying he was one of her great loves; most other femme stars at Warner Bros. (where he was a stalwart from '32 to '46) also liked sharing scenes with the big, handsome Irishman, for, while a strong, dependable presence, he lacked the fire to overpower any one of them; four wives also found him lacking as a husband and divorced him: Helen Campbell (1922–29), star Ruth Chatterton (1932–34), Australian actress Constance Worth (1937; eight weeks after marriage, he tried and failed to get a court-approved annulment; she won a divorce before the year's end), Ann Sheridan (1942–43; left him a few months after saying "I do," saying, "We didn't part friends"); was married from '47 until her death in '74 to model Janet Michaels; two children: Suzanne and Barry; what few fans knew: underneath that black dye, his hair, graying early, was as white as Santa's beard; only 7 when his newspaperman father died and 11 when his mother passed away, he and an older sister were sent to live with an aunt in New York; attended a prep school (Dwight) and the N.Y. High School of Commerce, quitting at 15; worked in a lumber camp and on a fruit farm in upstate New York to earn money for his voyage back home; joined the Abbey Theater while studying at the National University at Dublin; meeting the legendary Irish revolutionary Michael Collins, he volunteered, risking his life, to act as dispatch carrier between Collins and De Valera, another famous leader of the fighting Irish; when Collins was ambushed and killed in '22, he fled for his life to Belfast and then to Glasgow with the English intelligence service close on his heels; made his escape to America—to Montreal—on a tramp steamer; acting experience at the Abbey enabled him to find work with stock companies and, finally, on Broadway; made his movie debut at 26, in a George O'Brien Western, *Fair Warning*; fame came when, two years later, he romanced Ruth Chatterton in *The Rich Are Always with Us*.

MOVIE HIGHLIGHTS: *Miss Pinkerton, So Big, Lily Turner, The Painted Veil, Front Page Woman, The Case against Mrs. Ames, God's Country and the Woman, Submarine D-1, Jezebel, Dark Victory, The Old Maid, Wings of the Navy, The Rains Came, The Fighting 69th, 'Til We Meet Again, In This Our Life, The Great Lie, Twin Beds, The Gay Sisters, My Reputation, Tomorrow Is Forever, The Spiral Staircase, Lover Come Back, Out of the Blue.*

Barbara Britton

(b. Barbara Brantingham, Sep. 26, 1920, Long Beach, Calif.; d. Jan. 16, 1980) For seven years, starting as the heroine in a "Hopalong Cassidy" Western, *Secrets of the Wastelands*, the blue-eyed blonde was one of Paramount's most charming light leading ladies; went directly from Long Beach City College to a studio contract; prominently featured in many, she had her best outing in '44 when she co-starred with Ray Milland in *Till We Meet Again*, a WWII drama in which she played a lovely, spirited young nun helping a downed American flyer return to Allied lines; was hailed by critics as a "young Ingrid Bergman," but later roles did not give her the opportunity to fulfill that promise; she did, however, enter movie history books in '52, when she co-starred with Robert Stack in *Bwana Devil*, the first full-length 3-D picture; had a successful (1952–54) TV series, "Mr. & Mrs. North," in which she and a longtime Paramount pal, Richard Denning, played the title roles; gave up her screen career in '55 after headlining in *Ain't Misbehavin'* and a remake of *The Spoilers*; was married from '45 on to Dr. Eugene J. Czukor, an eminent psychiatrist, by whom she had two children, Theodore (an actor) and Christopher Eugenia (an opera singer); leaving Hollywood, she moved with her family to New York, where her husband was on the staff of the American Foundation of Religion and Psychiatry and she was on the board of directors; continued as an actress on Broadway (*Spofford* with Melvyn Douglas), on tour (*Forty Carats*), in dinner theaters (*The Marriage-Go-Round*), and, each year, summer stock (*No, No, Nanette*, etc.); more lucratively, she worked for 12 years—at a reported $100,000 per—for Revlon as its spokeswoman on TV ("The $64,000 Question") and doing other promotional activities.

MOVIE HIGHLIGHTS: *Louisiana Purchase, Wake Island, The Fleet's In, Mrs. Wiggs of the Cabbage Patch, So Proudly We Hail, Reap the Wild Wind, Young and Willing, The Story of Dr. Wassell, Captain Kidd, The Virginian, The Return of Monte Cristo, The Fabulous Suzanne, Albuquerque, The Great John L., I Shot Jesse James, Champagne for Caesar, Bandit Queen, Ride the Man Down, Dragonfly Squadron.*

Hillary Brooke

(b. Beatrice Sofia Mathilda Peterson, Sept. 8, 1914, Brooklyn, N.Y.) Many believed this cool blonde to be British because she was so often cast as young English women (*Ministry of Fear, Sherlock Holmes Faces Death*, etc.), and because of her precise, clipped speech; the accent, though, was something she'd picked up while acting for several months on stage in London in a musical comedy, *Transatlantic Rhythm*; born to middle-class parents, she was graduated from John Madison High in Brooklyn and for three years attended Columbia University, planning to become a dietician; then, for

23

more than three years, was one of John Robert Powers' most famous cover girls, while also making her debut on Broadway in *Set to Music* with Bea Lillie; never having studied drama, acting was instinctive with her; her Hollywood career lasted exactly two decades, from *New Faces of 1937* to 1957's *Spoilers of the Forest*; played minor parts for a number of years as casting directors maintained she had "no sex appeal"; that changed, thanks to *Jane Eyre* ('44) and its male star, Orson Welles; seeing her test for the second femme lead of Blanche (in which she wore a lush, off-the-shoulder black velvet gown), a dazzled Welles, who'd heard the no-sex-appeal rumor, dispatched a note to the front office that began, "Are you blind?"; she got the part; many prominent roles ensued, including leads in Bs; when in big-budget films, most often cast as the "other woman," more than one top-billed movie heroine discovered she was a classy force not to be taken lightly; a most unlikely role, and one she vastly enjoyed, was that of the high-kicking dance-hall queen in *The Road to Utopia*; her first marriage, to assistant director Jack Voglin, ended in divorce after four years in '47; their son, Donald, who uses his stepfather's name, became a movie director; in '60, she married Raymond A. Klune, former general manager and vice-president of MGM.

MOVIE HIGHLIGHTS: *Eternally Yours, And the Angels Sing, Practically Yours, Standing Room Only, The Crime Doctor's Courage, The Enchanted Cottage, Up Goes Maisie, Lady in the Dark, Earl Carroll's Sketchbook, Monsieur Beaucaire, The Strange Woman, Big Town, The Fuller Brush Man, Underworld Scandal, Vendetta, Never Wave at a WAC, Abbott & Costello Meet Captain Kidd.*

Rory Calhoun

(b. Francis Timothy McCown, Aug. 8, 1918, Los Angeles, Calif.) Alan Ladd discovered this lanky (6'3"), handsome guy with the prominent widow's peak on a Hollywood bridle path, and Ladd's wife, agent Sue Carol, promoted him to stardom; confided to the Ladds at the outset that he had a prison record, a fact that did not surface for years, until a scandal magazine reported it; had been brought up in Santa Cruz and L.A., in sometimes desperate circumstances, by his Spanish mother and stepfather, Nathaniel Durgin, after the death of his own father, a sailor; he'd been, he said, "a wild kid"; beginning at 13 with petty thievery and graduating to grand auto theft, he did time—several years—in various institutions: Whittier School for Boys, the Preston School of Industry, a federal prison at Springfield, Mo., and the Federal Reformatory in

El Reno, Okla.; was set on the straight path at the latter by the chaplain there, Father Donald J. Kanally, who became his friend and adviser; converting to Catholicism, he was baptised while still behind bars—and under armed guard; when released, he worked at a variety of jobs, including operating a crane in an ironworks, before falling into an acting career; began in '44 in an unbilled bit in *Something for the Boys*; was billed "Frank McCown" in *Nob Hill* and *The Great John L.*, in which, playing boxing champ Jim Corbett, he first attracted notice; final screen name change came in '47, with a second lead in *The Red House*; was long at 20th Century–Fox, where *Sand* was his first starring role; in later years, after his juvenile delinquency record was revealed, he answered many calls to reformatories to advise young inmates against a life of crime; in addition to acting, he has been a movie producer-director *(Hired Gun)*, a screen scriptwriter *(Domino Kid, Shotgun)*, and has penned a novel *(The Man from Padera)*; was married for 21 years, until their divorce in '69, to actress Lita Baron, by whom he has three daughters; was wed in '71 to Sue Rhodes Boswell, a newspaperwoman from Australia, by whom he also has a daughter.

MOVIE HIGHLIGHTS: *That Hagen Girl, Massacre River, Ticket to Tomahawk, I'd Climb the Highest Mountain, Meet Me After the Show, With a Song in My Heart, How to Marry a Millionaire, River of No Return, Way of a Gaucho, The Spoilers, Red Sundown, Raw Edge, Ride Out for Revenge, Black Spurs, Flight to Hong Kong, Saga of Hemp Brown, Apache Uprising.*

Judy Canova

(b. Juliet Canova, Nov. 20, 1916, Starke, Fla.; d. Aug. 5, 1983) Other than its cowboys, tiny Republic Pictures had only a handful of stars and, in Saturday afternoon yuk-getters, she was one of its brightest and biggest moneymakers; of course, at her home studio as elsewhere, she could only be seen as a straw-hatted, yodeling hillbilly comedienne in beribboned pigtails; no hillbilly, she had some illustrious ancestors, including, among other Italian artists, sculptor Antonio Canova, a favorite of Napoleon, and, on her mother's side, Commodore Matthew Perry; studied to be an opera singer—yet when, in one of her country bumpkin flicks, she did an operatic number, few could believe she did her own singing; discovering that comedy paid better than the classics, she began doing a hayseed act in nightclubs and in movies *(In Caliente)* with brother Zeke and sister Anne; sang on radio with Paul Whiteman's orchestra and wowed 'em on Broadway in *Calling All Stars* and the *Ziegfeld Follies*; once she'd donned the goofy country get-ups, there was no turning back—until, at least, in later years on TV, she more than once portrayed dignified redhaired matrons (and also was seen regularly as "Aunt Vivian" in dish detergent commercials); her "Judy Canova Show" was for 12 years one of the great hits on the NBC Radio network; a typical routine that garnered nationwide guffaws in the '40s—*Stooge:* "One of my ancestors was a Knight of the Royal Order of Bath—or don't you know the Order of Bath?" *Judy:* "Why shore—on Saturday night it was Paw first and then all the kids in the order of their ages"; none of her four marriages lasted; divorced William Burns in '39 after three years; had a surprise marriage in Honolulu in '41 to Army Cpl. James H. Ripley ("We were hit over the head by a moonbeam"), which was quickly annulled; divorced Chester England in '49 (one daughter: Julietta); was wed from '50 till '63, when they divorced, to Cuban-born bandleader-importer-realtor (and anti-Castro activist) Filiberto Rivero; their daughter, Diana (Canova), became popular on TV in "Soap" and other, strictly sophisticated comedy series.

MOVIE HIGHLIGHTS: *Artists and Models, Scatterbrain, Sis Hopkins, Puddin' Head, Sleepytime Gal, Joan of the Ozarks, Chatterbox, True to the Army, Sleepy Lagoon, Louisiana Hayride, Singin' in the Corn, Hit the Hay, Honeychile, The WAC from Walla Walla, Oklahoma Annie, Carolina Cannonball, Lay That Rifle Down.*

Macdonald Carey

(b. Edward Macdonald Carey, March 15, 1913, Sioux City, Iowa) Paramount leading man with a strong, intelligent, good-natured face who has enjoyed a well-rounded career in "medicine"; an early break in radio in the '30s was playing young Dr. Lee Markham on NBC in the "Woman in White" soap opera (written by Irna Phillips); in '65, the first major movie star to go into daytime TV, he began his decades-long stint as Dr. Tom Horton in NBC's "Days of Our Lives" (written by Irna Phillips); in between, he played a physician in his debut movie, *Dr. Broadway* ('42), had the same occupation when co-starring with Sandra Dee in *Tammy and the Doctor*, and, in TV's infant years, was the title lead in "Dr. Christian"; the early ambition of this judge's son, when he enrolled at the University of Wisconsin, was to have a career in—medicine; college plays changed his mind; first professional experience was with a Shakespearean troupe at the Texas Centennial in Dallas in '36, signing up shortly before getting his M.A. in drama at the University of

Iowa; 1937–39 saw him as an actor in radio ("First Nighter," etc.) in Chicago; fame came on Broadway in '41 when he played the wise guy editor in *Lady in the Dark*, opposite Gertrude Lawrence; signing a movie contract, he was soon romancing on screen all the top femme stars (Claudette Colbert, Rosalind Russell, Betty Hutton, etc.); enlisting in the Marines in '43, he saw action in the South Pacific and was discharged in '45 with the rank of captain; in '41 was married in a Catholic ceremony to Philadelphia debutante-aspiring actress Elizabeth Heckscher; separated in '65, they divorced soon afterwards; six children: Lynn (became the lead singer with the rock band Mama Lion), Lisa, Steve, Teresa, Macdonald, and Paul; personal favorite of his four dozen movies: 1950's *The Lawless*; a favorite tale he tells on himself: went to confession once in Ireland to a priest who, it turned out, had once served in Hollywood and was eager to hear all about his former parishioners; emerging from the booth after the hour-long session, he faced an Irishman, waiting to confess, who gasped, "My God, man, what have you done?"

MOVIE HIGHLIGHTS: *Take a Letter, Darling, Wake Island, Shadow of a Doubt, Suddenly It's Spring, Dream Girl, Hazard, Variety Girl, Streets of Laredo, Bride of Vengeance, The Great Gatsby, Copper Canyon, South Sea Sinner, Comanche Territory, Excuse My Dust, Let's Make It Legal, Meet Me after the Show, Outlaw Territory, The Great Missouri Raid, John Paul Jones, Blue Denim.*

Hoagy Carmichael

(b. Hoagland Howard Carmichael, Nov. 22, 1899, Bloomington, Ind.; d. Dec. 27, 1981) Wasn't it enough that he composed "Stardust" (the tune), the most recorded popular song in history?; dreamed that up in '27 while visiting the campus of his alma mater, Indiana U., but couldn't get it published for two years; then there were all the other great melodies: "Georgia on My Mind," "In the Still of the Night," "Skylark," etc., including the later "In the Cool, Cool, Cool of the Evening," which won an Oscar; no one could have guessed that this droll guy, with the hair hanging down over his forehead, would sing and act—so drily—his way to movie fame in '45; normally one of Hollywood's sleekest, best-groomed gents, he got the part of the laconic, match-chewing, baggy-suited honky-tonk piano player in *To Have and Have Not* by chance; next-door neighbor Howard Hawks, the film's director, happened to spot him gardening one day, dressed and looking like a refugee from the Bowery, and cast him as "Cricket"; he also ended up writing the background music for the film as well as its songs ("How Little We Know," "Hong Kong Blues"); this was not, actually, his screen debut; in '37 in *Topper*, nattily dressed, he played a tunesmith singing a song of his, "Old Man Moon"; *To Have and Have Not*, though, made him a great '40s favorite; of fans who were delighted by his strange, chanting-like song style, he jested: "Maybe they call me 'The Voiceless' "; a self-taught pianist (never learned to read music), he began composing tunes while studying law in college; his first recorded (by Paul Whiteman) song: "Washboard Blues"; its success prompted him to give up his law practice for Tin Pan Alley; was first married from '36 until her death to Ruth Meinardi (sons: Hoagy Bix and Randy Bob), and last to former B-picture leading lady Wanda McKay.

MOVIE HIGHLIGHTS: *Johnny Angel, Canyon Passage, The Best Years of Our Lives, Night Song, Johnny Holiday, Young Man with a Horn, The Las Vegas Story, Belles on Their Toes, Timberjack.*

John Carroll

(b. Julian La Faye, July 17, 1906, Mandeville, La.; d. April 24, 1979) Humor in the wrong mix can be deadly to a handsome man who aspires to being a top leading man; in photographs and repose, this big guy with a manicured moustache looked like a curly-haired Gable, but when animated, it was forget-it time; audiences were amused by his acrobatic eyebrows, the Cajun accent, the faces he pulled, and, often as not, his love scenes; with his adventure-filled past, though, perhaps he found it difficult to take moviemaking seriously; longtime friends swear the following is true; became a soldier of fortune at 12 when he ran away from home and landed in Houston, where he worked in a steel mill pulling hot bolts; soon headed south and found a profitable occupation carrying mysterious packages—until, caught by a Texas ranger, he learned he'd been innocently acting as a gun runner; next signed on a freighter as a wiper and for two years sailed the world—China, Germany, Russia, etc.; back in Houston, he was a porter, then a floorwalker at Foley Bros. Dry Goods store; at 17 in Chicago he went in for dirt track race driving; then in New Orleans voice coach Victor Chesnais persuaded a philanthropist, Mrs. S. O. Thomas, to invest $25,000 to send him to Europe to train his voice for opera; while studying, he also worked as a steeplejack and deep sea diver; later sang in Paris, Budapest, Rome, and points in between; starred and sang ("Song of the Open Road") in his debut movie, RKO's *Hi, Gaucho!* ('35); married his leading lady, Hungarian-born Steffi Duna, had a daughter

(Juliana), soon divorced; after many features and the serial *Zorro Rides Again*, was a star at MGM (1940–47); there met and was married—for 35 years to the end—to Lucille Ryman, head of talent at the studio; did a three-year stint as an Air Force pilot during WWII, suffering a broken back in a crash in North Africa, emerging as a captain; an extremely wealthy man (land investments), he quit movies in '59; piled up another fortune in "retirement" in Florida as owner of a shrimping fleet and a steel mill.

MOVIE HIGHLIGHTS: *Murder on the Bridle Path, Rose of the Rio Grande, Only Angels Have Wings, Congo Maisie, Susan and God, Go West, Hired Wife, Sunny, Lady Be Good, Rio Rita, Flying Tigers, Hit Parade of 1943, Bedside Manner, A Letter for Evie, Fiesta, Wyoming, The Fabulous Texan, Old Los Angeles, The Avenger, Belle le Grande, Two Grooms for a Bride Geraldine.*

Jack Carson

(b. John Elmer Carson, Oct. 27, 1910, Carmen, Canada; d. Jan. 2, 1963) One of his wives called him "Porky," and he had a few things in common with a prize boar, being large, seeming aggressive, looking well fed, having, literally, a thick skin, and winning blue ribbons; comedy made him a star, playing the patsy—the widecracking, fast-talking show-off who always got tripped up; clicked with this typecasting on radio, TV, and the screen, especially when teamed with best buddy Dennis Morgan in *Two Guys from Milwaukee, Two Guys from Texas*, etc.; was proudest, though, of his serious roles—the belligerent studio publicist in Garland's *A Star Is Born*, the husband who committed suicide over lost love Joan Leslie in *The Hard Way*; friends insisted that, unlike any man he ever played, he was actually "a shy and simple kind of guy" who blushed when filming love scenes; grew up in Milwaukee, Wis., and considered it home, but when Canada instituted its Motion Picture Hall of Fame in '73, he was one of the first four inductees (with Norma Shearer, Raymond Massey, and Mary Pickford); attended St. John's Military Academy in Wisconsin, Carleton College in Minnesota; failed when he tried to start an electric sign company in Milwaukee ("fizzled then burned out completely," he joked); went into vaudeville as a comic and then, in '36, to Hollywood for radio work and bits in movies; never had a screen test, worked his way gradually to stardom; first major break: the loudmouth fourflusher who stole Hayworth from Cagney in *The Strawberry Blonde*; was divorced by the first three of his wives: Betty Lynn (not the Fox actress), Kay St. Germaine (1940–50), the soloist on his radio show who presented him with a son (John Jr.) and a daughter (Germaine), and actress Lola Albright (1952–58); was wed in '61 to Sandra Tucker; asked when 35 what he'd like to be doing at 60, he said, "Breathing"; missed that goal by eight years when claimed by cancer, which he kept secret from his closest associates.

MOVIE HIGHLIGHTS: *Stage Door, Carefree, Quick Money, Vivacious Lady, Lucky Partners, I Take This Woman, Blues in the Night, The Male Animal, Navy Blues, Gentleman Jim, Princess O'Rourke, Shine On Harvest Moon, The Doughgirls, Arsenic and Old Lace, Mildred Pierce, Roughly Speaking, One More Tomorrow, April Showers, Romance on the High Seas, John Loves Mary, My Dream Is Yours, The Good Humor Man, The Groom Wore Spurs, Cat on a Hot Tin Roof.*

Joan Caulfield

(b. Joan Beatrice Caulfield, June 1, 1922, East Orange, N.J.) With blue eyes, blonde hair, and a nursery-pink complexion, she was readymade for Technicolor cameras, in front of which Paramount was prone to place her; Bing Crosby, though she was young enough to be his daughter, adored her; inevitably, she was his leading lady in two of his biggest hits, *Blue Skies* and *Welcome Stranger*; rarely created much heat on the screen, usually seeming to be exactly what she was: a sweet-tempered, charming girl born to silver spoons, golf, bridge, tennis—and easy success; her road to fame, truly, contained no rocky obstacles; the offspring of affluent parents, she participated in drama club productions at the private school she attended in her hometown; for two years at Columbia University she acted with the Morningside Players, then was a famous Conover cover girl; at 20 was starring on Broadway with Kirk Douglas and Richard Widmark, playing Corliss Archer in the smash comedy *Kiss and Tell*; co-starred with Veronica Lake and Sonny Tufts in her debut movie, *Miss Susie Slagle's* ('45); private life was sometimes a bit more dramatic than her performances; in '50 she married producer Frank Ross (once wed to Jean Arthur), who starred her in two movies and two TV series ("My Favorite Husband," and "Sally"); lived—not always serenely—in a hilltop Spanish hacienda that was once John Barrymore's home; discovered she was pregnant after filing for divorce in the spring of '59, but did not withdraw her suit; son Caulfield was born in November of that year; was married in '60 to Dr. Robert Peterson, a dentist, by whom she also had a son, John, in '62, and whom she divorced in '66; later starred on tour and in regional theaters in many plays (*Butterflies Are Free, Plaza Suite, Dream Girl*, etc.), but was not deluged with offers from film producers.

MOVIE HIGHLIGHTS: *Monsieur Beaucaire, Dear Ruth, The Unsuspected, Variety Girl, The Sainted Sisters, Dear Wife, Larceny, The Petty Girl, The Lady Says No, The Rains of Ranchipur, Cattle King, Red Tomahawk, Buckskin, The Doberman Heist.*

Lon Chaney Jr.

(b. Creighton Tull Chaney, Feb. 10, 1906, Oklahoma City, Okla.; d. July 12, 1973) *Of Mice and Men* ('40) gave him the chance to prove what he could really do; gave an admirable performance as dim-witted ranchhand Lennie, but it proved to be one of the few career-enhancement roles he ever had; it may have been inevitable that, given his name and being the son of the silent screen's immortal portrayer of gargoyles, he would become Universal's second-string king of horror flicks—in *The Wolf Man*, as the Monster in *The Ghost of Frankenstein*, as the Mummy in *The Mummy's Tomb*; "Death has been my living," he once said; had a traumatic childhood; his mother, Cleva Creighton, was a 15-year-old choir singer when she married his father, quickly becoming successful as a singer in cabarets; pressured by her husband to give up her career and care for their son, she attempted suicide; at 3, the son worked with his father in a circus trapeze act; was 8 when his soon-to-be-famous dad divorced his mother, won custody of him, soon wed another (Hazel Hastings, who reared the boy as her own), and told him his mother was dead; later came a long period of estrangement between father and son when this was revealed to be a lie; was a butcher's boy, boilermaker, fruit picker, and plumber before becoming an actor, first in stock companies; was billed Creighton Chaney for his first three years in movies, beginning with a dancing role in *Girl Crazy* ('32) and, later that year, the starring role in a Western serial, *The Last Frontier*; switched to Lon Chaney Jr. in '35 when playing supporting roles in *Accent on Youth, Captain Hurricane*, etc.; first of his starmaking horror films at Universal: *Man-Made Monster* ('41); remained at the studio through '45, after which he free-lanced; divorced from Dorothy Hinckley, by whom he had two sons (Ronald, Lon Jr.), he was married from '37 on to photographic model Patsy Beck; was portrayed by Roger Smith in *The Man of a Thousand Faces*, the movie based on his father's life with Cagney in the starring role.

MOVIE HIGHLIGHTS: *Midnight Taxi, Life Begins in College, Mr Moto's Gamble, Jesse James, Frontier Marshal, Union Pacific, Northwest Mounted Police, Badlands of Dakota, Billy the Kid, Calling Dr. Death, Crazy House, Son of Dracula, Dead Men's Eyes, Cobra Woman, Weird Woman, The Daltons Ride Again, The Frozen Ghost, My Favorite Brunette, The House of Dracula, Pillow of Death, High Noon, The Cyclops, Not as a Stranger.*

Cyd Charisse

(b. Tula Ellice Finklea, March 8, 1921, Amarillo, Texas) Dance star with the most gorgeous legs ever seen on film, as the "Gotta Dance" set-piece with Gene Kelly in *Singin' in the Rain* amply demonstrated; from '46 (*Ziegfeld Follies*; dancing role, no dialogue) to '57 (*Silk Stockings*), MGM could count itself fortunate to have her on the payroll; was first seen on screen, billed Lily Norwood (mother's maiden name was Lela Norwood), in '43 in a "dancing on clouds" number with ballet star David Lichine in *Something to Shout About*; was also a dancer that same year in *Mission to Moscow*; the daughter of a well-to-do Texas jeweler of French descent, she began ballet lessons at 6; at 12 was a student at the Hollywood Professional School, living with a family friend, going home only on holidays; Colonel de Basil of the Ballet Russe saw her dance at 14 and invited her to join his company in a tour of the U.S. and Europe; was sometimes billed Filea Sidorova and, on other occasions, Maria Istomina; her Ballet Russe dance instructor was French-born Nico Charisse; married him at 17, left the company with him when he opened a dance studio in Hollywood, had a son, Nicky, at 21; eventually chose to use her married name for her professional one ("Cyd" is a variation of Sid, which her younger brother called her as a child, being unable to enunciate "sister"); deciding to be an actress as well as a dancer, she won her Metro contract via a dramatic test in which she did a scene from *The Cradle Song*; spoke her first dialogue on screen in her second film at MGM, *The Harvey Girls*, playing a naïve, pretty lass named Deborah; divorced from Nico Charisse in '47, she has been married since '48 to singer Tony Martin (their mutual agent introduced them), by whom she also has a son, Tony Jr., born in '50; leaving movies, the dancer and singer teamed up for a perennially popular club act; a combined autobiography of them, *The Two of Us* (penned by Dick Kleiner), was published in '76; her dedication in the book was to her husband "for all the joy he has put in my life."

MOVIE HIGHLIGHTS: *Till the Clouds Roll By, Three Wise Fools, Unfinished Dance, Fiesta, On an Island with You, The Kissing Bandit, Words and Music, Tension, East Side, West Side, Sombrero, The Band Wagon, Brigadoon, Easy to Love, Deep in My Heart, It's Always Fair Weather, Meet Me in Las Vegas, Party Girl, Black Tights, Two Weeks in Another Town, The Silencers.*

Dane Clark

(b. Bernard Zanville, Feb. 18, 1913, New York, N.Y.) Dark-haired and wiry, with a pugnacious, Brooklyn-style charm, he was for seven years (1943–50) one of the busiest, most popular personalities on the Warners lot; the stars he most wanted to work with were Cagney, Bogart, and Ingrid Bergman ("the most exciting actors")—made it at least with Bogart in his first at the studio, *Action in the North Atlantic*; defined his approach to acting as "not artistic— just realistic", which may have come from hard knocks endured during the decade that led to movie fame; the son of a sporting goods store owner, he graduated from St. John's University Law School; preparing to take the bar exam, he worked briefly as a law clerk until dire financial conditions caused him to reevaluate his goals; never stagestruck, he became an actor—in the depths of the Depression—at the urging of friend John Garfield (they would later co-star in *Pride of the Marines* at Warners); started under his own name in '34, playing bits in a number of quick-flop Broadway shows (*Sailors of Cattaro, Till the Day I Die*, etc.); next toured for years—usually as an understudy—in a long list of plays (*Stage Door, Dead End, Of Mice and Men*, among others); many career setbacks and disappointments had put a slashing edge on his personality by the time he drove a flivver cross-country to launch an attack on Hollywood; talked his way first into minor roles at MGM (*The Sunday Punch*) and Paramount (*The Glass Key*) in '42; experiences during a stint in the Merchant Marines served him well when WB cast him repeatedly in wartime dramas; was married from '41 until her death in the '60s to Margo Yoder, a concert pianist who'd played with the Chicago and London Symphonies; in '72 was wed to a New York stockbroker, Geraldine Frank; starred for several years on Broadway (*A Thousand Clowns, Tchin-Tchin*) before returning to Hollywood and a new career as a television actor.

MOVIE HIGHLIGHTS: *Destination Tokyo, Rear Gunner, The Very Thought of You, God Is My Co-Pilot, Her Kind of Man, A Stolen Life, Dark*

Passage, Deep Valley, That Way with Women, Moonrise, Embraceable You, Whiplash, Fort Defiance, Without Honor, Backfire, The Gambler and the Lady, Paid to Kill, Highly Dangerous, The Toughest Man Alive, The McMasters.

Charles Coburn

(b. Charles Douville Coburn, June 19, 1877, Savannah, Ga.; d. Aug. 30, 1961) Character star, usually found with cigar and monocle, who could be delightfully droll (Niven's millionaire dad in *Bachelor Mother*), devilishly sly (Stanwyck's cardsharp father in *The Lady Eve*), or downright dangerous (the sadistic doctor in *Kings Row* who needlessly amputated Ronald Reagan's legs, giving the actor-turned-president his most famous movie line and the title of his autobiography, *"Where's the Rest of Me?"*); co-starring with Jean Arthur was lucky for him—won the Best Supporting Oscar for *The More the Merrier* and snagged a similar nomination for *The Devil and Miss Jones*; was also nominated later for *The Green Years*; like the best of the character people in Hollywood's Golden Era, he had been on stage for decades before entering movies; was first, at 18, the manager of a theater in his hometown; in 1906, the year he married Ivah Wills (who acted as Mrs. Charles Coburn), he organized and co-starred with his bride in the Coburn Players, a Shakespearean company that toured the South; were married until her death in '37; in the '20s, he and his wife appeared together on Broadway in a dozen plays (*French Leave, The Better 'Ole, The Yellow Jacket*, etc.), including several (*The Farmer's Wife, The Right to Marry*, etc.) that he also directed; made his screen debut in '33 in *Boss Tweed* but returned to the stage and only settled in as a movie actor in '38, when he was in four, including *Of Human Hearts* and *Vivacious Lady*; quite the gay blade in the '40s, he could be seen almost any Saturday night at Ciro's on the Sunset Strip doing a torrid tango with the loveliest starlet in the room; became a groom again in '59, marrying Winifred Natzka; his subtlety and versatility as an actor made him a pet with fans and such noted critics as Otis Ferguson, who once observed that "he always seems as though the part were made for him, as though he were there and not even thinking of acting—which of course demands the best and only true thinking about acting."

MOVIE HIGHLIGHTS: *Lord Jeff, Yellow Jack, Idiot's Delight, Made for Each Other, The Story of Alexander Graham Bell, Edison, the Man, H. M. Pulham, Esq., In This Our Life, The Constant Nymph, George Washington*

Slept Here, Heaven Can Wait, Princess O'Rourke, Wilson, Since You Went Away, Together Again, The Impatient Years, Col. Effingham's Raid, A Royal Scandal, The Paradine Case, B. F.'s Daughter, Green Grass of Wyoming, Monkey Business, Gentlemen Prefer Blondes, How to Be Very, Very Popular.

Richard Conte

(b. Nicholas Peter Conte, March 24, 1910, Jersey City, N.J.; d. April 15, 1975) Capitalizing on his brooding Sicilian looks, coiled-spring personality, and secretive smile, disarming but with a hint of suppressed violence, 20th Century–Fox starred him repeatedly as a military man—but of ever descending rank; was a captain in his debut movie, *Guadalcanal Diary* ('43), a lieutenant in *The Purple Heart*, a sergeant in *A Bell for Adano*, and, in *A Walk in the Sun*, a private (his real-life rank in the Army before being medically discharged); ironically, years after all these heroic roles, he wound up typecast in Mafia parts, like that of Barzini, one of Brando's malevolent rivals in *The Godfather*; further irony: Before Brando landed the part, he'd been the leading contender for the movie's title role; the son of a seamstress mother and barber father (in whose shop he worked as a youth), the black-eyed actor grew up in the slums of Jersey City, in a tenement sandwiched between a brass foundry and a coal yard; as a young man he worked as a truck driver, Wall Street messenger, shoe salesman, and as a combination waiter-barber–dancing partner for feminine guests at a summer resort; seeing a Clifford Odets play, *Waiting for Lefty*, turned him on to acting, and the Neighborhood Playhouse in New York gave him a scholarship; two years later, the Group Theater handed him a major role in Saroyan's *My Heart's in the Highlands* ('39); in '42 he played Saroyan in *Jason*, and critic George Jean Nathan, no pushover, hailed him as "the year's most outstanding actor"; *The Family* took him to Hollywood the following year; secret of his success on film was explained this way by Joseph MacDonald, cinematographer of many of his pictures: "He is mentally as well as physically photogenic; he projects his mental processes on the screen with an air of casualness which clicks with audiences"; personal favorite of his movies: *Full of Life* with Judy Holliday—a comedy.

MOVIE HIGHLIGHTS: *Captain Eddie, The Spider, Somewhere in the Night, 13 Rue Madeleine, The Other Love, Call Northside 777, House of Strangers, Cry of the City, Thieves' Highway, Whirlpool, The Sleeping City, Under the Gun, The Raiders, The Hollywood Story, The Blue Gardenia, New*

York Confidential, I'll Cry Tomorrow, The Brothers Rico, They Came to Cordura Ocean's Eleven, Assault on a Queen, Hotel, Tony Rome.

Wendell Corey

(b. Wendell Corey, March 20, 1914, Dracut, Mass.; d. Nov. 8, 1968) Unprepossessing Hal Wallis star who got off to a dying start—in '47 was killed off before the fadeout in both of his first pictures, *Desert Fury* (John Hodiak did the deed) and *I Walk Alone* (Kirk Douglas pulled the trigger); played conventional heroic roles and villainous ones, preferring the latter, saying, "If he's something special in the line of heels, I'd play him for nothing"; seemed like strange talk for a minister's son, but then, his father wasn't always a preacher—at 40, he abruptly quit his job as purchasing agent for a Boston contracting firm, enrolled in a theological seminary, and four years later was ordained for the ministry; after graduation from high school, the future star was selling washing machines in an appliance store in Providence, R.I., by day and acting with a local amateur theatrical group by night; first stage role: a Swedish janitor in *Street Scene*; later put in a season with the Red Barn Theater in Westboro, Mass., and went from there, in the Depression years, to the WPA Theater; of that experience, he later recalled "the long drives through raging blizzards in horse-drawn cutters to reach some one-room country school where we put on a performance"; in the company was actress Alice Wiley, to whom he was married from '39 until his death; four children: Lucy Robin, Jonathan, Jennifer, and Ronald; first play on Broadway, *The Life of Reilly*, lasted eight days; curtain rang down on his second, *Comes the Revolution*, after four; pattern continued for a decade (*Texas Town, But Not Goodbye,* etc.); finally in '45 came a smash hit, *Dream Girl*, in which he played a cynical newspaperman with a voice of acid and a heart of gold, and movie offers flooded in; postponed accepting one until he'd starred in London in *Voice of the Turtle*; a direct descendant of Presidents John Adams and John Quincy Adams, he also became president—of the Academy of Motion Picture Arts and Sciences.

MOVIE HIGHLIGHTS: *The Search, Sorry, Wrong Number, The Accused, File on Thelma Jordan, Any Number Can Play, Holiday Affair, The Furies, No Sad Songs for Me, Harriet Craig, Rich, Young and Pretty, Carbine Williams, The Wild Blue Yonder, The Wild North, Rear Window, Hell's Half Acre, The Big Knife, The Bold and the Brave, The Rainmaker, Light in the Forest, Blood on the Arrow, Loving You, Waco.*

Joseph Cotten

(b. Joseph Cheshire Cotten, May 15, 1905, Petersburg, Va.) His silken charm and butter-soft Southern accent, which he never entirely lost, made him a romantic rage in '44 when he shared love scenes with Ginger Rogers in *I'll Be Seeing You*—after eight earlier movies and four years in Hollywood; Orson Wells played a major role in his career; the two became lifelong friends when acting on radio together in the mid-1930s; becoming director of the Federal Theater Project, Welles starred him in the play *Horse Eats Hat*, after Cotten had appeared in a number of quick flops like *Absent Father* ('32) and *Jezebel* ('33); later, when Welles established his Mercury Theatre, Cotten was cast in starring roles in *Shoemakers' Holiday* and *Julius Caesar*; in '40, was one of the leads, of course, in Welles' historic *Citizen Kane*, marking the film debut of both actors, and there were still later movies for and with Welles; David O. Selznick soon snapped up Cotten's contract and astutely provided him with splendid opportunities to shine on screen; became almost as famous off screen for once booting gossip queen Hedda Hopper in the rear, after she made derogatory remarks about President Franklin D. Roosevelt; to the (rundown) manor born ("We had all the luxuries but none of the necessities"), he put himself through drama school in Washington, D.C., by playing semipro football; next acted in repertory in Miami, while also working as a paint salesman and part-time drama critic for the *Miami Herald*; in Florida, met pianist Lenore Kip, to whom he was married from '31 until her death in '60; was wed later that year to actress Patricia Medina, with whom he subsequently appeared in many touring plays; his lack of ego prompted one friend to say, at the height of the actor's fame, "It's amazing he has gotten as far as he has without the drive most actors have—he would have been just as happy being a professor of drama at some Midwestern university"; continued to star in movies until '82, when, after making *Screamers*, he was felled by a stroke.

MOVIE HIGHLIGHTS: *Lydia, The Magnificent Ambersons, Journey into Fear, Shadow of a Doubt, Hers to Hold, Gaslight, Since You Went Away, Love Letters, Duel in the Sun, The Farmer's Daughter, Portrait of Jennie, Under Capricorn, Beyond the Forest, The Third Man, September Affair, Walk Softly, Stranger, Niagara, Bottom of the Bottle, Hush . . . Hush . . . Sweet Charlotte, Tora! Tora! Tora!, Soylent Green, Twilight's Last Gleaming, Airport '77, Guyana: Cult of the Damned, Heaven's Gate.*

(b. James Henry Meador, Feb. 4, 1912, Nashville, Tenn.) Along with Robert Taylor and Clark Gable, whom he greatly resembled, this muscular, black-haired star was one of the handsomest men on the Metro lot; acted for Leo the Lion for five years, starting in '42; during that time he lived on a ranch north of Hollywood raising, annually, thousands of turkeys (which quite a number of his movies were); after finishing high school in his hometown, this son of a building contractor was a premed student at Texas' Rice Institute, where he played end on the football team (made All-Southern); quitting college after two years, he worked at a General Motors plant in Houston and began acting in amateur theatricals; one play he did, *Craig's Wife*, gave him his professional name; in Hollywood on a two-week vacation in '37, he presented himself at Paramount and was signed to a short-term contract; debuted in supporting roles in *Sophie Lang Goes West* and a Gilbert Roland Western, *Thunder Trail* (its heroine, Marsha Hunt, and Craig would get together again, romantically, six years later at Metro in *Lost Angel*); unhappy with his progress at this studio, he headed for New York in '38 and landed a minor role in *Missouri Legend* starring Katharine Cornell; returned West with a Columbia contract, which was soon followed by others at Universal and RKO; at the latter, he vied with Dennis Morgan for the affections of Ginger Rogers in *Kitty Foyle*, and his impressive performance attracted the interest of MGM moguls; his private life has been more complex than most of his roles: Mary Ray was his wife from '39 until '54, when they divorced; children: James Jr., Diane, and Robert (died when a toddler); was next married in '59 to starlet Jill Jarmyn; after their divorce in '62, he and his first wife remarried—but it didn't last; his '64 marriage to Jane Valentine ended in divorce within months (three years later she killed her young son by a previous marriage, then committed suicide); his present marriage, it is said, has been a happy one; in recent years, has done TV commercials, played character roles in movies and on TV, and worked as a realtor.

MOVIE HIGHLIGHTS: *The Buccaneer, Taming of the West, Seven Sinners, The Devil and Daniel Webster* (aka *All That Money Can Buy*), *Valley of the Sun, The Human Comedy, Swing Shift Maisie, The Heavenly Body, Kismet, Marriage Is a Private Affair, Our Vines Have Tender Grapes, Boys' Ranch, Northwest Stampede, Hurricane Smith, Code Two, While the City Sleeps, Naked in the Sun, If He Hollers, Let Him Go.*

Jeanne Crain

(b. Jeanne Crain, May 25, 1925, Barstow, Calif.) For more than a decade at 20th Century–Fox, with her red hair and gentle smile, she was the prettiest and, it was generally agreed, sweetest girl on the lot; "Miss Homespun America" they called her—and meant it as a compliment; at 27, could still convincingly play teen-age roles *(Belles on Their Toes)*; grew up near Hollywood and was named "Inglewood High Grid Queen of 1941" (recalls a classmate: "She was exceedingly shy, but great fun when you got to know her"); was chosen that same year as Miss Long Beach in the Miss America contest; a photographers' model after leaving high school, she made the rounds of the movie studios, without success, and was finally discovered by a talent scout at the Max Reinhardt Playhouse—while sitting in the audience; the daughter of two teachers, she later played one—a mulatto (a risk for both the studio and herself)—in *Pinky* and was Oscar-nominated as Best Actress; at 18, fell in love with Paul Brinkman, a handsome young actor (a Flynn lookalike) and a graduate engineer; he soon gave up movies, established his own firm, and eventually became a millionaire manufacturing missile parts and radar sets; they have been married since she was 20; announced when she was pregnant that their first two children would be boys and be named Paul and Michael—they were and they are; five others followed: Timothy, Jeanine, Betsy (Lisabette), Mia (Maria), and Christopher; screen career finally suffered as she turned down major roles to spend time with her family ("I have no regrets—you can't have everything, and I'm happy with what I have"); still acts occasionally on TV or the stage—in summer stock or at big city playhouses in proven hits like *The Philadelphia Story* and *Claudia*; is a professional painter whose oils—mostly portraits—have been exhibited in recent years at the Mascagni d'Italy and Westwood (Calif.) Art Association galleries.

MOVIE HIGHLIGHTS: *Home in Indiana, In the Meantime, Darling, Winged Victory, State Fair, Margie, Leave Her to Heaven, Centennial Summer, You Were Meant for Me, Apartment for Peggy, A Letter to Three Wives, The Fan, Cheaper by the Dozen, People Will Talk, Take Care of My Little Girl, O. Henry's Full House, The Model and the Marriage Broker, Vicki, Gentlemen Marry Brunettes.*

Broderick Crawford

(b. William Broderick Crawford, Dec. 9, 1911, Philadelphia, Pa.) Hardly a pretty-boy, with a creased face that looks like a Rand McNally road map, he played ruthless politico Willie Stark to a fare-thee-well in *All the King's Men* ('49) and won a Best Actor Oscar; made three other movies that same year, including one with Ronald Reagan *(Night unto Night)*, which didn't do a thing for him; got that picturesque broken schnozz as a kid—stage actor-father Lester Crawford delivered a haymaker once when he failed to call him "sir"; his mother, a stage-screen comedienne Helen Broderick, strongly discouraged his early acting ambitions and remained unconvinced of his talent even after Ethel Barrymore waxed enthusiastic over his stage work in *Point Valaine* in '35; his towering performance on Broadway in *Of Mice and Men*, as the retarded Lennie, changed his mother's mind; she lived to see him win the Academy Award and to hear Ethel Barrymore, congratulating him, say, "See? I told you so"; after graduation from Dean Academy in Massachusetts, he sailed for a while on an oil tanker, then did a short stint at Harvard before deciding to be an actor; first a radio actor ("20,000 Years in Sing Sing"), he had his first important stage role in support of Florence Reed in *Punches and Judy*; made his screen debut in '37 in Miriam Hopkins' *Woman Chases Man*; personal favorite of his 100-plus movies: *Born Yesterday*; a gentle (and sentimental) man despite his rugged appearance, he says, "As an actor, my face is something to work against—because I look tough, I have to work at bringing out the real feelings of the inner man"; was married first (1940–57) to movie actress Kay Griffith; adopting an infant boy in '47, he told the agency: "Give me the worst one—he needs me more"; the chosen child, Kim, had eyes that were crossed, deformed feet, and was believed—falsely—to be retarded; thousands were willingly spent correcting these physical ills, and Kim grew to be 6'4" and his father's pride, along with Kelly, the natural-born son the actor and Kay Griffith had later; second wife (1962–67) was actress Joan Tabor; in '73, married a Los Angeles widow, Mary Alice Michell.

MOVIE HIGHLIGHTS: *Submarine D-1, Beau Geste, The Real Glory, Slightly Honorable, Seven Sinners, When the Daltons Rode, Tight Shoes, Broadway, Butch Minds the Baby, The Black Angel, The Flame, Slave Girl, The Time of Your Life, Sealed Verdict, Anna Lucasta, The Mob, Stop! You're Killing Me, Night People, New York Confidential, Not as a Stranger, Big House U.S.A., The Decks Ran Red, A House Is Not a Home, The Oscar, Hell's Bloody Devils.*

Dan Dailey

(b. Dan Dailey Jr., Dec. 14, 1914, New York, N.Y.; d. Oct. 16, 1978) It was no disgrace when this lanky song-and-dance man, nominated for the Best Actor Oscar for *When My Baby Smiles at Me*, lost the race to Laurence Oliver in *Hamlet*; began his movie career, sans acting lessons, as a straight dramatic actor, playing a Nazi storm trooper in *The Mortal Storm* ('40); it was when he put on his tap shoes for *Panama Hattie*, however, that he really became a favorite with moviegoers; first performance was at 6, singing "Here Comes Danny O'Neill," in an impromptu stage show at a Long Island hotel ("really a glorified theatrical boarding house") managed by his father; determined in his teens to be a dancer—though, at 6'4", everyone said he was too tall—he quit high school and broke in as a hoofer in burlesque; later came hard times and many odd jobs—golf caddying, selling shoes at Macy's, jerking sodas; also was a bandleader on a cruise ship sailing between New York and South America and the social director at a Catskills resort; began on Broadway in *Babes in Arms* in '34, which was followed by other musicals, *Stars in Your Eyes* and *I Married an Angel*, which propelled him into an MGM contract; in '42, scheduled to star in *For Me and My Gal* (Gene Kelly replaced him), he was drafted; served with the Signal Corps, transferred to the cavalry and, finally, the 88th Infantry, winning a field promotion to captain before being discharged in '46; found no role waiting for him in Hollywood until '47, when Betty Grable desperately needed a singer-dancer-actor to co-star in *Mother Wore Tights*—which led to his 11-year run at 20th Century–Fox; suffered a nervous breakdown in mid-career and was able to return only after five months in the Menninger Clinic; first marriage, to Esther Rodier, ended in divorce in '41; in '42, married socialite Elizabeth Hofert (had show horses—jumpers—as a common interest), who divorced him in '51; son Dan III, his only child, committed suicide at 29; was married next (1955–62) to Gwen Carter (ironically, her ex was Donald O'Connor, and in '54 Dailey had played O'Connor's father in *There's No Business Like Show Business*); his fourth marriage, to Carol Warner, also failed.

MOVIE HIGHLIGHTS: *Dulcy, Ziegfeld Girl, Lady Be Good, The Getaway, Mokey, The Sunday Punch, Give My Regards to Broadway, You Were Meant for Me, Chicken Every Sunday, You're My Everything, When Willie Comes Marching Home, My Blue Heaven, I Can Get It for You Wholesale, Call Me Mister, The Pride of St. Louis, Meet Me at the Fair, What Price Glory?, It's Always Fair Weather, Taxi.*

Cass Daley

(b. Katherine Daley, July 17, 1915, Philadelphia, Pa.; d. March 23, 1975)
Raucous, knockabout comedienne with black hair and buck teeth, on which
she capitalized to hilarious effect; gimmick was to come on as a demure lass
ready to sing a song straight—then, explosively, she'd be swinging Tarzan-like
on a velvet curtain, chasing the nearest man, popping her teeth, walking on
the sides of her heels, and straddling the mike; the daughter of an Irish
streetcar conductor, she began working for $8 a week in a hosiery mill at 14
while going to school one day a week; fired for mimicking the boss, she was
next a hatcheck girl at a rundown nightclub in Camden, N.J., working for tips
and a chance to sing with the band; at 17, began a two-year singing engagement at Mary's Club in Tuckahoe, N.Y., where an agent, Frank Kinsella,
caught her act and persuaded her, against her will, to switch to mugging-
with-music; before they married in '41, he guided her to fame; in '36, was on
Broadway in *Ziegfeld Follies*; two years later, was a hit when touring English
and Scottish music halls; headlined on radio in "The Fitch Bandwagon" (was
named in polls as the most popular comedienne) and "The Maxwell House
Coffee Time," playing Frank Morgan's boisterous niece (her much-quoted
catch-phrase: "I said it and I'm glad!"); was next starring in the Broadway
comedy *Yokel Boy*, with Joe Penner, when Paramount signed her; made a
wildly memorable screen debut in '42 in *The Fleet's In*; after the birth of a son,
Dale, in '48, she and Kinsella retired to a 15-room mansion in exclusive
Newport Beach, Calif.; came back for one movie in the '50s, *Red Garters*,
and a trio of flops in the '60s; said then: "I made a horrible mistake when I
decided to forget about my career"; after divorcing Kinsella, was married to
building contractor Robert Williamson; was last seen in a Hollywood stage
production of *The Front Page* in '74; played Jenny, the cleaning lady, and
joked that she'd practiced by scrubbing her gold stars on Hollywood
Boulevard—had two, one for movies, another for radio work; her death was
bizarre—at home alone, she fell and shattered a glass on a coffee table,
embedding a shard of glass in her neck.

MOVIE HIGHLIGHTS: *Riding High, Star-Spangled Rhythm, Crazy
House, Duffy's Tavern, Out of This World, Ladies' Man, Variety Girl, The
Spirit Is Willing, Norwood, The Phynx.*

(b. Helmut Guttmann, Oct. 7, 1917, Vienna, Austria; d. May 3, 1982) Darkly handsome and unsmiling, with finely chiseled features, deep-set gray eyes, and a Continental accent, he had a corner on young Nazi roles—most memorably, the downed, wounded Luftwaffe flier in *Mrs. Miniver*—and, curiously, won the hearts of millions of femme fans; no Nazi, he was the son of an assistant to the Austrian Secretary of State; at 21, a graduate of both the Consular Academy and the University of Vienna, he had been appointed to the Austrian Embassy in London when Hitler's troops marched into his homeland; imprisoned in a concentration camp for three months, he was given the option of joining the Party and the German army or getting out of the country, which of course he did; (sequel: in '43 he attended a preview of *Desert Victory*, a British documentary containing scenes showing captured high-ranking German officers; a familiar face loomed on the screen, and he exclaimed, "That's him—Colonel Hufnagel, who was in charge of the camp at Rossauerlande when I was there!"); American Ambassador Messersmith in Vienna aided him in getting a visa, quota number, and passage to America on a German ship; with $2.50 (all he was allowed to bring) in his pocket, he arrived in New York on Christmas Eve, 1938, finding a railroad ticket awaiting him from relatives so that he might join them in California; after a single term of studying business administration at UCLA, he enrolled at the Pasadena Playhouse; was urged to become an actor by another Austrian refugee, friend Werner Klemperer (later famous on TV, as comic Nazi Col. Wilhelm Klink, in "Hogan's Heroes"); performance in a Playhouse production won him a contract at Warner Bros., where he made his debut (as a Nazi) in a bit in Ronald Reagan's *International Squadron* ('41), and where he remained—greatly popular—for seven years; was a frugal man—three years after becoming a star, he still lived in a one-room, furnished apartment with a monthly rental of $45; first marriage, to stage ingenue Gwen Anderson, ended in divorce after three years; was next married (1948–51) to oil heiress Charlene Wrightsman, by whom he had a daughter; from '58 on, was wed to Hollywood heiress (Loew's Inc.) Nicola Schenck, with whom he had two daughters; eventually produced several movies (*The Wilby Conspiracy*, etc.), in which he also acted.

MOVIE HIGHLIGHTS: *Casablanca, To Be or Not to Be, Edge of Darkness, Mission to Moscow, The Mask of Dimitrios, Northern Pursuit, Passage to Marseille, Hotel Berlin, Escape in the Desert, Whispering City, Call Me*

*Madam, Alexander the Great, War and Peace, Fraulein, Thundering Jets,
Operation Crossbow, Tarzan, the Ape Man.*

Linda Darnell

(b. Monetta Eloyse Darnell, Oct. 16, 1923, Dallas, Texas; d. April 10, 1965)
A great brunette beauty (with a face that, cameramen said, was "perfect from
every angle"), she was a most winning screen presence and deserved a fate
better than she had; died—destitute—in a fire in the home of a friend, her
onetime Hollywood secretary; before going to bed that fatal night, they had
watched (and she had laughed at) a TV showing of a movie she'd starred in
when 17, *Star Dust*—based, ironically, on her own "discovery" by a Hollywood scout; the ending was sad, the beginning beautiful; of French-Irish-
Cherokee heritage, she grew up in Dallas on a street named "Hollywood,"
one of five children of a postal clerk and a fiercely ambitious (for her) stage
mother; determined that her daughter would be a star, the mother carted her
off to the Coast twice before Linda was signed at 15 by 20th Century–Fox;
played leads (always adult roles) from the first, making her debut in *Hotel for
Women* ('39); in her second movie, replacing Loretta Young (who had left the
studio), she was cast as Tyrone Power's radiant young bride in *Daytime
Wife*—when not quite 16 and an 11th grader in the same Fox-lot school
attended by Shirley Temple and Jane Withers; studio publicity claimed she
was two years older; was a major star at Fox, headlining in 30 top films, for
exactly 12 years; made 14 other pictures elsewhere later (1951–65), not one of
which is memorable; at 19, declared her independence of her mother but did
not improve her lot; eloped with a much older, twice-divorced cameraman,
Peverell Marley (photographed her screen test and early films), a domineer-
ing, tight-fisted man who treated her like a child; in '48, adopted a daughter,
Charlotte ("Lola"); an affair with Howard Hughes caused the marriage to end
in divorce in '51; lost at the same time her Fox contract, popularity, and
lifetime savings (embezzled by her manager); two subsequent marriages also
ended in divorce—to Phillip Leibman (1954–55) and pilot Merle Robertson
(1957–63)—and led to a descent into alcoholism; was attempting to resurrect
her career with roles in touring plays when stricken with myasthenia gravis, a
debilitating muscular disease; cremated, as she requested, her ashes are buried
in a Pennsylvania cemetery near the home of her daughter.

MOVIE HIGHLIGHTS: *The Mark of Zorro, Brigham Young, Frontiersman,
Chad Hanna, Blood and Sand, The Loves of Edgar Allan Poe, Rise and*

Shine, It Happened Tomorrow, Summer Storm, Buffalo Bill, Sweet and Low-down, The Great John L., Hangover Square, Fallen Angel, Centennial Summer, Anna and the King of Siam, My Darling Clementine, Forever Amber, Unfaithfully Yours, The Walls of Jericho, A Letter to Three Wives, No Way Out, Slattery's Hurricane, Two Flags West, This Is My Love.

Laraine Day

(b. Loraine Johnson, Oct. 13, 1917, Roosevelt, Utah) Fresh-faced and a fascinating talent, she was a star at MGM for seven years (1939–45) and at RKO for another three (1946–48) before turning free-lance; private life may have kept her from achieving top-rank fame; early publicity put heavy emphasis on her devout Mormon faith (a fact) and on her being the mother of three adopted children (Angela, Christopher, and Michele), so fans were taken by surprise when, after five years, she divorced her first husband, musician Ray Hendricks, in '47; more, she created a legal furor by filing for divorce on January 20 in California (where divorce was not final until a year had passed) and, on January 21, marrying baseball's Leo "The Lip" Durocher after a quick divorce in Mexico; during her marriage to Durocher, she gave up a $1 million contract to be able to live with him in New York and paid scant attention to her career, making only a handful of pictures; late in '60, in a traditional Mormon ceremony (her first), she became the wife of TV exec Mike Grilikhes, later giving birth to two daughters, Dana Laraine and Gigi; *The Third Day* ('60) marked her departure from the screen, though she continued to act on TV; her early and only ambition was to be an actress; grew up, after 1931, in Long Beach, Calif., with her twin brother, Lamar, two older brothers, and a sister (two other children had died young); was the daughter of a contractor father and housewife mother whose grandfather, Charles C. Rich, was once sent by Brigham Young to found a Mormon colony in California; studied first with drama coach Elias Day (her screen name is in his honor) and was in many productions of the Long Beach Players' Guild; first professional stage role was in a touring production of *Conflict*, which led to bits in the movies *Stella Dallas* and *Scandal Sheet*; next, as Loraine Johnson, was the heroine in George O'Brien Westerns (*Border G-Men, The Painted Desert*, etc.); made her debut at Metro in *Sergeant Madden* ('39) with Wallace Beery, but it was her poignant performance the following year, on loan-out, in *My Son, My Son* that established her as a star.

MOVIE HIGHLIGHTS: *Tarzan Finds a Son, Calling Dr. Kildare* (and six others in the series), *I Take This Woman, Foreign Correspondent, And One*

Was Beautiful, The Bad Man, The Trial of Mary Dugan, Kathleen, Journey for Margaret, Mr. Lucky, The Story of Dr. Wassell, Bride by Mistake, Keep Your Powder Dry, Those Endearing Young Charms, The Locket, Tycoon, My Dear Secretary, Toy Tiger, The High and the Mighty.

Yvonne De Carlo

(b. Peggy Yvonne Middleton, Sept. 1, 1922, Vancouver, B.C.) "The Most Beautiful Girl in the World"—that was the legend beneath her name in ads for 1945's *Salome, Where She Danced*, her first starring movie; studio publicists claimed it was the sultry brunette's screen debut, but, starting in '42, she'd already played bits—as Peggy Middleton—in 17 films, including *For Whom the Bell Tolls* and *This Gun for Hire*; when *Salome* (with its dance of the seven veils) made her instantly famous, Universal sent her to New York for two months to learn how to act like a movie star—put her up at the Sherry-Netherland hotel and enrolled her at John Robert Powers model agency school, where she learned such things as how to make an entrance; starred sexily and exclusively at Universal until '51; working in many Technicolor Westerns, in which she learned to be an expert shot, led to an unladylike hobby—has acquired over the years a collection of guns (and knives) that would make Gene Autry green with envy; before the star's birth, her mother announced the baby would be a girl and grow up to be a dancer, an ambition that quickly became the star's own; has said that as a child, with Eleanor Powell as her idol, she would line up her dolls and teach them "dancing lessons"; trained as a dancer first at the June Roper studio in her hometown, and in her teens, quitting school, spent six months each year in Hollywood studying dance with Marge Champion's father and Fanchon & Marco; began dancing professionally at 14 as a soloist at Vancouver's Palomar Café; moved to Hollywood when 18 and worked at $37.50 a week as a specialty dancer at the Florentine Gardens nightclub; next did a stint in the chorus at Earl Carroll's until Paramount signed her to a starlet's contract; training there prepared her for *Salome* and all that followed; ardently wooed by many of the world's richest, most powerful men, including Arabian sheiks and Howard Hughes, she remained single until she was 33; then she married a stuntman, Robert Morgan, by whom she has two sons, Bruce and Michael; made her Broadway debut in '70 in the musical *Follies*, playing, splendidly, a movie star—those lessons at John Robert Powers paid off.

MOVIE HIGHLIGHTS: *Frontier Gal, Brute Force, Slave Girl, Black Bart, Song of Scheherazade, Casbah, River Lady, Criss Cross, Calamity Jane and Sam Bass, The Gal Who Took the West, The Desert Hawk, The Buccaneer's Girl, Tomahawk, Hotel Sahara, Silver City, Scarlet Angel, Hurricane Smith, The San Francisco Story, Sombrero, The Captain's Paradise, The Ten Commandments, Band of Angels, McLintock!, Munster, Go Home.*

Gloria De Haven

(b. Gloria Mildred De Haven, July 23, 1925, Los Angeles, Calif.) Movie careers can be curiously unpredictable; MGM starred her in '44 with June Allyson in *Two Girls and a Sailor*; was more beautiful than her co-star and had more screen experience, a better singing voice, and a "Petty Girl" figure, albeit pocket-size—yet Allyson became the bigger star; was the daughter of Mr. and Mrs. Carter De Haven, as they were billed when starring on stage and in silent movies; father's name actually was Francis O'Callahan, which he changed legally before Gloria, the youngest of three, was born; she laughs: "My mother was 43 when I came, and I think I was *supposed* to be born. She was a one-man woman and my father was quite a chaser. After 22 years of marriage, of her tolerating this, they divorced. One year and two months later, they got married again and lived together for exactly six months, during which time I was conceived"; adds that she, too, has a "surprise baby," her youngest daughter, "who enjoys teasing me about it"; was acting in movies at 11; a bit in Chaplin's *Modern Times* led to better juvenile roles in *Susan and God, Two-Faced Woman*, etc.; after graduation from Ken-Mar Professional School, she sang with the bands of Bob Crosby and Jan Savitt before becoming, at 18, Metro's curvaceous "Baby Blonde" (hair is naturally brown); got much publicity as a teen-aged leading lady by giving Sinatra his first screen kiss in *Step Lively*; on the last day of filming, he gave her her first piece of real jewelry, a rose-gold wristwatch studded with diamonds and rubies, and he had to turn on the charm to persuade her mother to let her keep it; marriages (four, but only three husbands) and time out for motherhood almost certainly retarded her career; marital record: actor John Payne (1944–50), by whom she has two children, Kathleen and Thomas; businessman Martin Kimmel (married for three 1953–54 months), and Richard Fincher, who became a Florida State Senator (married and divorced twice: 1957–63, 1964–68), father of her Harry and Faith; says, "I still see these men, am still friendly with them all";

when her youngest went off to college, she said, "From the time I was 15, I supported or was responsible for someone—a parent, a sister or my children. Now, for the first time in my life, I am free, alone. And it's a fabulous feeling."

MOVIE HIGHLIGHTS: *Best Foot Forward, Thousands Cheer, Broadway Rhythm, The Thin Man Goes Home, Manhattan Serenade, Between Two Women, Summer Holiday, The Doctor and the Girl, Yes Sir, That's My Baby, Scene of the Crime, I'll Get By, Summer Stock, The Yellow Cab Man, Three Little Words, Two Tickets to Broadway, So This Is Paris, Down Among the Sheltering Palms, The Girl Rush.*

Philip Dorn

(b. Hein Van Der Niet, Sept. 30, 1901, Schevenigen, Holland; d. May 9, 1975) Of all the European actors who left their imprint on Hollywood movies of the '40s, none was more gifted, or more handsome, than this big dark-haired Dutchman with that superb bass-cello speaking voice; his face was infinitely kind, but one never doubted that he dared to be gentle because at the center of his being was wisdom and strength; under another professional name, Frits Van Dongen (assumed because his own name translated, literally, "nothing"), he made several movies in Europe in the '30s but was far more renowned on the stage, which he regarded as his true métier; earlier career: boat builder; arrived in Hollywood in '39 with second wife Marianne; planned to do a picture or two at Universal and immediately return home, but the outbreak of the war in Europe precluded that; for the duration he acted in American films—and dreamed of a return to the stage; by an early marriage, which ended in divorce, he had a daughter, Femia, who accompanied him to Hollywood, and a son, who remained behind (at war's end, he learned that his son had died, at 16, in a Nazi prison after refusing to go to a German work camp); was under contract for six years at MGM, starting there in '40 when he co-starred with Norma Shearer in *Escape*, recalled by him as a pleasant experience; not so *Reunion in France* with Joan Crawford—mutual "sheer hate" was so evident in their voices that the stars had to redub every foot of their love scenes; in '51, he made his last American film, *Sealed Cargo*, and to the puzzlement of fans, simply vanished; fate had tragic surprises awaiting him; after making a number of pictures in Europe, he was back in Holland starring on stage in *The Fourposter* in '54 when he was struck by a heavy object falling from the roof of a building; a stroke followed this blow, and a bit later, he underwent surgery to relieve the buildup of water pressure on the brain, which left him with slurred speech; though director George Stevens besieged him to accept a major role in *The Diary of Anne Frank*, he refused out of professional pride—did not want audiences to be made aware of the change in him—and never acted again; on Thanksgiving Day 1964, the same day that Patricia Neal was similarly stricken, he suffered a massive stroke; even more fortunate than she, he finally, miraculously, recovered the full use of all his limbs.

MOVIE HIGHLIGHTS: *Ski Patrol, Enemy Agent, Ziegfeld Girl, Underground, Tarzan's Secret Treasure, Calling Dr. Gillespie, Random Harvest, Paris After Dark, Chetniks, Blonde Fever, Passage to Marseille, Escape in the Desert, I Remember Mama, Panther's Moon, The Fighting Kentuckian, Spy Hunt, Salto Mortale.*

Kirk Douglas

(b. Issur Danielovitch, Dec. 9 1916, Amsterdam, N.Y.) Rugged, two-fisted, durable star, filled with raw vitality, who garnered Best Actor Oscar nominations for *Champion, The Bad and the Beautiful*, and *Lust for Life*; after graduating from St. Lawrence University, worked his way through the American Academy of Dramatic Arts and went directly to Broadway in *Spring Again* ('41), *The Three Sisters*, etc.; went to Hollywood in '46 for *The Strange Love of Martha Ivers* after former Academy classmate Lauren Bacall recommended him to producer Hal Wallis; another classmate, Diana Dill, who acts as Diana Douglas, was his first wife (1943–51) and mother of his sons Michael and Joel; his eighth movie, *Champion* ('49), made him a box-office sensation; wisely chose to do this low-budget prizefight film though agents pressured him, instead, to accept a co-starring role with Gregory Peck and Ava Gardner in *The Great Sinner* at MGM; except for one year at Warners following *Champion*, he was never under contract at any studio; has said, "I've been a maverick—I've made my own way"; admits his judgment of roles hasn't always been infallible—rejected both *Stalag 17* and *Cat Ballou*, each of which won Oscars for its star; formed his own production company, Bryna (named for his mother), in '55, turning out such multimillion dollar epics as *Spartacus* and *The Vikings*, in which he starred; many films of his have had an identical plot device—the individual fighting against society; his understanding of this theme surely comes out of his own background, which he has termed "as corny as a B script"; once described himself as "the kid who worked up from abject poverty to become a champion," then added this success secret, "But you got to fight—success is a combination of hard work and luck"; was the middle child and only son of seven children born to Russian immigrant parents; his peddler father, who changed the family name to Demsky, deserted the family when he was a lad of 5, forcing him to become a wage earner while still in grade school; ever since, it's been "dukes up"; has been married since '54 to French-born Anne Buydens (mother of his Peter and Eric), who has characterized him as a "volcano" of a presence—"the tension spits out of him like sparks."

MOVIE HIGHLIGHTS: *I Walk Alone, Out of the Past, Mourning Becomes Electra, Walls of Jericho, A Letter to Three Wives, The Glass Menagerie, Young Man with a Horn, Ace in the Hole, Detective Story, The Big Sky, The Story of Three Loves, The Juggler, Act of Love, Ulysses, Paths of Glory, Gunfight at the O.K. Corral, The Devil's Disciple, A Town without Pity, Lonely Are the Brave, Seven Days in May, The Way West, The Brotherhood, The Arrangement, Saturn 3, The Man from Snowy River.*

Tom Drake

(b. Alfred Alderdice Jr., Aug. 5, 1918, Brooklyn, N.Y.; d. Aug. 11, 1982) Soft-spoken and pleasing, he was for six seasons (1944–49) MGM's perennial "Boy Next Door"; was literally and most winningly that in *Meet Me in St. Louis*; though he'd been on Broadway under his real name (in *June Night, Clean Beds,* etc.), Metro moguls insisted on a name change, first pegging him, for a couple of weeks, "Tom Blake"; had yet an earlier movie monicker, "Richard Alden," which he used just once, playing at 22 Cary Grant's 16-year-old son in *The Howards of Virginia*; friends always called him "Buddy"; first screen test for MGM, done in New York when he was playing the juvenile lead in *Janie*, was a flop—official report on it read: "A skinny kid on the Dead End type. Hard face to photograph"; deciding to give him another shot, the studio handed him a ticket to the Coast; arrived in Hollywood on a Tuesday, tested on Wednesday, and on Thursday was on camera with June Allyson and Gloria De Haven in *Two Girls and a Sailor*; seeing him in this, Judy Garland requested him for *Meet Me in St. Louis*, which made him a bobby-soxers' delight; at his peak, received 4,000 fan letters a week; grew up in New Rochelle, N.Y., where he sang in the church choir and attended Iona School; his English father, a wealthy international linen importer, died when he was 11, and his mother when he was 16, after which an uncle was his guardian; was a student at Mercerburg Academy in Pennsylvania, where he became interested in acting and went directly into stock companies; began acting on Broadway in his late teens; explaining his great popularity in movies, producer Joseph Pasternak said, "He has the same quality June Allyson has—he's just nice and average enough for the average girl to find a facsimile of him in her hometown"; was married just once, early and briefly, to stage actress Christopher Curtis; during his first years in Hollywood, he shared his Beverly Hills home with his sister Claire, a divorcee with two small children, and three Great Danes; the dogs were perhaps not a reflection on another named Lassie, with whom he starred in three movies, though he once candidly admitted being none too fond of the collie; continued to work in movies and on TV to the end, but his career took a sharp nose dive when he left MGM.

MOVIE HIGHLIGHTS: *The White Cliffs of Dover, Maisie Goes to Reno, Marriage Is a Private Affair, Mrs. Parkington, This Man's Navy, The Green Years, Courage of Lassie, Cass Timberlane, The Beginning or the End?, I'll Be Yours, Hills of Home, Words and Music, Mr. Belvedere Goes to College, Scene of the Crime, The Great Rupert, Disc Jockey, Sangaree, Raintree County, The Bramble Bush, The Singing Nun, The Sandpiper, Johnny Reno.*

Bobby Driscoll

(b. Robert Driscoll, March 3, 1937, Cedar Rapids, Iowa; d. March 30, 1968) Popular child star whose performance in *The Window* ('49) won him a special Academy Award as "the outstanding juvenile actor of the year"; the Oscar was handed to the 12-year-old, small for his age, dressed spiffily in his first tux, by Donald O'Connor—a former kid star himself, but one on whom the gods smiled more kindly; the only child of a businessman father and retired schoolteacher mother, Bobby was 6 when his family moved to Pasadena, Calif.; a barber there, impressed by the outgoing lad with an obviously high I.Q., urged his mother to put him in movies; took him to MGM where they were casting a Margaret O'Brien film, *Lost Angel*, and he was hired on the spot to play a bit; soon became a full-fledged juvenile star at Disney in *Song of the South*, etc., earning $50,000 a year, and was so well supervised at the studio that no one was allowed to utter a swear word in front of him; home life was equally circumspect—was sent to public schools (so he wouldn't be "spoiled"), attended church each Sunday with his parents, grace was said before meals, and he was regularly reminded that the talent which brought

51

him worldwide fame came from God; child stars do grow up—with sometimes tragic consequences; when 16, the bottom fell out of his career ("I was carried on a silver platter and then dumped into the garbage can"); at 17 a high school pusher introduced him to drugs, and the hard years began; police picked him up at 19 on a marijuana charge; was the first in a series of arrests—for possession of a deadly weapon, burglary, check forgery, and drugs again; after being sent to the State Narcotics Rehabilitation Center for six months, he worked for a while as a carpenter; married at 19, he now had three kids, a heroin habit, and no hope; alone, he went off to New York at 28 "to start a new life"—and just disappeared; when found dead in an abandoned Greenwich Village flat three years later, he had no identification, no money, and, going unrecognized, was buried in a pauper's grave; only through fingerprints a year and a half later did his mother—recently widowed—learn of his fate; warning other young people of the dangers of drugs then became her mission; after granting an interview about her son to *Movie Digest* magazine in '72, the mother wrote its editor (this book's author) "to ask if there would be some compensation to me. I don't want to seem mercenary—my sole aim is to help in the fight against narcotics. I am in pretty bad straits since all our money went down the drain trying to help Bobby. I didn't even have enough to pay for my husband's funeral."

MOVIE HIGHLIGHTS: *The Sullivans, Sunday Dinner for a Soldier, The Big Bonanza, Identity Unknown, From This Day Forward, Miss Susie Slagle's, O.S.S., So Goes My Love, So Dear to My Heart, Melody Time, Treasure Island, When I Grow Up, The Happy Time, The Party Crashers.*

Howard Duff

(b. Howard Duff, Nov. 24, 1917, Bremerton, Wash.) Brawny, blue-eyed actor who went from radio fame (title role in "Sam Spade, Detective") to the co-star spot in his first picture, 1947's *Brute Force*, and a long-standing romance with Ava Gardner that had gossip columnists predicting marriage; "We fought for three years," he said later; instead, he was married (sometimes stormily) from '51 to '73 to actress-director Ida Lupino, with whom he eventually co-starred in the successful TV sitcom "Mr. Adams and Eve"; said Lupino: "I fell in love with his voice on the radio before I ever met him"; when a mutual friend introduced them, though, she disliked him on sight, feeling he was "cold," before concluding that "his shyness gives you a false impression of him"; arrived at the latter opinion when, in '49, they co-starred in the movie *Woman in Hiding* (Ronald Reagan, scheduled to play opposite Lupino, broke his leg playing in a baseball game and was replaced by Duff); godfather of their only child, Bridget—Lupino's ex-husband, Collier Young; the future actor had moved with his family to Seattle when he was 4; because of his distinctive voice, the drama coach at Roosevelt High, from which he graduated in '34, encouraged him to pursue an acting career; began at the Seattle Repertory Playhouse, financing his training by working as a radio announcer at station KOMO; in '38, went to San Francisco and was an announcer at KFRC before winning the lead in a radio serial, "Phantom Pilot"; two years after the show, and after he moved to Hollywood, he entered the Army, eventually serving as a radio correspondent for Armed Forces Radio before being honorably discharged in '45; "Sam Spade," which he played for five years, even after becoming a movie favorite, opened all doors for him in Hollywood; eventually co-starred with Ida Lupino in five features, including *Private Hell No. 36* and *While the City Sleeps*; she also directed him in the pilot of his TV series "Dante," which ran for one season (1960–61) on NBC; he'd had much better luck earlier (1966–69), when starring in the "Felony Squad" series; in recent years, he's done, and enjoyed doing, voiceovers for television commercials, saying, "It takes me back to the days when I was playing Sam Spade; you come to the studio, read your lines and get paid royally—it's almost like stealing money."

MOVIE HIGHLIGHTS: *The Naked City, All My Sons, Calamity Jane and Sam Bass, Red Canyon, Johnny Stool Pigeon, Shakedown, The Lady from Texas, Steel Town, Models, Inc., Roar of the Crowd, Jennifer, Tanganyika, Yellow Mountain, Women's Prison, Broken Star, Blackjack Ketchum—Desperado, Boys' Night Out, The Late Show, Kramer vs. Kramer, A Wedding.*

Dan Duryea

(b. Dan Duryea, Jan. 23, 1907, White Plains, N.Y.; d. June 7, 1968) Thin, blond actor who often played a "good guy" on Broadway, such as the G-Man in *Dead End*, but became one of the screen's great villains, starting in '41 as Bette Davis's treacherous nephew, Leo Hubbard, in *The Little Foxes*; off screen, he was a quiet, reserved, popular man, the antithesis of the slippery characters he played so convincingly; was also regarded as a model husband and father, being married to one wife, non-pro Helen Bryan, from '31 until her death in '67; two sons: Peter, an actor, and Richard, who has been the manager of the singing Beach Boys; waited on tables to pay his way through

Cornell, where he played leads in several productions and, in his senior year, succeeded Franchot Tone as president of the drama society; upon graduation, at the urging of his parents, he became an ad salesman in New York, starting at $50 a week; stuck with it for six years, then illness made it expedient that he find work with less stress; turned to the stage, making his debut on Broadway at 28 in *Caesar and Cleopatra*; a number of other plays followed—*Many Mansions*, *Missouri Legend*, *The Virginian*, etc.; career on the boards was capped by *The Little Foxes* ('39), with movie producer Sam Goldwyn realizing that no other actor could improve on his sly portrayal of treacherous Leo and importing him to Hollywood; he later got to play yet another of playwright Lillian Hellman's scheming Hubbards—Leo's uncle Oscar—in *Another Part of the Forest* ('48); in the meantime, being a movie menace had made him a millionaire, with a lavish hillside Hollywood home and another at Lake Arrowhead, where he enjoyed a quite innocent favorite pastime, sailing; later had his own TV series, "Affairs of China Smith," in which he was a true-blue hero.

MOVIE HIGHLIGHTS: *Ball of Fire*, *The Pride of the Yankees*, *Sahara*, *Woman in the Window*, *Mrs. Parkington*, *None But the Lonely Heart*, *Ministry of Fear*, *The Valley of Decision*, *Lady on a Train*, *Along Came Jones*, *Scarlet Street*, *The Black Angel*, *River Lady*, *Black Bart*, *Larceny*, *Criss Cross*, *One Way Street*, *Winchester 73*, *Thunder Bay*, *Terror Street*, *Ride Clear of Diablo*, *Battle Hymn*, *Kathy O'*, *Six Black Horses*.

Faye Emerson

(b. Faye Margaret Emerson, July 8, 1917, Elizabeth, La.; d. March 9, 1983) Subtle, sexy, and a dynamite talent, the blonde actress was on screen from '41 to '50, under contract the entire time at Warner Bros., starting in small roles and working her way to stardom; after her parents divorced when she was 3, she was shuttled between her father, who had moved to Chicago, and her mother, then living in El Paso, Texas; began acting in church plays at 12; after attending San Diego State College, she trained for the stage with the St. James Repertory Company in Carmel, Calif., and went directly from there to a screen test and studio contract; her first marriage, before entering movies, to William W. Crawford Jr., by whom she had a son, William III (called "Scoop"), created no stir, nor did her third and last, to bandleader Skitch Henderson; her second wedding, though, made international headlines when, in '44, she became the bride of Brig. Gen. Elliott Roosevelt, son of the president of the United States; mother-in-law Eleanor Roosevelt grew quite fond of her, and when she left the White House after FDR's death and moved back to Hyde Park, she gave the actress many priceless family possessions; the fact that husband Elliott insisted upon hanging a buffalo head and having a stuffed mountain goat in their living room had nothing to do with their divorce in '50; of her marriages, she continued to say this one was the happiest and that if she had it to do over she "might have been wiser"; settled in New York after her Hollywood years and became even more celebrated as a TV talk-show hostess and quiz-show panelist; was noted for her charm, brains, cleavage (displayed in tasteful off-the-shoulder gowns with plunging V-necks), and distinctive hairdo (center-parted and pulled back into a bun); in '63, at the peak of this career, rich and weary of putting on makeup, she sailed to Spain; put down roots on the island of Majorca in a beautiful, white-washed house on a hillside, lived a life of leisure, allowed herself the luxury of growing fat and letting her hair turn silver, and never faced a movie or TV camera again; reportedly, she also penned her autobiography, in which the Roosevelt family figured prominently, but as of this date, no such book has been published.

MOVIE HIGHLIGHTS: *The Nurse's Secret, Bad Men of Missouri, Manpower, Blues in the Night, Juke Box Girl, Murder in the Big House, The Hard Way, The Desert Song, Air Force, Destination Tokyo, Between Two Worlds, The Very Thought of You, The Mask of Dimitrios, Hotel Berlin, Uncertain Glory, Danger Signal, Her Kind of Man, Nobody Lives Forever, Guilty Bystander.*

William Eythe

(b. William John Joseph Eythe, April 7, 1918, Mars, Pa.; d. Jan. 26, 1957) Without a "Tyrone Power" on its star roster—a black-haired, handsome young man with thick lashes and melancholy eyes—20th Century–Fox would not have been Fox; with the original Power in military uniform, the studio counted itself lucky to discover this talented guy—4-F because of punctured ear drums caused by a fight in a play on Broadway; springboard to Hollywood was the role of a good-looking, doomed Nazi soldier, Lt. Tonder, in Steinbeck's *The Moon Is Down*; studio veterans soon found he had a wacky sense of humor and never forgot the day he brought stripper Ann Corio around and, with a straight face, introduced her to all and sundry as "my mother"; unlike brother Howard "Dutch" Eythe (rhymes with scythe), a football hero who made All-American at Carnegie Tech, theater was in his blood from grade school days; was particularly interested in scenic-costume designing, songwriting, and directing, which he always preferred to acting; at the height of his movie fame, he was to be found directing (and starring in) such plays as *The Glass Menagerie* on Hollywood stages or producing (and appearing in) revues like *Lend an Ear*, which made a star of Carol Channing when he next took it to Broadway; put himself through Carnegie Tech via various jobs—was a bookkeeper, clerked in a dairy store, delivered lectures on astronomy (did not write his own material) at Pittsburgh's Buhl Planetarium, and staged musical fashion shows at a local department store, penning and playing on the piano his own tunes; upon graduation from college, he seriously considered entering a seminary to study for the priesthood but, deciding that wasn't meant to be, eventually followed his theatrical inclinations; became a song-and-dance man with the Pittsburgh Civic Playhouse, acted on local radio stations, then in the summer of '41, joined his first professional stock company at Cohasset, Mass., which was headed by former film star Ruth Chatterton; launched on Broadway in '42, he returned there eight years later, when he and 20th Century–Fox parted company, and starred in *The Liar* and *Out of This World*.

MOVIE HIGHLIGHTS: *The Ox-Bow Incident, The Song of Bernadette, The Eve of St. Mark, Wilson, A Wing and a Prayer, A Royal Scandal, Col. Effingham's Raid, The House on 92nd Street, Centennial Summer, Mr. Reckless, Meet Me at Dawn, Special Agent, Customs Agent.*

Betty Field

(b. Betty Field, Feb. 8, 1918, Boston, Mass.; d. Sept. 13, 1973) Versatile, uniquely talented star, with a voice totally distinctive in pitch and timbre, who, at any point in the '40s, could have given Bette Davis a run for the money as Hollywood's drama queen; unfortunately, she had three "handicaps": She chose never to play the same kind of character twice, making it hard for fans to get a peg on her (ranged from the sharecropper's gallant young wife in *The Southerner* to the sultry, trampish Mae in *Of Mice and Men*, a leading role for which, incidentally, she was paid a paltry $1,000), she was never a beauty (though she could play one), and she lacked the movie-star "mentality" (who ever heard of a star who preferred buses to studio limos?); the stage—not motion pictures—was her life; instead of high school, she elected to attend the American Academy of Dramatic Arts, going directly after her graduation there at 16 to a one-line role on Broadway in *Page Miss Glory*;

was in nine New York plays, with leads in *Room Service* and *The Primrose Path*, before going to Hollywood at 21 to co-star as Jackie Cooper's high school sweetheart in *What a Life*, the first Henry Aldrich comedy; sandwiched in many other plays during the decade she starred in movies; in '46, won the New York Drama Critics' Award in *Dream Girl*, written specially for her by husband Elmer Rice; married in '42, divorced in '55, they had three children: John, Paul, and Judith; was married in '56 to lawyer-criminologist Edwin Lukas, and then, from '68 on to illustrator-portrait painter Raymond L. Olivere; after *The Great Gatsby* ('49; as Alan Ladd's adored, unattainable Daisy), movie fans did not see her again for six years; returned then to play a middle-aged matron, Kim Novak's careworn Kansas mom, in *Picnic*—being all of 37; for the rest of her career, she alternated between the stage and movies, in which she always played character roles.

MOVIE HIGHLIGHTS: *Seventeen, Victory, The Shepherd of the Hills, Kings Row, Blues in the Night, Are Husbands Necessary?, Flesh and Fantasy, Tomorrow the World, The Great Moment, Bus Stop, Peyton Place, Hound-Dog Man, Butterfield 8, The Birdman of Alcatraz, Middle of the Night, Seven Women, Band of Gold, How to Save a Marriage—and Ruin Your Life, Coogan's Bluff.*

Barry Fitzgerald

(b. William Joseph Shields, March 10, 1888, Dublin, Ireland; d. Jan. 4, 1961) Wrinkled little leprechaun whose fey performance as the old Irish priest, Father Fitzgibbon, in *Going My Way* won him the Best Supporting Oscar—and soon afterwards, practicing golf swings in his living room, he knocked its head off; was not, incidentally, Catholic; co-starred again with Bing Crosby later in *Welcome Stranger* and *Top o' the Morning*; the brother of character actor Arthur Shields, with whom he often acted in movies (*The Long Voyage Home, How Green Was My Valley*, etc.), he got a late start as an actor; after graduation from Skerrys College, he worked for 20 years—still living at home with his parents—as an insurance clerk in the order department of the Labor Exchange in Dublin; at 28, while working there by day, he began acting by night with the Abbey Theater, appearing first in mob scenes; took the name by which he became famous to keep his civil service employers from knowing what he was up to; quit his job at 42 to act full-time with the Abbey; that same year ('30), he made his movie debut with the group in a bit part in *Juno and the Paycock*, directed by Alfred Hitchcock; made three tours of the United States with the company; was called to Hollywood in '36 by John Ford, who cast him as roistering Fluther Good in *The Plough and the Stars*; becoming a Ford "regular," he last acted for the director in *The Quiet Man* ('52); continued to act on Broadway (in *The White Steed, Tanyard Street*, etc.) even after he was an in-demand movie character actor; became an American citizen and thoroughly Americanized—getting to and from the studios on a motorcycle, haunting movie houses playing cowboy pictures (was overjoyed at 59 to finally act in a Western, *California*); never took his fame seriously—lived quietly, with his stand-in, in an old, vine-covered white house in the Hollywood hills, filled with books and symphonic records; returned to Ireland in '58 and stayed; always said, "I never want to marry; I don't want any woman around. I'm a bachelor and I'm going to stay that way"; kept his promise.

MOVIE HIGHLIGHTS: *Ebb Tide, Bringing Up Baby, The Dawn Patrol, Four Men and a Prayer, The Saint Strikes Back, The Sea Wolf, Tarzan's Secret Treasure, Corvette K-225, I Love a Soldier, None But the Lonely Heart, Incendiary Blonde, And Then There Were None, The Stork Club, Two Years before the Mast, Easy Come, Easy Go, The Naked City, The Sainted Sisters, Miss Tatlock's Millions, The Story of Seabiscuit, Union Station, Silver City, The Catered Affair, Rooney, Broth of a Boy.*

Rhonda Fleming

(b. Marilyn Louis, Aug. 10, 1923, Los Angeles, Calif.) If, in 1939, the beautiful green-eyed redhead had won radio's talent-finding *Gateway to Hollywood* competition—and she almost did—she would be known today as "Gale Storm"; was runner-up to Josephine Cottle, a Texas teen-ager, who won the name and a studio contract; a fatalist, she shed no tears ("I've always believed that those things destined for me will come to me"); a late bloomer, she was pegged a "newcomer" through most of the '40s, even after she began playing leads; first became famous when co-starring and singing with Bing Crosby in *A Connecticut Yankee in King Arthur's Court*, her first in Technicolor, for which she was ready-made; won the part over Ann Blyth and, it's said, 200 other contenders; broke through to stardom a short while later—after plastic surgery provided her with the most photogenic of noses (which her original wasn't); had a theatrical heritage; grandfather John C. Graham was a Mormon pioneer who, as a youth, crossed the plains to Utah with Brigham Young and acted on stage for many years at the old Salt Lake

Theater; her mother, Effie Graham, was a singer who appeared with Al Jolson in *Dancing in the Dark* on Broadway; after graduation from Beverly Hills High, she began her own career as a Paul Hesse photography model and, on stage, as a long-stemmed dancer in the first edition of Ken Murray's girly-girly *Blackouts*; at the same time was singing in oratorios and acting in religious plays at her church; studied acting at the Cumnock School and won a starlet's contract and her new name (first spelled Ronda)—but no roles—at 20th Century–Fox; made her screen debut as a dance hall girl in '43 in John Wayne's *In Old Oklahoma* (aka *War of the Wildcats*); David O. Selznick, signing her without a test, groomed her for stardom, eventually selling her contract to Paramount, which finished the job; married and divorced four husbands: builder Tom Lane (1940–42; son Kent Lane is an actor), Dr. Louis Morrill (1952–58), actor Lang Jeffries (1960–62), and producer-director Hall Bartlett (1966–72); in '78 was married to theater owner Ted Mann.

MOVIE HIGHLIGHTS: *Since You Went Away, When Strangers Marry, Spellbound* (bits), *Abilene Town, The Spiral Staircase, Out of the Past, The Great Lover, The Redhead and the Cowboy, The Eagle and the Hawk, Cross Winds, Little Egypt, Hong Kong, Golden Hawk, Tropic Zone, Pony Express, Those Redheads from Seattle, Yankee Pasha, Jivaro, Gunfight at the O.K. Corral, Home before Dark.*

Glenn Ford

(b. Gwyllyn Samuel Newton Ford, May 1, 1916, Quebec, Canada) In many of his nearly 200 movies, since making his debut in '39 (in *Heaven with a Barbed Wire Fence*), this star has played a variation of the strong, quiet man who takes it until he has had enough—and then it's "Bad guys, beware"; off the screen, he is also less than loquacious ("Actors talk too much") but, with one major role leading to another, he's rarely had much to fight about; even got along splendidly with Harry Cohn, tough (and disliked by many stars) boss at Columbia, where he was long under contract; private life, though, has occasionally given him problems; was married for 16 years (1943–59) to musical star Eleanor Powell (one son: Peter), and the divorce was not entirely amicable; for years, then, he was a swinging bachelor-about-town; of that period, a newspaperman pal, James Bacon, once jested, "Glenn promises to marry every girl he goes to bed with. . . . Sometimes it gets him into trouble"; Judy Garland was one of his conquests, and a photograph of her, still on view in his Beverly Hills home, is inscribed; "Now I can look upward and see the beauty of the sun and moon and the love you give to me"; nearby are photos of other screen lovelies, including Angie Dickinson and Hope Lange; second marriage, to soap opera actress Kathryn Hays, lasted two years (1966–68); at 61 was married to actress-model Cynthia Hayward, 29; grew up in Santa Monica, Calif., after age 5; was a stableboy at Will Rogers' ranch as a teen-ager, and later, a little theater stage manager before turning actor; took his screen name from the Canadian town of Glenford, in which his Welsh father, a building contractor, owned a paper mill; career was interrupted for three years (1942–45) for active duty in the Pacific as a Marine Corps captain; travel is a passion with him—likes best the films taking him to distant locations; among his proudest accomplishments: climbing Mont Blanc and graduating from the Cordon Bleu in Paris; guards his privacy, saying, "My life is my own."

MOVIE HIGHLIGHTS: *The Lady in Question, So Ends Our Night, Texas, The Desperadoes, A Stolen Life, Destroyer, Gilda, The Loves of Carmen, Lust for Gold, The White Tower, Follow the Sun, Secret of Convict Lake, Affair in Trinidad, The Big Heat, Interrupted Melody, The Blackboard Jungle, Trial, The Teahouse of the August Moon, The Cowboy, Cimarron, A Pocketful of Miracles, Is Paris Burning?, Santee, Midway, Superman.*

Susanna Foster

(b. Susanna DeLee Flanders Larson, Dec. 6, 1924, Chicago, Ill.) Blonde soprano who, in the '40s, was Universal's golden songbird and, as far as her career was concerned, her own worst enemy; walked out on her contract in '45 to star on stage in operettas with tenor Wilbur Evans, a much older man whom she married in '48; had two sons by him, Philip and Michael, and was divorced in '56; no longer in demand in Hollywood or in the theater, she lived in New York with her sons and, to support them, held many odd jobs—switchboard operator, swimming instructor, typist, receptionist—never earning more than $180 a week; finally returned to Hollywood, by bus, in '74 but did not receive a heartwarming welcome; her first arrival in the movie capital had been far different; growing up in Minneapolis, she began singing in imitation of her screen idol, Jeanette MacDonald; was discovered at 11 by a local bandleader, Carl Johnson; he brought her to the attention of Merle Potter, movie critic of the *Minneapolis Journal*, who arranged radio appear-ances for her; thanks to a record of hers that he sent to MGM executives, she was taken to Hollywood at 12; Metro moguls, astonished at the high-register range of her voice, immediately signed her, decided her screen name would be simply "Suzanne," announced that she would star in *B above High C*, never made the film, and quickly dropped her option; moving on to a contract at Paramount, she made a sensational film debut at 15, as Mary Martin's opera-singing daughter, in *The Great Victor Herbert*; disappointed with later roles she was given, and highly vocal about it, the teen-ager managed to make herself thoroughly unpopular at the studio, acquiring a reputation as "a brat to end all brats"; was indeed popular with fans and on the Universal lot after '43, until she decided—to her eventual regret—to take a powder from movie fame.

MOVIE HIGHLIGHTS: *There's Magic in Music* (aka *The Hard-Boiled Canary*), *Glamour Boy, Star Spangled Rhythm, Top Man, The Phantom of the Opera, The Climax, Bowery to Broadway, Follow the Boys, This Is the Life, Frisco Sal, That Night with You.*

Ava Gardner

(b. Ava Lavinia Gardner, Dec. 24, 1922, Grabtown, N.C.) Her longevity as a star—more than 80 films to date—is its own reprimand to those who labeled her an "opportunist" when at 19—gorgeous, naïve, and unknown—she became Mickey Rooney's first bride; he was the first star she met, when 17, on her first day at MGM; marriage lasted 16 months; next was briefly (1945–46) the fifth wife of bandleader Artie Shaw, who set out to "educate" her, forced her to read "good" books, threw away the "trashy" novels she preferred, including *Forever Amber* by Kathleen Winsor—the author was destined, ironically, to be the next Mrs. Shaw; Artie Shaw might be astonished to learn that Ava, a British resident since '68, regularly attends the opera and ballet in London; Frank Sinatra was her third groom (1951–57); his career was in the doldrums then and her being nominated for the Best Actress Oscar in *Mogambo* ('53) did nothing to enhance the marriage's chance for success; roster of her romances is endless: bullfighter Miguel Dominguin, Howard Hughes (offered her a fortune in cash to marry him), Howard Duff, Stewart Granger, Walter Chiari, George C. Scott, etc.; began at Metro in '40 at $50 a week and with much phony publicity, including the canard that she toiled in tobacco fields as a child; was 2 and the youngest of six when her father lost his farm, moved the family to Smithfield, and went to work in a sawmill; mother ran a boarding house for female schoolteachers; after graduating from Smithfield High, she studied typing and shorthand at Atlantic Christian College and went to New York, where a sister lived, in an unsuccessful search for a secretarial job; before she returned home, her brother-in-law, photographer Larry Tarr, took photos of her, which he showed to MGM execs; was brought back to New York, given a test (silent because of her cornpone accent) and a contract; for four years she posed for pinups and did unbilled bits (*We Were Dancing, Kid Glove Killer*, etc.); got her first screen credit in '44 in *Three Men in White*; playing George Raft's sweetheart in *Whistle Stop* ('45) and Burt Lancaster's in *The Killers* ('46) made her a star; leaving MGM after 17 years of "slavery" (her term), she admitted being "afraid," saying: "I never worked for any other company, I never had another job"; as time proved, she had no need to worry.

MOVIE HIGHLIGHTS: *Maisie Goes to Reno, The Hucksters, Singapore, One Touch of Venus, The Great Sinner, East Side, West Side, The Bribe, My Forbidden Past, Pandora and the Flying Dutchman, Show Boat, Lone Star, The Snows of Kilimanjaro, Ride, Vaquero!, Knights of the Round Table, The Barefoot Contessa, Bhowani Junction, The Little Hut, The Sun Also Rises, On the Beach, The Naked Maja, 55 Days at Peking, Seven Days in May, Night of the Iguana, Earthquake.*

Peggy Ann Garner

(b. Peggy Ann Garner, Feb. 3, 1932, Canton, Ohio; d. Oct. 16, 1984) Greatly talented blonde child star who received a special Oscar at 13 for her glowing portrayal of tenement child Francie Nolan in *A Tree Grows in Brooklyn*; a John Robert Powers model at 4 in New York, she made her movie debut at 6 in Ann Sheridan's *Little Miss Thoroughbred*; a brace of heavy dramas at RKO, *In Name Only* and *Abe Lincoln in Illinois*, won her a contract at 20th Century–Fox, where she starred throughout the '40s; also had her own radio show, "Meet Me in St. Louis"; years later, she said, "Unlike many others who began acting as children, I enjoyed every minute of it; nobody forced me into it, though my mother was a real 'movie mother,' and I was doing what I wanted to do"; a friend said of her when young: "She is as sturdy as an oak. She bends with the wind but she will never break"; proved this repeatedly through all her life; left Hollywood at 19 and spent the entire decade of the '50s in New York doing many "live" TV dramas (also had a TV series, "Two Girls Named Smith"), starring in four plays on Broadway (*First Lady, Home Is the Hero*, etc.), and flying to the Coast for an occasional film; was married first (1951–53) to singer-actor Richard Hayes and next (1956–63) to actor Albert Salmi, with whom she co-starred on tour in *Bus Stop*; after three miscarriages, finally had a daughter, Cassandra (Cas); in *Bus Stop*, she played Cherie, the honkytonk singer later portrayed in the movie by Marilyn Monroe; in her final role, in the 1980 TV drama "This Year's Blonde," based on the glamour star's life, Peggy Ann played the wife of the man that the illegitimate Marilyn believed to be her father; her final marriage ('64), to realtor Kenyon Foster Brown, also ended in divorce; having learned the business from him, she was a real estate agent for a while; went on to a highly successful career as an executive with General Motors in Los Angeles—selling, en masse, fleets of automobiles to major companies; her last movie role, after 11 years off screen, was in Robert Altman's *A Wedding* in '78; never had a chance to enjoy the fortune earned as a child; investments made for her by her mother proved disastrous—everything was lost.

MOVIE HIGHLIGHTS: *Eagle Squadron, The Pied Piper, Jane Eyre, Keys of the Kingdom, Nob Hill, Junior Miss, Home Sweet Homocide, Daisy Kenyon, Thunder in the Valley, The Sign of the Ram, The Big Cat, The Lovable Cheat, Teresa, Black Widow, Eight Witnesses, The Black Forest, The Cat.*

Greer Garson

(b. Greer Garson, Sept. 29, 1908, County Down, Ireland) An aristocrat in looks and manner, with green eyes and Florentine red hair, she was, of all the femme stars at MGM, Louis B. Mayer's admitted favorite; moviegoers also cherished her as the movies' "great lady," whose performances were marked by wifely virtue and restrained charm; between '42 and '46 was among the Box-Office Top Ten; in '45 she toppled Betty Grable from her throne as *the* most popular screen actress, and a wax effigy of her was installed in Madame Tussaud's London Waxworks; *Mrs. Miniver* ('42) won her the Best Actress Oscar (made the longest acceptance speech in history—45 minutes); was also nominated for *Goodbye, Mr. Chips* (her debut movie; a three-page role) and for five later pictures; of her first 11 films, nine premiered at the world's largest movie palace, Radio City Music Hall, playing a total of 64 weeks, a record never equalled by any other star; in 28 years before the cameras, she starred in only 24 films, and her decline in popularity was indeed swift; in '47, divorcing her much younger husband, Richard Ney (played her son in *Mrs. Miniver*), she testified in court that he had called her a has-been; movies that came later proved he wasn't far off the mark; once too often she had portrayed the courageous-under-adversity heroine, and when she next took a flyer at comedy, fans were not enchanted; is Scottish on her father's side (he was an importer who died when she was four months old) and Irish on her mother's; her given name is a corruption of her mother's maiden name (McGregor); family expected her to teach after getting her degree at London University; instead went to work at an advertising agency (future actor George Sanders was a colleague there), joining the firm's drama club; later experience with the Birmingham Repertory Theater led to stage roles in London; in the first, *Street Scene*, she played—in a black wig—a New York Jewish girl, and critics hailed her as "the new American actress"; was discovered personally by Louis B. Mayer in a later play, *Old Music*; arrived in Hollywood married (since '33) to barrister Edward Alec Abbot Snelson; divorced him in '41; has been married since '49 to millionaire Buddy Fogelson; two weeks before her MGM contract was due to expire, she landed the starmaking role of Mrs. Chips; tested for it with Walter Pidgeon—soon to be her "husband" in many films.

MOVIE HIGHLIGHTS: *Remember?, Pride and Prejudice, Blossoms in the Dust, When Ladies Meet, Random Harvest, Madame Curie, Mrs. Parkington, The Valley of Decision, Adventure, Desire Me, Julia Misbehaves, That Forsyte Woman, The Miniver Story, The Law and the Lady, Scandal at Scourie, Julius Caesar, Her Twelve Men, Strange Lady in Town, Sunrise at Campobello, The Nun, The Happiest Millionaire.*

Frances Gifford

(b. Mary Frances Gifford, Dec. 7, 1920, Long Beach, Calif.) Lovely and gifted brunette who starred as Nyoka in *Jungle Girl*, a 1941 Republic serial ("She was the dream girl of that serial year," recalls one film historian), and soon afterwards was one of MGM's most appealing leading ladies; was a 17-year-old freshman at UCLA, planning to study law, when she accepted a friend's invitation to visit a movie studio; producer Sam Goldwyn spotted her on the lot, volunteered a screen test, and gave her a small role in Miriam Hopkins' *Woman Chases Man*; her only training had been one semester of dramatics in high school; on Christmas Day, 1937, she married actor James Dunn and did not act again for three years, until they costarred in a B picture, *Mercy Plane*; divorced him—her only husband— in '42; was launched at Metro as a dramatic actress in *Cry Havoc* ('43), a film depicting the harrowing experiences of Army nurses in the battle of Bataan during the early days of WWII; career at this studio flourished to the end of the decade; made just two movies elsewhere later, then in '53 she simply disappeared, and fans were left to wonder where she was and what had happened; in the '70s, after returning to Hollywood where she worked as a librarian, she explained; for two decades she had been in California's Camarillo State Hospital (for the mentally ill), suffering from acute depression; the condition, she told reporter Colin Briggs, was brought on by a series of losses and upsets—the breakup of a longtime relationship with MGM executive Benny Thau, an auto accident causing some physical injury but leaving greater emotional scars, the almost simultaneous deaths of her parents (to whom she'd been close), and being dropped by MGM; said she became a voluntary patient at Camarillo after years of private treatment, "because I could no longer afford private nurses and expensive neurologists. It wasn't exactly a picnic, but it was no snake pit, either. . . . I went out to lunch every week, either with a friend or the doctor for whom I worked."

MOVIE HIGHLIGHTS: *New Faces of 1937, Hold That Woman, The Reluctant Dragon, West Point Widow, The Remarkable Andrew, American Empire, Beyond the Blue Horizon, The Glass Key, My Heart Belongs to Daddy, Marriage Is a Private Affair, Our Vines Have Tender Grapes, Thrill of a Romance, She Went to the Races, Little Mister Jim, The Arnelo Affair, Luxury Liner, Riding High, Sky Commando.*

Betty Grable

(b. Elizabeth Grable, Dec. 18, 1916, St. Louis, Mo.; d. July 2, 1973) *How to Be Very, Very Popular* was the title of the last movie she made—and if anyone knew that secret, it was this heavenly-bodied star; blonde and blue-eyed, with *Million Dollar Legs* (most appropriate title of an early film of hers) and a high-voltage smile that drove straight to the heart, she was, in every way, the queen—queen of 20th Century–Fox, queen of Technicolor musicals, queen of the pinup brigade, queen of the box-office; for ten consecutive years (1942–51), longer than any other femme star, she ranked high among the Box-Office Top Ten; usually she was the top woman on the list, and one year ('43), was the #1 star of all; Technicolor, and Alice Faye being taken ill, turned the trick for her; in 1940, Fox plucked her out of a Broadway hit, *Du Barry Was a Lady*, as a last-minute substitute for Alice Faye in *Down Argentine Way*, and the gold rush was on; had already been in pictures (usually campus comedies) for a full decade—and had been fired five times from four movie studios; she'd also had a failed marriage, to Jackie Coogan (1937–40); was groomed to be a star almost from birth; under a firm maternal thumb, she studied ballet, acrobatics, and tap dancing; at 13, with her mother pushing hard behind her, she went to Hollywood, lied about her age, and got a job in a Fox chorus (the movie was Lola Lane's *Let's Go Places*); between early movie roles, she sang with Ted Fio Rito's band and toured with the comedy team of Wheeler and Woolsey; sudden fame did not change her from the friendly, unaffected person she'd always been; said an intimate then, "Stardom means little to her, except enough money to buy all the Shalimar perfume in sight"; finally, with the $3 million she earned as a star, she could have bought the factory outright; always cited *The Dolly Sisters* as her personal favorite of the 55 movies in which she appeared; in '42, when bandleader Harry James was signed for her picture *Springtime in the Rockies*, it was mutual hate at first sight; the reaction was quickly reversed; were married for 22 years and had two daughters, Victoria and Jessica, before divorcing in '65; strange coincidences: they married on July 5, 1943, and on July 5, 1973, he was among the mourners at her funeral—and on July 5, 1983, he joined her in death.

MOVIE HIGHLIGHTS: *Follow the Fleet, Pigskin Parade, College Swing, Man about Town, Tin Pan Alley, Moon over Miami, I Wake Up Screaming* (aka *Hot Spot*), *Song of the Islands, A Yank in the R.A.F., Coney Island, Sweet Rosie O'Grady, Pin-Up Girl, Diamond Horseshoe, The Shocking Miss Pilgrim, Mother Wore Tights, That Lady in Ermine, When My Baby Smiles at Me, Wabash Avenue, My Blue Heaven, Call Me Mister, Meet Me after the Show, How to Marry a Millionaire.*

Gloria Grahame

(b. Gloria Grahame Hallward, Nov. 28, 1925, Los Angeles, Calif.; d. Oct. 5, 1981) Sultry, pouty blonde star, who, without nudity or vulgarity, was easily the most blatantly sensual actress on screen in the '40s and '50s ("It wasn't the way I looked at a man, but the thought behind it"); was nominated for a Best Supporting Oscar in '47 in *Crossfire* (a tart role filmed in two days) and won one in the same category (as a classier sexpot) in *The Bad and the Beautiful*; the daughter of a Scottish actress mother and an industrial designer father, she quit Hollywood High, just short of graduation, to join a touring show, *Good Night Ladies* (thought risqué in its day); later appearances in two Broadway plays (*The World's Full of Girls, A Highland Fling*), billed Gloria Hallward, won her a $250-a-week contract at MGM; began there in *Blonde Fever*, with Philip Dorn, in '44; was off to the races two years later, when she was the wayward miss who tempted Jimmy Stewart in *It's a Wonderful Life*; after reigning as a sexpot (and becoming a cult figure) for a decade and a half, she quit movies for seven years after *Odds Against Tomorrow* ('59); returning then for *Ride beyond Vengeance*, she dropped out once more for six years before coming back as a character actress in *The Loners*, *The Todd Killings*, *Mansion of the Doomed*, and other Bs; personal life was as complex as any role she ever played; was married and divorced four times; her first three husbands were actor Stanley Clements (1945–48), director Nick Ray (1948–52; had a son, Timothy), and writer Cy Howard (1954–57; had a daughter, Mariana); her fourth marriage was the shocker; in '61 she became the wife of a younger man, actor-producer Tony Ray; he was the son of Nick Ray and, of course, once her own stepson; before divorcing in the mid-1970s, they had a son and daughter; made for familial complications—such as the actress' being the sister-in-law of her own older son, and her younger children having a half-uncle who was also their half-brother, etc.; more than her Oscar-winning role, she will probably go down in screen history as the bad girl scalded with coffee by Lee Marvin in *The Big Heat*.

MOVIE HIGHLIGHTS: *Without Love, It Happened in Brooklyn, Merton of the Movies, Roughshod, A Woman's Secret, In a Lonely Place, The Greatest Show on Earth, Sudden Fear, The Glass Wall, Man on a Tightrope, Human Desire, Naked Alibi, The Good Die Young, The Cobweb, Not as a Stranger, Oklahoma!, The Man Who Never Was.*

Farley Granger

(b. Farley Earle Granger III, July 1, 1925, San Jose, Calif.) Late in 1942, producer Sam Goldwyn found himself in need of a new young actor to co-star with Anne Baxter in *The North Star*; a newspaper ad placed by his casting director was answered by a lean, rather Lincolnesque 17-year-old North Hollywood High senior with a bit of amateur experience; filled the bill, got the role, and overnight became the heartthrob of millions of teen-agers in anklets and saddle oxfords; they mourned when, after only one other film, he enlisted in the Navy, but were ready to swoon all over again when he returned three years later; hearts broke when Shelley Winters, then a blonde sexpot, became his fiancée—and rejoiced when the engagement was broken; one of the busiest, most highly-publicized young stars around, he played leads in two dozen big-budget films; two were for Alfred Hitchcock, *Rope* and *Strangers on a Train*, in which he was a tennis champion falsely suspected of murder; the director said later: "I wasn't too pleased with Farley Granger; he's a good actor, but I would have liked to see William Holden in the part"; also dissatisfied with his movie work, the actor was soon saying, "In my first few pictures, I was quite good. But it was pure instinct. Before long, I was playing each role the same way. The mannerisms that were charming at first became stupid and predictable. As my so-called 'box-office appeal' faded, so did my confidence"; buying out his contract for $200,000, he went to New York ("to learn my craft"), studied with the finest coaches, and starred in stock, "live" TV dramas and, finally, on Broadway (*The Warm Peninsula*, *Deathtrap*, etc.); after doing the classics with the National Repertory Theater, he lived for a period in Rome, making films and raising Airedale Terriers; recent times have found him, still a bachelor, back in New York, acting on stage, starring in the movie *Close Quarters* with old friend Shelley Winters, and saying they still talk about getting married; told a reporter, "She lives in this building and we see each other every day when we're both in town. Even if we married, I'm not sure we would live together. This way it's great. If we have a fight, I just get on the elevator."

MOVIE HIGHLIGHTS: *The Purple Heart, They Live by Night, Enchantment, Roseanna McCoy, Side Street, Our Very Own, Edge of Doom, Behave Yourself, I Want You, O. Henry's Full House, Hans Christian Andersen, The Story of Three Loves, Senso, Small Town Girl, The Naked Street, The Girl in the Red Velvet Swing, The Challengers, So Sweet, So Dead, Arnold, Death Is in Your Eyes, Widow, The Prowler* (aka *Rosemary's Killer*).

Kathryn Grayson

(b. Zelma Kathryn Elisabeth Hedrick, Feb. 9, 1922, Winston-Salem, N.C.) Bosomy, hazel-eyed brunette whose beautiful coloratura voice enchanted millions for 16 movie years; screen name is her mother's maiden name; always aspiring to singing grand opera, this daughter of a building contractor lived in many places (Tennessee, Ohio, Virginia, etc.) before the family settled for a while in St. Louis, Mo., where she received her first professional encouragement; as a prank on one midwinter day, she and a friend climbed over the fence at the outdoor amphitheater of the St. Louis Municipal Opera, where musicals are done only in the summer; on the huge empty stage, they sang a duet from *Lucia di Lammermoor* and were heard by Frances Marshall, star of the Chicago Civic Opera, who was visiting the theater's business office that day; coming down to the stage and learning it was Kathryn who sang soprano, Marshall accompanied her home, gave her lessons in voice production, and strongly urged her to go to New York to study with the celebrated

Sembrich; family finances did not permit this, but when the Hedricks moved next to Texas, the 12-year-old started her serious study of music; in Hollywood at 15 and a student at Manual Arts High, she enrolled for voice lessons with a noted teacher, Minna Letha White; with an older brother, she soon made an appearance on radio on "The Eddie Cantor Show," which gave opportunities to many new musical talents; an MGM exec heard her and took her to the office of Louis B. Mayer, who signed her to a long-term contract on the basis of her voice and appearance, without a test; a two-year grooming period led to her debut in '41 in *Andy Hardy's Private Secretary*, to her meeting and marrying (1940–46) another Metro newcomer, John Shelton, and to many well-recalled musicals; was married later (1947–51) to singer Johnnie Johnston; at their daughter Patricia's wedding in '69, the maid of honor was her best friend, Colleen Lanza—daughter of Mario Lanza, Grayson's co-star in *That Midnight Kiss* and *Toast of New Orleans*; after the early deaths of both Lanza and his wife, the actress took their children into her home; "She has been like a mother to me," says Colleen Lanza. "She is the most loving, beautiful, wonderful person in the world."

MOVIE HIGHLIGHTS: *Rio Rita, The Vanishing Virginian, Seven Sweethearts, Thousands Cheer, Anchors Aweigh, Ziegfeld Follies, Two Sisters from Boston, Till the Clouds Roll By, It Happened in Brooklyn, The Kissing Bandit, Grounds for Marriage, Show Boat, Lovely to Look At, The Desert Song, So This Is Love, Kiss Me Kate, The Vagabond King.*

Sydney Greenstreet

(b. Sydney Hughes Greenstreet, Dec. 27, 1879, Sandwich, Kent, England; d. Jan. 18, 1954) Portly character who, whether sitting glowering like a venomous frog or lurching about like a demented pachyderm, was a gem of a villain; privately, was a genial soul with a chuckly sense of humor, and his nickname was Tiny; began in movies at 61, and his Warner Bros. deal lasted from the beginning to the end of his screen career, from '41 to '49, from *The Maltese Falcon* to *Flamingo Road*; was written into his contract that his weight had to remain above 250 pounds; once, at his heaviest, he became wedged in a studio phone booth, and carpenters had to dismantle it to free him; was in 24 pictures, and only four times were other studios allowed (at a premium price) to borrow his services—for *The Hucksters, The Velvet Touch, Ruthless*, and *Malaya*; one of eight children born to a tanner, he was a strapping athlete at prep school, a tea planter in Ceylon, and an agent for a brewery in England before going on the stage at 23; his father opposed this career choice, but his mother advanced him the funds to study acting; made his debut at Ramsgate playing murderer Craigen in *Sherlock Holmes*; remaining on the boards for nearly 40 years, he toured the world, most often doing Shakespeare and usually, as the weight piled up, playing comedy roles; reportedly, he retained in memory more than 12,000 lines of Shakespeare; Broadway first saw him in 1905 as Good Fellowship in the morality play *Everyman*, and the U.S. was his home for the rest of his life; was married from '18 to the end to an American, Dorothy Marie Ogden, by whom he had one son, John Ogden; became a prime favorite with American theatergoers, acting not only in dramas but also such musical comedies as *Roberta*; from '35 on, Alfred Lunt and Lynn Fontanne claimed his services exclusively; appeared with them in many stage hits, including *The Taming of the Shrew*, *Idiot's Delight*, and *There Shall Be No Night*; director John Huston saw him in the latter and gave him the famemaking role of sinister Kasper Gutman in *The Maltese Falcon*, which won him a Best Supporting Oscar nomination; was photographed from the floor to make him appear even fatter than he was; longed to play comedy, saying after many evil roles, "I don't mind playing villains. But a musician who can play Beethoven wants to play something besides Beethoven once in a while"; never got to be a funnyman—or to play Benjamin Franklin, his other dream.

MOVIE HIGHLIGHTS: *They Died with Their Boots On, Across the Pacific, Casablanca, Background to Danger, Hollywood Canteen, Between Two Worlds, Passage to Marseille, The Mask of Dimitrios, The Conspirators, One Man's Secret, Conflict, Christmas in Connecticut, Pillow to Post, Devotion, Three Strangers, The Verdict, That Way with Women, The Woman in White.*

Charlotte Greenwood

(b. Frances Charlotte Greenwood, June 25, 1893, Philadelphia, Pa.; d. Jan. 18, 1978) Blonde, tall, and good-natured, with a gawky, loping gait, she was a fixture at 20th Century–Fox in the '40s and one of the period's best-loved character stars; was called "Long Legged Letty," because of her loose-jointed, skyscraping, absolutely vertical kicks (which she invariably showed off in movie musicals), and because she'd appeared in the popular "Letty" series of stage comedies in the teens and '20s (*So Long, Letty, Linger Longer, Letty*, etc); had reached her adult height of 5′10″ by the time she was 11; quit school in the seventh grade and went on the stage; at 12, billed Lottie Greenwood, was dancing in the chorus of *The White Cat* on Broadway; was next on the vaudeville circuit; at 16, played Tik-Tok in a stage production of *The Wizard of Oz* and, three years later, starred on Broadway in *The Passing Show of 1912*; in the '20s, was a headliner at the Palace; had an early screen career that later fans knew little or nothing about; in '15 starred in the silent comedy *Jane*; was back in pictures between '27 and '33, playing major comic roles in *Baby Mine* (with George K. Arthur and Karl Dane), *Palmy Days*, *Stepping Out*, etc., including the movie version of *So Long, Letty*; was afterwards a popular stage star in England *(Wild Violets)* and America before great movie fame came her way in the '40s, starting with Linda Darnell's *Star Dust*; screen commitments kept her from creating the part of Aunt Eller on Broadway in *Oklahoma!*, a role written specifically for her by Oscar Hammerstein II, but finally got to play it in the '55 film version; from '24 until his death many years later, was happily maried to Martin Broones (her second husband), who composed the songs for *LeMaire's Affairs* and other stage revues in which she starred; away from the spotlight, her life revolved around the Christian Science religion; a "reader" for years in the church, she regularly served in this capacity for stars such as Doris Day (whose sets she often visited) when they converted to this faith; was always amused by this anecdote involving her that someone once told on Groucho Marx: "Who else, one wonders, but Groucho, would go to a White House show, watch comedienne Charlotte Greenwood do a high kick that involved wrapping one leg around her neck, then turn to Mrs. Roosevelt and say, 'You could do that if you'd just put your mind to it.' "

MOVIE HIGHLIGHTS: *Down Argentine Way, Young People, Tall, Dark and Handsome, Moon over Miami, The Perfect Snob, Springtime in the Rockies, The Gang's All Here, Dixie Dugan, Up in Mabel's Room, Home in Indiana, Driftwood, Wake Up and Dream, The Great Dan Patch, Oh, You Beautiful Doll, Peggy, Dangerous When Wet, Glory, The Opposite Sex.*

Jane Greer

(b. Bettejane Greer, Sept. 9, 1924, Washington, D.C.) In *Out of the Past* ('47), perhaps her finest, this stunning brunette played an amoral young woman whose huge, trusting eyes and sweet lips made saps out of Kirk Douglas and Robert Mitchum; in '84 when they remade the film as *Against All Odds*, starring English actress Rachel Ward in that role, she came out of retirement to play the girl's equally devious mother; one critic noted that she was "still beautiful [and] with those amazing eyes as blandly treacherous as ever," while another said that she "looks far more glamorous than Ward, the movie's supposed *femme fatale*"; facial paralysis—finally overcome—threatened her acting ambitions as a teen-ager; began her career as a singer with Enric Madriguera's band in a club in her hometown, singing in Spanish (learned by phonetics); becoming a model, she appeared in a newsreel displaying the new WAC uniform; Howard Hughes saw the footage and took her, at 18, to Hollywood; learning that she was a twin, the producer was eager to sign up her sibling also—until he found out the twin was a brother; did not make her movie debut until three years later; meanwhile, she was briefly married (1943-45) to Rudy Vallee, with whose band she sometimes sang at military camps; Vallee, who said long after they divorced, "A more charming, talented and gracious person I shall never know," helped her get out of her Hughes contract and secure another at RKO; at this studio from '45 to '50, she appeared in 13 films, starting with a one-line role in *Pan-Americana* (billed Bettejane Greer) and working her way to stardom; in '47, she married Beverly Hills attorney–socialite Edward Lasker, bore him three sons (Albert, Lawrence, and Steven), and divorced him after 20 years; was ill for some time with a heart condition, which was surgically corrected; latter part of career has been stop-and-start; off the screen for seven years after *Man of a Thousand Faces*, she came back in '64 and made two movies; returned in '73 for a supporting role (Robert Duvall's grieving sister-in-law) in *The Outfit*, and was not seen again until *Against All Odds*; in the 1984–85 season on TV she played Susan Sullivan's mother on "Falcon Crest."

MOVIE HIGHLIGHTS: *George White's Scandals, Dick Tracy, The Falcon's Alibi, The Bamboo Blonde, Sinbad the Sailor, Sunset Pass, They Won't Believe Me, Station West, The Big Steal, The Company She Keeps, You're in the Navy Now, You for Me, The Prisoner of Zenda, Desperate Search, The Clown, Down among the Sheltering Palms, Run for the Sun, Where Love Has Gone, Billie.*

Edmund Gwenn

(b. Edmund Gwenn, Sept. 26, 1875, Glamorgan, Wales; d. Sept. 6, 1959) Small-sized (5'4") giant of a character star who, with a twinkle in his eye, snagged a Best Supporting Oscar as Kris Kringle in *The Miracle on 34th Street* ('47) and another nomination as the charming counterfeitor in 1950's *Mister 880*; when he started his scene-stealing in Hollywood in '35, in *The Bishop Misbehaves* with Maureen O'Sullivan, he had 40 years of stage experience behind him, plus many British films; stars had every right to fear sharing scenes with him; choice of a career was so strongly opposed by his father, a stern British civil servant, that he was disowned and turned out of the house at 17; made his first stage appearance at 20 in London at the Public Hall, Tottenham, and his West End debut in 1899 at the Globe Theater in *A Jealous Mistake*; had his first major success a bit later in George Bernard Shaw's *Man and Superman*; a favorite with the playwright, he was in the original casts of five other Shaw plays; following his debut movie, 1916's *The Real Thing at Last*, he fought in the Great War, enlisting as a private and being demobilized three years later as captain; did not become a regular on the screen until after '31, when he starred in the British film *How He Lied to Her Husband*; throughout the '20s was greatly popular on the stage both in England and America, where he made his Broadway debut in '20 in *The Skin Game* (also starred in the movie), with several other New York hits following it; in the '40s, his busiest screen years, he found time to return to Broadway for four plays (*The Wookey, The Three Sisters*, etc.); divorced after many years from actress Minnie Terry, he lived in a suite in a Beverly Hills hotel, attended by a manservant who—since the actor never learned to drive—was also his chauffeur; his most passionate interests were fine wines, sailing, the theater, and walking—would sometimes disappear from Hollywood for weeks to hole up at some mountain inn to indulge, with joyous abandon, in the latter.

MOVIE HIGHLIGHTS: *Anthony Adverse, Laburnum Grove, A Yank at Oxford, Earl of Chicago, Pride and Prejudice, Foreign Correspondent, The Doctor Takes a Wife, Cheers for Miss Bishop, Charley's Aunt, Forever and a Day, Lassie Come Home, Keys of the Kingdom, Between Two Worlds, Of Human Bondage, Undercurrent, Life with Father, Green Dolphin Street, Hills of Home, Apartment for Peggy, Challenge to Lassie, Mr. Scoutmaster, Them, The Trouble with Harry.*

Anne Gwynne

(b. Marguerite Gwynne Trice, Dec. 10, 1918, Waco, Texas) Vivacious red-head (photographed blonde) with a dimpled smile who was as charming a leading lady as Universal ever had; after attending Stephens College, where she studied drama with Maude Adams, she modeled and acted in little theater productions of *Stage Door, The Colonel's Lady*, etc.; began her film career in '39 in a small role in *Charlie McCarthy, Detective*; won her Universal contract a few months later after an interview—no test—and made her debut at this studio in *Unexpected Father*, starring Baby Sandy, receiving tenth billing; rapidly made her way from minor roles to leads; was publicized by Universal as the "T.N.T. Girl" (Trim, Neat, Terrific); became such a pinup favorite during World War II that a cavalry regiment voted her "The Girl We'd Most Like to Corral"; most of the movies she made in that period are forgettable— not so the actress herself; in '44, was married to Beverly Hills attorney Max Gilford, with Evelyn Ankers as her matron of honor and Peggy Ryan as a bridesmaid—both actresses being among her many intimate friends at Universal; had two children, Gwynne Gilford (an actress now) and Gregory Maxwell (a composer), by her (only) husband and remained married to him until his death in '65; selling her Beverly Hills house then and moving to an apartment in the San Fernando Valley, she put her children through college by working as a secretary and salesperson at the Bullock's Wilshire department store; in more recent years, she has operated a boutique in Westwood, Calif.; after a few minor films in the '50s, she was absent from the screen until '70, when she played Michael Douglas' mother in *Adam at 6 A.M.*, looking, as she still does, beautiful.

MOVIE HIGHLIGHTS: *Oklahoma Frontier, Sandy Is a Lady, Spring Parade, Black Friday, Give Us Wings, Nice Girl?, The Black Cat, Tight Shoes, Melody Lane, Mob Town, Broadway, Ride 'em, Cowboy, You're Telling Me, Men of Texas, We've Never Been Licked, Top Man, Jail House Blues, Ladies Courageous, Murder in the Blue Room, Moon Over Las Vegas, Weird Woman, House of Frankenstein, Babes on Swing Street, The Glass Alibi.*

Jon Hall

(b. Charles Locher, Feb. 26, 1913, Fresno, Calif.; d. Dec. 13, 1979) With muscles and strong, handsome features, it was inevitable that he would spend the larger part of his screen career clutching delectable damsels, like "sarong girl" Dorothy Lamour, to his brawny, often-bared chest; spent most of his youth in Tahiti before being splendidly educated at International University in Geneva, Switzerland, and England's Badingham College; besides a physique, he had a brilliant mind—after film fame, was an inventor-manufacturer of sophisticated underwater photographic equipment; had early experience on stage (*M'Lord, the Duke*, etc.); began in movies under his real name, acting in, among others, *Charlie Chan in Shanghai* ('35); next used the billing "Lloyd Crane" in *The Girl from Scotland Yard* and others; became famous as Jon Hall when playing the Polynesian hero in Goldwyn's *The Hurricane* ('37); final screen name was taken from that of his cousin, James Norman Hall, coauthor of the novel on which this movie was based; Goldwyn had been keen for Joel McCrea in this role, but director John Ford, Jon Hall's next-door neighbor, held out for his own choice; greater popularity came in the 1942–45 period when he and exotic Maria Montez teamed romantically and became Universal's king and queen of Technicolor via six fantasy epics: *Arabian Nights*, *White Savage*, *Ali Baba and the Forty Thieves*, *Cobra Woman*, *Gypsy Wildcat*, and *Sudan*; was married to petite singer Frances Langford in '38 and divorced by her in '55; parting was so amicable that later, after marrying others, they and their spouses often visited in California or Florida (where she lived); was engaged next to actress Carol Brewster, who recently recalled him as "a lovely guy, with a warm, upbeat way about him"; final marriage, in '59 to former actress Raquel Torres, ended in divorce; his sign was Pisces, which, to the astrologically inclined, means he was a homeloving man who would have liked having children and a marriage that lasted happily forever—but he had neither; committed suicide (gunshot) when stricken with cancer, because he "didn't want to be a burden" to anyone.

MOVIE HIGHLIGHTS: *Sailor's Lady*, *South of Pago Pago*, *Kit Carson*, *Aloma of the South Seas*, *Eagle Squadron*, *Lady in the Dark*, *The Invisible Man's Revenge*, *San Diego, I Love You*, *The Men in Her Diary*, *Prince of Thieves*, *Last of the Redmen*, *Hurricane Island*, *China Corsair*, *Eyes of the Jungle*, *Ramar and the Jungle Secrets* (and the TV series), *White Goddess*, *Hell Ship Mutiny*, *Forbidden Island*.

Rex Harrison

(b. Reginald Carey Harrison, March 5, 1908, Huyton, Cheshire, England) Hollywood got this charming rake in '46, after 17 years in British films, when he co-starred with Irene Dunne in *Anna and the King of Siam*; gossip maven Louella Parsons did him no favor by labeling him "Sexy Rexy"; following many movies not nearly so memorable as his American debut, his career got a shot in the arm when he was nominated as Best Actor for *Cleopatra* and won the Oscar the next year for *My Fair Lady*; had created the role of Prof. Henry Higgins in this musical on Broadway in '56; Warner Bros. decreed he was "too old" to play the same part in the film; he proved the contrary by impishly mailing director George Cukor a color snapshot of himself—in the nude; his off-screen loves and marriages often made headlines; has had six wives: model

Marjorie Collette Thomas (1933–42; one son, Noel), actress Lilli Palmer (1943–57; one son, Carey; Palmer stood by him in '48 when movie star Carole Landis committed suicide, allegedly over Harrison), screen comedienne Kay Kendall (1957–59; left him a widower, dying of leukemia), British actress Rachel Roberts (1962–71; who was nominated for a Best Actress Oscar for *This Sporting Life*), Richard Harris' ex-wife, Elizabeth (1971–75), and Mercia Tinker, whom he married late in '78; wrote with candor about his love affairs and first five marriages in *Rex: An Autobiography* ('75); reviewing the book, *Variety* said: "Harrison concludes that results of 'research' into his past have not been entirely flattering"; Lilli Palmer, wife #2, was less than complimentary to him in her own autobiography, *Change Lobsters and Dance*; wife #4, Rachel Roberts, who committed suicide in '80, left behind journals that were published as *No Bells on Sunday* ('84), containing a number of shockers about her failed marriage to the actor; born to well-to-do parents, he attended Liverpool College, began acting with the Liverpool Repertory, toured for nine years in road companies, and had his first great stage success in London in *French without Tears*; made his movie debut in England at 21 in *Get Your Man*.

MOVIE HIGHLIGHTS: *School for Scandal, The Constant Husband, Storm in a Teacup, The Citadel, Sidewalks of London, Major Barbara, Blithe Spirit, The Ghost and Mrs. Muir, The Foxes of Harrow, Unfaithfully Yours, The Long Dark Hall, The Fourposter, The Reluctant Debutante, Midnight Lace, The Yellow Rolls-Royce, The Agony and the Ecstasy, The Honey Pot, Dr. Dolittle, A Flea in Her Ear, Staircase, The Battle of Britain, The Prince and the Pauper.*

Hurd Hatfield

(b. William Rukard Hurd Hatfield, Dec. 7, 1918, New York, N.Y.) His second movie at MGM, *The Picture of Dorian Gray*, made him one of 1945's most talked about new stars; something about the role, a perennial bachelor who (as his portrait ages) remains forever youthful, surely rubbed off on him—he's still youthful and he has remained a bachelor; "Some people," he has said, "insist I must really have a picture in my attic"; the fact that he neither smokes nor drinks may account for his lasting good looks; had a silver-spoon background as the son of a prosperous attorney who read Shakespeare to him as encouragement of his early announced decision to act, and a painter mother (a descendant of the Randolphs of Virginia); was sent to the best private schools (Horace Mann, Morristown Prep, Riverdale Academy); at Columbia University, he appeared in a school production of *Cymbeline* and was seen by Tamara Daykarhanova; she was the U.S. representative for Russian actor-director Michael Chekhov, then teaching drama in England, and she strongly urged the hopeful actor to study with him; (Chekhov was later to be nominated for a Best Supporting Oscar as Ingrid Bergman's psychiatry professor-colleague in *Spellbound*); his training in England was interrupted by the outbreak of war, sending him home to New York where he appeared on Broadway in a few plays (*The Possessed, Twelfth Night,* etc.); went to Hollywood and was a regular on "Dr. Christian" on radio when signed by MGM; made his debut there, playing a Chinese, in *Dragon Seed;* a fellow actor in this movie, Turhan Bey, became and remains a close friend; years after scoring a sensation in *Dorian Gray,* he met his one idol, Greta Garbo, and learned that she had pleaded with MGM to let her play the role—dressed as a young man; left Hollywood in the early '50s, though he continued making movies there and in Europe, and returned to Broadway where he has starred in many plays (*Camino Real, Anastasia,* etc.); after years of residence in Segovia, Spain, he restored and moved into a pre-Georgian house near Cork, Ireland, the land of his ancestors; between movie-stage-TV assignments, he has served on both the Irish and Spanish committees of the International Fund for Monuments.

MOVIE HIGHLIGHTS: *Diary of a Chambermaid, The Beginning or the End?, The Unsuspected, The Checkered Coat, Joan of Arc, Chinatown at Midnight, Destination Murder, Tarzan and the Slave Girl, The Left-Handed Gun, El Cid, King of Kings, Mickey One, The Boston Strangler, Von Richthofen and Brown.*

June Haver

(b. June Stovenour, June 10, 1926, Rock Island, Ill.) 20th Century–Fox's blonde and blue-eyed "pocket Grable" (co-starred in *The Dolly Sisters*) discovered that life writes its own script; in '45, in *Where Do We Go From Here?*, she co-starred with Fred MacMurray, 19 years her senior; on June 28, 1954, she became Mrs. Fred MacMurray, the stepmother of his adopted children (Sue, then 14, and Rob, 11), and in '56, they adopted infant twin daughters (Katie and Laurie); in the years between their meeting and their marrying, much drama occurred in their lives; she eloped on March 9, 1947, with musician Jimmy Zito, her childhood sweetheart, married him again in a

Catholic Church ceremony on March 26th, was separated from him on June 16th, and was granted a divorce on March 25, 1948; was later engaged to a Beverly Hills dentist; early in '53, following his sudden death, she gave up her $3,500-a-week contract at Fox and entered the Sisters of Charity Convent in Xavier, Kansas, intending to become a nun; illness forced her to leave the convent later that year, though she planned to return when recovered; in June 1953, Fred MacMurray's wife, long ill, died; two nights before New Year's, 1954, June and the actor met socially for the first time, at a Hollywood costume party that each attended unescorted; the following evening at a party to which he invited her, they drank a champagne toast to the New Year and, two months after this first date, she has said, she proposed to him; now they are grandparents; throughout her life, events have occurred with great swiftness; made her stage debut with a Cincinnati little theater at 6; won the Cincinnati Conservatory of Music's Post Music Contest at 7, and, as its prize, the chance to play a piano solo with the Cincinnati Symphony conducted by Eugene Goosens; had her own radio show at 11; when 14, chaperoned by her mother, she began touring as the soloist with Ted Fio Rito's band; this took her to Hollywood where she sang in two musical shorts, one with Fio Rito, the other with Tommy Dorsey; signed to a $75-a-week contract at 20th Century–Fox, she made her debut when not quite 17 in Alice Faye's *The Gang's All Here*; it was a minor role—the only such she ever played.

MOVIE HIGHLIGHTS: *Home in Indiana, Irish Eyes Are Smiling, Three Little Girls in Blue, Wake Up and Dream, I Wonder Who's Kissing Her Now, Scudda-Hoo! Scudda-Hay!, Look for the Silver Lining, Oh, You Beautiful Doll, The Daughter of Rosie O'Grady, I'll Get By, Love Nest, The Girl Next Door.*

Sterling Hayden

(b. John Hamilton, March 26, 1916, Montclair, N.J.) "Aren't they beautiful?"; in '41 Paramount used this slogan on posters for *Bahama Passage*, showing big, blond, barechested Stirling (as he was then) Hayden in close embrace with flaxen-haired Madeleine Carroll—and indeed they were beautiful; time, as the world knows, wrought a few changes in Hayden, in looks and attitude; back then, he resisted being thought of as an actor; a few years later, wondering whether he had ever been anything *but* an actor, he would say, "I am flawed inside and I know it. Could it be perhaps that this is a trick of fate to compensate for my being tall and strong and good-looking enough to intrigue every girl I meet?"; the latter attributes were what made Paramount pull the bronzed young giant (6'4") off the high seas and put him into drydock on its Marathon Avenue sound stages; the son of a newspaper advertising manager, he dropped out of an exclusive prep school and ran off to sea at 17, dory trawling for haddock aboard schooners off the shores of Newfoundland; his first command as a 22-year-old master mariner was a brigantine, the *Florence C. Robinson*, which he sailed to Tahiti; at 24, after he got his skipper's papers, a story about him appeared in the *Boston Post* under the headline LOCAL SAILOR LIKE MOVIE IDOL; seeing this, movie director Edward H. Griffith interviewed him in New York and gave him a screen test (a scene from *Café Society*, which had starred Madeleine Carroll); the upshot: a $150-a-week Paramount contract; made his debut, in Technicolor, for which he was admirably suited, in *Virginia* ('41) opposite Madeleine Carroll; married her in '42, left her in '44 to go to war, and, with some bitterness on his part, divorced her in '46; was next married (1947–55) to socialite Betty DeNoon, by whom he has two sons and two daughters; another marriage, in '60 to Catherine McConnell, mother of his two other sons, also failed; returned to Hollywood and more starring roles in '47, earning at his peak $160,000 a year (most of which he spent on boats), but rapidly lost his godlike looks and has played character roles since; published his critically-acclaimed autobiography, *Wanderer*, in '63, and a novel, *Voyager*, some years later.

MOVIE HIGHLIGHTS: *Blaze of Noon, Variety Girl, El Paso, The Asphalt Jungle, The Denver & Rio Grande, Hellgate, Flat Top, The Star, So Big, Take Me to Town, Fighter Attack, Arrow in the Dust, Johnny Guitar, Prince Valiant, Suddenly, Naked Alibi, Battle Taxi, The Eternal Sea, Untamed, The Killing, Five Steps to Danger, Dr. Strangelove, Hard Contract, Loving, The Godfather, The Long Goodbye, 1900, Winter Kills.*

Dick Haymes

(b. Richard Haymes, Sept. 13, 1916, Buenos Aires, Argentina; d. March 28, 1980) "In My Arms (ain't I ever gonna get a girl in my arms)," he sang in that creamy tenor in '43, and millions of bobby-soxers swooned; the adulation increased to fever pitch the next year when, opposite June Haver, he made his starring debut in *Irish Eyes Are Smiling*; was never one of the world's handsomest men, but something about him spelled "lover" to the ladies; eventually had plenty of wives (six) and children to prove it; arrived in Hollywood married (in '41) to actress Joanne Dru, mother of his first brood (son, two daughters), who divorced him in '49; an earlier marriage at 21, to band singer Edith Harper, had been annulled; later had three two-year marriages—to pal Errol Flynn's ex, Nora Eddington ("an ego trip," the singer once confessed), to Rita Hayworth, and to vocalist Fran Jeffries (her ex, Richard Quine, had just directed Haymes in his final movie, *Cruising Down the River*), by whom he had a daughter; from '63 on, was wed to British model Wendy Smith, with whom he had a son and daughter; the son of an Englishman (cattle rancher) and a fashion salon proprietor mother, who soon divorced, he lived in Paris for a few childhood years before coming to America; in '44, claimed exemption from the draft as a citizen of Argentina, leading to an unsuccessful attempt by the Immigration Service in '54 to deport him; later became a U.S. citizen; peak years were 1946–47 when he averaged $25,000 a week via movies, records, and a radio show (personal appearances brought in more thousands); career took a nosedive in the mid-1950s because of alcoholism (which he conquered) and much adverse publicity (most particularly when he gave Rita Hayworth a black eye); did have a trigger temper and was not greatly loved by all professional associates; filed for bankruptcy in '60, claiming debts of nearly a half-million; never regained his oldtime popularity.

MOVIE HIGHLIGHTS: *Du Barry Was a Lady* (singing with Tommy Dorsey's band), *Four Jills in a Jeep, Billy Rose's Diamond Horseshoe, State Fair, Do You Love Me?, The Shocking Miss Pilgrim, Carnival in Costa Rica, Up in Central Park, One Touch of Venus, St. Benny the Dip, All Ashore.*

Susan Hayward

(b. Edythe Marrenner, June 30, 1917, Brooklyn, N.Y.; d. March 14, 1975) Volcanic redhead with a fierce talent and energy who went to Hollywood after a brief modeling career, was tested for Scarlett O'Hara, and made a lifetime career of playing spitfires; won her Best Actress Oscar portraying one (convicted murderess Barbara Graham) in *I Want to Live!*; earlier Academy Award nominations: *Smash-Up, My Foolish Heart, With a Song in My Heart*, and *I'll Cry Tomorrow*; made her debut in *Girls on Probation*; early career at Paramount (1938–45) was undistinguished, except for *Adam Had Four Sons* and *The Hairy Ape* (both made on loan-out); fame soared in '46 when producer Walter Wanger put her under personal contract and starred her in a string of big-budget hits (*Canyon Passage, Tap Roots*, etc.); buying up her contract for $200,000, 20th Century–Fox chief Darryl F. Zanuck made her the Technicolor queen of the lot; in '51, her first year at the studio, he called her "my $12 million baby," as he'd invested that amount (one-third of his annual filmmaking budget) in three movies starring her; made a mint for the company in the next five years, but Zanuck eventually came to dislike her passionately (reportedly because she flatly rejected his amorous propositions); was in the Box-Office Top Ten in '52, '53, '59; popularity waned greatly in the '60s; was stormily married (1944–53) to actor Jess Barker (two sons: Timothy and Gregory) and, from '57 until his death in '66 to Georgia businessman Floyd Eaton Chalkley; final public appearance, as a presenter on the '74 Academy Award telecast, was high drama; requested Frank Westmore to do her makeup; on the day of the show, going to her home to do so, he was shocked to find that cobalt treatments she was undergoing for a malignant brain tumor had destroyed her hair, eyebrows and eyelashes; had to reconstruct her as she had been decades earlier; Westmore later said, "I was never more proud of my craftsmanship than when I saw Susan walk out on that stage. . . . She looked not much different from the Susan Hayward of 1945, and that's how the world will remember her."

MOVIE HIGHLIGHTS: *Beau Geste, Reap the Wild Wind, I Married a Witch, The Forest Rangers, And Now Tomorrow, Deadline at Dawn, The Lost Moment, They Won't Believe Me, Tulsa, House of Strangers, I Can Get It for You Wholesale, Rawhide, I'd Climb the Highest Mountain, David and Bathsheba, The Snows of Kilimanjaro, The President's Lady, The Lusty Men, Demetrius and the Gladiators, The Conqueror, Back Street, The Marriage-Go-Round, Stolen Hours, Valley of the Dolls.*

Rita Hayworth

(b. Margarita Carmen Cansino, Oct. 17, 1918, New York, N.Y.) As a raven-haired, Spanish-dancing teen-ager, she was already a radiant beauty; when Columbia Pictures' makeup wizards finished remodeling her—raising her hairline an inch by electrolysis, creating a distinctive widow's peak, and giving her titian tresses—she was an 8 × 10 glossy, the very model of a love goddess; once the prototype was created, every starlet signed by the studio was "Hayworthized"; the first star to be discovered and developed by Columbia, where she started at $250 a week, she was under contract there for 20 years (1937–57); *Only Angels Have Wings* ('39) made fans aware of her, and *The Strawberry Blonde* ('41; on loan-out to Warners) made her a star; her first major musical, *You'll Never Get Rich* with Astaire (later in '41), made her a superstar; and that famous *Life* magazine photo of her in a sheer black nightgown encasing that flawless figure, kneeling atop a white satin bed, made her the pinup dream of millions of G.I.s; photograph was later taped to an atom bomb used in the Bikini tests; never did her own singing in any musical—in *Gilda*, her greatest hit, Anita Ellis dubbed "Put the Blame on Mame"; other Hayworth vocal "ghosts": Nan Wynn *(My Gal Sal)*, Martha Mears *(Tonight and Every Night)*, Jo Ann Greer *(Pal Joey)*—and most did more than one film; starting in movies at 17, with a dance specialty in *Dante's Inferno*, she made 11 pictures as Rita Cansino; name change came two years later at Columbia in *Criminals of the Air*; maiden name of her mother, a *Ziegfeld Follies* dancer, was Olga Haworth; began dancing professionally at 12 as the partner of her Seville-born father, Eduardo Cansino; was discovered by Hollywood when dancing at the Foreign Club in Agua Caliente; went through five husbands: promoter Edward Judson (1937–41), Orson Welles (1943–47; daughter, Rebecca), playboy–spiritual leader of Moslem millions Aly Khan (1949–51; daughter, Yasmin), Dick Haymes (1953–55), and producer James Hill (1958–61); "Basically, I am a good, gentle person," she said later, "but I am attracted to mean personalities"; said Judson, who guided her to stardom (and was 22 years her senior), threatened her "with bodily harm and exposure to public contempt and ridicule"; to give her a divorce, he demanded and got (from the studio) $30,000; of Orson Welles, she said he was "tormented, possessive . . . a genius, crazy"; torrid romance with Aly Khan, a married man, created a scandal and, marrying him, she gave up a salary of $248,000 a year; Dick Haymes dictated her every move, and James Hill wrote a none-too-kind book about her; alcoholism finally played havoc with her career; at 62 was diagnosed as suffering from Alzheimer's disease, a debilitating brain illness that causes victims to lose their intelligence, personality, and life; in New York, in an apartment next door to daughter Yasmin (her custodian), the star who left magical memories with millions is only existing—with no memory of who she was.

MOVIE HIGHLIGHTS: *The Lady in Question, Susan and God, Blood and Sand* (her first in color), *Tales of Manhattan, You Were Never Lovelier, Cover Girl, Down to Earth, The Lady from Shanghai, The Loves of Carmen, Affair in Trinidad, Salome, Miss Sadie Thompson, Fire Down Below, Separate Tables, They Came to Cordura, The Story on Page One, The Happy Thieves, Circus World, The Money Trap.*

Van Heflin

(b. Emmet Evan Heflin, Dec. 13, 1910, Walters, Okla.; d. July 23, 1971) An "actor's actor," he won a Best Supporting Oscar playing a hard-drinking newspaperman in *Johnny Eager*; used as his model his own father who, he once said, was "a fabulous character . . . and a drunk"; in performance, he was strong, soft-spoken, serious of manner; privately, he could also be stubborn—as millions of TV viewers saw for themselves when he was the subject of a "This Is Your Life" episode: visibly angry when surprised by host Ralph Edwards, he became a 30-minute illustration of icy noncooperation; acting was not an early ambition with him; after two years at the University of Oklahoma, he went to sea on tramp steamers for three years, sailing through the Orient to South America and Alaska; returned to the school, reasoning that an education would help his planned career in the Merchant Marine; doing two years' study in one, he got his degree and, thanks to college dramas, a yen to act; went on to get his master's in theater arts at Yale; appeared on Broadway in his 20s in a number of plays: *The Bride of Torozko* ("an unreasonably bad actor," said one noted critic), *Casey Jones*, *End of Summer*, etc.; Katharine Hepburn was "lucky" for him—supported her in his movie debut, 1936's *A Woman Rebels*; then, after minor roles in a number of others (*Annapolis Salute*, *Flight from Glory*, etc.), he returned to Broadway and became a top leading man when acting opposite Hepburn in *The Philadelphia Story* ('39); at the end of its two-year run, MGM gave him a screen test (with Donna Reed) and a contract; began at the studio in *The Feminine Touch* with Rosalind Russell; his next seven movies established him so firmly with fans that two years out for military duty did not dent his career; after serving in the Air Force as a combat photographer in Germany, he resumed as a star in *The Strange Love of Martha Ivers*; was married from '42 to '67, when they divorced, to starlet Frances Neal; two daughters, Vanna and Kate (an actress), and a son, Tracy; never lost his love of the sea—when he died, his ashes, as he had requested, were scattered over the Pacific.

MOVIE HIGHLIGHTS: *H. M. Pulham, Esq.*, *The Kid Glove Killer*, *Seven Sweethearts*, *Tennessee Johnson*, *Presenting Lily Mars*, *Till the Clouds Roll By*, *Possessed*, *Green Dolphin Street*, *B. F.'s Daughter*, *Act of Violence*, *Tap Roots*, *East Side, West Side*, *Madame Bovary*, *The Prowler*, *My Son John*, *Shane*, *Battle Cry*, *Patterns*, *3:10 to Yuma*, *They Came to Cordura*, *Under Ten Flags*, *Stagecoach*, *Airport*.

Paul Henreid

(b. Paul Hernreid Ritter von Wasel-Waldingau, Jan. 10, 1908, Trieste, Italy) On a Rio balcony with Bette Davis, he lit two cigarettes, so suavely, passed one to her and, moments later, swept her into his arms, kissed her tenderly, passionately—and a new romantic idol was born; the famous cigarette "bit" in *Now, Voyager* was his own idea, not in the script; he and his wife, Lisl (married since '36), had been doing it for years; says, "Back when cars didn't have lighters, and I was driving and wanted to smoke, she would light our cigarettes that way"; he and Davis were reunited four years later in *Deception* ('46); Warners had urged him to co-star with her in *Mr. Skeffington*, but he declined, insisting that only Claude Rains, who played it, was right for the part; 22 years after *Now, Voyager*, Henreid directed Davis in *Dead Ringer*; the well-educated son of a baron, he began acting in night classes at the Konservatorium of Dramatic Arts in Vienna, where his family moved soon after his birth in Trieste (which, incidentally, was in Austria then); was working by day as a salesman for a book publisher; made his movie debut at 20 in a minor role in *Only a Comedian*, starring German actor Emil Jannings; was a greatly popular leading man with the Max Reinhardt Theater in Vienna for several years and, at 27, wrote and starred in two Austrian films; emigrated to London in the late '30s and acted on stage and in films (*Goodbye, Mr. Chips*, in which he was billed Paul von Hernried, *Night Train*, etc.); starred on Broadway first in '40 in Elmer Rice's *Flight to the West* (and soon was a semiregular on the radio soap opera "Joyce Jordan: Girl Interne"); 1941 found him in Hollywood acting opposite Michele Morgan in *Joan of Paris*, a wartime drama—and a flop; became an American citizen in '45 and adopted two daughters: Monica (an actress) and Mimi; continuing to act, he directed his first feature, *For Men Only*, in '52 (later directed some 60 episodes of Alfred Hitchcock's TV series); his Viennese estates, confiscated by the Nazis during WWII because of his anti-Hitler activities and valued then at $100,000, were restored to him in the mid-1950s; a "people" person, he says, "Only on rare occasions have I met someone who didn't interest me in some manner. Each person has a story to tell."

MOVIE HIGHLIGHTS: *Casablanca, In Our Time, Between Two Worlds, The Conspirators, The Spanish Main, Devotion, Song of Love, Rope of Sand, Hollow Triumph, Last of the Buccaneers, So Young, So Bad, Thief of Damascus, Meet Me in Las Vegas, Holiday for Lovers, Never So Few, The Four Horsemen of the Apocalypse, Operation Crossbow, The Madwoman of Chaillot, Exorcist II: The Heretic.*

John Hodiak

(b. John Hodiak, April 16, 1914, Pittsburgh, Pa.; d. Oct. 19, 1955) Displaying his brawn and biceps in *Lifeboat*, this healthy-looking specimen of manhood was impressive; was even more so in military garb as Major Victor Joppolo in *A Bell for Adano*—strong, square-jawed, compassionate (all of which he himself was); got his starmaking role in *Lifeboat*, his seventh film, because of a favor he did for a friend; earlier in New York, he'd assisted black actor Canada Lee in his screen test; Hitchcock saw it and hired them both, reinforcing the star's long-held belief that "there is a law of compensation in life—you get back what you give"; after borrowing him from MGM for this film, 20th Century–Fox kept him around for another, *Sunday Dinner for a Soldier*, bringing him together with Anne Baxter; married for seven years (1946–53), they had a daughter, Katrina, who was 15 months old when they divorced; were opposites in background (poor on his part, rich on hers) and temperament (he was self-effacing and unruffled, while she, as once described by a friend, was "as often ruffled as an old-fashioned petticoat"); speaking of his "lack of confidence," Baxter later said, "He was a damned good actor, better than he realized. And I loved him very deeply. But two careers are murder, and two in the same profession are double murder"; proudly the son of Ukranian immigrants ("the salt of the earth"), he performed as a child in amateur foreign-language plays; family moved to Detroit when he was 8; following high school, and after seriously considering the preisthood, he joined his father as a worker in an auto factory (Chevrolet); with no training in speech, he auditioned at a radio station and was hired as an announcer; soon went to Chicago and acted on radio (lead in "Li'l Abner") while also attending Northwestern; signed his MGM contract (adamantly refusing to change his name) in '43, made his debut as the romantic lead in a B, *A Stranger in Town*, and promptly bought his parents a house in Tarzana; devoutly Catholic, he said, "I pray all the time; I count my blessings and thank God another day has passed with safety and comfort for my loved ones"; long before a massive heart attack struck him down at 41, he said, "When I die, I hope people will say just this of me: 'He always did his best. He liked people and enjoyed life. He always tried to share his happiness. So the world was a little better place for his having lived.' "

MOVIE HIGHLIGHTS: *Song of Russia, I Dood It, Marriage Is a Private Affair, Maisie Goes to Reno, The Harvey Girls, Somewhere in the Night, Two Smart People, The Arnelo Affair, Desert Fury, Homecoming, Command Decision, Malaya, The Bride, Battleground, The Miniver Story, Ambush, A Lady without a Passport, Across the Wide Missouri, Night unto Morning, The People against O'Hara, Dragonfly Squadron.*

William Holden

(b. William Franklin Beedle Jr., April 17, 1918, O'Fallon, Ill.; d. Nov. 16, 1981) An all-American-type star who began strong (title role in 1939's *Golden Boy*) and got even better with maturity; nominated for the Best Actor Oscar for *Sunset Boulevard* (Montgomery Clift had rejected the role), he won the statuette for *Stalag 17* and was nominated once more for *Network; Golden Boy,* publicized as his first film, actually wasn't; earlier that year, he had a two-word role ("Thank you") in Grable's *Million Dollar Legs;* began work on *Golden Boy* on his 21st birthday; once said, "I don't think anybody had as much determination and ambition as I did the day I started making that movie. Then I went to the opening and saw my name in lights. And I suddenly knew that it didn't mean a damn thing to me. It's been that way ever since"; a second cousin of President Warren G. Harding and the eldest of three sons of a chemist and a former teacher, he grew up in South Pasadena, Calif.; in bios, it was also said that his father was in the chemical analysis business—was actually a fertilizer-manufacturing firm; the future star studied chemistry at a local junior college and began acting at the Pasadena Playhouse at 18; at 20 he played an 80-year-old man (Madame Curie's father-in-law) in the play *Manya* and was signed by Paramount (which soon shared his contract with Columbia) at $50 a week; took his screen name from a prominent newspaper editor in Los Angeles (eventually had it legalized and also learned there had been an earlier movie actor by the same name); at 23, became the husband of actress Brenda Marshall, the stepfather of her three-year-old daughter (Virginia), and was soon the father of two sons (Peter Wesley and Scott); enlisted in the Army Air Corps in '42, found himself stuck in public relations for four years, and emerged as a first lieutenant; a backlog of three movies kept his popularity high while away; his best roles were still ahead of him, and one of them, in *Bridge on the River Kwai* (done on a percentage deal), made him a millionaire; was best man at the 1952 wedding of Hollywood pal Ronald Reagan to Nancy Davis; was 53 when, after a long separation, Brenda Marshall divorced him; Fredric March and Spencer Tracy were his idols—got to act with March in *Executive Suite;* a warts-and-all biography by Bob Thomas, *Golden Boy: The Untold Story,* was published after the actor's death.

MOVIE HIGHLIGHTS: *Invisible Stripes, Our Town, Arizona, I Wanted Wings, The Remarkable Andrew, Dear Ruth, Rachel and the Stranger, Apartment for Peggy, Miss Grant Takes Richmond, Born Yesterday, Union Station, The Turning Point, The Moon Is Blue, Sabrina, The Bridges at Toko-Ri, The Country Girl, Love Is a Many-Splendored Thing, Picnic, The Proud and Profane, The Horse Soldiers, The Counterfeit Traitor, The Wild Bunch, The Towering Inferno, Fedora, The Day the World Ended, S.O.B., The Earthling.*

Tim Holt

(b. John Charles Holt III, Feb. 5, 1918, Beverly Hills, Calif.; d. Feb. 15, 1973) Curly-haired, dimpled son of Jack Holt and RKO's most popular cowboy hero; a crack horseman, with twin six-shooters blazing and following along his father's trail, he was in the Box-Office Top Ten (of Western stars), 1941–43 and 1948–52; began in movies at 10, playing his father as a lad in *The Vanishing Pioneer*, and was later a leading romantic juvenile (*Stella Dallas, Spirit of Culver*, etc.); best roles as an adult were in *The Magnificent Ambersons* (arrogant young aristocrat George Amberson) and *Treasure of the Sierra Madre* (gold prospector Curtin); was in 149 films; perfected his horsemanship as a teen-ager at Indiana's Culver Military Academy, where he was in the cavalry branch and also played two years of varsity polo; returned to Hollywood, joined the Westwood Theater Guild, and made his stage debut with Mae Clark in *Papa Is All*, a play set in Pennsylvania Dutch country; played a half-witted boy and, he once humorously added, "The hard part was the dialect"; met producer Walter Wanger on the polo field, was given a screen test (actress Pat Paterson assisted) in which he played a young drunk, and, at 19, made his "official" screen debut in a bit in *History Is Made at Night*; said his father neither encouraged nor discouraged his career choice, but "when I definitely decided to be an actor, he helped me in any way he could—especially with tips on how to play a scene"; was away from movies for four years during WWII; enlisted as a private, served in the Pacific for 14 months with a Navy-Marine task force, and later, making lieutenant, flew 22 missions (several over Tokyo) as bombardier on a B-29 named The Reluctant Dragon; received a Purple Heart and was discharged as captain; eloped at 19 with a UCLA coed, Virginia May Ashcraft, by whom he had a son, Lance, before they divorced; was also divorced by his second wife, Helen, a California farmer's daughter; was survived by his third, Birdie, mother of his three other children; quit movies at 39, moved to Oklahoma, and was a rancher and sales manager of radio station KEBC-FM in Oklahoma City; when fatally ill with cancer, he said, "I've had a good life. I don't regret anything. I'm not afraid to die."

MOVIE HIGHLIGHTS: *Stagecoach, Fifth Avenue Girl, Swiss Family Robinson, Back Street, Riding the Wind, Six-Gun Gold, Bandit Ranger, Hitler's Children, My Darling Clementine, Thunder Mountain, Wild Horse Mesa, Indian Agent, Dynamite Pass, Western Heritage, Storm over Wyoming, Border Treasure, Overland Telegraph.*

Bob Hope

(b. Leslie Townes Hope, May 26, 1903, Eltham, England) Since the fifth of his seven sons was destined to become an American institution, it was foresighted of an English stonemason to move the family to Cleveland, Ohio, when the ski-nosed tad was 4; the future star became a U.S. citizen by virtue of his father's naturalization in '20; graduating from East High, he worked for an auto company and, determined to get into show business, studied dancing with a local instructor; also tried amateur boxing under the name "Packy East"; was first on stage in an act with a partner, George Byrne, the occasion being a Cleveland personal appearance of Hollywood comedian Fatty Arbuckle; the famed fat funnyman helped them get into a tab show, *Hurley's Jolly Follies*; two years later—dancing, singing, and doing comedy bits—they broke into vaudeville; discovering his gift as a stand-up comedian, he soon became a "single"; 1933 was a big year for him—starred on Broadway in *Roberta*, a friend (actor George Murphy) introduced him to singer Dolores Reade who was headlining at a nearby club (they wed early in '34), and he made his first appearance on radio (guesting on Rudy Vallee's show); 1938 was another milestone—starred in his own radio show and in his first movie, *The Big Broadcast of 1938* (sang "Thanks for the Memory" with Shirley Ross); has been riding the rainbow, and a whirlwind, ever since; starred in 55 films, on radio for 18 years (1,145 programs), and in 300 television shows; won many Emmys and received four honorary Academy Awards; was in the Box-Office Top Ten every year between '41 and '53, and one year ('49), was #1; endeared himself forever to G.I.s and their families by traveling more than a million miles to entertain some 20 million troops in every corner of the globe, at military bases and at the front, in three wars; also found time to adopt, and rear well, four children: Linda, Anthony, Nora, and Kelly; has received more than 800 awards and citations for his humanitarian and professional efforts, including the Congressional Gold Medal from President Kennedy and eight honorary university degrees; the "comedian's comedian" has cited these as the ten whose humor has delighted him most: Charlie Chaplin, Carol Burnett, Steve Martin, Lucille Ball, Johnny Carson, Gene Wilder, Shecky Greene, Lenny Bruce, Mel Brooks, and Woody Allen; has said he would like to be remembered "just for getting a few laughs and making people smile, that's all."

MOVIE HIGHLIGHTS: *College Swing, The Cat and the Canary, The Road to Singapore* (. . . *Zanzibar*, . . . *Morocco*, etc.), *The Ghost Breakers, Caught in the Draft, Nothing But the Truth, Louisiana Purchase, My Favorite Blonde, Star-Spangled Rhythm, They Got Me Covered, Let's Face It, The Princess and the Pirate, Monsieur Beaucaire, My Favorite Brunette, Paleface, Sorrowful Jones, Fancy Pants, The Lemon Drop Kid, My Favorite Spy, The Seven Little Foys, The Iron Petticoat, Beau James, Critic's Choice, Cancel My Reservation.*

Mary Beth Hughes

(b. Mary Elizabeth Hughes, Nov. 13, 1919, Alton, Ill.) She could sing, dance, and most definitely act, but looking like Betty Grable and being at the same studio (20th Century–Fox) in the early '40s was hardly a plus for this dishy blonde; so it was her lot to star in Bs or play the lovely, if sometimes bitchy, "other woman" in big-budget movies; the studio repeatedly promised to star her in a film based on the life of Jean Harlow ("my real inspiration"), but that never happened; a ballet student from childhood and with considerable stage experience in repertory theaters (notably the lead in *Alice in Wonderland*), she arrived in Hollywood at 19—weighing 172; no agent would even consider her until she'd lost 50 pounds; a short-term contract at MGM brought her a lot of beaux (Franchot Tone, Mickey Rooney, Jimmy Stewart) and a few bit parts (in *The Women, These Glamour Girls*, etc.); her handicap at Metro, though, was being too close in looks to Lana Turner; in '40 Fox bought up her contract; the dream of her maternal grandmother, who reared her in St. Louis after age 3 (when her parents separated), had come true; it was grandmother Flora Lucas, once on stage with Ethel Barrymore, who trained her for the theater and also made certain she was educated in Catholic convents; was discovered for movies by agent Johnny Hyde who, years later, would discover (and fall in love with) another blonde, Marilyn Monroe; her

Fox contract had a curious clause—she was forbidden to marry for three years; making *Charlie Chan in Rio*, she fell in love with her leading man, Ted (later Michael) North and in '43, the minute she was free of that contract stipulation, they married; had a son, Donald James, and divorced in '47; was next, for a few years, the wife of singer David Street, her *Holiday Rhythm* co-star; in '73, married her manager, Nicky Stewart; leaving 20th Century–Fox in '43, she remained a popular leading lady (and pinup favorite) through other pacts at Universal and Paramount; of her 60 movies, she cites *The Great Profile*, in which she co-starred with John Barrymore, as her favorite.

MOVIE HIGHLIGHTS: *Free, Blonde and 21, Four Sons, Star Dust, Lucky Cisco Kid, The Great American Broadcast, Dressed to Kill, The Cowboy and the Blonde, Blue, White and Perfect, Design for Scandal, Orchestra Wives, Over My Dead Body, Never a Dull Moment, The Ox-Bow Incident, Good Morning, Judge, The Great Flamarion, Young Man with a Horn, Riders in the Sky.*

Betty Hutton

(b. Elizabeth Thornburg; Feb. 26, 1921, Battle Creek, Mich.) Loud, frenetic, raucous, and fun, the singer–comedienne scaled the Paramount mountain in one swift leap (1942's *The Fleet's In*), and her downfall ten years later, after *Somebody Loves Me* and *The Greatest Show on Earth*, was, inexplicably, just as sudden; in the interim, though, the crowd-pleasing movies of the "blitzkrieg blonde" made a mint for the studio that only once let another company (MGM) borrow her services (as a last-minute replacement for Judy Garland, who had a nervous breakdown halfway through filming *Annie Get Your Gun*); began at Paramount at $750 a week—after screaming her way to fame to escape a poverty-stricken childhood; lived in Lansing, Mich., with her mother and older sister Marion until the police there, discovering that her mother was a bootlegger, forced them to leave town; in Detroit, unable to find work in those Depression years, her mother soon became an alcoholic, and Betty began singing for coins on street corners; next sang in speakeasies, with a band (Vincent Lopez's) at 15, and finally, in Broadway musicals (*Two for the Show* and Cole Porter's *Panama Hattie*); broke when she landed in Hollywood, she put up a flashy front—rented a penthouse, hired two maids, bought a mink coat and a snazzy convertible, all on credit; her boundless energy, though, in musical numbers like "My Rocking Horse Ran Away," made a greater impression; touching all bases, she proved her dramatic mettle in Preston Sturges' *The Miracle of Morgan's Creek* and was delightfully in step with Astaire in *Let's Dance*; less harmonious were her marriages, all four—to wealthy camera manufacturer Ted Briskin (1945–51; daughters: Lindsay and Candice), dance director Charles O'Curran (1952–55), record producer Alan Livingston (1955–58), and trumpet player Pete Candoli (1961–66; daughter: Carolyn); reviewing her marital fiascos, she said later, "It was always 'Betty Hutton'—no one's ever loved me for *me*"; made her last movie in '57—*Spring Reunion*, a flop—after being off screen for five years; after earning $9 million (her estimate) as a star, she learned in '67 that she was flat broke ("Someone absolutely stole me blind") and filed for bankruptcy, listing debts of about $150,000; cried a bit later, "I've been crucified in this racket, *crucified*, when I only gave out love. I bought houses, Cadillacs, furs, you name it, for people—even churches for my maids. But when the money went, everybody split"; found peace of mind later as a Catholic convert, working as a volunteer domestic at a rectory in Rhode Island.

MOVIE HIGHLIGHTS: *Star-Spangled Rhythm, Happy Go Lucky, Let's Face It, And the Angels Sing, Here Come the Waves, Incendiary Blonde, The Stork Club, Cross My Heart, The Perils of Pauline, Dream Girl, Red Hot and Blue.*

Claude Jarman Jr.

(b. Claude Jarman Jr., Sept. 27, 1934, Nashville, Tenn.) Engaging lad— blond, blue-eyed, and with a distinctive cowlick—who was discovered for *The Yearling* ('46) and received a special Oscar for his natural performance; the son of an accountant for the Nashville, Chattanooga & St. Louis railroad, he was plucked out of a fifth grade class at Eakin Elementary School in his hometown by the movie's director, Clarence Brown, after 12,000 other Southern boys had been interviewed for the role of Jody Baxter; what he may never have known: His good fortune was another adolescent's disappointment; in '42, MGM had spent more than $1 million and two months in the Florida Everglades trying to make *The Yearling* with an entirely different cast— Spencer Tracy and Anne Revere as the parents and juvenile actor Gene Eckman as Jody; the studio shelved the project when Tracy and director Victor Fleming had a violent disagreement; started again years later with a new Jody, as Eckman had outgrown the role, and, as the mother and father, Gregory Peck and newcomer Jacqueline White (quickly to be replaced by Jane Wyman as "Ma Baxter"); when new to Hollywood, Claude said his ambition was to go to college and play football, his favorite movie was *National Velvet* (saw it seven times), and young Elizabeth Taylor was his best-liked actress; while continuing to make movies—a couple of classics among them—until he was a young man, he commuted to Hollywood from Nashville, where he received his degree at Vanderbilt University before serving in the Navy; choosing public relations as his professional field, he settled in San Francisco in the '60s, founded a film production company, Medion, Inc., to make documentaries and TV commercials, and became director of the San Francisco International Film Festival; in the latter capacity, he found himself involved in a tempest in a teapot with another ex–child star, Shirley Temple, in '66; as one film to be shown at the festival, he and his committee had picked a Swedish film, *Night Games*, that dealt with incest; in protest, Temple promptly resigned from the management committee; a big man (6'2", 190 pounds), he has a big family; has three children by his first marriage, which ended in divorce, and two daughters—the first adopted, the second born in '72—with second wife Vanessa, whom he married in '68.

MOVIE HIGHLIGHTS: *High Barbaree, The Sun Comes Up, Roughshod, Intruder in the Dust, Rio Grande, The Outriders, Inside Straight, Hangman's Knot, Fair Wind to Java, The Great Locomotive Chase.*

Gloria Jean

(b. Gloria Jean Schoonover, April 14, 1927, Buffalo, N.Y.) Deanna Durbin put up a good front, but she was less than overjoyed when, in '38, Universal signed up a new soprano, who was all of 11, publicized her as the "next" Deanna, and soon starred her in *The Under-Pup*; "The press," Gloria Jean says, "was told I was Deanna's protégée—the truth is she never spoke to me"; studying opera in New York City at 10, she was discovered by the same producer who made Deanna Durbin a star, Joseph Pasternak; for *The Under-Pup*'s premiere, the studio chartered an entire train to take many of its stars (but not Deanna) from Hollywood to Scranton, Pa., where Gloria Jean grew up (and began singing and dancing at 5); 75,000 people, led by the mayor, turned out to meet the train and get a glimpse of their hometown Cinderella; in the next seven years she played leads in 18 movies, mostly Bs, before her contract expired; "When I was ejected from Universal, it was like a death in the family. More than that, I couldn't even get on the lot without a pass, and no one would give me one"; the studio had been both her home and school; got her high school diploma there in a class of three, with Ann Blyth and

Sabu ("For a short time, Elizabeth Taylor was in the school, and she was such a shy little girl that she used to hide under tables"); the co-star she liked best, and who reciprocated her affection ("though he *really* hated children"), was W. C. Fields; made five more pictures for other studios before '49; six years passed before she landed another lead, in a B, *Air Strike*; after another lull of six years, she was cast in a Jerry Lewis comedy, *Ladies' Man*, in what promised to be a major role but was trimmed to a bit in the cutting room; in the '50s what had been "a fairy tale come true" turned to cinders and ashes; Internal Revenue took her entire life savings ($30,000), claiming it was owed in back taxes; except for her three-bedroom home, little was left from her starring days but scrapbooks and an oil portrait of her in a party dress at 16; worked as a restaurant hostess, stood in unemployment lines, and gained weight; in '62, married a handsome man from Italy, Franco Cellini, who worked for the Italian government in Los Angeles; he returned to his native land without her before their son, Angelo, was born in '63; she has been employed in recent years as the switchboard operator-receptionist for a cosmetics firm (Redken Laboratories) in Van Nuys, Calif.; still sings—in the choir of Canoga Park's Church of the Valley.

MOVIE HIGHLIGHTS: *If I Had My Way, A Little Bit of Heaven, Never Give a Sucker an Even Break, What's Cookin'?, When Johnny Comes Marching Home, Get Hep to Love, Mr. Big, It Comes Up Love, Moonlight in Vermont, Pardon My Rhythm, Follow the Boys, Destiny, The Ghost Catchers, The Reckless Age, River Gang, I'll Remember April, Easy to Look At, Copacabana, An Old-Fashioned Girl.*

Van Johnson

(b. Charles Van Dell Johnson, Aug. 28, 1916, Newport, R.I.) Leo the Lion's very own Saint Bernard—big, friendly, and brave (on screen, for a fact—participated in the *Thirty Seconds over Tokyo* raid and, in *Battleground*, the Battle of the Bulge); actually was draft-deferred (4-F); studio publicists protected him from possible public criticism by issuing such dreams-of-peace quotes as the one that he wanted "to form an organization of friends who didn't go into the service to help those who did to find jobs when they return"; the idol of the bobby-soxers, he received more fan mail during the War than any other male star on the lot; was so popular that, in his first three years there, MGM rushed him through 13 movies ("I'd finish one on Saturday night and start the next on Monday morning"), and he sometimes worked on three at once; remained at Metro for 12 years (1942–54); in '45 and '46, was among the Box-Office Top Ten; reached a peak salary of $8,000 weekly; of Swedish descent and the son of a plumbing contractor, he was 3 when his mother abandoned the family, divorced his father, and remarried; when he was famous, his mother turned up at MGM, claiming to be sick and destitute, and demanded that he support her, which he did as long as she lived; had started acting with the drama society at Trinity Church in his hometown; after graduation from Rogers High, worked one year as a clerk in his father's office; at 19, went to New York, arriving with $5; soon landed a four-week job (at $15 a week) in a revue, *Entre Nous*, at the Cherry Lane Theater in Greenwich Village; was a chorus boy at the Roxy Theater, then a singer-dancer on the Borscht circuit; next came Broadway musicals: *New Faces of 1936*, *Too Many Girls* (understudied Eddie Bracken and Desi Arnaz), *Pal Joey* (understudied Gene Kelly and had a small role); an RKO screen test came to naught; Columbia gave him a test (opposite Janet Blair) and said no; Warners signed him, covered up his freckles (soon to be his trademark), died his carrot-top a dark brown, gave him a lead in *Murder in the Big House* opposite Faye Emerson, and dropped his option; at the urging of pal Lucille Ball, MGM's talent chief, Billy Grady, tested him (with an assist from Donna Reed), gave him a contract, and put him to work in a "Crime Doesn't Pay" short; next: a very minor role in Gable's *Somewhere I'll Find You*; his massive fan following began with *Dr. Gillespie's New Assistant*, in which he co-starred with Lionel Barrymore; in '43, was involved in a head-on auto collision in which he was almost decapitated; during his long months of recovery, Spencer Tracy and Irene Dunne were instrumental in saving his career by refusing to continue with *A Guy Named Joe* until he returned; was married once, in '47 to Evie Abbott Wynn (ex of his onetime best friend, Keenan Wynn, which shocked his fans); had a daughter, Schuyler, in '48, and divorced—bitterly—in '68, after a long separation; living in New York since the '60s, he stars in movies, on Broadway, in TV, and, particularly, in dinner theaters—performing in comedies to SRO audiences and earning a mint; in '85, he succeeded Gene Barry in the hit Broadway musical *La Cage Aux Folles*; says, "God has been good to me. I've led a charmed life."

MOVIE HIGHLIGHTS: *The War against Mrs. Hadley, Pilot No. 5, Dr. Gillespie's Criminal Case, The Human Comedy, Madame Curie, Three Men in White, Two Girls and a Sailor, The White Cliffs of Dover, Thrill of a Romance, Weekend at the Waldorf, Easy to Wed, No Leave, No Love, Till the Clouds Roll By, Romance of Rosy Ridge, High Barbaree, In the Good Old*

Summertime, Command Decision, Mother Is a Freshman, Three Guys Named Mike, The Caine Mutiny, Brigadoon.

Jennifer Jones

(b. Phyllis Lee Isley, March 2, 1919, Tulsa, Okla.) As Phyllis Isley, she got a false start in '39 at Republic as the heroine in a serial, *Dick Tracy's G-Men*, and a John Wayne Western, *New Frontier*; returned later under personal contract to David O. Selznick, who gave her a new name (he picked "Jennifer," a publicist came up with "Jones") and arranged for her to star at 20th Century–Fox in *The Song of Bernadette* ('43); won the Best Actress Oscar for this; was later nominated in the same category for *Love Letters, Duel in the Sun,* and *Love Is a Many-Splendored Thing,* and, as Best Support, for *Since You Went Away*; the daughter of a movie exhibitor, she had acted in tent theaters, studied at Northwestern and the American Academy of Dramatic Arts, performed in stock and on radio, and been a garment-district model in New York; in her first audition for Selznick she did a scene from *Claudia* ("and I was awful"); when signed by the producer in '41, she was married to actor Robert Walker and had two small sons (Robert Jr. and Michael); from their first meeting, Selznick was convinced he'd found the actress equivalent of the Hope Diamond, perfection in every facet, and she became an obsession with him; he gave as much time and attention to showcasing her talents as to his own production activities, finally with devastating results to his career (witness such flops as *Duel in the Sun,* a $10 million loser, and *A Farewell to Arms*); the day after winning the Oscar, while then filming romantic scenes with Robert Walker in *Since You Went Away,* the actress announced her intentions of divorcing the actor; in '45, the producer's wife, Irene, informed him she was leaving him; hoping to persuade her to stay, he confessed he was having an affair with the actress; in her autobiography, *A Private View,* Irene Selznick wrote: "Jennifer hadn't caused our situation. If it hadn't been her, it would have been someone else"; Selznick and his favorite star were married from '49 until his death in '65 (and, two years later, she survived a suicide attempt via sleeping pills); during their marriage, loaning her to other studios for major roles, Selznick bombarded directors, cameramen, designers, etc., with memos on ways to present his creation to dazzling effect; he told them in endless detail the best ways to light, direct, make up, and costume the actress; in '54 she and the producer became the parents of a daughter, Mary Jennifer, who, at 21, fell to her death from the roof of a 22-story building in Los

Angeles, an apparent suicide; in '71, one month after they met, the star became the wife of Norton Simon, a multimillionaire financier and art collector; asked early in her career what false impression people had of her, she replied: "They think I'm shy and retiring, when I'm not."

MOVIE HIGHLIGHTS: *Cluny Brown, Portrait of Jennie, We Were Strangers, Madame Bovary, The Wild Heart, Carrie, Ruby Gentry, Indiscretion of an American Wife, Beat the Devil, Good Morning, Miss Dove, The Man in the Gray Flannel Suit, The Barretts of Wimpole Street, Tender Is the Night, The Idol, Angel, Angel, Down We Go, The Towering Inferno.*

Louis Jourdan

(b. Louis Gendre, June 18, 1919, Marseilles, France) Tall and handsome—and the essence of elegance—he looks as though he would smell of chestnut trees in the Bois de Boulogne; yet, in his first American film, *The Paradine Case* ('47), he played a lowly stable hand whose mistress was the rich and murderous Mrs. Paradine (Valli); forced to use both players, director Alfred Hitchcock later complained that "the worst flaw in the casting was assigning Louis Jourdan to play the groom . . . [as he] should have been a manure-smelling stable hand, a man who really reeked of manure"; the actor's proper screen image was established forever in his next Hollywood movie, *Letter from an Unknown Woman*, and, a decade later, in the incomparable *Gigi*; the son of a well-to-do hotelkeeper, he attended fine schools in France, Turkey, and England—and laments that he still speaks English with an accent ("English is the most beautiful musical language in the world; I would want to speak English like John Gielgud"); trained for the theater at the Ecole Dramatique in Paris and had his first screen role in *Le Corsair* with Charles Boyer in '39; during the Occupation he made a number of nonpolitical films (*L'Arlesienne, La Vie de la Boheme*, etc.), then joined the Underground movement, having a most personal interest in France's liberation as his father had been arrested by the Gestapo; has been married since '44 to Berthe Frederique, known to friends as Quique (pronounced Keek); says of their long marriage, "It means we have weathered many difficulties. No lives or marriages are lasting without oppositions [but] if you feel that your wife or husband is an essential part of you, everything else is only peripheral"; their only child, Louis Henry, was found dead in '81, at 29, of a massive overdose of drugs and alcohol; in 1954–55, at the height of his movie fame, the actor took time out to star on Broadway in *The Immoralist* and *Tonight in Samarkand*;

pulling up stakes in Hollywood in the early '70s, he lived in Paris again for a decade before returning to America—to a mansion in Beverly Hills—to resume his career here.

MOVIE HIGHLIGHTS: *No Minor Vices, Madame Bovary, Anne of the Indies, Bird of Paradise, The Happy Time, Rue de l'Estrapade, Decameron Nights, Three Coins in the Fountain, The Swan, Julie, The Best of Everything, The Bride Is Much Too Beautiful, The V.I.P.s, Made in Paris, Cervantes, Peau d'Espion, A Flea in Her Ear, The Count of Monte Cristo, Silver Bears, Swamp Thing.*

Brenda Joyce

(b. Betty Graftina Leabo, Feb. 25, 1917, Kansas City, Mo.) Blondes may be a "dime a dozen" in Hollywood, but occasionally there is one like Brenda Joyce, unlike any other blonde in movies before or since; her fresh-scrubbed all-American-girl face, more than being merely beautiful, had interesting angular planes and was an admixture of naïveté and total self-confidence; in '39, at 20th Century–Fox, Darryl F. Zanuck had lined up an all-star cast (Tyrone Power, Myrna Loy, George Brent) for his $2½ million production of *The Rains Came*; what he didn't have, after testing 56 actresses, was someone to play the central role of unhappy Fern, an American girl of candor and fascinating ruthlessness, whose mother (Marjorie Rambeau) kept shoving her at the heads of all eligible males; Zanuck's problem was solved for him by Hollywood agent Frances Bailey; visiting a friend at UCLA, she was introduced to an English major at the university who was putting herself through school by working as a photographers' model; getting into movies had long been the goal of the young woman, soon to be famous as Brenda Joyce; after her parents separated when she was small, she lived with her mother in San Bernardino, Calif., and always planned to study at UCLA because it was near the movie studios; joining the dramatic society there, she played leads, such as Portia in *The Merchant of Venice*, and went unnoticed by talent scouts—only to be discovered by accident while playing tennis on the campus courts; once Zanuck's talent-hunt ended, he wisely issued orders to makeup men and coaches that his new star was not to be changed in any way; her naturalness carried her through a full decade of leading lady roles, the first four years being spent at 20th, the rest as a freelance; finally had the distinction of being the only actress to play Jane to two different Tarzans—Johnny Weissmuller in four pictures and Lex Barker in one; in the '40s, was married for several years, until they divorced, to high school sweetheart Owen Ward; he was an Army lieutenant when their daughter, Pamela Ann, was born in November 1942 and made the columns as Hollywood's first "war baby"; the actress quit movies in '49 and was later married to, and divorced from, a Naval officer; reportedly, she has lived in Washington, D.C., in recent years.

MOVIE HIGHLIGHTS: *Here I Am a Stranger, Little Old New York, Public Deb No. 1, Private Nurse, Marry the Boss's Daughter, Right to the Heart, Whispering Ghosts, The Postman Didn't Ring, Thumbs Up, Little Tokyo, U.S.A., Tarzan and the Amazons, I'll Tell the World, Strange Confession, The Enchanted Forest, The Spider Woman Strikes Back, Little Giant, Danger Woman, Springtime in the Sierras, Tarzan's Magic Fountain.*

Danny Kaye

(b. David Daniel Kaminsky, Jan. 18, 1913, Brooklyn, N.Y.) When Sam Goldwyn discovered this frenetic "git-gat-gittle" comedy star—a carrot top, a stringbean—he found a gold mine; it also cost the producer; for 1944's *Up in Arms*, his feature debut, the immediately popular funnyman was paid $100,000, a fortune then for an unproven star; refused to have his nose bobbed for the movies but didn't object when a screen character was created for him based on silent star Harold Lloyd—the shy, trouble-beset innocent who triumphs over all odds, mostly by accident, and wins the girl; had become famous on Broadway in '41 in the Gertrude Lawrence musical *Lady in the Dark* with one side-splitting patter song, "Tschaikovsky"—in which, in 39 seconds, he rattled off the names of Russian composers Malichevsky, Rubinstein, Arensky, Tschaikovsky, and some 50 others; two years earlier, a flop show, *The Straw Hat Revue*, marked his debut on Broadway, and getting there entailed a struggle; the son of an immigrant Ukrainian tailor, he grew up in a section of Brooklyn abounding in kids and poverty; quitting Thomas Jefferson High at 15, he worked for a while in a Manhattan insurance office; by 17, was a general handyman and part-time entertainer at summer resorts in the Catskills' Borscht belt; before he was 20, he was part of a rag-tag musical unit touring the Orient where, using pantomine and his mobile, expressive face, he learned to get laughs without words—a technique that later served him well; returning to the Catskills, to Camp Tamiment, he fell in love with a young songwriter and pianist, Sylvia Fine; made his movie debut long before getting to Hollywood—in a few 1937–38, New York-made Educational comedy shorts ("Cupid Takes a Holiday," "Dime a Dance," in which June Allyson also appeared, etc.); following his failed Broadway revue (which Sylvia Fine co-wrote), he scored a hit—accompanied by Sylvia at the piano—at La Martinique, a top Manhattan club, and was spotted there by producer-playwright Moss Hart, whose production of *Lady in the Dark* catapulted him to stardom at 28; married Sylvia in '40, and she became, as well as his lifelong partner, a major force in his career, writing his special material, etc.; their one child, Dena, born in '46, was named for a Hebrew song her father sang, and he named his own movie production company for her; growing up as Danny Kaye's daughter, she has said, was "a lot of laughs—my father is very spontaneous, and he is also very considerate"; before '63 he starred in 16 smash-hit movies and became very rich (real estate, radio stations, etc.), owning and piloting his own Lear jet, having a lavish Chinese kitchen built in his home, where, a celebrated chef, he exercised his culinary skills; for four years (1963–67), he starred in a music-variety series on CBS-TV, winning an Emmy; in later years, has been an international ambassador-at-large for UNICEF—the United Nations Children's Fund.

MOVIE HIGHLIGHTS: *Wonder Man, The Kid from Brooklyn, The Secret Life of Walter Mitty, A Song Is Born, Inspector General, On the Riviera, Hans Christian Andersen, Knock on Wood, White Christmas, The Court Jester, Merry Andrew, Me and the Colonel, The Five Pennies, On the Double, The Man from the Diner's Club, The Madwoman of Chaillot.*

Gene Kelly

(b. Eugene Curran Kelly, Aug. 23, 1912, Pittsburgh, Pa.) MGM's inimitable, ingratiating musical star—with a radiant Irish smile, a whiskey-tenor voice, and those nimble feet—who is irrefutably the greatest athletic dancer the screen has known; comparing himself to Fred Astaire, he once said, "I am the Marlon Brando of dancers, and he the Cary Grant"; nominated for a Best Actor Oscar for *Anchors Aweigh*, he was presented a special Academy Award in '51 "in appreciation of his versatility as an actor, singer, director and dancer, and specifically for his brilliant achievements in the art of choreography on film"; that dazzling, unprecedented 17-minute dance finale in *An American in Paris* had much to do with the honor; the son of a Columbia Gramophone salesman, he had dancing lessons from childhood; as kids, he and brother Fred (later the stage director of *This Is the Army*) were such gymnasts that they created an acrobatic hoofing-on-roller skates act and played in speakeasies and American Legion halls; a high school football star, he put himself through the University of Pittsburgh (prelaw student) by pumping gas and operating a dancing school; taught dance for seven years before he headed for New York, expecting to become a dance director; was for three years the choreographer at Billy Rose's Diamond Horseshoe (foreshadowing his later movie role in *Cover Girl*); played small parts in musicals: *One for the Money* and *Leave It to Me* (danced in the background as Mary Martin sang "My Heart Belongs to Daddy"); the part of the young hoofer in Saroyan's *The Time Of Your Life* in '39 made him well known and, the next year, the title role in *Pal Joey* made him a Broadway star; David O. Selznick signed him up, talked of starring him as the young priest in *Keys of the Kingdom*, then sold his contract to MGM; made his screen debut opposite Judy Garland in '42 in *For Me and My Gal*, replacing Dan Dailey, who'd been drafted; later served in the Navy himself (1944–46) and was lucky to have movies made prior to enlistment released while he was away; advanced the art of dance on film through adventurous experiments, the first being his "Alter Ego" number in *Cover Girl*, in which he and his shadow danced together via a split-screen matchup; next cavorted with a cartoon character, Jerry (of "Tom & Jerry"), in *Anchors Aweigh* (this novelty dance took two months to film); with pal Stanley Donen, he codirected (and starred in) *On the Town*, his personal favorite (puts *Singin' in the Rain* in second place); did many straight dramatic films (*The Cross of Lorraine*, *Christmas Holiday*, etc.); dancing career ended in '57 when he shattered his kneecap in a skiing mishap; in '80, he co-starred in *Xanadu*, a failed film with Olivia Newton-John, and was persuaded to appear in one musical number, but said, "I do a little moving, a couple of dance steps, but in all honesty they are just little flashes"; has directed movies in which he did not appear (*Hello, Dolly!*, *Tunnel of Love*, etc.) and Broadway musicals (*Flower Drum Song*); was first married from '40 to '57, when they divorced, to Betsy Blair (nominated for a Best Supporting Oscar for *Marty*); one daughter: Kerry; second wife was Jeanne Coyne, his longtime dance assistant (and once wed to Stanley Donen), by whom he has a son, Timothy, and a daughter, Bridget; had 13 years together (1960–73) before she died of leukemia; his biography, *Gene Kelly* by Clive Hirschhorn, was published in '75.

MOVIE HIGHLIGHTS: *Du Barry Was a Lady, Pilot No. 5, Thousands Cheer, Ziegfeld Follies, Living in a Big Way, The Pirate, The Three Musketeers, Words and Music, Take Me Out to the Ball Game, Summer Stock, It's a Big Country, The Devil Makes Three, Brigadoon, Crest of the Wave, It's Always Fair Weather, Invitation to the Dance, The Happy Road, Les Girls, Marjorie Morningstar, Inherit the Wind, What a Way to Go, Forty Carats.*

(b. Nancy Kelly, March 25, 1921, Lowell, Mass.) Greatly talented brunette beauty from Broadway who began playing romantic leads at 20th Century–Fox at 17, in *Submarine Patrol* and *Jesse James*, opposite Tyrone Power; the daughter of a theater ticket broker and an actress-model, she was trained for an acting career from infancy—as were her brother Jack (co-star of TV's "Maverick") and sister Carole (billed Karolee Kelly in such movies as *The Come On*); first a child model in New York and educated in private schools (St. Lawrence Academy, Bentley School for Girls), she made her movie debut at 5 in Gloria Swanson's *Untamed Lady*; was also seen that same year in other silents, *The Great Gatsby* and Warner Baxter's *Mismates*; was first on Broadway at 10 in A. A. Milne's *Give Me Yesterday*, which was followed by other plays and many appearances on radio ("Myrt and Marge," "The Shadow," etc.); major acclaim came at 16 when she gave a poignant performance as socialite Gertrude Lawrence's neglected daughter, Blossom, in *Susan and God*; movie career as an adult began well, but she soon drifted into Bs; was married twice during her Hollywood years—first, for one year (1941–42), to Edmond O'Brien, her leading man in *Parachute Battalion*, and next (1946–50) to cameraman Fred Jackman Jr.; after 1948's *Disaster*, perhaps the worst movie she ever did, she returned to Broadway and salvaged her career by starring in Clifford Odets' *The Big Knife*; the other stage successes followed (*Season in the Sun*, etc.), topped by 1955's *The Bad Seed*; performance as the distraught mother in this won her Broadway's Tony, Chicago's Sarah Siddons Award, when she toured in the play, and a Best Actress Oscar nomination when, returning to Hollywood in triumph, she starred in the movie version in '56; instead of capitalizing on this screen success, she chose to continue her career on the stage—later winning a second Sarah Siddons Award when she starred on tour in *Who's Afraid of Virginia Woolf?*; from '55 until they divorced in '68, was married to Theater Guild exec Warren Caro, by whom she has a daughter, Kelly, an actress; superstitious, she considers Friday her good luck day—was born on a Good Friday—and signs all her contracts on a Friday.

MOVIE HIGHLIGHTS: *Stanley and Livingstone, Tail Spin, He Married His Wife, Frontier Marshal, Private Affairs, One Night in the Tropics, Sailor's Lady, Scotland Yard, A Very Young Lady, To the Shores of Tripoli, Fly by Night, Friendly Enemies, Tornado, Women in Bondage, Show Business, Gambler's Choice, Double Exposure, The Woman Who Came Back, Betrayal from the East, Follow That Woman, Murder in the Music Hall.*

Arthur Kennedy

(b. John Arthur Kennedy, Feb. 17, 1914, Worcester, Mass.) Good-looking redhead, but no glamourpuss, who has the gift of making a scene come electrically alive when he's in it; made his debut in '40 as Cagney's sensitive, piano-playing brother in *City for Conquest*; has had exceptional luck in movies with "brother" roles—Alan Ladd's in *Chicago Deadline*, Kirk Douglas's in *Champion*, Jane Wyman's in *The Glass Menagerie*, etc.; "son" roles have done it for him on Broadway—was Ed Begley's in *All My Sons* and Lee J. Cobb's son Biff in *Death of a Salesman* (performance won him a Tony); was nominated for the Best Actor Oscar for *Bright Victory* and for the Best Supporting Oscar for *Champion*, *Trial*, *Some Came Running*, and *Peyton Place*; the latter remains one of his three favorite roles (other two: in *Boomerang* and *Adventures of a Young Man*); early career at Warner Bros. was interrupted when, after co-starring in *Air Force*, he was off the screen for three years for actual duty in the Air Force; resumed in '46, with Ida Lupino in *Devotion*, as though he'd never been away; of nontheatrical parents (father was a dentist), he first became interested in drama when in plays at Worcester Academy, a private school; got his degree in theater arts at Carnegie Tech in '36; that summer, at the Cleveland Great Lakes Exposition, he and other aspiring actor friends (David Brian, Macdonald Carey, San Wanamaker) acted with the Globe Theater in abbreviated Shakespearean plays—not profitably, financially; to the left of them on the midway was a lady snake charmer, to the right was a sideshow featuring an effigy of the Lindbergh baby's kidnapper with a circus barker yelling, "Why pay 40¢ to see *Julius Caesar* when you can see Bruno Hauptmann electrocuted for a dime?" (says the actor, "We couldn't afford a barker, so Hauptmann always won"); began his stage career as John Kennedy (in *Merrily We Roll Along*), was J. Arthur Kennedy next (in *Life and Death of an American*), and Arthur Kennedy first, in '40, in *International Incident*; married former actress Mary Cheffey in '38; has a son, Terence, and a daughter, Laurie, both of whom chose theatrical careers.

MOVIE HIGHLIGHTS: *High Sierra, Bad Men of Missouri, They Died with Their Boots On, Highway West, Desperate Journey, Cheyenne, The Window, Too Late for Tears, The Walking Hills, Red Mountain, Bend of the River, Rancho Notorious, The Lusty Men, The Girl in White, Desperate Hours, A Summer Place, Elmer Gantry, Home Is the Hero, Lawrence of Arabia, Cheyenne Autumn, Nevada Smith, Fantastic Voyage, Anzio.*

(b. Evelyn Louise Keyes, Nov. 20, 1917, Port Arthur, Texas) Blonde (and occasionally red-haired) star who was one of the most appealing light comediennes in movies (*A Thousand and One Nights, The Mating of Millie*) and no slouch at drama, either, (*Mrs. Mike, The Face Behind the Mask,* etc.); since her screen career, she has published a novel, *I Am a Billboard,* and, in '77, her best-selling autobiography, *Scarlett O'Hara's Younger Sister* (played Suellen in *Gone With the Wind*); besides being exceptionally well written, her autobiography was frank in the extreme (when playing her first bit in *The Buccaneer,* she wrote, star Frederic March tried to seduce her; when a starlet at Paramount, Anthony Quinn claimed her virginity; when a star at Columbia, studio boss Harry Cohn, who unsuccessfully lusted after her, often phoned to inquire about her dates' sexual talents, etc.); book also contained revelations about her many affairs, including the lengthy one with Mike Todd (lost him to Liz Taylor but had helped bankroll his *Around the World in 80 Days* and profited handsomely); not left out were intimate details about her four husbands; construction man Barton Bainbridge, an alcoholic who committed suicide in '40, Hungarian director Charles Vidor (1944–45), director John Huston (1946–50), and bandleader Artie Shaw (married in '57 but have been separated for many years); cited as one of her 20 lovers was David Niven; in his book *Bring on the Empty Horses,* he told this version of the breakup of her marriage to Huston—putting up for a while with a very ugly monkey the director insisted on keeping in the house, she finally informed him, "One of us has to go. . . . It's the monkey or me," to which Huston replied, after a long pause, "Honey . . . it's you!", after graduating from high school in Atlanta, where she grew up, she danced with a troupe touring the South; arrived in Hollywood, still a teen-ager, with a letter of introduction from bandleader Ted Fio Rito to a movie agent, who managed to get her a $50-a-week contract with Cecil B. De Mille; after a few minor roles for him, she moved on to Columbia in '40, where she rose to stardom and remained for a decade; "I could have been an important actress," says the star friends called Casey, i.e., Keysie, "but I didn't pay my dues."

MOVIE HIGHLIGHTS: *Union Pacific, The Lady in Question, Slightly Honorable, Here Comes Mr. Jordan, Ladies in Retirement, The Adventures of Martin Eden, Flight Lieutenant, The Desperadoes, Nine Girls, Something about a Soldier, Strange Affair, Thrill of Brazil, Renegades, The Jolson Story,*

Enchantment, Mr. Soft Touch, The Prowler, The Iron Man, The Killer That Stalked New York, 99 River Street, Shoot First, Hell's Half Acre, The Seven Year Itch.

Leonid Kinskey

(b. Leonid Kinskey, April 18, 1903, St. Petersburg, Russia) In the '40s ('30s, too), it was a rare week when moviegoers failed to witness a new performance by this fine character actor; did many serious roles (the murderous Russian peasant in *We Live Again*, the informer in *Algiers*, etc.), but the quintessential Kinskey was the inimitable comic—with his accent, pixilated look, acrobatic eyebrows, and half-moon grin wreathing a bell-pepper schnozz; was at his hilarious best as "Gigalo Galore" Tito in Grable's *Down Argentine Way* and, in *Rhythm on the Range*, singing (in fractured English) "I'm an Old Cowhand" with Bing Crosby, Martha Raye, and Bob Burns; his buffoonery masked a brilliant mind; between movie stints he taught drama at UCLA and, leaving the screen (by choice) after 1956's *Glory*, later wrote and directed industrial films for major firms; has also written articles for national magazines, one of which, a reminiscence of *Casablanca*, he titled "The Only Man Who Kissed Humphrey Bogart" (which he did, playing Sasha, the bartender, after Bogie, as Rick, did a rare kind deed for a young refugee couple in his club); began as a mime at the Alexandrinski Theater in St. Petersburg (Leningrad) and then had roles at other Imperial theaters; leaving Russia after the Revolution, he toured Europe and South America and finally performed in the U.S. as the comedy star in plays staged by the Firebird Theater troupe; movie debut was in a '26 silent film, *The Great Deception*, starring Ben Lyon and Aileen Pringle, which was made in New York; comedy antics in Jolson's *Wonder Bar* on Broadway took him to Hollywood, where his first talkie was the Lubitsch classic, *Trouble in Paradise*; next came dozens of roles as humorous professors *(Ball of Fire)*, frenetic Russian composers *(On Your Toes)*, waiters, cabbies, etc.; made so many films that, catching one on TV in later years, he would be surprised to find himself in it; was married four times; for two decades, until her death in '63, was the husband of the beautiful Viennese actress Iphigenia Castiglioni, and following their original wedding ceremony in Mexico City, they sentimentally married again three more times, every five years on their anniversary, and in a different country each time; movie fans may best recall Iphigenia Castiglioni for having several times protrayed Empress Eugenie, most notably in *The Story of Louis Pasteur*; marrying her, Leonid Kinskey, with no children of his own, acquired two stepdaughters—one of whom, the Marchesa de Companari of Italy, he has never met.

MOVIE HIGHLIGHTS: *Les Miserables, The Road to Glory, Café Metropolis, The Great Waltz, The Story of Vernon and Irene Castle, Everything Happens at Night, Daytime Wife, That Night in Rio, So Ends Our Night, Weekend in Havana, Lady for a Night, I Married an Angel, Talk of the Town, Presenting Lily Mars, The Fighting Seabees, Can't Help Singing, Monsieur Beaucaire, Honeychile, The Man with the Golden Arm.*

Alan Ladd

(b. Alan Walbridge Ladd, Sept. 3, 1913, Hot Springs, Ark.; d. Jan. 29, 1964) "Short guys don't make movie heroes"—so the movie moguls believed until Ladd—5'6", blond, and green-eyed—anchored at Paramount, starred in *This Gun for Hire* as Raven, a ruthless (yet somehow sympathetic) killer, and soon received 20,000 pieces of adoring fan mail each week (while still earning only $350 weekly); for almost a decade earlier, had played small parts (in *Souls at Sea, Goldwyn Follies*, etc.) without creating a ripple; was the only child of an accountant, who died when Ladd was 4, and an English immigrant mother, who took him following his father's death to California, where they lived in abject poverty; had a mother-fixation from which he never escaped and a lifelong melancholia aggravated by the nature of her death; becoming an alcoholic, she committed suicide when he was 23 by swallowing arsenic (ant paste); at North Hollywood High, he was a champion diver and swimmer and was first on stage at the school, singing the lead, Ko-Ko, in *The Mikado*; was briefly a laborer at Warner Bros.; became a radio actor, first at KFWB in Hollywood, graduating to supporting roles on such shows as "Hollywood Hotel" and "Lux Radio Theater"; when 25, was discovered via a radio performance by Sue Carol, a shrewd, driving woman, a latter-day Clara Bow-type in movies, who had been around the Hollywood track and became a top actors' agent; at their first meeting, she once said, she knew "he was for me"; though she was ten years older, they soon became lovers—but there were complications; in '79, ace reporter Beverly Linet penned the star's definitive biography, *Ladd: The Life, The Legend, The Legacy of Alan Ladd*, and rattled a few skeletons; revealed facts never mentioned in his studio bios; when Sue Carol and the actor met in '38, each was already married and had been, each of them, for two years—she to her third husband, Ladd to the shy sweetheart he'd met in school, Marjorie Jane ("Midge") Harrold, by whom he had an infant son, Alan Jr. (would grow up to be a movie studio exec); convinced he would be a big star, Sue Carol eventually landed a Paramount contract for him late in '41; earlier that year, he'd walked out on wife Midge, and in July she filed for divorce (reportedly, Sue hired the lawyer who represented her); Midge died of diabetes at 42—and not once in her lifetime was her name ever mentioned in connection with that of her ex; in March 1942, when *This Gun for Hire* was released and the actor (publicized as a bachelor) became an overnight sensation, Sue Carol divorced her writer husband and one week later was Mrs. Alan Ladd; she guided his career with an iron fist, accompanied him to the studio, collected his paychecks, invested his earnings (became a multimillionaire), and gave him two children (Alana and David); he became so popular that the studio built a $110,000 bungalow for him, and in '47, '53, and '54, he was among the Box-Office Top Ten; was a shy man with a deep-seated inferiority complex and perhaps was burdened by feelings of guilt; fame, fortune, and family finally were not enough; became an alcoholic— sometimes hiding his liquor at the studio in tonic bottles; in '62, recovered from an "accidental" self-inflicted gunshot wound; died less than two years later of a combination of alcohol and pills, also deemed by the coroner to be "accidental."

MOVIE HIGHLIGHTS: *The Glass Key, Lucky Jordan, China, And Now Tomorrow, Salty O'Rourke, Two Years before the Mast, The Blue Dahlia, O.S.S., Wild Harvest, Calcutta, Beyond Glory, Whispering Smith, Saigon, The Great Gatsby, Chicago Deadline, Branded, Captain Carey, U.S.A., Red Mountain, Appointment with Danger, The Iron Mistress, Shane, Desert Legion, Botany Bay, Hell Below Zero, Saskatchewan, The McConnell Story, The Proud Rebel, All the Young Men, The Carpetbaggers.*

Veronica Lake

(b. Constance Ockleman, Nov. 14, 1919, Brooklyn, N.Y.; d. July 7, 1973) Paramount's pint-sized (5'2"), curvaceous, silver-haired beauty with the world-famous "peekaboo" hairdo cascading over her right eye; like Alan Ladd, with whom she often co-starred *(This Gun for Hire, The Glass Key, The Blue Dahlia, Saigon)*, she drifted into alcoholism; unlike him, she died on the brink of poverty (a most trusted man in her life squandered her earnings); left Hollywood in '52 and moved to New York, saying, "I was never psychologically meant to be a picture star—I left to save my life"; with her went her children—Elaine (by art director John Detlie; 1940–43) and Michael and Diane (by director Andre DeToth; 1944–52); settled in Greenwich Village in a rundown apartment, the rent for which she was often in arrears, and worked at whatever job she could find; first labored in a factory for $75 a week, pasting felt flowers on lingerie hangers (used an assumed name; fellow workers never recognized her); next was a bar hostess at a second-rate hotel, then a bartender; acted in stock and an Off Broadway show (*Best Foot Forward*), and for a few months was in Baltimore as host of a TV show featuring old movies; marriage #3 (1955–59) was to songwriter Joe McCarthy (son of the composer of "You Made Me Love You"); from '61 to '65, when he died, she lived with a handsome merchant seaman, Andy Elickson, who'd not only never seen her on screen but had never heard of Veronica Lake; early in '72, was married to Robert Carleton-Munroe, a retired English sea captain, but filed for divorce within six months; the daughter of a ship's master, and first a premed student at McGill University, she studied acting at the Bliss-Hayden School in Hollywood; began on screen as Constance Keane (stepfather's name was Keane), playing bits in such 1939–40 films as *All Women Have Secrets*, *Sorority House*, and *Forty Little Mothers*; acquired her permanent screen name and the look that made her a pinup favorite with G.I.s when producer Arthur Hornblow Jr. starred her as a nightclub singer in *I Wanted Wings* ('41); starting salary: $350 a week; remained at Paramount to the end of the decade, finally earning a weekly wage of $4,000; between marriages, Aristotle Onassis wooed her and Howard Hughes proposed to her; with pale white makeup covering a million freckles, she moved through most roles like a sleepwalking miniature mannequin, speaking in a monotone; exceptions—two delightful comedy performances (in *Sullivan's Travels* and *I Married a Witch*) and a fine dramatic one as a tragic WWII nurse in *So Proudly We Hail*; temperamental, with a somewhat perverse streak in her nature, she was not greatly popular at the studio; except for acquiring a self-deprecating sense of humor ("I wasn't a sex symbol, I was a sex zombie"), nothing changed; in '71, *Veronica*, her autobiography (written by Donald Bain), was published; sending her on a cross-country publicity tour, the publisher rented her a mink coat—which she refused to return; her funeral in New York was attended by 30 friends—none from Hollywood.

MOVIE HIGHLIGHTS: *Star Spangled Rhythm*, *The Hour before the Dawn*, *Bring on the Girls*, *Hold That Blonde*, *Out of This World*, *Miss Susie Slagle's*, *Ramrod*, *Variety Girl*, *The Sainted Sisters*, *Isn't It Romantic?*, *Slattery's Hurricane*, *Stronghold*.

Hedy Lamarr

(b. Hedwig Eva Maria Kiesler, Nov. 9, 1913, Vienna, Austria) MGM's raven-haired, frozen-faced beauty, with the petulant-child's voice, whose ravishing looks were envied by every woman in America (that elegant nose— did it matter that it'd been "enhanced" by a plastic surgeon?); the private school-educated daughter of a director of the Bank of Vienna, she was first seen in five 1929–33 movies in Europe—*Geld auf der Strasse (Money on the Street)*, *Sturm im Wasserglas (Storm in a Water Glass)*, etc., including the notorious *Ekstase (Ecstasy)*, in which she romped in the nude; a Max Reinhardt protégée, she also appeared on the stage in Vienna in many plays (*Private Lives, The Weaker Sex, Queen Elizabeth*, etc.); first husband (1933–37) was multimillionaire munitions manufacturer Fritz Mandl, then a Hitler sycophant; fled from him to Paris, won her divorce, moved on to London; met American talent agent Bob Ritchie there, who agreed to manage her career and introduced her to Louis B. Mayer, who took her to Hollywood and named her after silent star Barbara La Marr, a beauty he greatly admired; became an international rage in her first American film, *Algiers* ('38), on loan-out from MGM, in a role originally meant for Sylvia Sidney; said *The Hollywood Reporter*: "She has more sex, more rare beauty than the screen has seen for many days and, with it, definite artistry"; her "artistry" later surfaced only rarely, most notably in *H. M. Pulham, Esq.* and Cecil B. De Mille's *Samson and Delilah*, the apex of her career; became equally famous for her marriages, all of which ended in divorce—to screenwriter Gene Markey, the ex of Joan Bennett (1939–40; adopted a son, James), actor John Loder (1943–47; had two children: Denise Hedy and Anthony), restaurateur Ted Stauffer (1951–52), oil millionaire W. Howard Lee (1953–59; later the husband of Gene Tierney), and Beverly Hills attorney Lewis Bowles (1963–65); little known talent: during WWII, was granted a patent as coinventor of a complex communications system designed to direct torpedoes at moving ship targets; when seeing her old movies on TV, she has said these are her memories: *Boom Town* (the warmth and friendliness of Clark Gable and Claudette Colbert), *I Take This Woman* (Spencer Tracy—"a great actor but there were times when he made me cry. He was not precisely my favorite person"), *Lady of the Tropics* ("teaching Bob Taylor how to kiss more convincingly for the movie cameras"), *Ziegfeld Girl* (parading down steep, glittery stairs, blinded by lights, burdened by a top-heavy, starry headdress, forbidden by the director to look anywhere but straight ahead—and terrified of falling); a redhead in recent times and still slender, she has long lived in New York in a small apartment on the fashionable East Side and vacations in Aruba; failing eyesight forced her to wear heavy-lensed glasses for a decade; condition was corrected in '80 when a Long Island opthamologist, Dr. Charles Kelman, performed surgery, removing cataracts from both eyes and implanting new lenses; in '84 she turned songwriter, penning tunes performed by singer Chris Taaj at a cabaret in Greenwich Village.

MOVIE HIGHLIGHTS: *Comrade X, Come Live with Me, Tortilla Flat, Crossroads, White Cargo, The Heavenly Body, The Conspirators, Experiment Perilous, Her Highness and the Bellboy, The Strange Woman, Dishonored Lady, Let's Live a Little, A Lady without a Passport, Copper Canyon, My Favorite Spy, The Story of Mankind, The Female Animal.*

Dorothy Lamour

(b. Mary Leta Dorothy Slaton, Dec. 10, 1914, New Orleans, La.) Languorous brunette, with a sultry singing voice and a whistle-bait shape, who, between '36 *(The Jungle Princess)* and '53 *(Road to Bali)*, reigned supreme as Paramount's "Sarong Girl"; Bob Hope once quipped: "She did more for a piece of cloth than any American woman since Betsy Ross"; her original sarong, which she held up by "muscle power," is in the Smithsonian Institution; favorite role, the gang moll in 1940's *Johnny Apollo*, came via a loan-out to 20th Century–Fox; "It proved that I wasn't limited to leaning against a palm tree or playing straight woman to Hope and Crosby"; she hit the "Road" with Hope and Crosby in seven comedies; they called her "Mommie"; has said, "I was closer to Bob than to Bing, whose moods were changeable—he'd be funny one day and quite remote the next"; a pinup queen during WWII, she earned $450,000 per movie at her peak and was famed for her many USO tours and for selling $300 million in war bonds; enormously popular in Hollywood, she was known as "the girl who never made an enemy"; friendship played a major role in her rise to fame; the daughter of a waiter and a waitress, and born in a charity ward, she longed to become a famous singer; in '30, with a childhood pal, the late movie actress Dorothy Dell *(Little Miss Marker)*, she entered a local beauty contest, which Dell won; Dell then signed with a Fanchon and Marco vaudeville act because they agreed to take her friend too; after a year's tour, Dell went into the *Ziegfeld Follies* in New York; Lamour returned home, worked as a secretary for a real estate firm, and won the Miss New Orleans beauty competition, leading nowhere; went to Chicago, became an elevator operator at Marshall Field's department store; when the *Follies* came through Chicago, Dell introduced her friend to a local agent, and soon she was singing torch songs with the band of Herbie Kaye; was married to him from '35 to '39; went to Hollywood in '35, tested for—and failed to get—the Helen Morgan role in *Show Boat*; won instead a Paramount contract starting at $200 a week; screen name is a variation of Lambour, her stepfather's name; "When I was young," she says, "I copied stars with class like Norma Shearer and Carole Lombard—and I felt like crying when asked to wear a sarong. The sarong may have done a lot for me but, truthfully, it was never my favorite wearing apparel"; admits just one serious romance with a Hollywood leading man of hers: Robert Preston; was married from '43 until his death in '78 to William Ross Howard III, handsome, polo-playing scion of an aristocratic Maryland family; an Air Force captain when they wed, he became a wealthy food manufacturer; lived in Baltimore most of those years, commuting to Hollywood for movies; had two sons: John Ridgely and Tom; back in Hollywood, she does TV, commercials, sings in clubs; has published her autobiography, *My Side of the Road*.

MOVIE HIGHLIGHTS: *High, Wide and Handsome, The Last Train from Madrid, The Hurricane, Her Jungle Love, Spawn of the North, Typhoon, The Road to Singapore* (. . . *to Zanzibar*, . . . *to Morocco*, . . . *to Utopia*, etc.), *Caught in the Draft, Chad Hanna, Aloma of the South Seas, The Fleet's In, Beyond the Blue Horizon, Riding High, They Got Me Covered, Dixie, And the Angels Sing, A Medal for Benny, Masquerade in Mexico, My Favorite Brunette, Wild Harvest, The Greatest Show on Earth*.

Burt Lancaster

(b. Burton Stephen Lancaster, Nov. 2, 1913, New York, N.Y.) *The Killers* ('46) made the tousle-haired muscleman a star, and playing the Bible-thumping charlatan evangelist in *Elmer Gantry* won him a Best Actor Oscar, but it's a sure bet he'll be remembered much longer as the Army sergeant who made adulterous love with Deborah Kerr on a wave-swept Hawaiian beach in *From Here to Eternity*; the latter rated him a Best Actor nomination, as did *Bird Man of Alcatraz* and, much later, *Atlantic City*; is such a complex man that playwright Clifford Odets once described him as being seven personalities in one package: Enigmatic Burt (for being unfathomably mysterious), Cocksure Burt, Wild Man Burt (boundless energy, extravagant enthusiasms), Old Father Burt (paternal to elders or weaker persons), Mr. Hyde (unexpected reverse side of his gentle Dr. Jekyll nature), the Marquis de Lancaster (aristocratic with superb manners), and Snake Oil Burt ("con man, mischief-maker, light-hearted rogue"); has convincingly played just about everything: cops *(Desert Fury)*, convicts *(Brute Force)*, con men *(The Rainmaker)*, cowboys *(Vera Cruz)*, Indians *(Apache)*, swashbucklers *(The Crimson Pirate)*, Germans *(Judgment at Nuremberg)*, Mexicans *(Valdez Is Coming)*, Italians— burly *(The Rose Tattoo)* and titled *(The Leopard)*, and circus stars *(Trapeze)*; the last came naturally; growing up in tough East Harlem, the son of a Manhattan postal clerk, he acquired his soon-famous physique at the Union Settlement House; winning a basketball scholarship at New York University, he dropped out at 18 and was for a decade a tank-town acrobat in a one-ring circus; at 22 was married briefly to June Ernst, a circus aerialist; next did pick-and-shovel jobs, was a singing waiter, a department store floorwalker, and a tie salesman; did a four-year stint in the Army during WWII; after discharge, a Broadway producer, looking for a physical type, spotted him on an elevator and gave him a small role in A *Sound of Hunting*; show lasted three weeks, and he got seven Hollywood offers; signed with Hal Wallis, who had to be persuaded not to rename him "Stuart Chase"; first movie was actually *Desert Fury*, which was held on the shelf until after the release of *The Killers*, made on loan-out; got the role of the big Swede in the latter because Warners demanded too much for the services of first choice Wayne Morris; from '46 until they divorced in '69, was married to former secretary Norma Anderson; five children: Joseph, William (the only one to follow him into show business—clicked as a screenwriter with his first film, *The Bad News Bears*), Susan, Joanna, and Sighle; to the first reporter who ever interviewed him, he said: "I've made up my mind that Hollywood isn't going to get me; I'm going to be one guy who won't let it rot his soul"; kept his dukes up—kept his promise.

MOVIE HIGHLIGHTS: *I Walk Alone, Sorry, Wrong Number, All My Sons, Criss Cross, Rope of Sand, Mr. 880, The Flame and the Arrow, Ten Tall Men, Jim Thorpe—All-American, Come Back, Little Sheba, South Sea Woman, His Majesty O'Keefe, The Kentuckian* (also directed), *Gunfight at the O.K. Corral, Sweet Smell of Success, Separate Tables, The Devil's Disciple, Seven Days in May, The Train, The Swimmer, Castle Keep, Scorpio, Twilight's Last Gleaming.*

Carole Landis

(b. Frances Lillian Mary Ridste, Jan. 1, 1919, Fairchild, Wis.; d. July 4, 1948) Throaty-voiced, blue-eyed blonde, gifted at screwball comedy (*Turna-*

bout, Out of the Blue, etc.), who exuded sex—decidedly a factor in her rise to stardom; off screen reputation of the "Ping Girl" was not the best; was a rebel, an outspoken free spirit, and Hollywood did not regard her as "a lady"; had four husbands; was married first at 15 for three weeks to one Irving Wheeler, though she didn't get around to divorcing him until six years later, in '40; that year, was married for a few months to yacht broker Willis Hunt (said then: "I learned one thing—marriage is still 90–10. The man gets 90 percent of the attention"); in '43, on a USO tour of North Africa, she met and, after a whirlwind courtship, married U.S. Army Air Forces Captain Thomas C. Wallace, an ex-Eagle Squadron flyer; she wrote a best seller about that tour and hasty wedding, *Four Jills in a Jeep,* which was made into a movie in which she starred; they parted after a few days and divorced two years later; in '45, she wed Manhattan millionaire Horace Schmidlapp and, though long estranged, was still married to him at the time of her death; had many lovers, one of whom, a producer, got her a contract at 20th Century–Fox and for a while was her protector there; another, her last, was Rex Harrison; in his autobiography, *Rex,* he observed that she was a "liberated woman" and had been "badly treated by the world in many ways"; he also noted that she "was ostracized and shunned by the people I used to meet in those California drawing rooms, shunned for the strange reason that she was, I think, ahead of her time"; the daughter of Polish immigrants who spoke little English (father was a railroad mechanic), she ran away from home at 14 and became a hula dancer at the Royal Hawaiian Club in San Francisco; at 18, was a Busby Berkeley showgirl in Warner Bros. musicals (*Gold Diggers in Paris, Varsity Show,* etc.); became famous in '40 in *One Million B.C.* with Victor Mature; was picked for this lead, as a sexy prehistoric femme, by legendary director D. W. Griffith (who expected to helm the movie but didn't) because she ran like a gazelle, with grace and energy; starred at Fox from '41 to '46; later came B pictures, a couple of low-budget films in England (*The Brass Monkey, The Silk Noose*), and finally, no offers at all; shortly before she committed suicide by an overdose of pills, she spoke of another star who died by her own hand, and said, "I know how Lupe Velez felt. You fight so hard and then what have you got to face? You begin to worry about being washed up. You get bitter and disillusioned. You fear the future because there's only one way to go, and that's down."

MOVIE HIGHLIGHTS: *Road Show, Topper Returns, Dance Hall, Moon over Miami, I Wake Up Screaming, Cadet Girl, A Gentleman at Heart, It Happened in Flatbush, My Gal Sal, Orchestra Wives, Manila Calling, The*

Powers Girl, Wintertime, Secret Command, Having Wonderful Crime, Behind Green Lights, It Shouldn't Happen to a Dog, Scandal in Paris.

Angela Lansbury

(b. Angela Brigid Lansbury, Oct. 16, 1925, London, England) At 18, she played the saucy, impertinent Victorian housemaid Nancy, hired by Charles Boyer, in *Gaslight* and made a quantum leap—from wrapping Christmas packages at Bullock's department store at $18 a week to fame and $500 a week at MGM, where she remained through the '40s; had never acted on screen before, though she started studying drama at 12; Metro moguls didn't want her in the part ("not sexy enough"), but director George Cukor, who had tested her, did ("I was delighted with her from the start. Suddenly I was watching real movie acting. She *became* this rather disagreeable little housemaid"); got a Best Supporting Oscar nomination—and later ones for *The Picture of Dorian Gray* (second movie, second Cockney role) and *The Manchurian Candidate*; in several movies she sang—"Goodbye, Little Yellow Bird" in *Dorian Gray*, "Sweetheart," when a nightclub star in *The Hoodlum Saint*, "How D'You Like to Spoon with Me?" in *Till the Clouds Roll By*, etc.; no one could have predicted, however, that, starting in her 40s, she would burst forth as one of the greats in American musical comedies, starring on Broadway in *Mame, Anyone Can Whistle, Sweeney Todd*; early ambition at MGM was to play comedy, "to be Jean Arthur"; was most often cast in dramas playing women much older than her actual age, becoming famous as Hollywood's "youngest character actress"—and for having "no temperament"; at 37, played two of the most diabolical mothers in movie history—Warren Beatty's (he was 25) in *All Fall Down* and Laurence Harvey's (he was three years younger than she) in *The Manchurian Candidate*, playing a scheming Communist who would sacrifice the life of her son for the Party; in '40, soon after the death of her father, a London merchant and politician, the Lansburys were blitzed out of their home by Hitler's bombs; her mother, actress Moyna MacGill, then packed up the children—Angela, 15, and her 9-year-old twin brothers, Bruce and Edgar—and took the next refugee boat to America; landed in Hollywood after brief stays in New York and Canada; after Angela was signed by MGM, her mother won a contract there, too, and was in many films, even appearing with her in both *Dorian Gray* and *Kind Lady*; the star admits that certain qualities of her talented Irish mother may often be spotted in her own characterizations ("a turn of my head, a motion of my body, or a way of saying a line"); her first marriage, to leading man Richard Cromwell, lasted one year (1945–46); has been married since '49 to Peter Shaw, onetime actor–turned–actors' agent, by whom she has two children: Anthony Peter and Dierdre Angela; asked in her teens what she expected of stardom, she replied: "Only one thing—security. We had six bad years after my father died. All I want now is freedom from financial worry, and to send the twins to college"; the twins grew up to become successful producers, and the star long ago became as financially secure as the Bank of England.

MOVIE HIGHLIGHTS: *National Velvet, The Harvey Girls, If Winter Comes, Private Affairs of Bel Ami, Tenth Avenue Angel, The Three Musketeers, State of the Union, The Red Danube, Samson and Delilah, Remains to Be Seen, The Court Jester, The Reluctant Debutante, The Long Hot Summer, The Dark at the Top of the Stairs, In the Cool of the Day, The World of Henry Orient, Death on the Nile, The Mirror Crack'd.*

Peter Lawford

(b. Peter Sydney Ernest Lawford, Sept. 7, 1923, London, England; d. Dec. 24, 1984) A handsome youth, tanned, dimpled, and bushy browed, he seemed more mature than his years and began playing romantic roles before he was 20; what he lacked in talent, he made up for with sophisticated wit, a nonchalant air, and British charm; if he kept his feet on the ground during the decade he was a pampered MGM star, much credit was due his late father, Lieut. Gen. Sir Sidney Turning Barlow Lawford, who was the general officer commanding the Lahore district of India in the '20s; at the first sign of his being seduced by fame, Sir Sidney would say, "You're not taking all of this too seriously, are you? You know, it can be taken away as quickly as it was given"; announced at 7 that he wanted to be an actor; a family friend, Sir Thomas Polson, introduced him to director Monty Banks at London's Elstree Studio, and Banks gave him a small role in *Old Bill*; educated by private tutors (never spent a day in any school), he spent the next few years traveling the world—Tahiti, New Zealand, Australia, Ceylon—with his parents; when 15, they stopped briefly in California, and he wangled a role in *Lord Jeff*, starring Mickey Rooney; the Lawfords were living in Florida in '39 when war broke out in Europe, cutting off their income from England; confident he could make it in movies and determined to get back to Hollywood, he earned money for their fares to the Coast by parking cars at a concession behind the Palm Beach branch of Saks Fifth Avenue; appeared on the movie scene at precisely the right moment, when the studios were turning out many "British" films; a small part in *Mrs. Miniver* ('42) led to ten other pictures in the next two years before MGM gave him a term contract and the starmaking role of Irene Dunne's son in *The White Cliffs of Dover*; became so idolized that every bobby-soxer in the country could recite his vital statistics: 6'1", 155 lbs., wavy brown hair, blue-gray eyes; they also could name (with envy) the girls he dated—Anne Baxter, Gloria De Haven, Marilyn Maxwell, Judy Garland—and reel off his hobbies (photography, playing the drums), his favorite sports (surfing, tennis), and the fact that he drove a red Ford convertible; once engaged to Sharman Douglas, daughter of the U.S. ambassador to Great Britain, he eventually married (and was divorced by) three other women: wife #1 was Patricia Kennedy (1954–66; sister of the president), by whom he had four children: Christopher, Sydney, Victoria, and Robin; wife #2 was Mary Rowan (1971–73; daughter of "Laugh-In" star Dan Rowan), who, when they wed, was 22 to his 48; wife #3, for seven weeks in '76, was Deborah Gould, 25, of Miami; was married from July 1984 on to Patricia Seaton; early on, MGM assured him he'd become the "new" Ronald Colman and that his time would come when he was 30; was 34 when a producer turned him down for a role as being "too old"; Lawford asked, "What happened to that time when I'd be perfect?"; said the producer, "I guess it just went by."

MOVIE HIGHLIGHTS: *Eagle Squadron, Mrs. Parkington, The Canterville Ghost, Son of Lassie, The Picture of Dorian Gray, Cluny Brown, Two Sisters from Boston, Good News, It Happened in Brooklyn, On an Island with You, Easter Parade, Julia Misbehaves, Little Women, The Red Danube, Please Believe Me, Royal Wedding, Kangaroo, You for Me, Never So Few, Exodus, Ocean's Eleven, Sergeants Three, Advise and Consent.*

Janet Leigh

(b. Jeanette Helen Morrison, July 6, 1927, Merced, Calif.) In 1947's *The Romance of Rosy Ridge*, her first film, she was the leading lady of established star Van Johnson; in '84 her autobiography, *There Really Was a Hollywood*, was published, and the New York book party for it was hosted by—Van Johnson; it was he who suggested "Janet" for her screen name, as she had a piquant quality similar to Janet Gaynor's—"Leigh" was for Vivien Leigh; as revealed in her book, she has lived a full life and had a longer career than might have been anticipated by those who launched her at MGM; had no show biz aspirations; was the only child of working parents who, moving frequently, followed job opportunities from town to town in central California; father (who nicknamed her "Stinky") was a grocery clerk, insurance salesman, shipyard worker, etc.; mother, a sometime waitress, was for a while a journeyman electrician at a military airfield; had an average childhood (in many ways): piano lessons and dance recitals (tap, ballet), sang in a Presbyterian church choir, worked part-time in Kress's five-and-dime and, a top student, skipped a couple of grades; entered high school at 13; at 15, eloped to Reno with her school beau, Kenneth Carlyle, 19; parents quickly whisked her home to Stockton, Calif., had the marriage annulled, and, reportedly, she never saw her groom again; attended the College of the Pacific as a music major; between 18 and 21, was married to Stanley Reames Jr., a Navy man when she met him and later, in Hollywood, the hopeful leader of a band (she worked as its business manager); her discovery for movies was a fairy tale—and true; MGM star Norma Shearer vacationed at the Sugar Bowl Ski Lodge, near Truckee, where at the time Janet's mother was the receptionist and her father the auditor; impressed by a snapshot of Janet she saw in the lodge album, the veteran star borrowed it to show her Hollywood agent, Lew Wasserman; also struck by her natural beauty and, after meeting her, her intelligence, he took her to MGM; signed her $50 a week contract there on Aug. 7, 1946, and stayed there seven years; eventually earned $100,000 per picture; in '50 Howard Hughes, wildly infatuated, borrowed her to co-star with John Wayne in *Jet Pilot*, a movie he kept in production (on and off) for years (was finally released in '57); *Jet Pilot* gave her what she hadn't had before—a sexy screen image—but the billionaire's ardent pursuit of her led to naught; instead, after a brief engagement to Robert Stack and a sizzling romance with actor Barry Nelson, she married Tony Curtis in '51, with whom she made six films (*The Vikings, Who Was That Lady?*, etc.); before they divorced in '62, she gave birth to two daughters: Kelly and Jamie Lew (named for agent Lew Wasserman, her godfather; she changed it to Jamie Lee when she, too, became an actress); has been the wife of stockbroker Robert Brandt since '62, marrying him one day after receiving her decree from Curtis; her best-known movie, *Psycho*, with that famous murder-in-the-shower scene (not nude; wore a flesh-colored moleskin bikini), rated her a Best Supporting Oscar nomination.

MOVIE HIGHLIGHTS: *If Winter Comes, Hills of Home, Words and Music, Little Women, The Doctor and the Girl, The Red Danube, That Forsyte Woman, Holiday Affair, Two Tickets to Broadway Angels in the Outfield, Just This Once, Scaramouche, Houdini, Prince Valiant, Living It Up, My Sister Eileen, Pete Kelly's Blues, Touch of Evil, The Perfect Furlough, Bye Bye Birdie, The Manchurian Candidate, Harper.*

Joan Leslie

(b. Joan Agnes Theresa Sadie Brodel, Jan. 26, 1925, Detroit, Mich.) Warner Bros.' perennial "typical" American girl, she was the leading lady of Gary Cooper in 1941's *Sergeant York* (he copped an Oscar), of James Cagney in 1942's *Yankee Doodle Dandy* (he won, too), and of Fred Astaire in 1943's *The Sky's the Limit* (becoming at 18 his youngest-ever dancing partner in movies); in 1944's morale-boosting *Hollywood Canteen*, make-believe "soldier boy" Robert Hutton lost his heart to "movie star" Joan Leslie—something thousands of real-life G.I.s had already done; with her smiling face and merry hazel eyes (they could flash spiritedly on the right screen occasion), and her modified pageboy hairdo neatly combed, she was so winningly natural—the screen's ideal girl-next-door; something she never was; with three musically talented daughters (Betty, Mary, and Joan, the youngest), their mother aimed them for the vaudeville stage and hit the road with them when Joan was 2; the future star's big number: "Let a Smile Be Your Umbrella"; accompanied by Mom on the piano, the girls sang and danced (clog dancing first, tapping later) all over Canada, the Midwest, and the Eastern seaboard; were appearing at the Paradise Club in New York City when an MGM scout signed Joan, 11, for her first small movie part, as Robert Taylor's kid sister in *Camille*; was billed Joan Brodel, as she was in 11 other minor roles (in *Foreign Correspondent, Love Affair, Nancy Drew, Reporter*, etc.); signed her Warner Bros. pact at 15; studio execs changed her name first to Joan Brooks (never used it on screen), then to Joan Leslie; scored sensationally in her first featured role, as the lame girl befriended by Bogart in *High Sierra* ('41); soon proved she could play anything well—comedy *(The Male Animal)*, heavy drama *(The Hard Way)*, musicals *(Where Do We Go from Here?)*; *This Is the Army* was her first in Technicolor, and fans discovered she was, as fan mags had told them, a redhead; career ran a strange course—beginning in mature roles, she finally was playing post-adolescents *(Janie Gets Married)*; at 21, weary of battling for better opportunities, she asked to be let out of her contract and was refused; she and the studio fought it out legally, with the Superior Court of Los Angeles and the District Court of Appeals ruling in her favor; her first film as a free lance, Eagle-Lion's *Repeat Performance*, was a winner; afterwards, it was downhill all the way; while at Warners, she has said, she acquired "a reputation for being uncooperative" because she rejected "wicked roles" and refused to "date" actors for publicity purposes; has been married since March 17, 1950, to Dr. William G. Caldwell, a leading obstetrician and gynecologist, who, like herself, is devoutly Catholic; they have identical twin daughters, Patrice and Ellen; gave up her movie career after 1956's *The Revolt of Mamie Stover* but, in later years, has done TV commercials (for Avon) and occasionally played mother roles in television dramas.

MOVIE HIGHLIGHTS: *The Wagons Roll at Night, The Great Mr. Nobody, Thieves Fall Out, Thank Your Lucky Stars, Rhapsody in Blue, Too Young to Know, Cinderella Jones, Two Guys from Milwaukee, Northwest Stampede, Born to Be Bad, The Skipper Surprised His Wife, Man in the Saddle, Hellgate, Toughest Man in Arizona, The Woman They Almost Lynched, Jubilee Trail.*

Paul Lukas

(b. Pal Lukacs, May 26, 1891, Budapest, Hungary; d. Aug. 16, 1971) An actor of distinction who, in '43, played Kurt Mueller, Bette Davis's anti-Nazi German husband, in *Watch on the Rhine* and won the Best Actor Oscar; marked the zenith of his movie career; when anyone told him his was the year's best performance, he replied: "I know. That's why I voted for myself"; had created the role in the '41 Broadway production of Lillian Hellman's drama; in WWI, ironically, he had fought on the other side; to avoid going into his father's advertising business, he enlisted in the Austro-Hungarian Army in '13, serving as an aviator; injured and discharged, he studied for the stage at the Actors' Academy of Hungary, making his Budapest debut in '16 in the title role of *Liliom*; did many classic plays at the Comedy Theater over the next nine years; made his film debut in Germany in '17, in the role of Samson in *Samson and Delilah*; impressed by his stage performance in *Antonia* in Budapest, Paramount's Adolph Zukor took him to Hollywood where, in '28, he co-starred in a late silent, *Loves of an Actress*, opposite Pola Negri; recalling this film, the great screen temptress has said, "As Paul spoke no English and I spoke no Hungarian, we approached our love scenes with an intensity born of lack of communication. We would each murmur intimacies in a language unintelligible to the other and try to compensate for this with a greater emphasis on physical passion"; blessed with a dry humor, he loved telling tales about the wild shenanigans in Hollywood in the late '20s; would remark that the swimming pools were filled with champagne so that stars could exercise, bathe, and get drunk simultaneously—"and sometimes without shedding your clothes"; eight months of intensive English lessons saved him when talkies came in—just as Paramount was set to drop his option; made scores of films in the '30s, few of which are memorable; exceptions: *Little Women* (as Hepburn's professor-mentor), *Shopworn Angel, Dodsworth;*

in most he played "the other man" in romantic triangles, as he epitomized Continental suavity, or as the villain (*Confessions of a Nazi Spy*); had a lackluster Hollywood career after winning the Oscar; proved his talent anew in '51 by co-starring with Ethel Merman in the Broadway musical *Call Me Madam*; had a cancer scare (a polyp on his larynx) while working on stage; awaiting biopsy results, he made a prayerful promise that if the test proved negative, which it did, he would help those who suffered from the disease; later contributed a portion of his income to the Cancer Society and, while appearing in a play, worked six hours each week as a volunteer orderly at New York's Memorial Hospital; continued in films in character roles through 1968's *Sol Madrid*; widowed by his first wife, Gizella ("Daisy") Benes in '62, after 35 years together, he was next married, in '63, to Annette Driesens.

MOVIE HIGHLIGHTS: *Dinner at the Ritz, The Lady Vanishes, Strange Cargo, The Ghost Breakers, Hostages, Uncertain Glory, Experiment Perilous, Address Unknown, Deadline at Dawn, Temptation, Berlin Express, Kim, 20,000 Leagues under the Sea, The Roots of Heaven, Scent of Mystery, The Four Horsemen of the Apocalypse, 55 Days at Peking, Tender Is the Night, Fun in Acapulco, Lord Jim.*

William Lundigan

(b. William Lundigan, June 12, 1914, Syracuse, N.Y.; d. Dec. 20, 1975) His sandy-haired good looks and friendly Irish face weren't enough to win him major stardom, but for two decades, they took him a long way as the hero of Bs (which most of his 125 films were); even when he appeared in big-budget movies, he once laughingly said, "I was always turning up as Olivia de Havilland's weak brother"; began on radio; one of his father's many shoe stores was in the building (which he also owned) that housed Syracuse's radio station, WFBL; began appearing in plays at the station, finally giving up his prelaw studies at Syracuse University to accept a staff position there as an announcer; four years later was heard by a visiting film exec who, impressed by his crisp, resonant voice, got him a screen test in New York, which resulted in a Universal contract; made his debut at 23 in *Armored Car*; brought his father (retired), mother, and three younger brothers to Hollywood to share his house; "Dimples," which he had, was his nickname, to his chagrin; was engaged early on to Margaret Lindsay, a bit later to Marguerite Chapman, then, in '45, was married—lastingly—to Rena Morgan, the adopted daughter of singer Helen Morgan, with whom he adopted a daughter, Anastacia (Stacy); enlisting in the Marines in WWII, he fought with the First Division in the most hazardous campaigns in the South Pacific; many years later, was hospitalized for extensive surgery on his limbs, required because of injuries received in the war; following contracts at Universal, Warners, and MGM, successively, he was at 20th Century–Fox for five years (1949–53); made numerous top-grade films then but, as elsewhere, the attention went to his femme co-stars: Jeanne Crain in *Pinky*, Susan Hayward in *I'd Climb the Highest Mountain*, June Haver in *Love Nest*, etc.; dropping out of movies in '54, he returned for three in the '60s, then, after *Where Angels Go, Trouble Follows* ('66), quit the big screen for good; acted just twice more, on TV in an episode each of "Marcus Welby" ('70) and "Medical Center" ('71); in '72, having been a tireless Republican Party supporter for three decades, he was urged—and was tempted—to run for mayor of Los Angeles but withdrew at the last minute.

MOVIE HIGHLIGHTS: *The Black Doll, Danger on the Air, Missing Guest, Three Smart Girls Grow Up, Forgotten Woman, The Old Maid, Dodge City, The Fighting 69th, Three Cheers for the Irish, The Sea Hawk, Santa Fe Trail, The Case of the Black Parrot, International Squadron, The Courtship of Andy Hardy, Dr. Gillespie's Criminal Case, Salute to the Marines, The Fabulous Dorseys, Dishonored Lady, Mother Didn't Tell Me, I'll Get By, The House on Telegraph Hill.*

Ida Lupino

(b. Ida Lupino, Jan. 1, 1914, London, England) It's easy to forget her first six years in Hollywood, when she was a dizzy blonde (peroxided) bundle from Britain starring in *Search for Beauty, Ready for Love*, and two dozen others just like them; everyone, however, remembers 1939's *The Light That Failed*; playing Bessie, the Cockney guttersnipe who spitefully destroyed Ronald Colman's glorious portrait of her, she went for the jugular; for the next decade, she lit up the screen with that unique Lupino lightning; not once, though, was she nominated for an Oscar, not for any one of her high velocity performances—in *High Sierra, They Drive By Night, The Hard Way, Ladies in Retirement* (her personal favorite), or *The Big Knife*; credit for her remarkable string of successes might go to her father, stage star Stanley Lupino (who was of an illustrious theatrical family dating back two centuries); was a teenager when he told her: "Don't ever think you are good; go on trying to be a little less worse than your last performance"; in the garden of the family home at Streatham, outside London, was a fully equipped playhouse where the

Lupinos staged workshop productions in which she first played Camille and Juliet; quit school at 13, worked as an extra in British films (*The Love Race*, etc.), earning a weekly wage of one pound (about $5 then); acted in repertory, then began playing leads in English movies at 17; in one, *The Ghost Camera*, she co-starred with John Mills; decades later, she directed him in two episodes of a TV series he did in Hollywood, "Dundee and the Culhane," directed one of his daughters, Hayley, in the movie *The Trouble with Angels* and appeared with his other daughter, Juliet, in an episode of her series, "Nanny and the Professor"; Hollywood director Allan Dwan, who helmed her debut film in London, *Her First Affaire*, took her to California to test for the title role in *Alice in Wonderland*; Charlotte Henry got the part, and Ida became Paramount's "baby vamp"—and, off screen, "queen of the nightclubs"; actor Louis Hayward, her first husband (1938–45), effected the change that made such a difference, urging: "Wash your face. Stop curling your hair. Quit playing the nightclub baby. Don't be a perpetual Wampas star. Be a real human being"; once in high gear, with blue eyes blazing, she was often pegged a "second Bette Davis"; "I'm as flattered as if someone had presented me a bouquet of diamonds," she would say, then usually add, a bit fiercely, "but what I do is *me*"; insisted her many neurotic roles gave her "a wretched case of insomnia"; her best male friend, strictly platonically, was Errol Flynn, who called her "Mad Eyes" and believed, as they were so much alike, they must have been twins in another life; was expected to, but didn't, marry Helmut Dantine after divorcing Louis Hayward; second husband (1948–50) was Collier Young, with whom she established a production company, Filmakers; after they divorced, she directed his next wife, Joan Fontaine (one of her best friends), in *The Bigamist*; was later married (1951–73) to Howard Duff, by whom she has a daughter, Bridget.

MOVIE HIGHLIGHTS: *The Adventures of Sherlock Holmes, Out of the Fog, Moontide, Life Begins at 8:30, In Our Time, Forever and a Day, Pillow to Post, Devotion, Escape Me Never, The Man I Love, Deep Valley, Road House, Lust for Gold, Woman in Hiding, On Dangerous Ground, Beware My Lovely, Jennifer, Private Hell 36, Women's Prison, While the City Sleeps, Strange Intruder, The Devil's Rain, The Food of the Gods, Junior Bonner.*

Diana Lynn

(b. Dolores Loehr, Oct. 7, 1926, Los Angeles, Calif.; d. Dec. 18, 1971) Late in '71, after 16 years off the screen, she returned to Hollywood to co-star as

Anthony Perkins' wife in *Play It As It Lays* but suffered a fatal stroke before filming began; had given up her career in '56 when she became the wife of wealthy Mortimer Hall, treasurer of a Manhattan daily, the *New York Post* (owned by his mother); had four children: Matthew, Dorothy, Mary, and Margaret; first husband (1948–54) was architect John C. Lindsay; starred in several plays on Broadway during her years in New York—*The Wild Duck*, *Mary, Mary* (taking over the Barbara Bel Geddes role), etc.; was the daughter of a well-to-do oil-supply concern executive and a concert pianist; a child prodigy on the piano (and a "Quiz Kid" on radio), she began in movies at 13 as Dolly Loehr, at the keyboard, in *They Shall Have Music*, which was followed two years later by *There's Magic in Music*; discovering her other gift—an unerring instinct for light comedy—Paramount put her under contract at 15 and kept her busy from '41 to '50; first won the critics over as the brainy teen-ager who saw through Ginger Rogers' phony kid impersonation in *The Major and the Minor*; became a full-fledged star when not quite 18, playing youthful Emily Kimbrough in the delightful flapper-era comedy *Our Hearts Were Young and Gay*; continuing her musical studies, she recorded albums and made her concert debut in Los Angeles in '43; *And the Angels Sing* and *Out of This World*, in which she got her first screen kiss (from Eddie Bracken), were among the few later films in which she was given a chance to display her skill as a pianist; closest studio friends: Gail Russell, her co-star in *Our Hearts* and its sequel, *Our Hearts Were Growing Up*, and Mona Freeman; an idol, with whom she never got to work, was Deanna Durbin; once said of her career ambitions: "If I could once do a Jean Arthur type of comedy role the way she does, I'd die happy"; minor claim to fame—was Ronald Reagan's leading lady in *Bedtime for Bonzo*.

MOVIE HIGHLIGHTS: *Star-Spangled Rhythm, The Miracle of Morgan's Creek, Henry Aldrich Gets Glamour, Duffy's Tavern, The Bride Wore Boots, Variety Girl, Easy Come, Easy Go, Ruthless, Texas, Brooklyn and Heaven, Every Girl Should Be Married, My Friend Irma, Paid in Full, Rogues of Sherwood Forest, Peggy, The People against O'Hara, Meet Me at the Fair, Plunder of the Sun, An Annapolis Story, The Kentuckian, You're Never Too Young.*

Jeffrey Lynn

(b. Ragnar Godfrey Lind, Feb. 16, 1909, Auburn, Mass.) He was the acme of young American manhood, the kind of handsome guy every mom wanted her daughter to marry, an Arrow-shirted, wavy-haired gentleman—smiling, earnest, charming—and born to be a professional man; femme fans by the thousands thought Priscilla Lane a fool to turn him down in favor of street-smart John Garfield in *Four Daughters*, and they later heartily approved when, in *Four Wives*, he and Priscilla finally got together; WWII played havoc with his highly promising movie career; served 1942–46 with the U.S. Army Signal Corps and USAAF (as a combat and intelligence officer) in North Africa, Italy, and Austria; was mustered out with the rank of captain and awarded both the Air Medal and the Bronze Star; returned to a changed Hollywood; "nice guys" were out—"tough guys" (Burt Lancaster, Kirk Douglas, and, soon, Marlon Brando) were in; continued playing leads, but the boat had sailed; despite Anglo-Saxon looks, is of Swedish descent; acting was his fourth career choice; got his B.A. degree (prelaw) at Maine's Bates College in '30; worked two years as a bill collector for the New England Telephone Co., and for one year was head of the English department of the Lisbon (Maine) High School; a lead in an amateur play put on by the Auburn Tennis Club, *Her Temporary Husband*, turned him on to acting; studied in New York at the Theodora Irvine School, was a barker outside the Embassy Newsreel Theater, clerked in Macy's sporting goods section, and acted with a repertory company (Virginia's Barter Theater); in '35, was on Broadway—billed Geoffrey Lind—in small parts in two failures, A *Slight Case of Murder* and *Stick-in-the-Mud*; after other flops, landed a role in the road company of *Brother Rat* and was spotted by talent scouts when it played Los Angeles; MGM signed and quickly dropped him, and Warners picked up the ball—changing his name to Jeffrey Lynn; until then ('38) had never earned more than $30 a week; debut movie: *Cowboy from Brooklyn*; was in 21 films—and tested for the role of Ashley Wilkes in GWTW—before going into the military; was once engaged to movie actress Margaret Hayes (aka Dana Dale); first wife (1946–57) was Robin Chandler (she later married millionaire Angier Biddle Duke), by whom he has two children; Letitia and Jeffrey Jr.; from '67 to '74, when they divorced, he was wed to former actress Patricia Davis and was the stepfather of her seven children; when his movie career fizzled in the '50s, he returned to the stage, starring in literally dozens of plays—on tour, in stock, and on Broadway (*Two for the Seesaw, Dinner at Eight*, etc.); also starred for years, starting in '67, as newspaper publisher Charles Clemens in the daytime soap opera "The Secret Storm"; later career: real estate agent.

MOVIE HIGHLIGHTS: *When Were You Born?, Yes, My Darling Daughter, Daughters Courageous, The Roaring Twenties, Espionage Agent, A Child Is Born, The Fighting 69th, All This and Heaven Too, It All Came True, My*

Love Came Back, Flight from Destiny, Million Dollar Baby, Underground, Law of the Tropics, The Body Disappears, For the Love of Mary, Black Bart, A Letter to Three Wives, Captain China.

Marjorie Main

(b. Mary Tomlinson, Feb. 24, 1890, Acton, Ind.; d. April 10, 1975) On screen for 25 years (1932–57), she was a sardonic, raucous, gravel-voiced delight in most of her 82 movies, but she didn't start that way; in early pictures, was often typecast as a slum mother—of "Dead End Kid" Billy Halop (*Little Tough Guy*), Jackie Cooper (*Boy of the Streets*), killer Bogart (walloping him in *Dead End*, she snarled, "Ya dirty yellow dog"); the fun part started in '40 when MGM cast her as a lady blacksmith—with dry wit and frosty smile—in *Wyoming*, opposite equally unkempt Wallace Beery; studio execs quickly realized they'd finally found a worthy successor to his former combative co-star, the late Marie Dressler; were teamed, hilariously, six more times (*Barnacle Bill, Jackass Mail, Bad Bascomb*, etc.), but she was never fond of him (thought him "unprofessional" for changing the dialogue in mid-scene) and they never socialized off the set; cared far more for nasal Percy Kilbride, her drawling colleague in seven greatly popular "Ma and Pa Kettle" comedies that she made on loan-out to Universal; series began in '49 with *Ma and Pa Kettle*, after the characters had clicked two years earlier in *The Egg and I*, which won her a Best Supporting Oscar nomination; had made her Hollywood debut in a bit in Walter Huston's *A House Divided* after long experience on the stage; was the daughter of a Church of Christ minister who strongly opposed her career choice; attended Franklin College and the Hamilton School of Dramatic Expression in Lexington, Ky.; spent another year studying dramatic art in Chicago and New York, then taught drama for one year at Bourbon College in Paris, Ky.; joining a Shakespearean repertory company playing a Chautauqua circuit, she met Dr. Stanley LeFevre Krebs, a psychologist–author who lectured on personality development; was married to him from '21 until his death in '35 (no children); was active on Broadway in the '20s, supporting Pauline Lord in *Salvation*, Barbara Stanwyck in *Burlesque*, etc.; hit her stride in movies in '39 in *The Women*, in a role she'd created on Broadway—the no-nonsense owner of a Reno dude ranch patronized by society women waiting out their divorces; MGM kept her under contract for the next 14 years; became so popular with old and young that, in '46, the 96th Infantry Division named her its "Occupation Girl"; no spendthrift, she economized by taking a public bus to the studio and eating most of her meals in cafeterias ("I like being with people, and studying people," she said); finally owned three homes in California—in Beverly Hills, Idyllwild (a mountain resort), and Palm Springs, in each of which she did her own housework.

MOVIE HIGHLIGHTS: *Angels Wash Their Faces, Another Thin Man, Susan and God, The Trial of Mary Dugan, A Woman's Face, Honky Tonk, Shepherd of the Hills, The Bugle Sounds, Tennessee Johnson, Woman of the Town, Heaven Can Wait, Rationing, Meet Me in St. Louis, Murder, He Says, The Heavenly Body, Undercurrent, The Wistful Widow of Wagon Gap, Big Jack, Summer Stock, Ma and Pa Kettle Back on the Farm, The Belle of New York, Rose Marie, The Long, Long Trailer, Friendly Persuasion.*

Dorothy Malone

(b. Dorothy E. Maloney, Jan. 30, 1925, Chicago, Ill.) All it took for this willowy, dark-haired (later blonde) actress was one play, *Star Bound*, about a movie hopeful, during her freshman year at Southern Methodist University; an RKO scout discovered her in it, gave her a screen test in Dallas (her hometown from infancy) and, at 18, she was whisked off to Hollywood with a contract; for the first two years, she played unbilled bits (in *The Falcon and the Coeds, Seven Days Ashore*, etc.); for the next five years (1944–49), with her name shortened, she was a Warners leading lady—and one of the studio's busiest; on reflection, the veteran of 70 films says, "I was making big movies and little ones, sometimes as many as six a year; I was the John Wayne of the girls. I always enjoyed the Westerns most, except for *Written on the Wind*. That was my most 'fun' movie"; it also won her a Best Supporting Oscar; *The Big Sleep* ('46) with Bogart, in which she was a sexy bookshop owner, made her reputation as a dramatic actress, others later made her a fan favorite, but her greatest popularity came at the tag end of her movie career, on TV, as the $250,000 a year star of *Peyton Place* (1964–68); her miraculous recovery then, after suffering a multiple pulmonary embolism, also made her something of a national heroine; the Catholic convent-educated daughter of a Southern Bell Telephone Co. executive, she had not anticipated having a screen career; once said what she liked best about making movies was that "it's a lovely feminine occupation—the makeup, the hairdos, the clothes"; even in the midst of her stardom, she would often pull up stakes and return to Texas and work at quite different careers—as an interior decorator, touring spokesperson for the Guardian Insurance Co., and features reporter on an FM radio station; has said, "I was always torn between Hollywood, which I have loved from the start, and Dallas—family vs. career," hence the shuttling back and forth; after a five-year engagement to actor Scott Brady, she was married in '59 to Ginger Rogers' ex, Jacques Bergerac; had an acrimonious divorce in '63 ("After knowing so many winners, I picked a loser"), followed by bitter court battles, which she won, over custody of their daughters, Mimi and Diane; for a few months in '69, until the marriage was annulled, she was wed to jet-setter stockbroker Robert Tomarkin (later, convicted for his role in a giant $2 million swindle of the now-defunct Franklin National Bank in New York, Tomarkin served 40 months in prisons such as Attica, Greenhaven, and Sing Sing); the actress's third marriage, in '71 to motel-chain exec Charles Huston Bell, ended in divorce; asked if she will marry again, she said, "I don't really think so. Dallas [where she mostly lives] has a lot of interesting men, but the worthwhile ones are all happily married."

MOVIE HIGHLIGHTS: *Too Young to Know, Night and Day, Janie Gets Married, To the Victor, Two Guys from Texas, One Sunday Afternoon, Flaxy Martin, Colorado Territory, South of St. Louis, The Killer That Stalked New York, Saddle Legion, Jack Slade, Torpedo Alley, Young at Heart, Battle Cry, Man of a Thousand Faces, Too Much, Too Soon, Tip on a Dead Jockey, Tarnished Angels, Warlock, The Last Voyage.*

Brenda Marshall

(b. Ardis Ankerson, Sept. 29, 1915, Isle of Negros, the Philippines) This dark beauty's career, which began with 1939's *Espionage Agent* and ended after 1950's *The Iroquois Trail*, meant more to her admirers than to her; has said of moviemaking, "I *hated* it. One year they made me do eight pictures and I wound up with a nervous breakdown"; yet being an actress was her youthful goal; was 15 when her sugar plantation-owner father sent her and her sister to live in San Antonio, Texas, where they attended high school and Texas State College for Women; next went to New York and studied at Madame Maria Ouspenskaya's dramatic school, where she met and married her instructor, character actor Richard Gaines (recalled by movie fans as Jean Arthur's nerdy fiancé in *The More the Merrier*); made her Broadway debut, as Ardis Gaines, in '37 in *Wives of Tomorrow*; the following year, she had a daughter, Virginia, and was again on the New York stage in a WPA production of Shaw's *On the Rocks*; a screen test for Paramount, which turned her down, was seen by Warner Bros., which signed her, gave her a new name, and started her in leading roles; was newly divorced from Gaines when a friend introduced her to William Holden, who once said he "fell in love the minute we met"; was earning five times Holden's salary when they eloped in '41 to Las Vegas, with Brian Donlevy as best man; newlyweds spent their honeymoon in the hospital—both with appendicitis; eight months after marriage, Holden, who had legally adopted her daughter, enlisted in the Army Air Forces; after the births of their sons, Peter (called "West") and Scott, he asked his wife to give up her career, which she did; finding themselves deeply in debt after his discharge, she just as readily went back to work to help out with the family finances; their dispositions were vastly different—she was calm and quiet, and he excitable and explosive (said a friend of hers, "This has to be the genius-woman of all time—to live with a man like him day in and day out"); also, he drank heavily and was a rogue with the ladies (one of whom, Shelley Winters, told in her autobiography of spending romantic Christmas Eves with him, after which he would jump into his car, loaded with toys, and race home to play Santa); in '59 the Holdens took up residence in Switzerland; when they separated in '63, there were reports that he had fallen in love with Capucine, his co-star in *The Lion* (and in his will, he left Capucine $50,000); they reconciled later that year, about the time Brenda Marshall's daughter, who had married, made her a grandmother, but in '66 she left Switzerland—and Holden—and returned to California for good; the actor once said that the divorce settlement in '71 "cost me a small fortune"; he later declared, "For me marriage was just a phase—and I grew out of it"; to date, Brenda Marshall has not remarried.

MOVIE HIGHLIGHTS: *The Sea Hawk, The Man Who Talked Too Much, Money and the Woman, East of the River, South of Suez, Footsteps in the Dark, Highway West, The Smiling Ghost, Captains of the Clouds, You Can't Escape Forever, The Constant Nymph, Paris after Dark, Background to Danger, Something for the Boys, Strange Impersonation, Whispering Smith.*

Mary Martin

(b. Mary Virginia Martin, Dec. 1, 1913, Weatherford, Texas) Compared with her glorious Broadway successes (*South Pacific, Peter Pan, The Sound of Music,* etc.), her 1939–43 starring career at Paramount was merely a prelude to fame; at the time, though, made up as a tuneful carbon copy of Claudette Colbert, she was quite a beguiling screen presence; has said in later years, "I try to forget the movies I did. I loathed making pictures because that is not my medium. My medium is the stage, with an audience, the real thing"; did not always know that; when young, Hollywood was her destination; made her first stage appearance at 5 singing "When Apples Grow on the Lilac Tree" at a hometown fireman's ball—and has been going like a house afire ever since; "I have to be careful of my wishes," she says, "because they have all come true. I always get what I want. I'm Sagittarius. And the Sagittarius sign is a bow and arrow; when you pull back that string, the arrow goes to its destination"; as a teen-ager, was briefly at Ward-Belmont finishing school in Nashville, Tenn., until officials there discovered she was secretly married to young Texas attorney Ben Hagman and pregnant; returned home to await the birth of son Larry in '31; he grew up to star in "Dallas" on TV, giving her additional fame as "J.R.'s mother"; for years, as a young divorcee, she operated a dance studio in Weatherford, while also singing on radio; with a loan from her parents, she went to Hollywood and, over many discouraging months, became known as "Audition Mary"; though promoted by advocates like gossip queen Hedda Hopper, movie moguls agreed that the voice was sensational but the face was not photogenic; a talent night contest at a Hollywood nightclub brought her to the attention of producer Lawrence Schwab; next stop: Broadway; the show was 1938's *Leave It to Me*, and her big moment in it was a three-minute so-called "strip tease" while singing "My Heart Belongs to Daddy"; becoming the toast of the town overnight, she returned to Hollywood as a star; was married from '40 until his death in '73 to Richard Halliday, onetime Paramount story editor who became her mentor-manager-stage producer; in '41 they sent a minor shock wave through the country by naming their daughter Heller; returned to Broadway in '43 and started her climb to the top of the mountain in *One Touch of Venus*, followed by *Lute Song* and *South Pacific* (in it, in April 1949, she began to "wash that man right outta my hair" and shampooed through 1,866 performances); in a much later hit musical, *I Do, I Do*, she was reunited with Robert Preston, who had been her young leading man in Hollywood in 1941's *New York Town*; when she retired from the musical stage, she and her husband lived for years on a 12,000-acre estate in Brazil's remote Goias Valley, near the headwaters of the Amazon; later, living alone in Palm Springs, Calif., she became the host of a San Francisco–based TV talk-show, "Over Easy"; published her sentimental autobiography, *My Heart Belongs*, in '76.

MOVIE HIGHLIGHTS: *The Great Victor Herbert, Rhythm on the River, Love Thy Neighbor, Kiss the Boys Goodbye, Birth of the Blues, Star-Spangled Rhythm, Happy Go Lucky, Night and Day* (cameo as herself), *Main Street to Broadway* (a similar cameo).

James Mason

(b. James Neville Mason, May 15, 1909, Huddersfield, England; d. July 27, 1984) Curious—from the moment this moody, brooding (on screen) fellow smashed his cane across the fingers of the girl he loved, pianist Ann Todd, in *The Seventh Veil*, he was a matinee idol; the year was 1945, and he'd already been a movie actor for a full decade, in 26 earlier British films—starting with *Late Extra*; later came many hits, including *The Mill on the Floss*, *Thunder Rock*, and the greatly popular *The Man in Grey*, establishing him as a sadistic charmer, after which he was England's #1 male star; the son of a Yorkshire wool merchant, he won a Cambridge degree in architecture but, finding no demand for his services, went on the stage in England at 22; arrived in Hollywood, suave and tweedy, in '46 with novelist-actress wife Pamela Kellino; they had co-starred in *I Met a Murderer* ('39), were married two years later, and later appeared together on screen in *They Were Sisters*, *Lady Possessed*, etc.; Hollywood found them a mite eccentric—kept a houseful of cats (27 at one point), Pamela's ex-husband, director–cinematographer Roy Kellino, lived for a while above the garage on their Beverly Hills estate, and when they had children, they reared them European-style, treating them "as adults"; daughter Portland, achieving a certain notoriety for smoking cigars when young, played a juvenile role in *The Man in the Gray Flannel Suit*; son Morgan, seen on screen as Elizabeth Taylor's son in *The Sandpiper*, was eventually on the White House staff of President Reagan; Mason was nominated for a Best Actor Oscar for *A Star Is Born* ("I didn't get a single offer for a grade-A film for one year after that"); was nominated later, as Best Support, for *Georgy Girl* and *The Verdict*; always regarded *Five Fingers* as his best in Hollywood; he and wife Pamela were divorced in '64 after a two-year legal wrestling match, during which she asked for a property settlement of $1 million and $14,000 a month for child support (she later, for whatever reason, named one of her cats "Dirty Jim"); *Lolita* ('62) marked his deliberate switch to character roles; settled in Switzerland, made scores of international films subsequently, but rarely returned to Hollywood; his autobiography, *Before I Forget*, was published only in England ("American publishers claimed it was too polite"); a lighthearted memoir, it contained many delightful self-drawn caricatures, plus an amusing list of all the movies in which he died an untimely death, and how: "*Fire over England*—sword thrust, *The Upturned Glass*—suicide leap from cliff, *Botany Bay*—spear from aborigine," etc.; making a movie in Australia, *Age of Consent*, which was never released, he met actress Clarissa Kaye; they later co-starred on Broadway in *The Faith Healer*, which failed, and had a marriage, which succeeded, from '71 on.

MOVIE HIGHLIGHTS: *Odd Man Out, Caught, Madame Bovary, The Reckless Moment, East Side, West Side, One Way Street, Pandora and the Flying Dutchman, The Desert Fox, The Prisoner of Zenda, Face to Face, Charade, The Man Between, The Desert Rats, Julius Caesar, 20,000 Leagues under the Sea, Bigger Than Life, Island in the Sun, North by Northwest, The Marriage-Go-Round, The Pumpkin Eater, Child's Play.*

Ilona Massey

(b. Ilona Hajmassey, June 16, 1910, Budapest, Hungary; d. Aug. 10, 1974) A Hungarian rhapsody in human form, she was perhaps the loveliest singing actress ever on Hollywood screens—with her flaxen hair, famous beauty mark, contagious smile, and personal gaiety; since many critics agreed with the one who hailed her as "a singing Garbo," her career, encompassing a mere ten movies between '37 and '49, plus one more in '59, remains a puzzlement; MGM executive Benjamin Thau met her at a party in Vienna, at which she sang, and signed her to a studio contract; arrived in Hollywood as part of a shipment of 36 European screen hopefuls, one of whom was Hedy Lamarr (and with whom, at first, she shared a Hollywood apartment)—the other 34 did not succeed; unable to speak English then, she made her debut as Eleanor Powell's friend in *Rosalie*, singing and reciting her lines phonetically; her second film, *Balalaika*, in which she sang with Nelson Eddy, made her a popular favorite; never hid her humble origins; was born in the slums of Budapest to a disabled father (an unemployed typesetter) and a peasant mother; "My salvation," she said once, "is that I have known misery and hunger. Now, if I'm well fed, well-dressed, and have a home, what else is there for me to want?"; began work at 14 as a seamstress in a tailor shop; at 16, living in one room with her parents and younger sister, she supported the family on her monthly earnings of 60 pengo (about $12) as a chorus girl at Kiraly Szinhaz, Budapest's leading opera house; later went to Vienna, played minor roles in two films (*Knox und die Lustigen, Der Himmel auf Erden*), was briefly married to Nicholas Szavozd, a doctor of philosophy, and studied opera; Felix von Weingartner, manager of the Vienna State Opera House, witnessed her performance in a small theater production of *Tosca*, gave her minor singing parts, and finally, the title role in *Empress Josephine*, which brought her operatic fame; in Hollywood, fell in love with her *New Wine* leading man, Alan Curtis, and was married to him for one year (1941–42); was married later (1952–55) to Manhattan jeweler Charles Walker, and from '55 on to wealthy Washington, D.C., attorney (and former USAF major general) Donald S. Dawson, who once served as special executive assistant to President Truman; took time out from movies to star on Broadway in the *Ziegfeld Follies* (1943–44) with Milton Berle; proudly became an American citizen in '46, and was dismayed by the "permissive society" that flowered in the '60s; in public appeals for a return to higher moral standards, she said, "God created this country with a smile on His face, but it is headed for a great disaster unless it changes"; also remained fiercely loyal to her homeland; during the Hungarian Revolution, she helped organize and served as the president of Hungarian Coordinated Relief, Inc., and "tried to focus attention on the sad plight of that wonderful country and her people, now under enforced Communist domination"; when Nikita Khruschev visited here, she was among those on picket lines before the White House and the United Nations building in New York, carrying a sign demanding his expulsion from the U.S.

MOVIE HIGHLIGHTS: *International Lady, Invisible Agent, Frankenstein Meets the Wolf Man, Holiday in Mexico, Northwest Outpost, The Plunderers, Love Happy, Jet over the Atlantic.*

Victor Mature

(b. Victor Mature, Jan. 29, 1916, Louisville, Ky.) Huge, with a hawk-like profile, shirt-bursting biceps, a headful of batwing curls, and an arrogant toothy smile, he was, as studio publicists persistently trumpeted, "a beautiful hunk of man"; was a virile womanizer and served with honor in the Coast Guard but was surprisingly gentle (not to mention intelligent) for a muscleman; working with him in *Footlight Serenade*, in which he played a heavyweight champ, comic Phil Silvers observed that "he abhorred violence, couldn't stand anyone hitting him with a glove or even touching him"; Cecil B. De Mille, directing him in *Samson and Delilah*, discovered he was a walking bundle of phobias (fearing lions, swords, fire, falling temple columns, etc.); castigating him before the entire cast and crew, the director thundered that he was "100 percent yellow"; the easygoing star (his conceited look was highly misleading) took it with a laugh; once said of himself, "I am a devout coward—I wouldn't walk up a wet step"; his father was an Austrian immigrant who arrived in America with six cents in his pocket, unable to speak English, and made a fortune by establishing a refrigeration plant—a place where, after attending Kentucky Military Institute, his heir chose not to work; ran off to California at 19, was given a working student fellowship at the Pasadena

Playhouse, lived in a tent (borrowed from the theater) pitched on the corner of a friend's garden and, in less than five years, appeared in more than 100 plays; discovered by movie producer Hal Roach, he made his debut in '39 opposite Joan Bennett in *The Housekeeper's Daughter*; consolidated his instantaneous fame in *One Million B.C.* the following year, about the time his first marriage, to nonpro Frances Evans, was annulled; contract was bought up in '41 by 20th Century–Fox, where he starred well into the '50s, most notably in *Kiss of Death* and *My Darling Clementine*, before turning free-lance; became Hollywood's beefcake king and was equally famous for his torrid off-screen romances (with Rita Hayworth, prior to her elopement with Orson Welles, Anne Shirley et al.), as well as his wives and divorces: Martha Stevenson Kemp, Pasadena socialite Dorothy Berry, Adrianne Joy Urwich; in the '60s, a very wealthy man (real estate, electronics firm, restaurants), he retired, after 72 films, to a luxurious 11-acre spread at Rancho Santa Fe, 125 miles from Hollywood, where his passion is golf; at 59, became a first-time father; daughter Victoria is by his fifth wife (since '72), Lorey; has been coaxed out of retirement to play small roles at big salaries in such movies as *After the Fox*, *Every Little Crook and Nanny*, *Firepower*, etc.; returned in '84 to appear in the television drama "Samson and Delilah," as Manoah, Samson's father; remarked then: "When I was asked to play the role, I said, 'If the price is right, I'll play his mother.' As it turned out, I was like a Yiddishe mama, anyway, running around yelling, 'Don't marry that girl' "; sometimes they used to say that to Victor Mature—occasionally he listened.

MOVIE HIGHLIGHTS: *I Wake Up Screaming* (aka *Hot Spot*), *The Shanghai Gesture*, *Song of the Islands*, *My Gal Sal*, *Seven Days' Leave*, *Moss Rose*, *Cry of the City*, *Martin Rome*, *Fury at Furnace Creek*, *Easy Living*, *Wabash Avenue*, *Stella*, *Androcles and the Lion*, *Million Dollar Mermaid*, *The Robe*, *Affair with a Stranger*, *Demetrius and the Gladiators*, *The Egyptian*, *Chief Crazy Horse*, *Safari*.

Virginia Mayo

(b. Virginia Clara Jones, Nov. 30, 1920, St. Louis, Mo.) One of producer Sam Goldwyn's loveliest discoveries, a Technicolor-ready blonde with hazel-green eyes, she is an all-American beauty, not only in looks but ancestry; her great, great, great-grandfather, Capt. James Piggott, served with General Washington in the Revolutionary War and later founded the city of East St. Louis, Ill.; the daughter of a *St. Louis Globe Democrat* newspaper reporter, she began preparing for a show business career at age 6, studying dance and the stage arts in her hometown's Wientge School of Dramatic Expression, owned and operated by her aunt; following high school graduation in '37, she spent the summer as a member of the ballet of the St. Louis Municipal Opera, then signed to appear with a well-known vaudeville act called Pansy the Horse; toured for five years as the ringmaster of this antic "equine" (two comedians inside the suit), taking her professional name from that of Andy Mayo, star of the act; Pansy and friend made it to Broadway in Eddie Cantor's *Banjo Eyes*, then went into a revue at Billy Rose's Diamond Horseshoe in New York, where Virginia was spotted by a David O. Selznick talent scout; the producer gave her a screen test (a scene from Noel Coward's sophisticated comedy *Private Lives*, in which she was considerably out of her depth) and turned her down; seeing the test, Sam Goldwyn put her under contract expecting her to be merely one of his decorative "Goldwyn Girls," which she was in Danny Kaye's *Up in Arms*; the producer soon discovered her talents extended far beyond mere beauty; earliest dramatic role was a small part in *Jack London*, starring a new actor, a redhead named Michael O'Shea, heralded then as the "new" Spencer Tracy; on the day in '43 when he first saw her on a studio sound stage, O'Shea approached and kissed her, before they were even introduced, then informed her, "You're the girl I'm going to marry some day"; the ensuing romance raised a few eyebrows; he was 14 years older than she and, back in Connecticut, he had a teen-aged son and daughter and a wife to whom he'd been married since '26; four years after they met, Virginia became the second Mrs. Edward Francis Michael Joseph O'Shea; their daughter, Mary Catherine, was born in '53, the actor soon afterwards chose a career other than acting (became a plainclothes detective with the sheriff's office in Ventura County, Calif.), and they remained happily married until his death in '73; long famous as comedian Danny Kaye's perennial leading lady (*Wonder Man*, *The Kid from Brooklyn*, etc.), the actress was similarly occupied in *The Princess and the Pirate* with Bob Hope; comparing the two funnymen, she once said, "Danny is moody, either down in the dumps or up in the clouds. Bob is always the same, wise-cracking, happy, fun to be with"; for the record, it was she—playing the trampish young wife—who delivered to returning G.I. "husband" Dana Andrews the ironic title line in *The Best Years of Our Lives*.

MOVIE HIGHLIGHTS: *Seven Days Ashore, The Secret Life of Walter Mitty, Out of the Blue, A Song Is Born, The Girl from Jones Beach, Colorado Territory, Flaxy Martin, Always Leave Them Laughing, White Heat, The West Point Story, The Flame and the Arrow, Captain Horatio Hornblower,*

Painting the Clouds with Sunshine, She's Working Her Way through College, She's Back on Broadway, The Iron Mistress.

Lon McCallister

(b. Herbert Alonzo McCallister Jr., April 17, 1923, Los Angeles, Calif.) Something unexpected happened with 1943's *Stage Door Canteen*; in the script, the ostensible leading man was a G.I. called "Dakota" (played by William Terry) who, at the Canteen, left his heart with "a girl named Eileen" (Cheryl Walker); the camera, however, which "picks" people, singled out a different hero, a kid nicknamed "California"—this not-tall (5'6"), 20-year-old with wavy hair, dimples, a modest manner, and a most engaging shy smile; popular novelist James Hilton once called him "the most charming boy" the screen had seen; while a "new face" to movie audiences, he'd already been in movies for seven years, first as an extra and then in bit parts as a juvenile (*Gentleman Jim, Babes in Arms*, etc.); director George Cukor—a confirmed bachelor, as this actor proved to be—was his lifelong friend; the director gave him his first minor role at 13 in *Romeo and Juliet*, later directed him in the lead in *Winged Victory*, and once termed him "the perfect choir boy"; bobby-soxers found him an object of desire, judging by fan mail volume and their squeals of joy at his personal appearances; was born into a wealthy family (grandfather was a real estate tycoon) that lost its fortune in the Depression; left its mark on him; saw his grandfather become a night watchman at a movie studio, his mother lose her dressmaking establishment and go to work as a waitress; soon earning $1,500 a week as a star, he lived frugally and invested his money in land, apartment houses, and a beach house at Malibu, becoming independently wealthy; after serving two years in the Army in WWII, he resumed moviemaking and set a deadline of 1950 as the year he would quit the screen; had other ambitions, which he fulfilled; inspired by the sea stories of Joseph Conrad, he said, "I want to write and travel"; actually continued in movies through 1953's *Combat Squad*, quitting without a backward glance, and has written mysteries and plays and traveled the world over, sometimes as a merchant seaman; labeling himself "one of the original loners," he also lives a "free, unencumbered life" by land, journeying for several months each year wherever he likes in a motor home—solo; admits no regrets at not having had a family; says, "Most of my friends have children and I love playing uncle to them. But it's kind of a cop-out, because I can always go wandering off. I have all the pleasures of being with children and none of the responsibilities."

MOVIE HIGHLIGHTS: *Home in Indiana, Thunder in the Valley, The Red House, Scudda Hoo! Scudda Hay!, The Story of Seabiscuit, The Big Cat, A Yank in Korea, Montana Territory.*

Roddy McDowall

(b. Roderick Andrew McDowall, Sept. 17, 1928, London, England) His boyish charm, British accent, and mix of youthful courage and vulnerability made him a greatly popular child star of the '40s in Hollywood; English movie fans were acquainted with his talents first, having seen him from age 8 in 17 films, including *Scruffy* (his debut), *Murder in the Family, Yellow Sands*, and *Just William*; his Scottish father, an officer in the British Merchant Marines, evacuated the family to America at the height of the London Blitz in '40; signed immediately to a term contract at 20th Century–Fox (remained there through '48), the adolescent actor made his U.S. debut early in '41 in *Man Hunt*, starring Walter Pidgeon; later that year, playing Huw, the Welsh lad who had to leave school and go to work in the mines, in *How Green Was My Valley*, he was reunited with Pidgeon—and became a star; perhaps inevitably, in several of his best he had to share the screen with animals—horses *(My Friend Flicka, Green Grass of Wyoming)* or dogs *(Lassie Come Home)*; working with him in the latter was a beautiful child, Elizabeth Taylor, who became and remains his closest friend; besides working together in later films *(The White Cliffs of Dover*, as children, and *Cleopatra*, as adults), he has taken photographs of her (photography being a second career of his) that have appeared in many magazines; played a number of adult stars as lads before they grew up and became Gregory Peck *(The Keys of the Kingdom)* or Tyrone Power *(Son of Fury)*; unimpressed by his own youthful accomplishments on screen, he still says, "Jackie Cooper was the best child actor ever"; eventually finding it difficult to make the transition from kid parts to leading man roles, he left Hollywood for New York in '52; spent years doing "live" TV (won a supporting Emmy in the drama "Not without Honor") and acting on the stage (22 plays—*Misalliance, No Time for Sergeants, Camelot*, etc.—and was accorded a supporting Tony for his performance in Anouilh's *The Fighting Cock*); resumed his screen career in 1960's *The Subterraneans* and *Midnight Lace*; movie credits now total more than 100, including the highly successful *Planet of the Apes* and its three sequels, in which he starred as the scholarly Cornelius; a voracious collector of cinematic memorabilia, he has also directed movies *(Tam Lin*, starring Ava Gardner) and published a book of photographs of such famous friends as Judy Garland and Mary Martin, *Double Exposure*; a confirmed bachelor, he has such a gift for friendship—and such an "extended family" of intimates—that Ruth Gordon once said of him, "I don't know anyone who has such a following, except maybe Queen Elizabeth."

MOVIE HIGHLIGHTS: *Confirm or Deny, On the Sunny Side, The Pied Piper, Hangover Square, Thunderhead, Son of Flicka, Molly and Me, Holiday in Mexico, Rocky, Macbeth, Kidnapped, Black Midnight, Tuna Clipper, Killer Shark, Everybody's Dancin', The Steel Fist, The Third Day, That Darned Cat, The Loved One, Inside Daisy Clover, Lord Love a Duck, The Life and Times of Judge Roy Bean.*

Dorothy McGuire

(b. Dorothy Hackett McGuire, June 14, 1918, Omaha, Neb.) *Claudia*, in which she portrayed Rose Franken's adorable creation, the scatterbrained, naïve young wife, made her a star on Broadway in '41 and, two years later, did the same for her in movies; of Irish-Scottish-English ancestry, she was the daughter and only child of a well-to-do attorney (who committed suicide when she was in her teens); started her career at 13, playing the Maude Adams role in *A Kiss for Cinderella* at the Omaha Community Playhouse; her leading man was visiting actor Henry Fonda, himself an alumnus of that theater; completed her schooling at Ladywood Convent in Indianapolis and Pine Manor Junior College in Wellesley, Mass.; went directly to New York, where she won a leading role in a radio soap opera, "Big Sister," acted in a number of plays—*Stop-Over, My Dear Children* (padded to play a tweedy, fat frump in this John Barrymore vehicle), *Swingin' the Dream*—then understudied, and finally replaced, Martha Scott (when she went to Hollywood) in *Our Town*; won the role of the irrepressible Claudia over a reported 208 other contenders, thanks to her "fresh, wind-blown quality" (in the words of the playwright) and childlike manner that made the play's producers believe she didn't know what time it was (they were mistaken); though David O. Selznick bought movie rights to *Claudia* and signed McGuire to a personal contract, she almost lost the screen role to another new discovery of his, Jennifer Jones, who tested—most impressively—for it; Selznick finally sold *Claudia* and half of McGuire's contract to 20th Century–Fox, demanding that the studio not glamorize her or tamper with her "pixie kind of personality"; admittedly once awed by movie personalities, she has said her strangest early experience in

Hollywood was going to a Selznick dinner party and seeing Kay Francis sitting in the drawing room, cocktail glass in hand, "just as she always did in pictures"; was the only Selznick player who never once appeared in a feature film produced by him; when new at 20th Century–Fox, was given Loretta Young's old dressing room, an opulent, satin-padded affair, which she said reminded her of a coffin and which she promptly had redecorated; was nominated for a Best Actress Oscar for *Gentleman's Agreement*, the last movie she made in the '40s; had a happy marriage from '43 until his death in '79 to *Life* magazine photographer-theatrical producer John Swope, son of the president of General Electric; it was strictly a coincidence that, when young, he'd been active in the University Players, whose members included his close friend Henry Fonda, her first leading man; she and Swope had two children: Mary (an actress now known as Topo Swope) and Mark; in later years she has been more active in television dramas (*Rich Man, Poor Man, The Runaways*, etc.) than in films.

MOVIE HIGHLIGHTS: *A Tree Grows in Brooklyn, The Enchanted Cottage, The Spiral Staircase, Claudia and David, Till the End of Time, Mother Didn't Tell Me, Mister 880, Callaway Went Thataway, Invitation, I Want You, Three Coins in the Fountain, Trial, Friendly Persuasion, Old Yeller, The Remarkable Mr. Pennypacker, A Summer Place, The Dark at the Top of the Stairs, Swiss Family Robinson, Susan Slade, Summer Magic, The Greatest Story Ever Told, Flight of the Doves.*

Ann Miller

(b. Johnnie Lucille Collier, April 12, 1923, Houston, Texas) Brunette, long-limbed, and ever youthful, she was the second-best femme tap dancer in the history of movies—second only to Eleanor Powell; had a three-tiered career: secondary parts at RKO (1937–40), starring roles in Bs at Columbia (1941–46), and major musicals at MGM (1948–56); Metro nabob Louis B. Mayer, much older, fell madly in love with her ("It was a big thrill for me to be courted by a man of such eminence"), but "all hell broke loose" when he proposed marriage (" 'Absolutely no way,' said my mother"); later, when she announced she planned to marry a younger man, a distraught Mayer attempted suicide with sleeping pills; had three failed marriages, giving up her career before and resuming it after each; first husband (1946–47): multimillionaire (Consolidated Steel heir) Reese L. Milner—she accidentally fell down a flight of stairs when nine months pregnant and her child (a girl) was born dead; husband #2 (1958–61) was Texas oil millionaire Bill Moss—ex of Jane Withers; #3 (1961–62) was another Texas oil magnate, playboy Arthur Cameron ("He had 16 mistresses when we got married and he never gave them up")—marriage was annulled; got her first tap-dancing lesson—impromptu fashion—from the great Bill "Bojangles" Robinson; he made a personal appearance at Houston's Majestic Theater, her mother took her backstage to meet him, and he, singing "Bye, Bye, Blues," showed her how it was done; was 11 when her mother and father, a Texas lawyer, separated and then divorced; that same year her mother (her lifelong companion until her death in '81) took her to Hollywood; was a child extra in *Anne of Green Gables* ('34) and *The Good Fairy*; dancing debut on screen was in 1936's *The Devil on Horseback*; won her RKO contract at 14—claiming to be 18—and was featured in *New Faces of 1937*; got an RKO contract with the help of Lucille Ball, then a starlet at the studio, who had seen her on stage; left the studio and scored a great hit on Broadway in the '39 edition of *George White's Scandals*; returned to RKO, where she'd been earning $250 weekly, with a $3,000-a-week contract and a glamorous, new, highly photogenic nosejob—and co-starred with pal Lucille Ball in *Too Many Girls*; next did two pictures at Republic, in one of which, *Melody Ranch*, she made history as the one who gave cowboy star Gene Autry his first screen kiss; following many fondly recalled wartime Bs at Columbia, she began making tap history—at last in Technicolor, for which she was a natural—in *Easter Parade*; two interesting books about her have been published: *Tops in Taps*, a pictorial history by Jim Connor, and her autobiography, *Miller's High Life* (done in collaboration with Norma Lee Browning); the first line in the latter: "I became a Hollywood star on my talent, not on casting couches. If I had gone that route, I could have been a bigger star"; fans would surely say she did all right—on talent.

MOVIE HIGHLIGHTS: *The Life of the Party, Stage Door, Radio City Revels, Having Wonderful Time, You Can't Take It with You, Go West, Young Lady, Time Out for Rhythm, Priorities on Parade, True to the Army, Reveille with Beverly, Jam Session, Hey Rookie, Eadie Was a Lady, Eve Knew Her Apples, The Thrill of Brazil, The Kissing Bandit, On the Town, Texas Carnival, Two Tickets to Broadway, Lovely to Look At, Small Town Girl, Kiss Me Kate, Hit the Deck, The Opposite Sex, The Great American Pastime.*

Carmen Miranda

(b. Maria Da Carmo Miranda Da Cunha, Feb. 9, 1909, Marco Canavezes, Portugal; d. Aug. 5, 1959) 20th Century–Fox's Technicolored musical smorgasbord—petite (only 5′, hence the six-inch wedgies), English-mangling, eyeball-rolling, peppery Brazilian bombshell (aka "the lady in the tutti-frutti hat"); was camp long before the word was coined, but she brought joy to a war-weary world; introduced in 1940's *Down Argentine Way*, she was steadily on screen through 1953's *Scared Stiff*; wore bare-midriff costumes even after a gall-bladder operation left her with a scar ("Een peecture I hang a flower or butterfly over eet"); most of her garish movie getups were based on her own costume designs; knowledge of fabrics came of firsthand experience; born "veree poor," she was taken to Brazil as a child and, between 14 and 19, was apprenticed to a French dressmaker in Rio—and sewing remained a lasting passion; began singing professionally on records and in clubs in her 20s and, between '34 and '38, appeared in Brazilian films (*Alo, Alo, Carnaval, Banana la Terra*, etc.); was starring at Rio's sumptuous Casino when discovered by New York producer Lee Schubert who presented her on Broadway with explosive results in 1939's *Streets of Paris*; took with her to Hollywood her mother and six married sisters and their families, and they all lived harmoniously in the same mansion; in '47, she added a husband of her own, producer David Sebastian, to the domicile; despite her *outré* screen persona, she is recalled by Hollywood friends as "a simple, sincere and unaffected woman with a tremendous verve and enjoyment of life"; also, loyal to Brazil, and the best known entertainer ever produced by her country, she always insisted on at least one song in Portuguese in every movie she did; career at 20th Century–Fox came to an abrupt, unpredicted end; a "real lady," in the words of studio chief Darryl F. Zanuck, she never wore anything under her costumes, as that would affect the line of the garment and restrict her movements; unfortunately, one day a free-lance still photographer had his camera set at a low angle as she danced—and millions of copies of his all-revealing snapshot found their way onto the black market; "super-puritanical pressure groups" (women's organizations of the time), said Zanuck, ganged up on the studio, forcing it to drop her option; made just four more films elsewhere; visitors to Rio de Janeiro today are pleased—and perhaps a little surprised—to discover in a park across Botafogo Bay from Sugar Loaf Mountain a modern cement building, the Carmen Miranda Museum; displayed inside, in glass cases, are the elaborate costumes, turbans, and platform shoes—a riot of color—worn by the star in her Hollywood movies; "She was, after all," explains a museum official, "an ambassador of Brazilian popular culture."

MOVIE HIGHLIGHTS: *That Night in Rio, Weekend in Havana, Springtime in the Rockies, The Gang's All Here, Four Jills in a Jeep, Greenwich Village, Something for the Boys, Doll Face, If I'm Lucky, Copacabana, A Date with Judy, Nancy Goes to Rio.*

Robert Mitchum

(b. Robert Mitchum, Aug. 6, 1917, Bridgeport, Conn.) Maverick star—rugged, forceful, and sleepy-eyed—who has always said and done just what he pleased, take it or leave it; pattern began early; once said, "When the other kids in school had shoes to wear, and I didn't, I had to make a routine of nonconforming. It was a matter of salvation of my pride and self-respect"; was 2 when his father, a railroad switchman, died after a train-yard accident, leaving the family in straitened circumstances; for the next ten years, he, his brother (actor John Mitchum), and his sister were farmed out to various relatives; admittedly a juvenile delinquent, he was expelled from schools in New York City and Delaware; at 14, lying about his age, he shipped as an engine wiper on a European-bound freighter; next hitchhiked to Los Angeles ("When I got to California, I lay on the beach and rolled drunks; I didn't know any better"); hopping a freight back East, he was arrested for vagrancy in Georgia and served a short-term sentence on a chain gang; later did a stint in the CCC, worked in a factory in Toledo, Ohio, and went West once more; in Long Beach, Calif., was a stevedore on the docks, wrote, directed, and acted in shows for the Long Beach Players Guild, did a two-year tour as manager of famous astrologer Carroll Righter, wrote for radio and nightclub comics; at 22, in Delaware, he married his one wife, Dorothy Spence—by whom he now has three children: Jim, Chris (both actors), and Petrine; in the spring of '40, he and his wife arrived in California, where he found work as a shaper operator at Lockheed Aircraft; in '42, convincing an agent he was an expert rider (had never been on a horse), he crashed movies as a heavy in eight "Hopalong Cassidy" Westerns (*Hoppy Serves a Writ, Bar 20*, etc.); played bits in many other movies (*The Human Comedy, We've Never Been Licked, Gung Ho!*, etc.) before winning an RKO contract in '44; made his reputation in '45 (being nominated for a Best Supporting Oscar) in *The Story of G.I. Joe*—and was promptly inducted into the army; returning to pictures in *Till the End of Time*, he quickly became such a fan favorite that an arrest for marijuana possession in '48 damaged him little, if at all; many in Hollywood remain convinced the "bust" was a frame-up, that he was merely being used as a famous "example"—and, three years later, a California court did indeed set aside the guilty verdict; served 59 days of a 60-day sentence at the Los Angeles County honor farm; as Howard Hughes, owner of RKO, had loyally declined to cancel his contract, he began work at once in *The Big Steal*, after which there was no stopping him; looking back on a career encompassing more than 100 films, he cites his favorites as *The Sundowners* and *Heaven Knows Mr. Allison*.

MOVIE HIGHLIGHTS: *Undercurrent, The Locket, Pursued, Crossfire, Out of the Past, Rachel and the Stranger, Blood on the Moon, The Red Pony, Holiday Affair, Where Danger Lives, The Racket, The Lusty Men, White Witch Doctor, River of No Return, Track of the Cat, Night of the Hunter, Home before Dark, The Enemy Below, Home from the Hill, Cape Fear, The Longest Day, El Dorado, Ryan's Daughter, Farewell, My Lovely, The Big Sleep, That Championship Season.*

Maria Montez

(b. Maria Antonia Africa Gracia Vidal da Santo Silas, June 6, 1918, Barahona, Dominican Republic; d. Sept. 7, 1951) Except for a few pictures at the end, this volatile beauty was (1940–47) a one-studio star—Universal's dark, exotic tropical flower; left a lasting impression in a series of sex-and-sand epics; uninhibited and fiercely ambitious, she got what she wanted by going after it with the zeal of a Spanish conquistadore; her philosophy: "It is far better to make an attempt and fail than fail to make the attempt"; when new in Hollywood, and just another $125-a-week contract player, she announced: "I am going to be a great star"; won early attention by making her appearances at the studio commissary flashier than a floor show; each noon's sparkly outfit was more outlandishly original than the previous day's (and some were so daring they would have given movie censors a stroke); following her entrance came a "performance"; a witness has recalled: "She put tragedy in the slicing of a steak, passion in the way she consumed her dessert. When she left, the dining room lost its sparkle"; a *Saturday Evening Post* scribe found her such a "ball of fire" that "in her own drawing room she is Halley's Comet colliding with a super nova"; was one of the ten children (five boys, five girls) of the Spanish consul in the Dominican Republic; was married at 17 to William G. McFeeters, an officer in the British Army, with whom she lived, briefly, on his family estate in Ireland; going on to New York, she met the owner of the Monte Carlo nightclub, who thought she was movie material and who had studio contacts; RKO paid for her dramatic and diction lessons, but Universal signed her and took her to Hollywood; screen name came from Lola Montez, the nineteenth century Spanish dancer; studio soon discovered, as did a newspaper reporter, who wrote, "She has been a press agent all her life. And what she advertises is Maria Montez exclusively"; began in small parts but quickly graduated to starring roles, in which there was always some variation of the line "How-dare-you-spik-to-me-zat-way-do-you-not-know-I-am-ze-Queen?"; her second and last husband, from '43 on, was Jean-Pierre Aumont; their daughter, Maria-Christine (named for the Spanish queen from whom the star reportedly was descended), has had a screen career of her own (started as Tina Marquand when married to French actor Christian Marquand and made her debut in Dean Martin's *Texas Across the River* for Universal; is now billed Tina Aumont); Montez was a confirmed believer in astrology ("I follow eet like a barometer"), and many astrological forecasts made for her came true; a happy one was the birth of her daughter, as predicted, on Valentine's Day; later, consulting Hollywood astrologer Blanca Holmes, she insisted on knowing details about her final days; reluctantly, the woman told her that, according to the charts, her life would be short and the end would come suddenly; prediction was fulfilled two years later in Paris; while taking a bath, she suffered a fatal heart attack.

MOVIE HIGHLIGHTS: *Boss of Bullion City, The Invisible Woman, South of Tahiti, The Mystery of Marie Roget, Arabian Nights, White Savage, Ali Baba and the Forty Thieves, Cobra Woman, Gypsy Wildcat, Bowery to Broadway, Sudan, Tangier, The Exile, Pirates of Monterey, Siren of Atlantis, The Thief of Venice.*

George Montgomery

(b. George Letz, Aug. 29, 1916, Brady, Mont.) Born on a ranch, of Russian immigrant parents, this brawny guy first studied architecture at the University of Montana, then, at 21, lit out for Hollywood determined to be a movie cowboy; if Montana's Gary Cooper could do it, so could he; immediately landed a one-day job (at $75) riding a horse, as a Cossack, in Garbo's *Conquest*; after months as a combination bartender-dishwasher at a Hollywood Boulevard café, was signed by Republic to star in a serial, *The Lone Ranger*, which he made under his real name; this stardom proved fleeting; for the next two years he did bits, was the stunt double for John Wayne and Randolph Scott, and did a stint as the stand-in for Ralph ("Dick Tracy") Byrd; finally made it as a leading man in '40 when he signed a contract at 20th Century–

Fox, where he stayed for the next seven years before turning free-lance; made his debut at the studio in *The Cisco Kid and the Lady*; soon arrived at the point where even established stars like Henry Fonda were complaining that the choice assignments were going to him; as he was rugged and handsome, every femme star on the lot vied for his services; Gene Tierney got him for *China Girl*, Betty Grable for *Coney Island*, Ginger Rogers for *Roxie Hart* (a real-life romance followed that, as did a brief "official" engagement to Hedy Lamarr); Dinah Shore, however, lassoed him in '43, and they were together until their divorce 19 years later; two children: Melissa and an adopted son, John David (Jody); did not marry again, and, in recent years, has said he is "looking for a young Dinah Shore" to wed; with three years out for military duty (Signal Corps), he returned to the screen in '46 in *Three Little Girls in Blue*; picture was three weeks into production, with Victor Mature in the lead, when studio chief Darryl F. Zanuck learned Montgomery would be available, scrapped it, and started over; this was a blessing and a curse; Montgomery's agent demanded and got him a new deal—$2,750 a week; an angry Zanuck retaliated by eliminating all his close-ups and giving him just one subsequent role, in *The Brasher Doubloon*; a decade later, after many movies at other studios, the star became an independent producer; turned out more than a dozen pictures in which he starred (*Black Patch, War Kill*, etc.) and some of which he also directed (*Samar, The Steel Claw*); also headlined in a 1958–60 NBC-TV series, "Cimarron City"; never losing his youthful interest in architecture, he has designed and built numerous Hollywood homes; lives now—alone—in a magnificent, tri-level modern Spanish mansion in California's Trousdale Estates, filled with furniture of his own making, which boasts a massive swimming pool fed by a waterfall—all done according to his specifications and with his active, physical participation.

MOVIE HIGHLIGHTS: *Star Dust, Young People, The Cowboy and the Blonde, Cadet Girl, Ten Gentlemen from West Point, Orchestra Wives, Bomber's Moon, The High Window, Lulu Belle, Davy Crockett—Indian Scout, Dakota Lil, Indian Uprising, Cripple Creek, Fort Ti, Battle of Rogue River, Pawnee, Gun Duel in Durango, Badman's Country, Man from God's Country, Watusi.*

Constance Moore

(b. Constance Moore, Jan. 18, 1920, Sioux City, Iowa) With her sparkle, sophisticated dark-blonde beauty, and a lovely singing voice, she made many

B musicals classier than they had any right to be; was an eye-filling charmer whether singing before a band in a form-fitting white gown with sequins or being romanced by some handsome leading man like Robert Paige; famed illustrator Russell Patterson once termed her "the typical American girl"; seemed destined to star at the smaller studios; after some 20 low-budget movies at Universal (1937–41), she escaped to Paramount and RKO for a couple of As, then it was on to Republic for the rest of her career; the daughter of an Iowa father (family owned a grocery chain and a candy factory) and a Texas mother, she was 4 when her parents divorced; grew up in Dallas, where she attended private schools (Miss Gray's Day School, Miss Hockaday's Junior College); began singing on a local radio station at 15 on programs sponsored by her wealthy godfather, Jack Marvin, who owned a chain of drug stores; was 17 when Universal talent scout Rufus LeMaire visited Dallas; arranging to meet and sing for him, she snagged a $125-a-week studio contract, sans screen test; made her debut in a minor role (her no-name character being simply credited as "Girl") in a Wendy Barrie programmer, *Prescription for Romance*; worked in seven movies and one serial (*Buck Rogers* with Buster Crabbe) before she was allowed to sing a note on screen; in '39 she became (and remained) the wife of Johnny Maschio, then a top Hollywood agent and later a real-estate exec; two children: Mary Constance ("Gina") and Michael; in addition to movies, had careers in other media in the early '40s—on the radio series "Ceiling Unlimited" with Joseph Cotten and on Broadway with Ray Bolger in a Rodgers and Hart musical, *By Jupiter*; quit movies after *Hit Parade of 1947* and later starred in nightclubs; on TV in the '60s, had a leading role in a daytime soap opera, "The Young Marrieds," and co-starred with Robert Young in a short-lived prime time series, "Window on Main Street"; always had many friends among the socially elite of Beverly Hills (Cary Grant, Olivia de Havilland, Reginald Gardiner, etc.), but one of them was not Veronica Lake; Moore and Lake were the femme leads in 1941's *I Wanted Wings*, and if the tales that the "peekaboo blonde" told in *Veronica*, her autobiography, are true, their relationship was less than harmonious.

MOVIE HIGHLIGHTS: *State Police, The Crime of Dr. Hallet, Prison Break, A Letter of Introduction, Swing That Cheer, You Can't Cheat an Honest Man, Hawaiian Nights, Charlie McCarthy, Detective, Ma, He's Making Eyes at Me, La Conga Nights, I'm Nobody's Sweetheart Now, Argentine Nights, Buy Me That Town, Take a Letter, Darling, Show Business, Atlantic City, Delightfully Dangerous, Mexicana, Earl Carroll's Sketchbook, In Old Sacramento.*

Agnes Moorehead

(b. Agnes Robertson Moorehead, Dec. 6, 1906, Clinton, Mass.; d. April 30, 1974) Sterling character star, best at playing authoritative or soured women, who was four times nominated for a Best Supporting Oscar—for *The Magnificent Ambersons*, *Mrs. Parkington*, *Johnny Belinda*, and *Hush . . . Hush . . . Sweet Charlotte*; most often dowdy on the screen, this striking green-eyed redhead was a fashion plate off it, having the closets of her Italian-style Beverly Hills villa filled with the latest creations of Givenchy and Dior; was such an imaginative child that her mother (who, incidentally, survived her) greeted her each morning with: "Well, Agnes, who are you today?"; grew up in St. Louis, Mo., and Reedsburg, Wis., the daughter of a Presbyterian minister; remained a fundamentalist and often said she believed literally every word of the Bible; father offered no objection to her career choice, provided she completed her education; acted in summer stock at 10, spent four summers as a singer-dancer with the St. Louis Municipal Opera, then racked up a series of degrees: B.A. at Ohio's Muskingum College, a master's (in English and public speaking) at the University of Wisconsin, and a doctorate (in literature) at Bradley University; taught in a public school in Soldiers Grove, Wis., to earn tuition money, then attended and graduated with honors (in '29) from the American Academy of Dramatic Arts (along with Rosalind Russell, who remained her lifelong friend); went directly to Broadway for many plays: *Marco Millions*, *Scarlet Pages*, etc.; also appeared on hundreds of radio shows, most notably "The March of Time," where she was the voice of some 40 famous women (Eleanor Roosevelt, Mme. Chiang Kai-shek, etc.); in '39, with Orson Welles and Joseph Cotten, was a founder and charter member of the Mercury Theater Players; was among those Welles took with him to Hollywood in '41 for *Citizen Kane*, his directing-starring debut in which she played Kane's mother; her first spine-tingling radio performance in "Sorry, Wrong Number" (on "Suspense") came in '43; repeated the drama on the air more than 20 times over the years and later recorded it; was seen in more than 90 films, the last being 1972's *Dear Dead Delilah*; for years starred on TV as Endora, the wickedly delightful witch, in "Bewitched"; an outspoken woman, she had nothing but contempt for avant-garde drama, saying, "I'm not interested in blasphemous, dirty, ugly theater. I loathe *Who's Afraid of Virginia Woolf?* I believe drama should lift the spirits of man"; expressed just as strongly her admiration for people with drive and ambition ("That's why I adore Debbie Reynolds"—one of her closest friends, with whom she co-starred in *The Singing Nun*); final professional engagement was in the

Broadway musical *Gigi*, in which she played Aunt Alicia; had an adopted son, Sean, and two marriages that ended in divorce—to John Griffith Lee (1930–52), a radio actor, and Robert Gist (1953–58), an actor–turned–TV director.

MOVIE HIGHLIGHTS: *Journey into Fear, The Big Street, Jane Eyre, Dragon Seed, Since You Went Away, Tomorrow the World, Keep Your Powder Dry, Our Vines Have Tender Grapes, Her Highness and the Bellboy, The Lost Moment, Dark Passage, Summer Holiday, The Woman in White, The Stratton Story, The Great Sinner, Caged, Fourteen Hours, Show Boat, The Blue Veil, Magnificent Obsession, The Swan, Raintree County.*

Dennis Morgan

(b. Stanley Morner, Dec. 10, 1910, Prentice, Wis.) Curly-haired, well-built star, with a splendid baritone voice, who handled with verve whatever Warner Bros. threw at him—comedy *(Two Guys from Milwaukee)*, Westerns *(Cheyenne)*, musicals *(Shine On, Harvest Moon)*, dramas *(God Is My Co-Pilot)*; starred exclusively at this one studio (except for a single loan-out to RKO for *Kitty Foyle*, which made him a star) between '39 and '52; at one point was the highest-salaried star on the lot; appeared elsewhere later in only five more films before quitting the screen; had two earlier names as a movie actor; made his debut under his real name in '36 in a B picture, *I Conquer the Sea*, produced by a small-time outfit, Academy Pictures; was still Stanley Morner during his one year (1936–37) at MGM, where he had small roles in, among others, *Old Hutch, Navy Blue and Gold,* and *The Great Ziegfeld,* in which he appeared to sing (studio belatedly realized Ziegfeld's lead male singer had to be a tenor; Allan Jones' voice was dubbed in); in '38 Paramount billed him as Richard Stanley in *King of Alcatraz, Persons in Hiding,* etc.; final Irish monicker, by which he became famous, was given him by Warners, where he first screen tested for the role of The Red Shadow in *The Desert Song* (in which he finally starred after 16 earlier films); the son of a banker of Swedish descent (eventually his business manager), he grew up in Marshfield, Wis., was a basketball and football star in high school, won a statewide singing competition, and planned a career in grand opera; John Charles Thomas was his idol, and he owned every record the singer ever made; began dating Lillian Vedder when both were high school seniors, and they went on together to attend Carroll College (Waukesha, Wis.), where he was a glee club soloist; while in college, he worked for $35 a week on Milwaukee's radio station WTMJ, playing records, reading poetry, and inviting listeners to tune in his own music show to hear "Tomorrow's star . . . the Prince of Song"; married his high school sweetheart (his one wife) at 23; three children: Stanley Jr., Kristin, and James; moving on to Chicago to study at the Chicago Musical College, he began his career at the State Lake Theater, was a hit as a solo attraction at the Empire Room of the Palmer House, was heard on a coast-to-coast NBC radio show ("Silken Strings"), sang the leads in two operas, *Faust* and Handel's *Xerxes* (the first to do it in English), and became the protégé of veteran opera star Mary Garden; she pulled strings to get him a screen test; had the easy charm and face of a playboy, which he never was; when a star, receiving 1,000 fan letters a day, he settled his family in conservative La Canada, a hilly country community 20 miles from Hollywood where his children attended public schools; was known there by his real name (which he never changed), never frequented nightclubs (preferred hunting and fishing), and, with his brood, attended Hollywood's Presbyterian Church, where he sang in the choir.

MOVIE HIGHLIGHTS: *Waterfront, The Fighting 69th, Three Cheers for the Irish, River's End, Affectionately Yours, Kisses for Breakfast, In This Our Life, Captains of the Clouds, Wings for the Eagle, The Hard Way, The Very Thought of You, Christmas in Connecticut, One More Tomorrow, The Time, the Place, and the Girl, My Wild Irish Rose, Two Guys from Texas, One Sunday Afternoon, It's a Great Feeling, Perfect Strangers.*

Wayne Morris

(b. Bertram deWayne Morris, Feb. 17, 1914, Los Angeles, Calif.; d. Sept. 14, 1959) No other leading man played the part quite so well, the big handsome guy with rippling muscles who was just a bit slow on the uptake; *Kid Galahad*, in which he was a naïve boxer, established the pattern, *Brother Rat* consolidated it, and so it went; if he looked like a modern young Viking (blond, blue-eyed, brawny, and 6'2"), there was good reason—traced his ancestry back to King Olaf of the tenth century; always had, perhaps to his detriment, an easy-does-it attitude; at Los Angeles Junior College, where he "majored" in football, he calculatedly got himself elected freshman-class president because "I'd learned that if you held some student body office, the teachers just naturally assumed you must also be a leader in your studies—and that's how I got by"; next shipped as a waiter on a two-month cruise to Australia and the South Seas; after another nine months as a forest ranger in California's Sierra Madre mountains, he signed on at the Pasadena

Playhouse; over the next three years, was in 42 plays and in 41 of them "played old men with beards and aches in their backs"; the one exception was his last, *Yellow Jack*, in which, as young Private Dean, he had a role that gave him his first chance to be himself; skipping a screen test, Warner Bros. talent scout Irving Kumin signed him to a $50-a-week contract; made his debut in '36 in a walk-through role in Pat O'Brien's *China Clipper* (his close-up and one line ended up on the cutting room floor); spoke his first line—just one—on screen in Joe E. Brown's *Polo Joe*; soon came several good-luck castings opposite equally blonde Priscilla Lane (*Men Are Such Fools, Brother Rat*, etc.) that brought him great popularity as a romantic idol; said then the person he most admired in Hollywood was great character actor Harry Carey who, after 30 years of fame, had "stayed such a fine man"; also said he envied the way Carey lived—"so simply, on a ranch with his wife, and he has so many friends; that's the kind of life I'd like"; never found that lifestyle; was married first (1939–40) to New York socialite Leonora "Bubbles" Schinasi, by whom he had a son, Bert Jr.; second wife (from '42 on) was Patricia O'Rourke; two daughters: Patricia and Melinda; had racked up 25 movies and was riding the crest of the wave by the time America entered WWII; enlisted in the Navy as a cadet, became a fighter pilot, and served with such valor that, before his discharge five years later, he was twice awarded the Distinguished Service Cross; returning a hero, he found the Hollywood parade had passed him by and his days of glory were over; after a few second leads (*The Voice of the Turtle*, etc.), drifted into character roles, which he played to the end; was last seen on TV in an episode of "Adventures in Paradise"—looking bloated, haggard, older than his years, and utterly disillusioned.

MOVIE HIGHLIGHTS: *Smart Blonde, Submarine D-1, Valley of the Giants, The Kid from Kokomo, Brother Rat and a Baby, The Return of Dr. X, Flight Angels, Ladies Must Live, An Angel from Texas, The Quarterback, I Wanted Wings, Gambling on the High Seas, Three Sons o' Guns, Deep Valley, The Time of Your Life, The Big Punch, A Kiss in the Dark, The Younger Brothers, John Loves Mary, Task Force, Johnny One-Eye, Riding Shotgun, Paths of Glory.*

Margaret O'Brien

(b. Angela Maxine O'Brien, Jan. 15, 1937, Los Angeles, Calif.) At 5, accent-perfect as an English child, she played a wartime waif in *Journey for Margaret*, zeroed in on the hearts of millions, and became, with no near rivals, the #1 child star of the '40s; where Shirley Temple had been a golden-haired dream child, an undiluted shot of glucose, she was noted for her "naturalness"—pigtails, freckled button nose, woebegone expression, and enchanting (if sometimes astonishingly cunning) smile; was reared by her widowed mother, onetime dancer Gladys Flores; father Larry O'Brien, a circus performer, died months before the future juvenile star was born; began modeling for famed photographer Paul Hesse at 3; made her movie debut at 4 as the daughter of James Cagney and Ann Sothern in an eight-minute Office of War Information short, *You, John Jones*; also played a bit in *Babes in Arms*; got her screen name via *Journey for Margaret*, her first lead; was accorded a special Oscar at 7 for her role of baby sister Tootie in *Meet Me in St. Louis*; performance was aided by a cruel trick; in one big scene she had to go tearfully berserk, demolishing the family's backyard snowman with a broomstick; to make certain that she gave the moment a maximum of anger, grief, and tears, she was told that her pet dog had just been killed; was among the Box-Office Top Ten in '45 and '46; many co-stars at MGM had affectionate nicknames for her—Mickey Rooney ("Little Lamb Chop"), comic Rags Ragland ("The Old Hag"), etc.; Mary Astor, however, who played her mother both in *Meet Me in St. Louis* and *Little Women*, wasn't overly fond of her; once said, "She was a quiet, almost too-well-behaved child when her mother was on the set. When Mother was absent, it was another story and she was a pain in the neck"; Margaret herself had little affection for Wallace Beery, her *Bad Bascomb* co-star ("He pinched my bottom because he thought I was stealing a scene, and one day he even stole my lunch"); at 12, had a stepfather who, within months, threw in the towel, blaming his marital woes on tantrums Margaret allegedly threw because she had to share her mother with someone else; was 21 when her mother died and she came into a trust fund worth a quarter of a million dollars; as her movie fame faded, she toured in comedies (*Barefoot in the Park*, etc.), did TV, and ventured to Broadway in two plays, which flopped; first marriage, to advertising art director Robert Allen Jr., ended in divorce in '68 after nine years; lived for a while in Lima, Peru, where, in English, she starred in two locally made films, and, in Spanish, hosted a daily soap opera; next had a lengthy relationship, first in Lima and later in Hollywood, with wealthy Peruvian Julio Tijero; in '74, in Los Angeles, she married Scandinavian steel executive Roy Thorvald Thorsen and, two years later, at 39, became the mother of her only child, Mara Tolene; the youngster got a perfect present on her fourth birthday, a mint-condition Margaret O'Brien doll that, located after a lengthy search, was such a collector's curio that it cost the movies' onetime pigtailed princess (who didn't own one) $450.

MOVIE HIGHLIGHTS: *Dr. Gillespie's Criminal Case, Lost Angel, Thousands Cheer, Madame Curie, The Canterville Ghost, Jane Eyre, Music for Millions, Our Vines Have Tender Grapes, Three Wise Fools, Unfinished Dance, Tenth Avenue Angel, The Big City, The Secret Garden, Her First Romance, Glory, Heller in Pink Tights.*

Donald O'Connor

(b. Donald David Dixon Ronald O'Connor, Aug. 28, 1925, Chicago, Ill.) Just as in the Judy Garland song, he was "Born in a Trunk"; the offspring of show biz veterans, he began in vaudeville himself at the age of 13 months and started in movies at 12—doing a tap number with brother Jack—in a minor Warner Bros. musical, *Melody for Two*, starring tenor James Melton; the following year he was Bing Crosby's feisty, accordian-playing kid brother in *Sing You Sinners*, usually credited as his debut film; many other juvenile roles followed—in *Men With Wings*, *Beau Geste* (playing Gary Cooper, age 12), *Tom Sawyer, Detective*, etc.; fame came in a rush at Universal between '42 and '45 when, usually paired with tap-happy Peggy Ryan, he starred in a long string of "teen musicals"—low-budgeters turning huge profits—such as *What's Cookin'*, *Mr. Big*, *Chip Off the Old Block*; following this came the durable series of "Francis, the Talking Mule" comedies (*Francis Goes to the Races*, *Francis Covers the Big Town*, etc.); in '52, MGM borrowed him for *Singin' in the Rain* and, in light of his major comedic contribution to this classic (especially the "Make 'Em Laugh" routine), it was generally believed that the studio would buy out his contract; has said, "You know the secret of why Gene Kelly and I looked good together? While most performers turn to the right when dancing, Gene and I both turn to the left"; after claiming his services for one more film, *I Love Melvin*, MGM surprised many by looking the other way while he returned to Universal, to *Francis Joins the WACs*, etc.; when finally finished with that long-term contract, he sailed off to better things at bigger studios—*There's No Business Like Show Business* at 20th Century–Fox and *Anything Goes* at Paramount; was luckier than "star" Francis himself who, after playing the title role in six blockbusters, was reduced to carrying machine guns on his back in bit parts in war pictures; since '56, O'Connor has been married to former starlet Gloria Noble, by whom he has three children: Don Frederick, Alicia, and Kevin; a highlight of their nuptial year was when he conducted the Dallas Symphony in the debut performance of *Reflexions d'un Comique*, a tone poem that he composed; an earlier marriage, to Gwen Carter, mother of his daughter Donna, ended in divorce in '53

150

after nine years; quit movies in '65 after *That Funny Feeling* ("Musicals were dying out, and besides, I was making so much money from other forms of show business that it didn't seem important to keep on"); did not return until 16 years later when he appeared in *Ragtime*; that same year ('81), this veteran of every show business medium finally made his debut on Broadway, as the star of *Bring Back Birdie*; at that time, he disclosed with pride his personal triumph over booze after "a 25-year championship bout with alcoholism that almost destroyed me."

MOVIE HIGHLIGHTS: *Private Buckaroo, Give Out, Sisters, Get Hep to Love, When Johnny Comes Marching Home, It Comes Up Love, Top Man, This Is the Life, Patrick the Great, The Merry Monahans, Something in the Wind, Are You with It?, Yes Sir, That's My Baby, The Milkman, Call Me Madam, Walking My Baby Back Home, The Buster Keaton Story, Cry for Happy, The Wonders of Aladdin.*

Cathy O'Donnell

(b. Ann Steely, July 6, 1923, Siluria, Ala.; d. April 11, 1970) In *The Best Years of Our Lives*, G.I. Homer Parrish (Harold Russell) returned from the war with both hands missing, and this gentle beauty, as Wilma, proved her love by insisting that they marry anyway; began her career in '46 with this memorable performance under the direction of William Wyler, was directed by him later in *Detective Story*, and again in *Ben-Hur* ('59), her final film, in which she portrayed Tirzah; he also became her brother-in-law; from '48 on, she was married to his older brother, writer-associate producer Robert Wyler, who was 25 years her senior; this was the only marriage for each; was determined from childhood to act in movies and, devoutly religious throughout her life, believed that "if you pray for what you want, work hard for it, and it's right for you, you will get it"; was 9 when her parents separated and she and a brother were sent to Oklahoma City to live with an aunt; following graduation from high school, she attended business college and took a stenographer's job at the local Army induction center; earned the tuition for an acting course at Oklahoma City University, where drama instructors quickly realized that, with her childlike charm and dark, luminous eyes, she would make an ideal Juliet; reading the novel *Portrait of Jennie*, and learning that a movie version of it was planned, she set out for Hollywood to try for the lead in it; acquired a small nest egg by working for a hardware concern and paid a local family, driving to California, $20 to let her share the ride; Lana Turner wasn't discovered sipping a soda at Schwab's Drug Store, but O'Donnell was—by agent Ben Medford; took her to Sam Goldwyn, pointing out that "she talks with her eyes"; a screen test proved this, plus the fact that her Southern-accented voice was high and thin; undaunted, Goldwyn signed her, named her Cathy after the character Merle Oberon played in his successful movie *Wuthering Heights*, and sent her to New York for a year's study at the American Academy of Dramatic Arts; with this training, she next toured in the road company of *Life with Father*, in the role created by an earlier Goldwyn discovery, Teresa Wright, with whom she soon appeared in *The Best Years of Our Lives*; back in Hollywood, she tested—five times—for the same part in the movie, losing out to Elizabeth Taylor; a mystic by nature, she repeatedly read Kahlil Gibran's *The Prophet* and believed profoundly a statement she found in it on love: "Think not you can direct the course of love, for love, if it finds you worthy, directs your course"; love, and Robert Wyler, came into her life with her debut film; though they had no children, the 22 years they had together were happy, even the long, final ones when she was critically ill with cancer; nine months after her passing, he suffered a massive heart attack and followed her in death; speaking then of his "human warmth and courage," a friend noted that "he was a sick man pretending that he was well. And he did a magnificent job. He pretended to his wife . . . who died of a lingering illness. . . . He stood by her for years, always festive and acrobatic in his talk, always the lighthouse grin of youth and confidence on his face."

MOVIE HIGHLIGHTS: *They Live by Night, Bury Me Dead, The Spiritualist, Side Street, The Miniver Story, Never Trust a Gambler, Eight O'Clock Walk, Mad at the World, The Man from Laramie, The Deerslayer, The Story of Mankind.*

Martha O'Driscoll

(b. Martha O'Driscoll, March 4, 1922, Tulsa, Okla.) For exactly a dozen years, before retiring at 25, this hazel-eyed blonde was always a pleasure to see, and the opportunity came often; went directly from one studio contract to another: Paramount (1935–37), Universal (1937–38), MGM (1938–40), RKO (1940–41), Paramount (1941–42), Universal (1942–46), after which she free-lanced in three and, following *Carnegie Hall*, left the screen; the daughter of nonprofessionals, she began studying dance at 3, started modeling when 4, and at 9, was acting in little theater productions: looking more mature than her years, she broke into movies at 13, playing a co-ed—a bit—in Jack Oakie's

Collegiate; was mostly used as decoration until at 17, she was cast by RKO in *Li'l Abner*; was decorative there, too, but with a difference—played Daisy Mae, the handsome hillbilly's true love; soon returned to Universal, where she starred in many Bs (most often opposite the young Noah Beery Jr.) and spent the major portion of her career; dissatisfied with the roles she got, she tried to void her contract on the basis that she'd been underage when she signed; studio contested the suit and won; was not her only appearance in court; after a seven-year romance with actor William Lundigan, the first man she dated in Hollywood, she eloped with Navy Commander Richard D. Adams; in '45, after less than a year of marriage, she filed suit for divorce in Los Angeles, which the officer opposed; finally obtained a Reno divorce in '47, shortly after which she became—and has remained—the wife of wealthy Chicago businessman Arthur Appleton, chairman and president of Appleton Electric Co.; the mother of four (Jim, John, Linda, and Bill), she has been highly active in Chicago society—as past president of both the Sarah Siddons Society (which presents the prestigious theatrical award that is the regional equivalent of Broadway's Tony) and the Women's Board of the Chicago Boys Clubs, in addition to holding other offices of the Chicago Junior League; she has also served on the board of directors of her husband's company and the Gulf Stream Race Track in Florida, where they have a winter home and breed thoroughbred race horses; says, "My life has been very full since I left Hollywood"; also adds, with a note of maternal pride, that while attending Wellesley College, her daughter was chosen as Dartmouth's Winter Carnival Queen; heredity, obviously, still tells.

MOVIE HIGHLIGHTS: *Champagne Waltz, Mad About Music, The Secret of Dr. Kildare, Judge Hardy and Son, Forty Little Mothers, Laddie, Wagon Train, The Lady Eve, Pacific Blackout, Reap the Wild Wind, My Heart Belongs to Daddy, Young and Willing, The Fallen Sparrow, Crazy House, We've Never Been Licked, Hi, Beautiful!, Allergic to Love, Ghost Catchers, The Daltons Ride Again, Her Lucky Night, Here Come the Coeds, Shady Lady, Blonde Alibi.*

Maureen O'Hara

(b. Maureen FitzSimons, Aug. 17, 1920, Milltown, Ireland) Titian-haired with flashing green eyes, this colleen arrived in Hollywood at 19 as shiningly beautiful as a bit of Irish lake dropped from the skies; the full effect was not perceived by moviegoers, though, until three years later when Technicolor cameras first focused on her in *To the Shores of Tripoli* and *The Black Swan*; still, she was such an immediate sensation that the first story about her to appear in an American magazine was titled "All the World Will Be Talking About Her"; the second eldest of six (two boys, four girls), she inherited her love of drama from her mother, Rita Lilburn, an opera singer who was also a member of the Abbey Players, Ireland's national theater group; while a student in private schools, she began acting in radio plays in Dublin at 12; became an Abbey player herself at 14, while going on to attend Dominican College and Burke's School of Elocution; won a beauty contest at 17, the judge being American nightclub star Harry Richman, who encouraged her to take a movie screen test, which a London producer promptly offered; Charles Laughton, looking for a leading lady for his movie *Jamaica Inn*, saw the test, liked her but not it, gave her a second test, and signed her; "No, I was not nervous when I met him," she said back then. "I have never been nervous in my life, not of anyone or anything have I ever been nervous"; while waiting for the film to start, she met and fell in love with a young movie production manager, George Brown; Laughton always enjoyed telling how he and fellow cast members Leslie Banks and Emlyn Williams were set to help the beautiful newcomer with bits of acting advice when they began *Jamaica Inn*; he would then add, with a chuckle, "But after the first day's shooting we gathered back of the set and said, to a man, 'Did *you* see her?' That's when we knew we had something in the gel"; took her to Hollywood next to co-star with him in *The Hunchback of Notre Dame*; one hour before sailing to America, the actress impulsively married George Brown, who remained behind; while admitting to Hollywood reporters that this hasty marriage "may not have been wise," she never hid the fact that she was married ("Black is black for me, and white is white; I never stand on middle ground"); had the marriage annulled in August 1941, and in December of that year became the wife of Hollywood dialogue director Will Price; one daughter: Bronwyn; though they divorced in '53, she, being devoutly Catholic, did not remarry until after his death in '62; over her three-decade career, she starred in 52 films and cites as her favorites *The Long Gray Line*, *Sentimental Journey*, *The Quiet Man* (one of five with close friend John Wayne), and *How Green Was My Valley*; the latter contains her favorite scene—on the Welsh mountain slope with Walter Pidgeon, the minister who loves her but will not ask her to share his hardships, who tenderly explains why they must go their separate ways; "It was," she says, "a romantic scene to remember—quiet, without even a kiss, yet eloquent with the deepest emotions"; from '68 until his plane-crash death ten years later, she was most harmoniously married to Charles F. Blair Jr., a retired Air Force brigadier general and Pan Am pilot who had his own airline (Antilles Air Boats) with its headquarters in St. Croix, Virgin Islands, where they made their home.

MOVIE HIGHLIGHTS: A *Bill of Divorcement, Dance, Girl, Dance, Ten Gentlemen from West Point, This Land Is Mine, The Immortal Sergeant, The Fallen Sparrow, Buffalo Bill, Do You Love Me?, Miracle on 34th Street, The Foxes of Harrow, Sinbad the Sailor, The Homestretch, Sitting Pretty, Forbidden Street, Father Is a Fullback, Rio Grande, The Parent Trap, Wings of Eagles, McLintock!, Big Jake.*

Dennis O'Keefe

(b. Edward James Flanagan Jr., March 28, 1908, Fort Madison, Iowa; d. Aug. 31, 1968) Brawny and blond (with a distinctive "worry wrinkle" right between the brows), he served a long apprenticeship in scores of bits—billed as Bud Flanagan—before landing his first lead in 1938's *Bad Man of Brimstone*, for which he was indebted to Clark Gable; one short scene they did together at MGM in *Saratoga* so impressed Gable that he voluntarily went to bat for him and got him a contract; Metro execs promptly gave him a new monicker "because, when I told them my real name, they said Flanagan was too Irish"; was hailed at the start as the "new" Wallace Reid; a versatile actor, he alternately starred in dramas *(Hangmen Also Die)*, two-fisted action epics *(The Fighting Seabees)*, and farces, at which he was particularly gifted, such as *Up in Mabel's Room* and *Getting Gertie's Garter*; comedy talent came from his father, Edward Flanagan, who was half of the famous vaudeville act "Off and On," teamed with Neely Edwards; his mother, Charlotte Ravenscroft, a singing violinist, was also a big variety name; happened to be born in Iowa only because, between tours, his mother went there, to her mother's home, for the event; raised in theaters where his parents performed, he hit every town in America that boasted a vaudeville stage during the palmy days of two-a-day; was 12 when the family moved to Hollywood, where his father and his partner starred in a silent comedy series, "The Hall Room Boys"; expelled from Hollywood High, he completed his education at the Los Angeles Coaching School (private, for kids of professional entertainers) and USC's prep school; first movie job in his late teens: writer of "Our Gang" comedies; next was briefly in vaudeville, using his dad's old act, "A Lesson in Golf," and then on stage in *The Family Upstairs, The Broken Wing*, etc.; at the urging of his mother, he gave up show business and worked for two years at a Los Angeles wholesale plumbing supply house, but the smell of greasepaint proved too alluring to ignore; at 23, began playing bits (first in Irene Dunne's *Cimarron*), which he did for the next six years; in that time he also wrote screenplays, usually under the name Jonathan Ricks; wrote one titled *Don't Pull Your Punches*, about a young prizefighter, in which he hoped to play the lead; Warner Bros. bought it and filmed it as *The Kid Comes Back*, starring—Wayne Morris; for a short while in the '30s, was wed to Louise Stanley; was married from '40 on to Hungarian-born actress Steffi Duna, his leading lady in *The Girl from Havana* and the former wife of his friend John Carroll; gave up her career to care for O'Keefe, their son James, and Juliana, her daughter by John Carroll.

MOVIE HIGHLIGHTS: *Burn 'em Up O'Connor, Unexpected Father, That's Right, You're Wrong, La Conga Nights, Topper Returns, Lady Scarface, The Affairs of Jimmy Valentine, The Leopard Man, Hi Diddle Diddle, Abroad with Two Yanks, The Story of Dr. Wassell, Sensations of 1945, Affairs of Susan, Earl Carroll's Vanities, Brewster's Millions, Doll Face, T-Men, Walk a Crooked Mile, Mr. District Attorney, Raw Deal, The Great Dan Patch, Everything I Have Is Yours.*

Laurence Olivier

(b. Laurence Kerr Olivier, May 22, 1907, Dorking, England) "The greatest actor in the English language" is how this star, now Lord Olivier, is almost universally acclaimed; won the Best Actor Oscar for *Hamlet* ('48); has been nominated in the same category for *Wuthering Heights, Rebecca, Henry V, Richard III, The Entertainer, Othello, Sleuth, The Boys from Brazil*; was nominated as Best Support in *The Marathon Man*; regards Othello as the most difficult role in drama ("Woe betide anybody who plays Othello and thinks it's not going to kill him, because if it doesn't, he's no good"); has been steadily on screen since '30, when he appeared in three: *Two Many Crooks, The Temporary Widow, Murder for Sale*; was married that same year to actress Jill Esmond—mother of his son Tarquin—from whom he was divorced in '40; when first in Hollywood, under contract to RKO (1931–32), he made no lasting impression in the three leads he played—in *Friends and Lovers* with Lili Damita, *The Yellow Ticket* with Elissa Landi, and *Westward Passage* with Ann Harding; returned to England for other films, including *No Funny*

Business with Jill Esmond, before MGM lured him back to America with the promise of the lead opposite Greta Garbo in *Queen Christina*; tested with "The Great Swede," but she insisted the role go to her onetime love, John Gilbert; Hollywood did not see him again until '39, when, as Heathcliff, he established himself for all time as a great romantic star in *Wuthering Heights*; was accompanied to the Coast then by his new love, and future wife (1940–60), Vivien Leigh; beginning their romance while making *Fire Over England* ('37), they also co-starred in *21 Days Together* ('39) and again in *That Hamilton Woman* ('42), their final joint effort on the screen; their many later stage appearances together, mainly in the classics, became legend; after appearing in the failed *As You Like It* ('36), he expressed his conviction that Shakespeare could not be adapted to the screen; eight years later, it was he who directed and starred in *Henry V*, a film classic, as are *Hamlet* (received an Oscar as Best Picture of the Year) and *Richard III*, for which he also performed in this dual capacity; born to parents who "couldn't afford the theater" (father was a Church of England curate), his first exposure to drama came by observing his father in the pulpit and discovering "the difference between acting and being"; was still a child and already stagestruck when the family moved to London; attended All Saints Choir School and, at 9, played Brutus in a school production of *Julius Caesar*; was next at St. Edward's in Oxford; at 15 he made his first appearance on a professional stage, playing Katharine in *The Taming of the Shrew*—the production being part of the 1922 "Birthday Week" celebration at the Shakespeare Memorial Theater in Stratford-on-Avon; encouraged by his father, who had suppressed his own acting ambitions, he began studying for a theatrical career at 17 on a scholarship at London's Central School of Speech Training and Dramatic Art; then joined a Birmingham repertory theater, where he played juvenile leads for two years; next appeared in several flops in London and New York (*Murder on the Second Floor*); Noel Coward (whom he claims as one of the greatest influences in his life) then offered him the secondary role of Victor in *Private Lives*, which he reluctantly accepted only after the playwright drily commented: "You could do with being in a success for a change"; the play, a hit both in London and New York, altered forever his professional life, in which he found fame, honors, and wives; while filming *The Entertainer*, he fell in love with Joan Plowright, who played his daughter; married since '61, they have a son, Richard, and two daughters, Tamsin and Julie Kate; no longer physically able to star on stage, after having had cancer and a heart attack, he has played cameo roles in movies (many of them potboilers) in recent years, saying it is for his children: "I've got nothing to leave them but the money, which I can only make from films. . . . Nothing is beneath me if it pays well. I've earned the right to grab whatever I can in the time I've got left."

MOVIE HIGHLIGHTS: *The Divorce of Lady X, Q Planes* (aka *Clouds over Europe*), *Pride and Prejudice, The Invaders* (aka *The 49th Parallel*), *The Magic Box, Carrie, The Beggar's Opera, The Prince and the Showgirl, The Devil's Disciple, Spartacus, Team of Trial, Bunny Lake Is Missing, Khartoum, The Shoes of the Fisherman, Nicholas and Alexandra, The Seven Per Cent Solution, A Bridge Too Far, The Betsy, A Little Romance, Inchon, The Jazz Singer, Dracula, Clash of the Titans, The Bounty.*

Maria Ouspenskaya

(b. Maria Ouspenskaya, July 29, 1867, Tula, Russia; d. Dec. 3, 1949) Along with her wrinkled little face, quavery voice, and Tartar features, she had an attention-commanding way about her that was surely instructive to every star with whom she worked; to say "shared scenes" would be inaccurate—in any acting situation, the spotlight seemed only to be on her; made her first film, *Dodsworth*, at 69 and received an Oscar nomination as Best Support; played the Baroness von Obersdorf, who rigidly forbade older woman Ruth Chatterton to marry her son, recreating the role she had played on Broadway two years earlier; never married, except to her art, her main interest in movies was to earn money to support her School of Dramatic Art in New York (and, later, Hollywood), which she founded in '29; her own school was an offshoot of another, the American Laboratory Theater, which she and Richard Boleslavsky had established a few years earlier; the daughter of a lawyer, she studied singing at the Warsaw Conservatory and acting in Moscow at Adasheff's School of the Drama; in 1911, after performing in the Russian provinces, she joined the Moscow Art Theater, directed by Stanislavsky, whose methods she would teach throughout her life; came to America with the Art Theater in '22 and remained here after the troupe returned to Moscow; was a dominant figure on Broadway for more than a decade—in *The Saint, The Jest, The Three Sisters*, etc.; resided in Hollywood after '37, won a second Best Supporting Oscar nomination for *Love Affair* (as Boyer's grandmother), and, besides movie work, taught many future stars (Anne Baxter, Marie Windsor, etc.); the "real" Madame Ouspenskaya was not the kindly grandmother in *Kings Row*, though she was not an unkind person; closer to the mark was the demanding ballet mistress in *Waterloo Bridge*—the majordomo, the taskmaster, to whom the perfection of one's art was the only goal worth pursuing;

158

outspoken, she did not suffer fools lightly; after being directed by Josef von Sternberg in *The Shanghai Gesture*, she curled her lip and sniffed, "The man was an idiot"; eclectic in her choice of movie roles, she later appeared in a Western at Republic, *Wyoming*, with Vera Hruba Ralston; explained, "I did it for the same reason I did *The Wolf Man*; it was something I hadn't done before; I wanted to see what it was like—and I enjoyed it"; cigarettes were her only known vice, and she was a chainsmoker; died of burns suffered while smoking in bed.

MOVIE HIGHLIGHTS: *Conquest, The Rains Came, Judge Hardy and Son, Dr. Ehrlich's Magic Bullet, Beyond Tomorrow, Dance, Girl, Dance, The Mortal Storm, The Man I Married, The Mystery of Marie Roget, Frankenstein Meets the Wolf Man, Tarzan and the Amazons, I've Always Loved You, A Kiss in the Dark.*

Lilli Palmer

(b. Maria Lilli Peiser, March 12, 1914, Posen, Germany) Lovely and uniquely gifted star, with great serious eyes, whose apparently pragmatic view of the world has pervaded many of her performances; married Rex Harrison in '43, had a son (Carey), acted in movies with him *(The Rake's Progress, The Fourposter)*, starred with him on stage *(Bell, Book and Candle)*, stood by him through the Carole Landis suicide scandal, separated from him in '54, divorced him in '57; told this story about their divorce in the internationally best-selling autobiography *Change Lobsters and Dance*: Harrison, having an affair with actress Kay Kendall, learned she was terminally ill with leukemia, but he would not marry her unless his wife promised to come back to him after Kendall died ("I lied and pledged myself to return to him when all was over"); by the time Kendall died in '59, Palmer had been married for a year to Argentinean Carlos Thompson, a onetime Hollywood heartthrob *(Flame and the Flesh* with Lana Turner) and later an author, to whom she remains married; growing up in Berlin in a bourgeois Jewish home (father was a surgeon), she began her career on the stage of the State Theater of Darmstadt; escaping the Nazis and the threat of being taken to a concentration camp, she fled to Paris with her sister Irene; there, as refugees, the teen-aged sisters literally sang for their supper in cabarets and strip clubs in homemade dresses of green taffeta; a fellow German Jew who knew Palmer in Paris has recalled her as being "fiercely ambitious"; made her way to England and worked there in her first picture, *Crime Unlimited*, in '35, which was followed by 16 other

British films; went to Hollywood with Rex Harrison in '46, making her U.S. debut opposite Gary Cooper ("my girlhood idol" who became "a dear friend") in *Cloak and Dagger*; leaving California in '53, she has been back for only an occasional movie (*But Not for Me* with Gable, *The Pleasure of His Company* with Astaire), while making dozens elsewhere for European as well as American companies; performance opposite William Holden in *The Counterfeit Traitor*, filmed abroad, may well stand as her finest; besides her autobiography, she has written such outstandingly successful novels as *The Red Raven* and *A Time to Embrace* (writes them in her first language, German, and translates them into English); when her ex-husband penned his memoirs, *Rex*, in '75, she was less than pleased by "the distortions" and by "his treatment of me as some kind of Prussian nurse in the background"; as for his contention that she has no sense of humor, she retorted: "If a man who epitomizes English humor lived with a humorless woman for 14 years, he should either be sanctified or have a medal struck in his honor"; returned to Germany in '74 to receive the Grand Cross of the Order of Merit (Germany's highest civilian award), presented by the then West German President Gustav Heinemann.

MOVIE HIGHLIGHTS: *Secret Agent, Thunder Rock, English without Tears, My Girl Tisa, Body and Soul, No Minor Vices, The Long Dark Hall, La Vie a Deux, The Glass Tower, Maedchen in Uniform, Adorable Julia, The Miracle of the White Stallions, Operation Crossbow, Sebastian, Torpedo Bay, The Amorous Adventures of Moll Flanders, Oedipus, Hard Contract, The House That Screamed, Lotte in Weimer, The Boys from Brazil.*

Eleanor Parker

(b. Eleanor Parker, June 26, 1922, Cedarville, Ohio) As an ash blonde, with a low, whispery voice and a generally doleful air, she was at Warner Bros. throughout the '40s, beginning as a starlet and developing into a powerful dramatic star and winning a Best Actress Oscar nomination for *Caged*; that performance won her the "World's Best Actress" award at the Venice Film Festival; a second Oscar nomination came the next year ('51) for *Detective Story* at Paramount, followed by another four years later, for *Interrupted Melody* at MGM; played polo-crippled opera star Marjorie Lawrence in the latter, and her singing was supplied by Eileen Farrell; burst forth in the '50s as a glorious, spirited redhead in a spate of starring roles at MGM; made marriages as well as movies—four to date; first husband: Navy dentist Fred Losee

(1943–44); second: movie producer Bert Friedlob (1946–53; children: Susan, Sharon, and Richard); third: artist Paul Clemens (1954–64; son: Paul Jr.); in '66, became the wife of theater manager Raymond N. Hirsch; the youngest of three children of a high school mathematics teacher, she studied as a child (already determined to act) at the Tucker School of Expression in Cleveland, where the family then lived; once said it was a Frankie Darro movie serial, *Burn 'em Up Barnes*, that turned her on to acting; during two school vacations, served an apprenticeship with a stock company on Martha's Vineyard, paying her way by ushering and waiting on tables; as a youngster, she kept scrapbooks on movie personalities, including one on Ann Harding, who later played her mother in *Mission to Moscow*; went directly from high school to the Pasadena Playhouse in California; had been there only one semester when, sitting in the audience at a Main Stage production, she caught the eye of Irving Kunin, an assistant casting director at Warners; made her screen test on June 24, 1941, and signed her contract two days later, on her 19th birthday; moved into a small apartment near the Burbank studio on Hollywood Way, where Amelia Earhart once lived, but her flight to fame was a bit bumpier than that of the famous aviatrix; paid her dues in bits *(Busses Roar)* and Bs *(Mysterious Doctor)*; first major film lead was in 1944's *The Very Thought of You* with Dennis Morgan; even after other prominent roles, her screen personality still was not fixed, and she was spoken of as "the star least recognized off screen"; in the '46 remake of Maugham's *Of Human Bondage*, she played Mildred, the tarty, utterly selfish Cockney waitress, the same role that had catapulted Bette Davis to stardom; "No one can look at me after this," she said, "and decide I'd be just perfect as the ingenue in the next picture they're casting"; they never did; bigger and ever better opportunities lay just ahead, and every moviegoer knew her by name *and* face.

MOVIE HIGHLIGHTS: *Hollywood Canteen, Between Two Worlds, Crime by Night, Pride of the Marines, Never Say Goodbye, Escape Me Never, The Woman in White, Voice of the Turtle, Three Secrets, Chain Lightning, Valentino, Scaramouche, Above and Beyond, Escape from Fort Bravo, Valley of the Kings, The Naked Jungle, Many Rivers to Cross, The Man with the Golden Arm, Lizzie, The King and Four Queens, A Hole in the Head, The Sound of Music.*

Larry Parks

(b. Samuel Klausman, Dec. 13, 1914, Olathe, Kans.; d. April 13, 1975) Appearing before the House Committee on Un-American Activities in '51, he was the first star to admit, tearfully, that he had been a Communist—from 1941 to 1945; pleaded—unsuccessfully—that he not be forced to implicate others; that day his career as a star died; records indicate that he made just two more movies—*Cross-Up*, a '58 B picture made abroad in which he played the lead, and John Huston's *Freud*, in which he had a character role; five years before that fateful day in Washington, D.C., he'd starred in and been nominated for a Best Actor Oscar for *The Jolson Story*; Al Jolson, though far too old then, had wanted to portray himself in his life story and gave the young actor only grudging assistance in his performance (though, of course, he did the songs on the soundtrack); as filming progressed, Jolson opined, "The guy gives me the creeps watching him—the way he has all my little mannerisms and habits down so pat"; Parks later played the "Mammy" singer a second time, in *Jolson Sings Again*; born of well-to-do German-Irish parents, he grew up in Joliet, Ill.; planning to study medicine, he got his B.S. in chemistry in '36 at the University of Illinois; appearances in college plays inspired a change of career, though advisers urged against it; had a physical handicap about which movie fans never knew—a childhood illness had left him with not only a weakened heart, but one leg shorter than the other, which he camouflaged with special shoes; spent one year (at $30 a week) with the Manhattan Stock Co. of Fitchburg, Mass., then another two years in Manhattan itself, playing small roles with the Group Theater; death of his father caused him to return to Illinois to care for his mother; worked as a dining car inspector for the New York Central in Chicago and next as a copywriter in an advertising agency; John Garfield, a friend from the Group Theater, then encouraged him to give movies a try; arrived in Hollywood on Sept. 16, 1940, and scraped by at first as a $3-a-day actor in Biblical shorts made by an independent producer; Columbia Pictures casting director Max Arnow finally used him to assist in a screen test of character actor Barry Fitzgerald for *Here Comes Mr. Jordan*; Fitzgerald didn't get the part (Claude Rains did), but Parks got a stock contract; was at Columbia, first in many Bs, from '41 to '51, when, after his appearance before the House Un-American Activities Committee, his contract was abruptly terminated ("by mutual consent," claimed the studio); in a '46 magazine profile on him, it was stated that "His one great hobby is his active interest in the Hollywood Actors' Lab"; testifying before the Committee, he acknowledged there were Communists attached to some organizations with which he had been affiliated—"the Actors' Lab, for instance . . ."; was married from '44 on to actress Betty Garrett, by whom he had two sons, Garrett Christopher and Andrew Lawrence, who, as Andy Parks, has acted on TV.

MOVIE HIGHLIGHTS: *Mystery Ship, Harmon of Michigan, Three Girls about Town, Blondie Goes to College, Flight Lieutenant, Atlantic Convoy, You Were Never Lovelier, Alias Boston Blackie, They All Kissed the Bride, Reveille with Beverly, The Black Parachute, Sergeant Mike, Counter-Attack, Renegades, Down to Earth, The Swordsman, The Gallant Blade, Emergency Wedding, Love Is Better Than Ever.*

John Payne

(b. John Payne, May 23, 1912, Roanoke, Va.) An Adonis in face and physique (not to mention having an agreeable singing voice), he set femme hearts aflutter from coast-to-coast, especially after going to 20th Century–Fox in '40; was *the* male pinup of 1942–43, when starring in Technicolor musicals like *Springtime in the Rockies* and *Hello, Frisco, Hello* (romancing Alice Faye, with whom he starred on Broadway in '73 in the musical *Good News)*; a big guy (6′3″, 190 lbs.), he had no choice when singing in nightclubs but to stay in cheap hotel rooms, sleeping in dinky beds too small for his frame; gave himself a special reward once he'd made it in movies: "I swore then that some day I was going to have a bed big enough for me. The first thing I did after getting my first big role in a picture was to have one especially made—8 feet long and 7 feet wide"; inherited his musical talents—is a direct descendant of John Howard Payne, composer of "Home, Sweet Home," and his mother was an opera singer; his family, once wealthy, lost its fortune early in the Depression; to earn tuition money to attend Mercersburg (Pa.) Academy and Roanoke College (which, in the '70s, gave him an honorary Ph.D), he worked as a dishwasher on a ship sailing to Cuba, Mexico, and South America; went on to get his degree at the Pulitzer School of Journalism at Columbia University, paying his way by working as a male nurse to a widower's two children; was next in burlesque singing "A Pretty Girl Is Like a Melody" during the tableaux, then a boxer, a wrestler (known as Tiger John Payne, later as Alexei Petroff, the Savage of the Steppes), a radio and band singer; on Broadway, he landed a bit in *At Home Abroad*, starring Bea Lillie and Reginald Gardiner (also was his understudy; Gardiner later supported him in the movie *The Dolly Sisters)*; was noticed in this show by producer Sam Goldwyn, who put him under contract; movie debut was a bit in 1936's *Dodsworth*; soon dropped by Goldwyn, he moved along to Warners (1938–

39), where he scored a hit in *Garden of the Moon* with Margaret Lindsay (in a singing bandleader role rejected by Dick Powell), followed by kid-brother parts in *Wings of the Navy* and *Indianapolis Speedway*; major fame came next at Fox, where he starred for seven years, with time out for Air Force service; a dichotomy existed between the man and his image—often cast in cocky roles, he was actually an extraordinarily shy person, and, far from being the man-about-town he seemed, he preferred privacy and short-story writing to night-clubbing; was married first (1937–43) to Anne Shirley, by whom he has a daughter, Julie (a sometime actress), and next (1944–50) to Gloria De Haven, mother of his Kathie and Thomas; has been married since '53 to Alexandra Curtis; extremely wealthy (many kinds of investments), he lives with her in a hilltop mansion overlooking the Pacific at Malibu, acts when he feels like it, serves on the vestry of St. Aidan's Episcopal Church, and writes poetry.

MOVIE HIGHLIGHTS: *Maryland, Star Dust, Tin Pan Alley, The Great Profile, The Great American Broadcast, Sun Valley Serenade, Weekend in Havana, Remember the Day, To the Shores of Tripoli, Iceland, The Dolly Sisters, Sentimental Journey, Wake Up and Dream, The Razor's Edge, The Miracle on 34th Street, Larceny, The Saxon Charm, El Paso, The Crooked Way, The Eagle and the Hawk, 99 River Street.*

Gregory Peck

(b. Eldred Gregory Peck, April 5, 1916, La Jolla, Calif.) "Lincolnesque," they labeled him, because of his rangy size (6′3″) and rough-hewn hand-someness; the first in Hollywood to spot this was producer David O. Selznick who, after viewing Peck's earliest screen test (in '41), observed: "He photographs like Abe Lincoln, but if he has a great personality, I don't think it comes through"; had ordered a test on the actor on the recommendation of a studio scout who had seen him on stage; Peck did two scenes—one from the script of *This Above All*, a movie about to be made ("Satisfactory," said the producer, but it was "nothing to get excited about"), and another from *The Young in Heart* (referring to the actor who had played the part in the movie, Selznick said, "My respect for Doug Fairbanks Jr. goes up after seeing Peck"); the actor went on to score a personal hit in a short-lived 1942 Broadway play, *The Morning Star*, with Katharine Cornell; the day after it closed, he was married to Greta Rice, who had done Miss Cornell's hair and makeup; had three sons: Jonathan (committed suicide in '75), Stephen, and Carey; divorced in '54; both of his subsequent plays, *The Willow and I* and *Sons and Soldiers*, were flops but rated him a raft of movie offers; signed with Casey Robinson and starred in his independent production of *Days of Glory* in '44—taking second billing to the producer's ballerina-actress wife, Tamara Toumanova; his first moment on the screen was a knockout: entering a darkened room, he struck a match and lighted an oil lamp, the soft rays perfectly illuminating the splendidly photogenic planes of his face, then he spoke, in that deep, assured voice, and a star was born; was such an immediate hit that his contract was soon being shared by MGM, 20th Century–Fox, RKO, and—David O. Selznick; "integrity," from the start, was the keynote of his screen personality (his off screen one, too) and was a main reason for his enormous public appeal; that characteristic had much to do with his winning a Best Actor Oscar eventually, and belatedly, for *To Kill a Mockingbird* ('62); had been nominated earlier for *The Keys of the Kingdom*, *The Yearling*, *Gentleman's Agreement*, and *Twelve O'Clock High*; was among the Box-Office Top Ten in '47 and '52; the son of a druggist, he attended St. John's Military School in Los Angeles, completed high school in San Diego, attended San Diego State College for one year before quitting to drive a truck for an oil company; a year later, he entered the University of California at Berkeley as a premed student but became an English major before graduating; acting in a play (his first ever) during his senior year fired his interest in acting; the play was *Moby Dick*, in which he was the First Mate, never guessing that one day he would star as Captain Ahab in the movie; aiming for Broadway, he went East in the summer of '40 and worked first as a barker for the Meteor Speedway ride at the World's Fair; next was a tour guide at Rockefeller Center, a Sears-Roebuck catalogue model, a scholarship student at the Neighborhood Playhouse, and a trainee actor at Virginia's Barter Theater; toured with Katharine Cornell in both *The Doctor's Dilemma* and *Rose Burke* before she hired him for the Broadway play that put him on the road to fame—but he never got to act with his boyhood movie–dream girl, Madge Evans; has been married since '55 to Veronique Passani, by whom he has a son, Anthony, and a daughter, Cecilia; has said of his children: "I hope they inherit my luck."

MOVIE HIGHLIGHTS: *The Keys of the Kingdom, The Valley of Decisions, Spellbound, Duel in the Sun, The Yearling, The Macomber Affair, Gentleman's Agreement, The Paradine Case, Yellow Sky, The Walls of Jericho, Twelve O'Clock High, The Gunfighter, David and Bathsheba, Captain Horatio Hornblower, The Snows of Kilimanjaro, Roman Holiday, Night People, The Man with a Million, The Man in the Gray Flannel Suit, The Big Country, On the Beach, The Guns of Navarone.*

Susan Peters

(b. Suzanne Carnahan, July 3, 1921, Spokane, Wash.; d. Oct. 23, 1952) A brilliant future—which wasn't to be—was predicted for this delicate beauty in '42 after *Random Harvest*, in which she was Kitty, the young English aristocrat in love with Ronald Colman during his period of amnesia; performance won her an Oscar nomination as Best Support; indeed poignant in retrospect are these lines from the first magazine profile ever published on her: "She looks as if sorrow and defeat have never crossed her path; you sense that nothing would get her down—that she would go on enjoying every minute of her life"; years later, on New Year's Day, 1945, as her career was reaching its peak, she and her husband, Richard Quine, were on a dove-hunting trip; picked up a rifle—its safety catch not being on—that discharged, sending a bullet coursing upward to pierce a lung and lodge against her spine; was permanently paralyzed from the waist down; put up a brave front afterwards, pointing out that, in her own family, she'd had two examples of women triumphing over sorrow and handicaps; was 7 when her father was killed in an automobile accident; her mother (a grand-niece of Gen. Robert E. Lee), who had never held a job, took her children—Susan and Bob—to California and started a new life, working first in a dress shop and later managing an apartment house; "My mother's life was not easy but she never complained; we were poor but we managed, and had fun"; also, there was her French-born grandmother, Madame Marie Patteneaude, who established a famous method of facial contouring having to do with the beauty of both face and spirit; for the final ten years of her life, Mme. Patteneaude was almost totally blind, but even close friends, seeing her move about with assured grace, did not know her vision was impaired; confined to a wheelchair, Susan starred in a movie, *The Sign of the Ram* (playing a paralyzed murderess), adopted and cared for a child (Timothy), acted on radio, toured in plays (*The Glass Menagerie, The Barretts of Wimpole Street*), wrote for magazines, and had her own "live" TV series, "Miss Susan"; added sorrow was hers when her mother died of a heart attack; a Catholic, born and reared, she was at a convent school, Flintridge Sacred Heart, for several years before graduating from Hollywood High; a family friend with connections at MGM then helped her get a small part in *Susan and God*; next, while attending Max Reinhardt's School of Dramatic Arts on a scholarship, she was seen by a Warner Bros. scout in a showcase production and given a stock contract; at this studio from '40 to '42, she played minor roles in a number of movies (starting in *River's End* with Dennis Morgan) under her own name before making still other pictures (*The Big Shot, Three Sons o' Guns*) as Susan Peters; began her contract at MGM in '42 in a B picture, *Tish*, in which she and Richard Quine, her future husband (and destined to be a director), played the romantic leads; had gone on to more substantial roles (notably in *Song of Russia* opposite Robert Taylor) when her tragedy occurred; MGM paid her hospital bills and for two years, until she asked to terminate the contract, kept her on a token $100 weekly salary; in '48, to her husband's distress, she insisted upon a divorce; after her death a close friend, RKO talent coach Lillian Albertson, said, "Susan simply lost the will to live and, making it even sadder, she also lost her faith in God."

MOVIE HIGHLIGHTS: *Santa Fe Trail*, *Sockaroo*, *Meet John Doe*, *Here Comes Happiness* (all as Suzanne Carnahan), *Andy Hardy's Double Life*, *Dr. Gillespie's New Assistant*, *Young Ideas*, *Assignment in Brittany*, *Keep Your Powder Dry*.

Walter Pidgeon

(b. Walter Pidgeon, Sept. 23, 1897, East St. John, New Brunswick, Canada; d. Sept. 25, 1984) Solid, pipe-smoking star, with a deep, mellifluous speaking voice, whose popularity owed much to the eight classy, mature love dramas at MGM in which he and Greer Garson co-starred; among them were *Mrs. Miniver* and *Madame Curie*, both of which brought him Academy Award nominations as Best Actor; their perennial teaming began in '41 with *Blossoms in the Dust* and continued through 1953's *Scandal at Scourie*; remained lifelong friends and, after he suffered an inner ear-destroying fall at 80, she would visit him at his Bel Air home and call often; a veteran of more than 100 movies, he regarded *Madame Curie* and *Command Decision*, with Gable, as his best; had a well-off start in life as the son of a man who owned a chain of mercantile stores; lied about his age to get into the Canadian Army for the first World War; after attending the University of New Brunswick, worked for a Boston bank, studied singing on the side, and hoped for a theatrical career; at 25, married childhood sweetheart Edna Pickles, who died two years later after giving birth to his only child, Edna; was later married, from '30 on, to the former Ruth Walker; Fred Astaire heard him sing at a Boston social gathering, insisted his baritone voice deserved to be heard from a stage, and got him an audition, at which he sang "The Rosary," with which he was later long associated; made his singing debut with Elsie Janis at New York's Aeolian Concert Hall; first stage appearance was in *You Never Can Tell* with Janis, after which he toured with her and her *At Home* revue in England and throughout Europe;

returned to New York to vaudeville, Broadway *(Puzzles of 1925)*, and a contract with Victor Records, where he recorded and introduced such popular hits as "What'll I Do?" and "All Alone"; made his movie debut in a '25 silent, *Mannequin*, in which he played the lead opposite Dolores Costello; did many other silents *(Mlle. Modiste, The Girl from Rio,* etc.); first talkie: *Melody of Love* ('28) at Universal; worked at various studios before signing with MGM in '37, starting his 20-year stint there in Jean Harlow's swan song, *Saratoga*; heyday as a star began in '41 with *Man Hunt* and *How Green Was My Valley*, both made, ironically, on loan-out to 20th Century–Fox; became an American citizen in '43; served on the Screen Actors Guild Board of Directors for 33 years; left MGM after 1956's *The Rack*, with a handsome pension, after which he returned to Broadway *(The Happiest Millionaire)* and starred in a lengthy roster of films at other studios; final role was a cameo in Mae West's *Sextette* ('78); oddity; had a great memory for faces but none for names— called all but his friends "Joe," and the name stencilled on the back of his canvas chair at the studio was "Joe Pidgeon."

MOVIE HIGHLIGHTS: *Man-Proof, Too Hot to Handle, The Shopworn Angel, Society Lawyer, Stronger Than Desire, Nick Carter, Master Detective, It's a Date, Design for Scandal, White Cargo, Mrs. Parkington, Weekend at the Waldorf, Holiday in Mexico, The Secret Heart, If Winter Comes, Julia Misbehaves, That Forsyte Woman, The Miniver Story, Million Dollar Mermaid, The Bad and the Beautiful, Executive Suite, Funny Girl.*

Jane Powell

(b. Suzanne Burce, April 1, 1928, Portland, Ore.) Petite (5'2"), blue-eyed soprano whose Technicolor musicals for MGM made a mint and whose marriages and divorces (four) made headlines; first husband was ice skater Geary Steffen (1949–53; children: Geary Jr. and Suzanne); second was auto dealer Pat Nerney (1954–63; daughter: Lindsay); third was artists' manager James Fitzgerald (1965–76), who continued to be her manager; and fourth was writer David Parlour (1979–81); when she filed for divorce, Parlour told the court she had total assets of $1.7 million, that he had "helped" her career (an assertion denied by her manager), and asked for $3,915 a month alimony, plus other sums including $25,000 for his lawyer's fee; the upshot: She agreed to pay $1,000 a month alimony for a year; in '82, she began a relationship with another former child star, Dickie Moore, with whom she bought a house in Wilton, Conn.; columnist Earl Wilson quoted her as saying then: "No more marriages, no more babies, and no more puppies"; met Moore when he interviewed her for his book, *Twinkle, Twinkle, Little Star*, about ex–kid stars; first sang on a children's radio program at 7 in her hometown; started voice lessons at 11 and soon had her own show on local radio; went to Hollywood at 14 with her parents, ostensibly for a three-week vacation, but actually to try for an audition on a CBS Radio show, "Hollywood Showcase," hosted by Janet Gaynor, which spotlighted new talent; got on, sang "Il Bacio," and was such a hit that she appeared on the program for six consecutive weeks (breaking a record); said Hedda Hopper, who had replaced Gaynor as host in the midst of this excitement, "All Hollywood talent scouts were asked to listen in. They did. And both David Selznick and Metro were competing for Jane"; she signed with MGM, her dad opened a small malt shop on Sunset Boulevard (the unfashionable end), and both succeeded; first two movies, *Song of the Open Road* (in which she played a girl named Jane Powell) and *Delightfully Dangerous*, were made on loan-out to independent producer Charles R. Rogers; *Holiday in Mexico* ('46), with Walter Pidgeon (her favorite actor) playing her father, was her first at MGM and her first in color; was typecast as a perennial juvenile until *Royal Wedding* ('51), in which, as the dance partner–sister of Fred Astaire romanced by Peter Lawford, she had her first grown-up role; was a last-minute replacement for Judy Garland; one of her hit pictures, *Small Town Girl*, was, interestingly, a remake of one in which Janet Gaynor had starred; hit her peak with 1954's *Seven Brides for Seven Brothers*, remained at MGM for one more year, and then starred in a few additional pictures elsewhere before leaving the screen after 1958's *Enchanted Island*; next did TV, concerts, and nightclub work; revitalized her career in '74 when Debbie Reynolds (who'd played her older sister in *Two Weeks with Love*) left the Broadway hit *Irene* and she took over the starring role; remains a star in dinner theaters and summer musicals; possible explanation for her forever-youthful looks: "I take care of myself: vitamins, exercise, no booze or cigarettes—everything in moderation."

MOVIE HIGHLIGHTS: *Three Daring Daughters, Luxury Liner, A Date with Judy, Nancy Goes to Rio, Rich, Young and Pretty, Three Girls and a Sailor, Athena, Deep in My Heart, Hit the Deck, The Girl Most Likely, The Female Animal.*

Tyrone Power

(b. Tyrone Edmund Power, May 5, 1914, Cincinnati, Ohio; d. Nov. 15, 1958) "My God, he looks like a chimp!" exclaimed 20th Century–Fox chief Darryl F. Zanuck after viewing the actor's screen test; spotting the problem, eyebrows that grew together across his forehead, Zanuck's wife, Virginia, quietly suggested: "Shave them"; with shaven brows, becoming perhaps the most photogenic male in movies, the actor starred at the studio for 19 years (1936–55), with time out, three years, for wartime duty in the Marines—going from private to first lieutenant-pilot of C-46 transports over Japan-held areas; was forever and indisputably the prince of the Fox lot; was considered first for every major role; admirably suited for any type of part, he did costume epics *(Marie Antoinette)*, Westerns *(Jesse James)*, swashbucklers *(Captain from Castile)*, war films *(Crash Dive)*, musicals *(Alexander's Ragtime Band)*, contemporary comedies *(That Wonderful Urge)*, and dramas *(Johnny Apollo)*; was among the Box-Office Top Ten 1938–40; descended from actors from the Irish county of Tyrone, he was the third, after his father (a stage matinee idol who also was in many movies) and his great-grandfather, to carry the name Tyrone Power; his Indiana-born mother, Helen Emma Reaume, acted on the stage as Patia Power; also a drama teacher, she trained him from childhood for the theater; at 17, after graduating from a Cincinnati high school, he played supporting parts in Shakespearean plays in which his father starred at the Chicago Civic Auditorium; later that year, went to Hollywood with his father who, playing a major role in *The Miracle Man*, died on the set of a heart attack—in the arms of his son; did bits in two movies: *Tom Brown of Culver* and *Flirtation Walk*; returning to Chicago, he acted on radio and in stage shows at the Century of Progress Exposition, then in a play, *Romance*, in a downtown theater; next went to New York and played Benvolio, friend of Romeo, in Katharine Cornell's production of *Romeo and Juliet*, followed by another role in her next, *Saint Joan*; discovered by 20th Century–Fox, he made his debut there in '36 in a small role in Simone Simon's *Girls' Dormitory* and became a star later that year in *Lloyds of London*; studio rigged up a series of highly publicized "romances" with its femme stars and starlets—Sonja Henie, Loretta Young, Janet Gaynor, Marjorie Weaver, Nancy Kelly, and Arleen Whelan; was married to and divorced from other actresses: France's Annabella (1939–48; adopted her daughter, Anne) and Linda Christian (1949–55; daughters: Romina and Taryn); between marriages, had a headline-making romance with Lana Turner; when he died of a heart attack while filming *Solomon and Sheba* (a movie that was started over again with Yul Brynner starring), he'd been married for a few months to non-pro Debbie

Minardos; she gave birth to his son, Tyrone IV, after his death; this lookalike son made his movie debut in '85 in a leading role in *Cocoon* at, appropriately, 20th Century–Fox, and heading the supporting cast, adding to the deja vu aspect of it, was his father's frequent co-star Don Ameche; reportedly, the young actor "was not especially moved to probe Don Ameche for anecdotes about his parent"; in her autobiography, *Linda*, Linda Christian wrote: "A woman can love a man for his character, his intelligence and capability. Or love him for his beauty. Or for his sensitivity and understanding. If all those qualities are embodied in the one man, the woman he loves is incredibly fortunate. I married such a man"; at the end of her marriage to Power, she added, he seemed greatly changed and "sensitivity had been abandoned wholly for sensuality"; whispers that he was bisexual began early in his career, and confirmation was offered in Hector Arce's book *The Secret Life of Tyrone Power*; Joan Fontaine, his co-star in *This Above All*, has said: "Of course we all heard stories about Ty. But he was such a fine man, such a gentleman, that it made no difference to us; his private life was his own business."

MOVIE HIGHLIGHTS: *Thin Ice, Second Honeymoon, In Old Chicago, Suez, Rose of Washington Square, The Rains Came, Brigham Young— Frontiersman, The Mark of Zorro, Blood and Sand, A Yank in the R.A.F., Son of Fury, The Black Swan, The Razor's Edge, Nightmare Alley, Luck of the Irish, Prince of Foxes, The Black Rose, An American Guerrilla in the Philippines, Mississippi Gambler, The Long Gray Line, The Eddy Duchin Story, The Sun Also Rises, Witness for the Prosecution.*

Robert Preston

(b. Robert Preston Meservey, June 8, 1918, Newton Highlands, Mass.) "Vital, virile, excitingly alive—a powerhouse of a man," said a *New York Times* critic, expressing a view long held by movie fans; except for a short time in his teens, when a parking lot attendant at the Santa Anita race track, he has never been anything but an actor; "Acting," he says still, "is a joy, a goddam joy!"; family moved to California when he was 2; a drama coach at Lincoln High (in the tenderloin district of Los Angeles) had him playing Hamlet when only 15; the following year—already mature looking and 6'1", with a rich voice and rugged physique—he turned professional and did the title role in *Julius Caesar* for a repertory company headed by Patia Power (Tyrone's mother); at 18, joined the Pasadena Playhouse and remained there for two years and 42 plays; doing one play, *Night over Taos*, in which he played the villain, he fell in love with the ingenue, Kay Feltus, from Indiana; was still not quite 20 when, in '38, Paramount put him under contract, fibbed to the press about his age, had him grow a moustache to seem older, and put him in a few Bs (*King of Alcatraz, Illegal Traffic*) to gain experience; became a star at 21 when Cecil B. De Mille cast him as Barbara Stanwyck's gambler husband in *Union Pacific*; the actress gave him a medal of the martyred St. Genesius which, for luck, he still wears on a gold chain around his neck; says of Stanwyck: "Nobody else was or is like her; if St. Genesius was the patron saint of actors, she is the patroness"; following him into movies, Kay Feltus, taking Catherine Craig as her screen name, did one lead at Monogram, then was given a test at Paramount, with Preston assisting in a scene from *Skylark*; "It was the first and last time we worked together in film," she says. "We did the test on Monday, I signed a contract on Thursday, and on Friday we were married in Las Vegas"; the year was 1940—they are still married; before going to war, Preston became a popular favorite via leads in nearly two dozen pictures; was away for three years as an intelligence officer (captain, finally) with the Air Forces' 555th Bombardment Squadron in England, France, and Belgium; later, with a few exceptions (*The Macomber Affair*, "The Bride Comes to Yellow Sky" segment of *Face to Face*, etc.), the roles that came his way left him dissatisfied; for three decades after '51, movies took a back seat to his work on Broadway; starred in almost 20 shows, including the two musicals that won him Tony Awards: *The Music Man* (as con artist Professor Harold Hill, singing "76 Trombones," he fast-talked his way through 882 performances before marching on to do the movie version) and *I Do! I Do!* with Mary Martin (his leading lady at Paramount in 1941's *New York Town*); favorite role, on stage and screen, was in *The Dark at the Top of the Stairs*; was nominated for the Best Supporting Oscar in *Victor/Victoria* ('82), playing (most unlikely casting) a homosexual; saying he's had "a charmed, wonderful life," the exuberant star adds, "Every move I've made in my life has somehow or other been related to being in the right place at the right time."

MOVIE HIGHLIGHTS: *Beau Geste, Typhoon, North West Mounted Police, The Lady from Cheyenne, Parachute Battalion, The Night of January 16th, This Gun for Hire, Reap the Wild Wind, Wake Island, Wild Harvest, Whispering Smith, Blood on the Moon, The Big City, Tulsa, The Sundowners, When I Grow Up, My Outlaw Brother, Best of the Bad Men, How the West Was Won, All the Way Home, Child's Play, Junior Bonner, Mame, Semi-Tough, S.O.B.*

Ella Raines

(b. Ella Wallace Raubes, Aug. 6, 1921, Snoqualmie Falls, Wash.) Green-eyed, with a distinctive shoulder-length dark mane worn in a loose, "natural" way, she began at the top in '43 as the feminine lead (and only woman) in *Corvette K-225*, with no prior professional experience; in high school and at the University of Washington, though, this only child of a lumber company engineer had been in numerous plays; because it would interfere with her dramatic studies, she'd even declined to join a sorority; four months in New York after receiving her college degree did not bring any stage offers but did result in an introduction to a Hollywood agent, Charles Feldman, who arranged a test, a contract, and her debut role at Universal, where she remained a star through '47; less than frightened at facing a camera for the first time, she said then, "I've never been shy or at a loss, ever"; never a "starving starlet," she lived from the start in a posh Beverly Hills apartment, drove a flashy green Dodge convertible, had many highly placed movieland friends (Spencer Tracy, 20th Century–Fox bigwig Joseph Schenck, director Sam Wood's actress daughter, K. T. Stevens, etc.), and was squired about town by a hand-some young actor named John Forsythe (of later "Dynasty" fame), though their "dates" were strictly for publicity; suppressed by her studio for a while was the fact that in the summer of '42, months before arriving in Hollywood, she had married her high school sweetheart, Lt. Kenneth Trout; a bomber pilot, he'd made major by the time they divorced in '45; 1944 was her best screen year, when she played leads in three that, in their respective genres, are regarded as classics: *The Suspect* with Charles Laughton, *Phantom Lady*, and the Preston Sturges comedy *Hail the Conquering Hero*; in '47, she became the wife of Air Force Major Robin Olds, by whom she has two daughters, Christina and Susan; a jet pilot hero of the Korean War, Olds eventually was promoted to brigadier general and became commandant of the Air Force Academy at Colorado Springs, Colo.; the actress actively continued her work in movies through '52; five years later, while her husband was on duty in England, she starred in one picture there, *The Man in the Road*; after she and Olds were divorced in the early '80s, she returned to Hollywood to live and, besides teaching acting, resumed her career—as a character actress.

MOVIE HIGHLIGHTS: *Cry Havoc, Tall in the Saddle, Enter Arsene Lupin, The Strange Affair of Uncle Harry, The Runaround, White Tie and Tails, Brute Force, Time Out of Mind, The Web, The Senator Was Indiscreet, Impact, The Walking Hills, A Dangerous Profession, The Second Face, Singing Guns, The Fighting Coast Guard, Ride the Man Down.*

(b. Vera Hruba, July 19, 1919, Prague, Czechoslovakia) For *Ice-Capades of 1941*, at tiny, dusty Republic (famous for its Westerns), studio president Herbert J. Yates signed this 22-year-old skating star, who was runner-up to Sonja Henie in the '36 Olympics, and, though 40 years older, soon fell in love with her; first billed Vera Hruba, she was next Vera Hruba Ralston (a moniker dearly loved by nightclub comics), and, finally, simply Vera Ralston; dazzling on the ice, she was less so as an actress and was not readymade for motion picture cameras—nose was a bit long, face was somewhat thin, and her accent was decidedly thick; starred in one picture after another and soon became known as "the actress most damned by the critics" (and her fan mail never caused June Allyson sleepless nights); unable to marry her until '52 (he already had a wife), and perhaps to compensate for the love she didn't get from the public, Yates (his studio flock affectionately called him "Papa") showered her with costly baubles; after interviewing her, one writer (Thomas Wiseman) reported: "On her fingers she wears diamonds large enough to pass for knuckledusters. On her wrist she is sporting something which . . . looks like a portable rainbow and . . . proves to be a watch deeply imbedded in sapphires, pearls, diamonds, amethysts"; during her 17-year tenure at Republic, no other actress was given a big-star build-up by the studio; still, being a warm and witty (not to mention deeply religious) woman, she was well-liked by her colleagues, many of whom (co-star John Carroll, actress Blanche Yurka, etc.) became lasting friends; John Wayne became, by chance, a first-time millionaire thanks to her; to persuade a reluctant Wayne to co-star with her (at her request) in *Dakota*, Herbert Yates promised the actor he'd next star him in a million-dollar epic; before filming on that one began, Yates talked Wayne into waiving his $150,000 salary in exchange for a percentage of the movie's profits; *Wake of the Red Witch* was such a huge success that the actor's share was $1 million-plus—the highest single-picture fee ever earned by a star up to that time ('48); married to Herbert J. Yates for 14 years, until his death at 85, Vera Ralston revealed herself to be the most economically minded actress ever to wed a nabob; as the mistress of a mansion filled with art treasures, she said, "I don't believe in throwing money around. I buy half a cow and put it in the deep freeze. That way I save twenty cents on a pound of beef. . . . My home in Hollywood is entirely floored in marble. This way I save on carpets. The cost of things is terrible"; Republic stockholders eventually declared war on the studio chief and the actress; in a '56 lawsuit, it was claimed that of all Vera Ralston's starring vehicles (22 at the time), only two had even made back their negative costs; during the two years the bitter proxy fight lasted, Yates presented her in four more pictures, the last of which was *The Man Who Died Twice*; in '58 he was deposed, and she simultaneously retired from the screen; when he died in '66, Yates left her half of his estate, which was valued at more than $10 million.

MOVIE HIGHLIGHTS: *The Lady and the Monster, Storm over Lisbon, Lake Placid Serenade, Murder in the Music Hall, The Plainsman and the Lady, Wyoming, The Flame, Angel on the Amazon, I, Jane Doe, The Fighting Kentuckian, Surrender, The Wild Blue Yonder, Belle Le Grand, Hoodlum Empire, Fair Wind to Java, A Perilous Journey, Jubilee Trail, Timberjack, Accused of Murder.*

Ronald Reagan

(b. Ronald Wilson Reagan, Feb. 6, 1911, Tampico, Ill.) During his years at Warner Bros., studio casting directors put many actors in the "White House"—Victor Kilian as Lincoln in *Virginia City*, Joseph Crehan as Grant in *They Died with Their Boots On*, Captain Jack Young as Franklin D. Roosevelt in *Yankee Doodle Dandy*, and, in *Princess O'Rourke*, an anonymous stand-in for FDR (a figure hovering outside a door and nodding approval at the White House wedding of Olivia de Havilland and Robert Cummings, with a second-lead actress named Jane Wyman in attendance); not once, though, was Ronald Reagan considered as a likely occupant of the Oval Office; made it there all the same in '80, the electorate voting a landslide approval of his performance again in '84; earlier, was twice elected governor of California ('66 and '70); the son of an itinerant alcoholic shoe salesman, he played football and was in plays at the high school in Dixon, Ill. (lived there after age 10); first job at 14, as a construction worker on a house-remodeling project, was followed by others as a laborer; said in '47: "I'm a born clock-watcher. Once when I had a job as a ditchdigger I raised the pickax over my head and had it suspended for a downward blow when the whistle blew. . . . I just opened my hands and let it fall behind me"; got his degree in '32 in sociology and economics at Illinois' Eureka College, where he was on many teams (football, debating, swimming), was a member of Tau Kappa Epsilon fraternity (wore its ring for decades) and acted in plays; performance as a Greek shepherd boy in *Aria da Capo* won him an award in a Northwestern University School of Speech one-act play contest; a lifeguard for seven summers, he made 77 rescues; became a football announcer at radio station WOC (World of Chiropractic) in Davenport, Iowa; said later, "I figured that a ball game usually lasts about two hours. That's the shortest working day I could find"; next announced baseball games at WHO in Des Moines and, in '37, went to California for the station to cover the Chicago Cubs' spring training on Catalina Island; never went home; a friend from Des Moines, singer–starlet Joy Hodges, introduced him to agent Bill Meikeljohn, who introduced him to Warners casting director Max Arnow; was tested and given a contract starting at $200 a week (was earning $1,650 weekly when he left for military duty; returned to a new starting salary of $3,500 a week; finally earned $75,000 per picture); soon learned the studio hired him because his voice was similar to that of actor Ross Alexander, who'd committed suicide when on the verge of becoming a Warner star; studio's makeup wizards, the Westmore brothers, were appalled by his looks ("What are we going to *do* with him? With his hair parted in the middle like that, he looks like Joe E. Brown with a small mouth"); played the lead (radio announcer) in his first movie, *Love Is on the Air* ('37); soon became known as "the Errol Flynn of the Bs"; was briefly engaged to blonde Ila Rhodes, his leading lady in *Secret Service of the Air*; fell in love with Jane Wyman, also blonde (later naturally dark-haired, at his request), when they played sweethearts in *Brother Rat*; she was a Republican, and he was then "a hemophilic liberal" Democrat; were together in three later movies: *Brother Rat and a Baby, An Angel from Texas, Tugboat Annie Sails Again*; he called her "Button Nose," she called him "The Wild Irishman," and, while they were married, columnists called them "Hollywood's Nicest Couple"; wedding was at Wee Kirk o' Heather, a church in a cemetery (Forest Lawn); date: Jan. 26, 1940; daughter Maureen was born the next year on Wyman's 27th birthday (Jan. 4), they adopted son Michael in '45, and in '47, had a baby daughter who, born three months premature, lived just two days; was in the Army Air Force for four years, mostly as a personnel officer (captain) with a G.I. training film unit (nicknamed "Fort Roach") in Culver City, Calif.; Wyman divorced him in '48 (claimed his interest in politics bored her); the future politician served six terms as president of the Screen Actors Guild; in '52, married starlet Nancy Davis (who, he said, "was more than disinterested in Leftist causes; she was violently opposed to such shenani-gans"); that year, for the first time, he voted Republican; he and Nancy co-starred in '57's *Hellcats of the Navy*; their children: Patricia Ann and Ronald Prescott; made his 55th and final movie in '64, *The Killers*, playing his first bad-guy role, a killer; *Kings Row* ('42), his own favorite film, contained his best performance (as a small-town Lothario whose legs are needlessly amputated by an unscrupulous doctor) and most famous line of dialogue; the line became the title of his '65 autobiography, *"Where's the Rest of Me?"*; a collector's item now (and something of an embarrassment to his political advisers), the book opens with these words: "The story begins with a close-up of a bottom. . . . My face was blue . . . my bottom was red . . . and my father claimed afterward that he was white. . . . Ever since . . . I have been particularly fond of the colors that were exhibited—red, white, and blue."

MOVIE HIGHLIGHTS: *Hollywood Hotel, Girls on Probation, Boy Meets Girl, Dark Victory, Angels Wash Their Faces, Knute Rockne, All American, Santa Fe Trail, Million Dollar Baby, International Squadron, Juke Girl, Desperate Journey, This Is the Army, Stallion Road, That Hagen Girl, The Voice of the Turtle, Night unto Night, The Girl from Jones Beach, The Hasty Heart, Storm Warning, Bedtime for Bonzo, The Winning Team, Cattle Queen of Montana.*

Donna Reed

(b. Donna Belle Mullenger, Jan. 27, 1921, Denison, Iowa) A country girl, with reddish-brown hair and a gentle face (and sometimes surprisingly flinty opinions, privately expressed) she built a long career on playing wholesome sweethearts and wives; straying from "type" in '53, she portrayed prostitute Lorene (Alma before going into the profession) in *From Here to Eternity* and won the Best Supporting Oscar; then it was back to "nice girl" roles; was under contract at MGM from '41 (played the lead in her first, *The Getaway*, with Dan Dailey) through '47 *(Green Dolphin Street)*, free-lancing later till '60 *(Pepe)*; also starred on TV for eight seasons (1958–66) in "The Donna Reed Show," produced by her second husband (1945–71), Tony Owen; was married first (1943–45) to MGM makeup artist William Tuttle, and, in '74, to U.S. Army Colonel (Ret.) Grover Asmus; the daughter of a farmer and the eldest of five children, she attended a country grammar school (Nishabotany School No. 3; total enrollment: 12); at 13, she moved seven miles away to town (Denison), where she lived with her grandmother, went to high school, and because of strict parents, was not permitted to date until she was 17; first school play: *The Night of January 16th*; was voted School Queen in her senior year; at 18, in an aging jalopy, with $60 to her name, she went to Los Angeles, lived with an aunt, and enrolled in stenographic courses at L.A. City College; worked as a school librarian and washed dishes in a nearby boarding house to pay her way; expected to become a schoolteacher; acted in two college plays: *The Intruder* and *Happy Journey*; being elected Campus Queen two years later and getting her picture in the papers brought her to the attention of MGM talent scouts; screen test (February '41) was with another young hopeful, Van Heflin; has never liked the name the studio chose for her, but prefers it to Donna Adams, the monicker with which she began filming her debut picture; her agreeable personality found favor with movie fans from the start, though she did not have a truly demanding role until '46 when, on loan-out, she played James Stewart's wife, going from youth to middle age, in *It's a Wonderful Life*; shortly after she and Tony Owen married, they adopted two youngsters (not related), Penny and Tony Jr. (as Owen, after an accident, believed he could not become a father), then had two of their own, Timothy and Mary Ann; made one movie for her producer husband, *Beyond Mombasa*, a great flop ("She put me out of business," he later laughed); after a long absence from the cameras, she resumed her career in the autumn of '84 on TV's "Dallas," assuming the role of Miss Ellie, matriarch of Southfork Ranch, which illness had forced Barbara Bel Geddes to surrender.

MOVIE HIGHLIGHTS: *Shadow of the Thin Man, The Bugle Sounds, The Courtship of Andy Hardy, Eyes in the Night, Apache Trail, Calling Dr. Gillespie, The Human Comedy, The Man from Down Under, Thousands Cheer, See Here, Private Hargrove, Mrs. Parkington, The Picture of Dorian Gray, They Were Expendable, Faithful in My Fashion, Beyond Glory, Chicago Deadline, Saturday's Hero, Scandal Sheet, Hangman's Knot, Trouble Along the Way, The Caddy, They Rode West, The Last Time I Saw Paris, Ransom, The Benny Goodman Story.*

Roy Rogers

(b. Leonard Slye, Nov. 5, 1911, Cincinnati, Ohio) Gene Autry went off to war, and he took over the reins as "king of the cowboys"; was on the roster of Western moneymakers, 1939–42, but the older favorite firmly held the #1 spot from '37 to '42; seizing the position then, Rogers and Trigger, his handsome palomino steed, galloped at the head of the posse for 11 years, until Hollywood ceased making Saturday afternoon shoot-'em-ups; in '45, at the height of his fame, received 74,852 fan letters in one month—a record; of German and Irish stock (with a Choctaw Indian great-great grandmother), he grew up in the small Ohio towns of Portsmouth (family lived on a houseboat) and Duck Run (on a farm), where his education stopped at the 11th grade; early ambition was to be a dentist, but weekly visits to the local "picture show" inspired him with dreams of cowboy glory as portrayed by heroes Hoot Gibson and Tom Mix; in '31, in the depths of the Depression, he went to California with his family, clutching a guitar he'd picked up for $20 in a Cincinnati pawn shop; worked as a migratory fruit picker and drove a gravel truck; next teamed up with a cousin, Stanley Slye, in a cowboy musical act (The Slye Brothers) that appeared for the first time on radio's "Uncle Tom's Hollywood Hillbillies"; in '34, created, with Bob Nolan and Tim Spencer, the Sons of the Pioneers, which first became popular on radio and at barn dances; was seen with this musical group in several Western movies: *The Old Homestead* ('35), *The Big Show* ('36) starring Gene Autry, etc.; left the Pioneers in '37 when he signed a movie contract with Republic, which changed his name, first, to Dick Weston and falsely publicized his birthplace as Cody, Wyo.; played bits as Weston in The Three Mesquiteers' *Wild Horse Rodeo* and Gene Autry's *The Old Barn Dance*; as Roy Rogers, he became instantly famous in the spring of '38 when he starred in *Under Western Skies* (singing "Cool Water"), the first of four pictures he did that year—and the stampede was on; in '38, also bought for $2,500 a five-year-old trick pony named Golden Cloud, soon renamed Trigger, which lived to be 33; horse eventually had six doubles and, when reaching retirement age, was replaced by Trigger Jr.; Rogers was married in '36 to Arlene Wilkins, with whom he adopted a daughter (Cheryl), had one (Linda), and then had a son (Roy Jr.); soon after his son's birth in '46, Rogers' wife died; the cowboy star has been married since Dec. 31, 1947, to Dale Evans, who became his perennial screen leading lady after first appearing with him in '43 in *Hoosier Holiday* and *In Old Oklahoma*; their only child, a frail Mongoloid girl named Robin, born in '50, lived to be 2—and was the subject of a book written by her mother, *Angel Unaware*, the proceeds of which go to the National Association for Retarded Children; adopted three children: Mary Little Doe ("Dodie," who is part Choctaw), Deborah (a Korean war orphan who, at 12, was killed in a church bus crash; in her memory, Dale Evans wrote another book, *Dearest Debbie*, donating its royalties to World Vision, Inc., a welfare agency supporting orphans in many lands), and John David ("Sandy," who died at 18 during a choking seizure while serving with the U.S. Army in Germany); also reared as their own a Scottish orphan, Marion Fleming, whom they were unable to adopt because of British laws blocking it; a profoundly religious man, the cowboy star says, despite the tragedies in his life, "God has been good to me and given me happiness. . . . I can't help but thank God every time I get the chance."

MOVIE HIGHLIGHTS: *Billy the Kid Returns, Come On, Rangers!, In Old Caliente, The Arizona Kid, Robin Hood of the Pecos, Red River Valley,*

Romance on the Range, Heart of the Golden West, Idaho, King of the Cowboys, Silver Spurs, The Man from Music Mountain, Song of Nevada, Yellow Rose of Texas, Utah, Along the Navajo Trail, My Pal Trigger.

Mickey Rooney

(b. Joe Yule Jr., Sept. 23, 1920, Brooklyn, N.Y.) One thing only is small about this giant talent—his 5'1" frame; his achievements as a star remain incomparable; in '83 the Motion Picture Academy presented him a special Academy Award, saluting his lifetime contribution to the screen; was his second honorary Oscar—the first, in '38, being a special juvenile award; he also was nominated for the Best Actor Oscar for *Babes in Arms* and *The Human Comedy* and for the Best Supporting Award for *The Bold and the Brave* and *The Black Stallion*; for three consecutive years, 1939–41, was #1 among the Box-Office Top Ten and was also on the list in '38, '42, and '43; made his debut in vaudeville at 2, dressed in a miniature tux, in a sketch with his late parents, Joe Yule and Nell Brown; was given a special work permit (in order to comply with New York laws) by Gov. Alfred E. Smith; worked up a dance act with another kid, Sid Gold, that soon was featured in *Will Morrissey's Revue* in New York; discovered then by a movie scout, he made his screen debut in '26 in *Not To Be Trusted*, playing a cigar-smoking midget, which he was again the following year in Colleen Moore's *Orchids and Ermine*; next, as Mickey McGuire, he starred in his own series of two-reel comedies (*Mickey's Movies, Mickey the Detective*, etc.) as a talent-loaded moppet with an ever-present cigar; first screen name came from a comic strip, "The Toonerville Trolley"; billing as Mickey Rooney began in '32 at Universal when in *Fast Companions*; signed his MGM contract, which lasted 14 years, in '34; studio quickly capitalized on his ability to not only act but also sing, dance, clown, compose songs, and play virtually every musical instrument; playing Andy Hardy, the exuberant, "typical" small-town American teen-ager, made him a star; did the role 15 times between '37 and '46, starting with a A *Family Affair*, followed by *Love Finds Andy Hardy, Andy Hardy Gets Spring Fever* et al., and returned to it in '58 for the series' final "reunion" edition, *Andy Hardy Comes Home*; incidentally, another boy actor, Frankie Thomas, was almost signed for the role; Rooney, earning $300,000 a year before he was 20, actually had little in common with the kid from the fictional town of Carvel that he played; as noted by one Hollywood observer, "Off screen he was betting on horses, cultivating a taste for hard liquor, carousing with Hollywood starlets"; author Anita (*Gentlemen Prefer Blondes*) Loos, who worked at the studio then, once asked: "Could you guess the greatest lover on the MGM lot? Mickey Rooney. He was catnip to the girls"; eventually fathered seven children, racking up a prodigious marital record; wives: Ava Gardner (1942–43), Alabama beauty queen Betty Jane Rase (1944–47; mother of Mickey Jr. and Timothy), starlet Martha Vickers (1949–51; mother of Ted), model Elaine Mahnken (1952–59), starlet Barbara Ann Thomason (1959–66; mother of Kelly, Kerry, and Kimmy; was still married to Rooney when she was murdered by an alleged lover), author Margaret Lane (1966–67), Carolyn Zack (1969–74; mother of Jonelle; Rooney also legally adopted her son, Jimmy, by a previous marriage); in '78, was married to C&W singer Jan Chamberlain, a divorcee with two sons (quipped the actor: "If it doesn't last, I'll go and find wife No. 9"); "I have married often because I have searched for perfect love," he has said, as well as, "I've paid a lot of child support, true, but I never paid any alimony in my life—never mind what you've read"; speaking of his greatest love, he says: "Show business is like a beautiful woman. I've found her cheating on me. I've found her fickle. But no matter what she does to me, I've been in love with her all my life, and I always will be."

MOVIE HIGHLIGHTS: *Captains Courageous, Thoroughbreds Don't Cry, Boys Town, Stablemates, Young Tom Edison, Strike Up the Band, Babes on Broadway, Men of Boys Town, A Yank at Eton, Girl Crazy, National Velvet, Summer Holiday, Words and Music, Killer McCoy, Off Limits, The Bridges at Toko-Ri, Operation Madball, Baby Face Nelson, Breakfast at Tiffany's, Requiem for a Heavyweight, It's a Mad Mad Mad Mad World, The Magic of Lassie.*

Gail Russell

(b. Gail Russell, Sept. 23, 1924, Chicago, Ill.; d. Aug. 26[?], 1961) Two California teen-agers did this blue-eyed brunette no favor in '43 when, hitching a ride with a Paramount casting director, they waxed ecstatic about attending school with the "Hedy Lamarr of Santa Monica High"; the overnight fame that ensued brought her little happiness; after minor roles in *Henry Aldrich Gets Glamour* and *Lady in the Dark*, she was handed the romantic lead—requiring a British accent—opposite Ray Milland in a superior mystery, *The Uninvited*, and was proclaimed a star; credited Milland's kindness for her success, saying, "When he saw I was scared, he'd say, 'Come on, you can do it' "; stellar status was confirmed when she proved a delight as teen-aged Cornelia Otis Skinner in the comedy *Our Hearts Were Young and Gay*; was so painfully shy—no act—that in early movies, she did her emoting concealed from the view of the crew behind folding screens; a commercial art student whose father was a worker at Lockheed Aircraft, she'd had no training or aspiration for a movie career, but she had a mysterious, dreamy quality the camera found interesting; an early interviewer, Charles Samuels, discovered her to be "a strange young person. There is something soft and pathetic in her eyes. You feel you'd like to protect her"; her mother, describing her highly introverted nature, said, "It is difficult even for me to understand how it is possible for Gail to be an actress"; said the star: "I don't know where my career will take me. What I really want is to go barefooted and run a little motorboat"; career took her into unexpected and, finally, deep waters; in '47, when co-starring with John Wayne in *The Angel and the Badman*, there were rumors of a love affair—he'd given her a convertible—to the fury of his insanely jealous wife, Esperanza Baur; already she had begun to drink heavily—to overcome her fears, said friends—and Wayne's defenders insisted that his gestures were only to reassure her that "someone cared"; in '49 she married teen idol Guy Madison, in '50 Paramount dropped her option, in '53 she was arrested for drunk driving and entered a drying-out clinic, in '54 Madison divorced her, arguing that she discouraged visitors to their house and cared nothing for him or for their marriage; in '57 there was another drunk driving arrest; completely off the screen for five years after '51, she was in three minor movies, one each year, between '56 and '58—being hired each time only after reassuring producers she was no longer drinking; starred the year of her death in a B picture, *The Silent Call*, after being unemployed for three years; died alone, her body being found among empty vodka bottles on the floor of her furnished apartment in West Los Angeles; exact date of her death is not known—police could only estimate that she had died "some time between 6 P.M. Thursday [Aug. 24] and 11 P.M. Saturday [Aug. 26]."

MOVIE HIGHLIGHTS: *The Unseen, Salty O'Rourke, Our Hearts Were Growing Up, The Virginian, The Bachelor's Daughters, Calcutta, Moonrise, The Night Has a Thousand Eyes, Wake of the Red Witch, El Paso, The Great Dan Patch, Captain China, Song of India, The Lawless, Air Cadet, Seven Men from Now, The Tattered Dress, No Place to Land.*

Jane Russell

(b. Ernestine Jane Geraldine Russell, June 21, 1921, Bemidji, Minn.) Howard Hughes was—no secret—a "breast man," and one look at the bosom of this 19-year-old raven-haired beauty was enough to convince him he'd discovered the treasure chest of the century; publicity for *The Outlaw*, her first movie, came straight to the point: "What are the two reasons for Jane Russell's rise to stardom?"; the better to display her visible gifts, Hughes designed a special brassiere for her; what's more, over the years she was under contract to him (36 in all)—and when loaned out to other movie companies—directors, designers, and cameramen grew accustomed to receiving memoes from Hughes stressing how she and her famous bust should be costumed, photographed, and positioned in scenes; while visually a sexpot, with sulky, fascinating features, it eventually became evident that she had the attitude, voice, and behavior of a tomboy (which, having grown up with four younger brothers, she was); this aspect of her personality finally made her most appealing to fans when she spoofed sex in comedies like *Gentlemen Prefer Blondes*; inherited her looks from her mother, a onetime stage ingenue and a great beauty, a painting of whom hung in the White House when Woodrow Wilson resided there; Russell's parents, both American, were living in Canada when she was due to be born; her mother crossed the border to her family's summer house in Minnesota so that the child would be an American citizen; was ten months old when the family moved to California; grew up in Burbank and, later, Van Nuys, where her father was general manager of the Andrew Jergens Co.'s West Coast factory; given dramatic lessons from early childhood by her mother, who intended her to be an actress, she later performed in school plays—but her own goal was to be a dress designer; this ambition was thwarted when she was 16 and her father died; took a job as a chiropodist's receptionist ($10 a week); next modeled for photographer Tom Kelley (later famous for his nude calendar shot of Marilyn Monroe), then studied drama at the Max Reinhardt Theatrical Workshop and with Maria Ouspenskaya; an agent got her screen tests at Warner Bros. and 20th Century–Fox (both turned her down) and, finally, the one for Howard Hughes, who, searching for an unknown to star in *The Outlaw*, put her under contract at $50 a week; earnings from this contract, which became the longest in Hollywood history, finally totaled more than $1 million; an immediate pinup favorite with G.I.s, she was seen by the public in thousands of photos in magazines and newspapers and in another movie, *Young Widow*, before *The Outlaw* (made in '41 and long beset by censorship problems) reached the screen in '46; was married to high school sweetheart (and pro football star) Bob Waterfield from '43 until they were divorced in '68; children (adopted): Tracy, Thomas, and Robert; within weeks of the divorce was married to actor Roger Barrett, who died three months later; since '74, has been the wife of John Calvin Peoples, a Texas-born realtor; "I was never a sex symbol—not in my head I wasn't," she says; has often been offered a fortune—always refused—to write a book about Howard Hughes, but she has loyally insisted, "I'm not going to be any information center about the man."

MOVIE HIGHLIGHTS: *The Paleface, His Kind of Woman, Double Dynamite, Montana Belle, Macao, Las Vegas Story, Son of Paleface, The French Line, Underwater, Foxfire, Gentlemen Marry Brunettes, The Tall Men, Hot Blood, The Revolt of Mamie Stover, The Fuzzy Pink Nightgown, Fame Is the Hunter, Johnny Reno, Waco.*

Rosalind Russell

(b. Rosalind Russell, June 4, 1907, Waterbury, Conn.; d. Nov. 28, 1976) Sex, this elegant, lanky brunette did not convey, and when she tried, as in *They Met in Bombay* with Gable, the result was nothing to set pulses pounding; fun—whether raucous *(The Women)* or sophisticated *(Design for Scandal)*—was something else; was most humorously dazzling, in tailored pin-striped suits and with that proud tilt of her handsome head, when besting the opposite sex in whirling dervish comedies like *His Girl Friday* and *Take a Letter, Darling*; was nominated for the Best Actress Oscar for two comedies, *My Sister Eileen* and *Auntie Mame*, and, no slouch at heavy theatrics, for *Sister Kenny* (a personally engineered project dear to her heart) and *Mourning Becomes Electra*; both of these dramas were box-office disasters; said then, "I've no desire to return to tragedy, ever"—and she never did; the daughter of a well-to-do lawyer and named for the S.S. Rosalind, on which her parents once took a cruise, she discovered her acting gift when she played a bearded St. Francis in a school play; after receiving her B.A. from Barnard, persuaded her parents to send her to the American Academy of Dramatic Arts, where she auditioned with a scene from *Camille*; graduated in '29 and gave herself five years to succeed or become a teacher; spent two summers in stock; was on Broadway for three years after '30 in the *Garrick Gaieties, Company's Coming!*, etc.; was taken to Hollywood by Universal but, after nine unhappy days of tests there, managed to get out of the deal; won a test at MGM and a top supporting role in William Powell's *Evelyn Prentice*; she and Robert Taylor (with whom she soon worked in *West Point of the Air*) began their contracts on the same day; remained at the studio for seven years—usually playing "other women" or "cats"—until '42, when she chose to free-lance; gave up a fortune for her freedom: the offer of a new seven-year contract, without options, at $7,500 a week; in '43, had a nervous breakdown, about which her fans never knew, caused by grief over the deaths of several members of her family; was married for 35 years, from '41 on, to her one husband, Danish-born stage-movie producer Fred Brisson (produced several of her later films, including *Never Wave at a WAC*); over a long courtship, she several times rejected his proposals, until finally, in desperation, he announced he was writing to her mother to ask for her hand, which he did; one child: Lance; Brisson recalled in later years: "We had the most marvelous time together, because Rosalind was a life affirmer . . . and like Scaramouche, she had been 'born with the gift of laughter and the sense that the world was mad' "; a proper New Englander and Catholic, with an inborn inclination to serve others, she was actively involved over the years (by her husband's count) in 94 civic and public-spirited associations; between '60 and '69, she had two mastectomies and was afflicted by severe rheumatoid arthritis, yet, in those years, she starred in eight films; cancer recurred in '75, and in July of the following year she had to have a hip replacement; gave one of her most memorable performances in *Auntie Mame* on both stage and screen, in which she spoke the line: "Life is a banquet, and most of you poor suckers are starving to death"; completed her autobiography in her final months, which was published posthumously, and titled it *Life Is a Banquet*.

MOVIE HIGHLIGHTS: *China Seas, Reckless, Craig's Wife, Night Must Fall, Man-Proof, The Citadel, Four's a Crowd, Fast and Loose, Hired Wife, No Time for Comedy, This Thing Called Love, The Feminine Touch, Flight for Freedom, What a Woman, Roughly Speaking, She Wouldn't Say Yes, The Guilt of Janet Ames, The Velvet Touch, Tell It to the Judge, A Woman of Distinction, Girl Rush, Picnic, A Majority of One, Five Finger Exercise, Gypsy, The Trouble with Angels, Rosie, Mrs. Pollifax, Spy.*

Ann Rutherford

(b. Therese Ann Rutherford, Nov. 2, 1917, Toronto, Canada) In an even dozen Andy Hardy movies between *You're Only Young Once* ('38) and *Andy Hardy's Double Life* ('42), she was Mickey Rooney's adored Polly Benedict—brunette, with big flashing eyes, and just a bit bossy; scripts of the series intimated that these small-town sweethearts would grow up and "marry," but when Andy returned to Carvel in 1958's *Andy Hardy Comes Home*, his "wife" was someone named "Jane" (actress Patricia Breslin); Rutherford was offered the role first but, after reading the script, begged off ("It just didn't work. I had to make up an excuse about going on a business trip to get out of it. You just can't go back again"); off screen, she has been married twice—from '42 to '53, though they'd separated years before divorcing, to David May (heir of the Los Angeles May Co. department store, with whom she adopted daughter Gloria) and from '53 on to producer William Dozier; came of a theatrical background; her father, John Dufferin Rutherford, an operatic tenor, sang with the Met and on concert stages under the name of Juan Guilberti; mother, a cousin of famed Shakespearean star Richard Mansfield, acted on stage and in silent movies under two names—Lucille Mansfield and Pauline Daly; older sister Judith Arlen was a "Wampas Baby Star" of 1934 (appeared in *Young and Beautiful, Kiss and Make Up*), later married Al Simon, producer of TV's "Beverly Hillbillies," and died in '68; Rutherford was transplanted from Canada to San Francisco when four months old; began acting on radio in Hollywood at 11 in a series titled "Nancy and Dick in the Spirit of '76"; on radio in her teens, played everything from a crying baby to the wife of a hillbilly; made her movie debut at Mascot (later renamed Republic) at 17 as the romantic lead opposite Frank Albertson in *Waterfront Lady*; did 12 pictures, mostly Westerns, at this studio; was Gene Autry's first leading lady, in *The Singing Vagabond* and *Melody Trail*, and says, "It's not true he only kissed his horse—he kissed me three times"; first of her 34 features for Leo the Lion was 1937's *Espionage*, starring Edmund Lowe; in '39, was loaned to Selznick to play Scarlett O'Hara's baby sister, Carreen, in *Gone With the Wind*, a role for which Judy Garland was first considered; left MGM in '43, after *Whistling in Brooklyn* with Red Skelton, then free-lanced through 1950's *Operation Haylift*; did not return to MGM (or to movies) until 1972 when, with June Allyson and Peter Lawford, other studio alumni, she did a cameo in *They Only Kill Their Masters*; it was the last picture ever made on MGM's old back lot, and many of its scenes were filmed on the street where Andy Hardy once "lived" and dreamed of "popping the question" to Polly Benedict.

MOVIE HIGHLIGHTS: *Of Human Hearts, Judge Hardy's Children, Dramatic School, Love Finds Andy Hardy, These Glamour Girls, Dancing Coed, Pride and Prejudice, Wyoming, Andy Hardy Meets Debutante, Washington Melodrama, Badlands of Dakota, Whistling in the Dark, This Time for Keeps, Orchestra Wives, Happy Land, Bermuda Mystery, Bedside*

Manner, Murder in the Music Hall, The Secret Life of Walter Mitty, The Adventures of Don Juan.

Robert Ryan

(b. Robert Ryan, Nov. 11, 1909, Chicago, Ill.; d. July 11, 1973) Big (6'4", with the physique of a heavyweight champ), dark and handsome, he first played minor roles—as a $75-a-week contract player—in several films at Paramount in '40 (*Golden Gloves, North West Mounted Police, Queen of the Mob*); became a star at RKO, where he was under contract from 1943 (*Bombardier*) to 1952 (*Beware My Lovely*); between studio deals he acted in stock on the East Coast and played the juvenile lead opposite Tallulah Bankhead on Broadway in *Clash by Night* (starred in the movie version a decade later but in a different role, that of the older lover); was nominated for a Best Supporting Oscar for his portrayal of the murderous, psychotic soldier in 1947's *Crossfire*; though he'd played Hamlet as a kid in parochial school, he didn't decide to be an actor until he was 28; the son of a well-to-do Irish-American contractor, he had expected to be a newspaper reporter after graduation from Dartmouth in '32; finding no such opportunity during the Depression, he worked at other jobs for several years—as a sandhog, seaman (one trip to Africa as a ship's janitor), salesman (steel company), ranch hand (in Montana), cemetery lot salesman, photographer's model, WPA laborer, bootlegger's bodyguard, etc.; was back in his hometown working as a school supplies superintendent when a girl friend, a model, persuaded him to join an amateur theatrical group; soon headed for Hollywood, where he studied acting with Max Reinhardt, and met and married another student, Jessica Cadwalader; she gave up acting to rear their children—two sons, Timothy and Cheney, and a daughter, Lisa—and, after a career as a magazine writer, became a novelist (*The Crack in the Ring, Exit Harlequin,* etc.); the actor and she were married from '39 until her death in '72; soon after getting his big break at RKO—the romantic lead opposite Ginger Rogers in *Tender Comrade* (making him a fan favorite)—Ryan's career was interrupted for two years' stateside duty in the Marines; later came a few other romantic roles (in *Woman on the Beach, Born to Be Bad,* etc.), but his stardom took a curious turn; this actor, who had all the equipment for a movie career to parallel Gary Cooper's, found himself typecast for years in neurotic and/or killer roles; never stopped making pictures (final count: 81) but regularly returned to Broadway to star in plays—

Shakespeare's *Coriolanus* (to mixed reviews), *Mr. President* (an Irving Berlin musical), a revival of *The Front Page* with Helen Hayes, etc.; always said his favorite film role was that of the washed-up fighter in *The Set-Up* ('49); three movies in which he starred *(The Outfit, The Iceman Cometh, Executive Action)* were released the year of his death.

MOVIE HIGHLIGHTS: *The Iron Major, Behind the Rising Sun, Marine Raiders, Trail Street, Berlin Express, Return of the Bad Men, Act of Violence, The Boy with Green Hair, Caught, Flying Leathernecks, The Racket, Horizons West, The Naked Spur, About Mrs. Leslie, Her Twelve Men, Bad Day at Black Rock, The Tall Men, God's Little Acre, Lonelyhearts, Odds against Tomorrow, King of Kings, Billy Budd, The Dirty Dozen.*

Sabu

(b. Sabu Dastagir, Jan. 27, 1924, Karapur, Mysore, India; d. Dec. 2, 1963) Athletically racing about in "Arabian nights" fantasies of the '40s— barechested, in colorful turbans, and usually in the friendly company of beautiful lovers Maria Montez and Jon Hall—this smallish actor was one of Universal's most popular stars; no such future could have been predicted for him when born in the Karapur jungle 45 miles from Mysore in southern India; soon became the Maharajah's smallest pensioner orphan, his father having been killed while working the royal elephants; roaming the bazaars of Mysore, he called once a day at the Maharajah's elephant stables for his allowance of rice; there, at 11, he was found for movies by Robert J. Flaherty; the filmmaker, world-famous for his documentaries *(Nanook of the North,* etc.), and sent to India by English producer Alexander Korda to make a documentary about elephants, was overjoyed to discover this "natural actor"; the youngster proved himself utterly fearless in scenes with the gigantic elephant Kala Nag and in the picture's many life-risking episodes (the director reportedly "nearly went frantic watching Sabu riding his swimming elephant across a flood-swollen river"); taken to England, where the London Films production was completed at Denham Studios, Sabu never returned to India; becoming an international (and unexpected) star in *Elephant Boy,* as the movie finally was titled, he attended boarding school at Beaconsfield, was an ace player on the institution's soccer team, the Rovers, mastered English, and longed to become a famous racing-car driver like his idol, Prince Bira; *Drums,* his second starring picture, found him playing a pro-British Indian prince in a melodrama about the British Army in India; the movie gave the young actor a hint of what he would soon find in Hollywood; *Drums*, relates Michael Korda, the producer's nephew, "was filmed in the hills of South Wales, with circus elephants and horses from the local riding stables, and an army of Welsh miners and sheep farmers in blackface to portray the troops of the evil Prince Ghul"; 1940's *Thief of Bagdad*, his next, was started in England and completed in Hollywood, which would be nis home for the rest of his life; became a Cadillac-driving U.S. citizen, served with distinction in WWII as a gunner on a B-24, married former stage actress Marilyn Cooper, and became the father of a son, Paul, and a daughter, Jasmine.

MOVIE HIGHLIGHTS: *Arabian Nights, White Savage, Cobra Woman, Tangier, Black Narcissus, Man-Eater of Kumaon, The End of the River, Song of India, Savage Drums, Jungle Hell, The Black Panther, Jaguar, Sabu and the Magic Ring, Rampage, A Tiger Walks.*

S. Z. Sakall

(b. Szdke Szakall, Feb. 2, 1883, Budapest, Hungary; d. Feb. 12, 1955) Of all the talented European refugees who fled the Nazis and found a safe harbor in Hollywood, this yellow-haired, jowls-patting kewpie doll in the round specs was the most lovable; "Cuddles," they nicknamed him, on screen and off, for cause; an informal, fun-loving man, he played the drums and the trumpet (in the best Harry James fashion), and, pudgy or no, cut a svelte figure-eight as an ice-skater; also looked for small adventures in life; driving off a movie lot (usually Warners) after a day's work, he forever sought new routes that would take him home; a graduate of the University of Hungary, he was first a playwright and stage director; turning comedian, his reputation was made when his antics made Emperor Franz Josef guffaw with delight; quickly became the rage of the Hungarian stage, earning 3,000 pengos a week; offered the comic lead in a musical in Vienna, he demurred, pointing out, "I don't know three words in German"; learned the role by ear, scored a hit, mastered the language, and became one of the top-ranking comedians in German (and other European) films; seeing him on stage in Vienna, Universal producer Joseph Pasternak invited him to make films in America, but he argued, "I don't know three words in English"; having little choice eventually but to leave Europe, he stopped first in England where, in a '37 movie starring Hollywood's June Knight, *The Lilac Domino*, he clicked as a comic Gypsy band leader—and was billed Szocke Szakall; arriving in Hollywood in '39, he worked first in two Deanna Durbin musicals, *It's a Date* and *Spring Parade*, both produced by Pasternak, for which he had to learn his dialogue phonetically; from the start, fans were captivated by his perpetual consternation, eternal bewilderment, and apple-cheeked warmth; published his autobiography, *The Story of Cuddles*, in '53; was happily married from '22 on to wife Boeszike.

MOVIE HIGHLIGHTS: *Why Cry at Parting?* (German), *My Love Came Back, Florian, The Devil and Miss Jones, That Night in Rio, The Man Who Lost Himself, Ball of Fire, Seven Sweethearts, Yankee Doodle Dandy, Broadway, Casablanca, The Human Comedy, Wintertime, Shine On, Harvest Moon, Christmas in Connecticut, Wonder Man, The Dolly Sisters, Romance on the High Seas, Look for the Silver Lining, In the Good Old Summertime, Oh, You Beautiful Doll, The Student Prince.*

George Sanders

(b. George Sanders Jr., July 3, 1906, St. Petersburg, Russia; d. April 25, 1972) With a cynical air, a dissolute manner, and impeccable British diction, he was a natural to be Hollywood's consummate cad; could sneer in five languages, which he spoke fluently—Russian, English, Spanish, French, and German; often played, and actually was a misogynist; said, "Women are strange little beasts. I agree with the old verse: A woman, a dog, and a walnut tree—the more you beat them the better they be"; had four marriages, the third apparently being the happiest; wife #1 (1940–47); Susan Larson (aka Elsie M. Pool), who'd been a waitress at the Brown Derby; #2 (1949–54): Zsa Zsa Gabor, who, seven months pregnant by husband Conrad Hilton, saw Sanders in a movie *(The Moon and Sixpence)* and announced—though she had yet to meet him—he would be her next husband; he complained when she divorced him that she had discarded him "like a squeezed grapefruit"; #3, from '58 until her death in '67, was Ronald Colman's widow, actress Benita Hume, a joyful woman (while married, the actor, always obsessed with escaping taxes, turned their lives into a continual worldwide excursion and lost over a million dollars in speculative business deals); #4, for two months in '70, was his onetime sister-in-law, Magda Gabor; this son of a British father (a rope manufacturer) and a Russian mother fled with his family to England during the Communist revolution; following graduation from Brighton College and Manchester Technical School, was in the textile manufacturing business; next came a venture into the tobacco industry in South America; returned to England after being wounded in a pistol duel by a jealous husband; went on the stage in a musical revue, *Ballyhoo*, at the suggestion of an opera singer uncle; made his screen debut in '29 in a British film, *Strange Cargo*; several movies later, he went to Hollywood in '36, allowed 20th Century–Fox to cap his teeth (and long regretted it), and played Madeleine Carroll's pernicious husband in *Lloyds of London*; with such rare later exceptions as "The Saint" and "The Falcon" series, he became rigidly typecast; friends (there were a few) knew this mercurial and quixotic man to be a mechanical genius (invented successful water toys and devised elaborate lighting systems) and a first-class sailor (skippered a yacht christened, to no one's surprise, *Frustration*); snagged a Best Supporting Oscar for his performance as sardonic theater critic Addison DeWitt in *All About Eve*; his life has been well documented in books—his own *Memoirs of a Professional Cad*, Zsa Zsa's autobiography, and an affectionate volume about him by his friend Brian Aherne, *A Dreadful Man*; fearing boredom above all, he sought perpetual change, because, he once said, "Variety, and only variety, is worth the price of admission to this vale of tears"; committing suicide, he left behind a note that read: "Dear World: I am leaving because I am bored. . . ."

MOVIE HIGHLIGHTS: *Lancer Spy, The Saint in London, Nurse Edith Cavell, Confessions of a Nazi Spy, Rebecca, Foreign Correspondent, Bitter Sweet, Man Hunt, Tales of Manhattan, The Black Swan, This Land Is Mine, The Lodger, Summer Storm, The Picture of Dorian Gray, Hangover Square, The Strange Affair of Uncle Harry, Death of a Scoundrel, The Strange Woman, Forever Amber, The Private Affairs of Bel Ami, The Ghost and Mrs. Muir, Samson and Delilah, Ivanhoe.*

Lizabeth Scott

(b. Emma Matzo, Sept. 29, 1922, Scranton, Pa.) A star from her first picture, 1945's *You Came Along*, she had an ear-arresting husky voice, an eye-catching cascade of tawny blonde hair—and the misfortune to follow a much-too-similar Lauren Bacall to the screen; to her disadvantage, was even labeled "The Threat" when new in movies; starting in Mae Desmond's stock company and at the Abingdon Theater in Virginia, she then played in skits in the touring company of *Hellzapoppin'*, understudied Tallulah Bankhead (and Miriam Hopkins) in *The Skin of Our Teeth*, and was a photographer's model when movie agent Charles Feldman spotted her in a skirt-and-sweater ad in *Harper's Bazaar*; had two failed screen tests—at the now defunct International Studios and Warner Bros. (did a comedy scene from *The Male Animal*); had a "look," though, that intrigued Hal Wallis, then WB's production chief; leaving the studio to become an independent producer at Paramount, he took her along as his first personal contractee and supervised her career for the next 12 years; after the death of his wife, actress Louise Fazenda, there were rumors they would wed, but, even now, she remains unmarried; became typecast as a moll—often a torch singer in clinging black satin with a cigarette dangling from her lips and, sometimes, a smoking pistol in her hand; unlike the slinky, somnolent femme she usually played, her off-screen personality was energetic and forceful; the eldest of six children of ambitious immigrant parents from Ungvar, Czechoslovakia, she worked as a youngster in her father's grocery, on the ground floor of the small brick building in which the family lived; when her ambition to be a "movie star" blossomed early, her parents scrimped to give her dancing, singing, elocution, and piano lessons; of her family, she has said fondly, "It was just like the one in *You Can't Take It with You*"; appeared in Christmas pageants at the Catholic church they attended, in grammar school, and at Scranton High, but school drama coaches predicted no great future for her; after a brief stay at Marywood Seminary in her hometown, went to New York (with a $12-a-week allowance), studied at the Alviene School of the Theater ("They didn't like my low voice and kept after me to raise it"), and changed her name to Elizabeth ("just because I always liked the name"; soon dropped the "E") Scott (for a favorite play, *Mary of Scotland*); success in her chosen field may have been an inspiration to her younger siblings, who, achievers all, became engineers, writers, private-school teachers, etc., with some college-tuition assistance from her; early studio publicity "phonied up" her background, claiming she was the post-deb daughter of a Manhattan banker, though her legitimate climb-to-fame story would surely have appealed more to fans; having a "literary crush" on Aldous Huxley, she once seriously considered joining a Danteism cult of which he was an ardent supporter—"but when they came to the part about 'forswearing all worldly goods,' I had to bow out; even for Huxley, that was going too far."

MOVIE HIGHLIGHTS: *The Strange Love of Martha Ivers, Desert Fury, Dead Reckoning, Pitfall, I Walk Alone, Too Late for Tears, Easy Living, Dark City, Paid in Full, The Company She Keeps, The Racket, Two of a Kind, A Stolen Face, Scared Stiff, Bad for Each Other, Silver Lode, The Weapon, Loving You, Pulp.*

Randolph Scott

(b. George Randolph Scott, Jan. 23, 1903, Orange County, Va.) In the '30s, when repeatedly cast in Westerns like *The Texans* and *Wild Horse Mesa*, the rangy, virile blond with the gentle Southern accent said, "It's a fine life, but I want to be doing something better. I want to *act*, not just ride a horse"; never became an Oscar winner like fellow cowpoke Gary Cooper, but in the '40s and '50s, starring in a string of 39 big-budget "oaters," he discovered that wearing buckskins can be highly profitable; riding the range, he began earning a fortune even before landing among the Box-Office Top Ten for four consecutive years (1950–53); investing his movie salary in tungsten mines and Utah uranium, plus San Fernando Valley real estate, he rose to dizzying financial heights (estimated worth today: $50 million); educated in private schools and at the University of North Carolina, he first went into the textile manufacturing business with his engineer father (a descendant of early Virginia pioneers); admitting a secret yen to act, he went to California at 25, studied for two years at the Pasadena Playhouse and, while acting on stage with the El Capitan Stock Company in Hollywood, was given minor roles in a number of Westerns because he was a demon on horseback; initially nervous before the camera, he made a series of unsuccessful screen tests—always under different names, at his agent's insistence, to keep each studio from checking out his previous failures elsewhere; "Randolph Scott" struck out at MGM, despite Louis B. Mayer's opinion that he looked "like an Adonis"; Radio Pictures vetoed "George Randolph" as a no-talent, but Paramount thought one "George Scott" was a sure bet for fame; forgiving the deception, they signed him—under his rightful name—at $100 a week; in '36, climbing fast at this studio, he married years-older Mariana duPont (of *the* duPonts) Somerville, following her divorce from her millionaire husband; kept secret for months, the marriage was of short duration; they separated in '38, but for years she refused to give him a divorce; rise to stardom began in earnest in '38 when he signed separate deals with both 20th Century–Fox and Universal; one major role followed another, including, at 20th, that of the tough Marine officer in *To the Shores of Tripoli*, long his favorite film; the part of his private life he regards as "the happiest" began in '44 when he was finally free to marry Los Angeles society beauty Patricia Stillman; still married, they have two adopted children: Christopher and Sandra; the year of this marriage, he also began co-producing his own pictures—starting with *Belle of the Yukon*, followed by *Abilene Town*, etc.; perhaps his finest film, and certainly the one in which he gave his most assured performance, was his last, 1962's *Ride the High Country*—#97 on his credits roster; because "it illustrates the kind of human being he is," a friend has offered this: "Every night before he retires—just as he was taught when he was young—he gets down on his knees and says his prayers."

MOVIE HIGHLIGHTS: *So Red the Rose, Rocky Mountain Mystery, Jesse James, Frontier Marshal, Coast Guard, Virginia City, My Favorite Wife, Western Union, Belle Starr, The Spoilers, Pittsburgh, Bombardier, The Desperadoes, Corvette K-225, Gung Ho!, Captain Kidd, Badman's Territory, China Sky, Trail Street, Coroner Creek, Albuquerque, The Walking Hills, Fighting Man of the Plains, Colt .45, Fort Worth, Carson City.*

Zachary Scott

(b. Zachary Thomson Scott Jr., Feb. 24, 1914, Austin, Texas; d. Oct. 3, 1965) Playing a dinner-jacketed sophisticate was second nature to this lean, darkly handsome star, for he was to the manor born—the son of a wealthy surgeon, the grandson of a self-made cattle baron; wore cufflinks fashioned from the first gold dollars ever earned by his grandfather, who presented them to him; at Warner Bros., stocked with rough-edged customers like Bogart and Garfield, he was not "one of the boys"—not with that fine gold stud in his pierced left ear (long before such was common); was also the only actor on the lot with eyelashes so thick and long they had to be powdered down to keep them from casting shadows in scenes; arrived in Hollywood in '44 with a wife, Elaine (married on his 21st birthday), and a six-year-old daughter, Waverly; after he and Elaine divorced in '50, she became the wife (and eventually the widow) of John Steinbeck, and he was married ('52) to actress Ruth Ford, by whom he had another daughter, Shelley; first stage experience was at 4, when he impersonated Chaplin in a local talent show; decided on an acting career at 14; trained for it at the University of Texas, where he was a principal member of the Curtain Club, along with one Elaine Anderson of Fort Worth; each broke engagements to others to marry; after three years at the university, went to England on a cotton freighter out of New Orleans; claiming to be an Aussie, he joined the English Repertory Company, won the juvenile lead in *The Outsider*, and stayed with the troupe for 13 months before returning to Texas; while completing his education, worked for a refining company, taught dramatics at a convent school, and acted with his wife at the Austin Little Theater; later went together to New York, hoping to emulate the Lunts on stage; he acted in stock and she, soon forsaking acting ambitions, worked for the Theatre Guild and eventually was the stage manager of *Oklahoma!*;

after '41 he was on Broadway in several shows (debut: *A Circle of Chalk*), including *Those Endearing Young Charms*, in which he was discovered by Warner Bros.; studio gave him a moustache and the starring role in *The Mask of Dimitrios* (rejected by Joel McCrea), as a scoundrel who ruthlessly used women and was a cold-blooded killer; fortunately (as he was soon typecast), had a preference for villainy, provided it was "villainy with charm, evil with originality"; what he did not like was profile shots ("The tip of my nose wiggles when I talk"); most famous role was perhaps that of the suave Pasadena socialite–gigolo Joan Crawford "bought" and married in *Mildred Pierce*; best performance—and most atypical casting—was as the dirt-poor Texas share-cropper in *The Southerner* (his second film); in later years, continuing in movies, he was on Broadway in many, including a revival of *The King and I* and *Requiem for a Nun*, co-starring with his second wife, who also wrote the stage adaptation of this Faulkner novel; at 32, professed this as his philosophy: "Life is short. There isn't enough time to be bored"; made the most of the 19 years he had left.

MOVIE HIGHLIGHTS: *San Antonio, Danger Signal, Her Kind of Man, Stallion Road, The Unfaithful, Cass Timberlane, Ruthless, Whiplash, Flaxy Martin, South of St. Louis, Born to Be Bad, Pretty Baby, Lightning Strikes Twice, Shadow on the Wall, The Secret of Convict Lake, Let's Make It Legal, Stronghold, Appointment in Honduras, Flame of the Islands, Shotgun.*

Ann Sheridan

(b. Clara Lou Sheridan, Feb. 21, 1915, Dallas, Texas; d. Jan. 21, 1967) Ronald Reagan, in *Kings Row*, adored this redhead; at Warner Bros., at all times, so did everyone on the lot—with the possible exception of Jack L. Warner, with whom she often fought for better roles; humorous as well as sexy, she was a regular guy, a straight shooter, the poker pal of Errol Flynn—and part-Cherokee; was the studio's foremost glamour girl, publicized as "The Oomph Girl" (which she hated), but nature had made a couple of mistakes, about which she joked; there was a great gap between her front teeth (always wore a porcelain cap when being photographed) and, being a "flattie," her much-admired bosom came courtesy of a studio-designed bra; all else was real, including her frankness; for a few weeks in '42, was married to star George Brent; when asked by Louella Parsons why they broke up so soon, the actress succinctly replied, "Brent bent" (credit for the story goes to screenwriter Stuart Jerome, who was there); said of her earlier (1936–39) marriage to actor Edward Norris, "I was just another one of Eddie's many redheaded wives"; later came a long relationship with publicist Steve Hannagan, who died in '53, leaving her $218,399; the daughter of an auto mechanic, she grew up—the youngest of five children—in Denton, the small Texas town to which her family moved soon after her birth; ever a tomboy, she was a sophomore at North Texas State Teachers' College (and an ace basketball player), planning a teaching career, when a sister sent a bathing-suit photo of her to Paramount's "Search for Beauty" contest; signed by the studio at 19, she acted first under her real name and had minor roles in nearly two dozen movies (*Notorious Sophie Lang, Wagon Wheels*, etc.) before being billed as Ann; Warner Bros., where she stayed through the '40s, took over her contract ($75 a week) in '36; only began playing leads there in the late '30s (*Angels With Dirty Faces, They Made Me a Criminal*, etc.); Rex Harrison, who never met her, once cited her as one of Hollywood's ten most exciting women; like her fans, he said he "was struck by her extraordinary magnetism and directness. . . . She is warm and human—with a distinctive quality of earthiness that never descends to blatant sexiness"; her sex appeal, though, made her a top pinup favorite with G.I.s; off screen, dancing was her passion, and she was to be found on many evenings at Ciro's or the Mocambo, doing the conga or the rhumba—"the" dances of the '40s—with favorite partner Cesar Romero; after '48, lived for nearly a decade in Mexico, commuting from south of the border for film commitments; when her movie career came to an abrupt end in '57 (after *Woman and the Hunter*), she moved to New York and took whatever acting jobs she could find; toured in plays (met actor Scott McKay, whom she married in '66, while doing *Kind Sir*), did TV guest appearances ("Playhouse 90," "Climax"), was featured in a daytime TV soap opera (NBC's "Another World"); took it all in stride, saying with a laugh, "There are a few good parts being written for women my age. But Roz Russell gets those. The rest of us stand in line"; went back to Hollywood at 51 in style, as the star of TV's "Pistols 'n' Petticoats," a Western comedy series; she and the show were hits—but she did not live to finish the first season.

MOVIE HIGHLIGHTS: *The Great O'Malley, San Quentin, Dodge City, Indianapolis Speedway, Angels Wash Their Faces, Torrid Zone, They Drive by Night, City for Conquest, Navy Blues, Honeymoon for Three, The Man Who Came to Dinner, Juke Girl, George Washington Slept Here, The Animal Kingdom, Edge of Darkness, Shine On, Harvest Moon, The Doughgirls, One More Tomorrow, The Unfaithful, Nora Prentiss, Good Sam, Silver River, I Was a Male War Bride, Stella, Take Me to Town, Come Next Spring, The Opposite Sex.*

Frank Sinatra

(b. Francis Albert Sinatra, Dec. 12, 1915, Hoboken, N.J.) At the Paramount Theater in New York in the early '40s, hysterical girls in saddle-shoes and "sloppy Joe" sweaters screamed so loudly (the earliest paid to do so by his press agent) over a skinny singer—in a big bow tie, with an Adam's apple and caved-in cheeks—that an idol was born; over the decades, the idol became a legend; "The Voice," they called this son—only child—of an Italian immigrant fireman; in time, the voice—first heard nationally on radio's "Major Bowes Amateur Hour"—would soar to magical heights and rain a fortune on its owner (via movies, records, radio, TV, supper clubs), be lost, then gloriously regained; on the "Amateur Hour," Sinatra sang his "lucky" song, "Night and Day," which won him a spot on Major Bowes' touring show and remains his favorite song ("I always include it when I open an engagement anywhere"); early career (after trying sportswriting): sustaining (no sponsor) radio shows—18 a week at one point—in New York (salary: 70¢ carfare from New Jersey to the Mutual studios); first paying job ($15 a week) was as the singer-emcee at the Rustic Cabin, a dance hall in Englewood, N.J.; early influences on his singing style were all women: Billie Holiday, Mabel Mercer, Ella Fitzgerald, and Lee Wiley; Harry James heard him on the air (singing "Begin the Beguine" with Harold Arden's band), interviewed him at the Paramount Theater, and hired him; was on the road with James's band for the second half of '39; next (1940–42), was featured with Tommy Dorsey's orchestra; first appeared on screen as a singer with this band—in *Las Vegas Nights* ('41) and *Ship Ahoy* ('42); has said: "My greatest teacher was not a vocal coach . . . but the way Tommy Dorsey breathed and phrased on the trombone"; first movie as a soloist after becoming a star in his own right: Ann Miller's *Reveille with Beverly* (in which he had no lines); later that year ('43) made his starring debut as a singer-actor in *Higher and Higher*, at RKO, where he was next in *Step Lively* (and got his first screen kiss—from Gloria De Haven); movie career went into high gear at MGM, where he remained to the end of the decade, starting with *Anchors Aweigh* ('45) with Gene Kelly; also made a short subject on intolerance that year, *The House I Live In*, that won a special Oscar; the Hollywood star who, at the start, made the greatest impression on him: "Norma Shearer. So feminine and lovely—but as smart as a man" (voiced in pre-Lib days); first straight acting role was that of a priest in 1948's *The Miracle of the Bells* (did one song, unaccompanied, "Ever Homeward"); earnings climbed to more than $1 million a year; hard times came in the early '50s when his vocal cords abruptly hemorrhaged, movies like *Meet Danny Wilson* flopped, and his agency dropped him; determined to make it as an actor, he campaigned for and got the role of Maggio in *From Here to Eternity* (salary: $8,000); won the 1953 Best Supporting Oscar; two years later was nominated as Best Actor for *The Man with the Golden Arm*; recovering his singing voice, he alternated between musicals and dramatic films; soon was earning annually $7 million–plus; fans were not pleased when, in '51, he and first wife Nancy Barbato (married since '39) were divorced—at his request; children: Nancy Jr., Frank Jr., and Christina; wife #2 (1951–57) was Ava Gardner; #3 (1966–68) was Mia Farrow (who was less than half his age; long after the divorce, his ex–mother-in-law, Maureen O'Sullivan, volunteered: "Nice man. He used to ring me up when he was in New York"); married his fourth wife, Barbara Marx (ex of Zeppo Marx), in '76; the song he requests orchestras to play for her: "The Most Beautiful Girl in the World"; once summed up his career this way: "Fruitful, busy, uptight, loose, sometimes boisterous, occasionally sad, but always exciting."

MOVIE HIGHLIGHTS: *Till the Clouds Roll By, Words and Music, It Happened in Brooklyn, The Kissing Bandit, Take Me Out to the Ballgame, On the Town, Double Dynamite, Suddenly, Young at Heart, Not as a Stranger, Guys and Dolls, The Tender Trap, High Society, The Joker Is Wild, The Pride and the Passion, Pal Joey, Kings Go Forth, Some Came Running, A Hole in the Head, Never So Few, Can-Can, Ocean's 11, The Manchurian Candidate, None But the Brave.*

Red Skelton

(b. Richard Bernard Skelton, July 18, 1910, Vincennes, Ind.) MGM's rusty-haired, rubber-faced knockabout comedy star who created such wacko characters as Clem Kaddiddlehopper and Cauliflower McPugg, and whose catchphrases ("I dood it" and "I'm a mean widdle kid") swept the nation; audiences warmed to him because, as noted by producer Marty Rackin (who grew up with him), "He's never been anything but the childlike country boy"; had his quirks—insisted on a clause in his contract that he never had to pick up a telephone because he's always had a deathly fear of phones; another oddity—he is often seen with a cigar in his mouth, but he never smokes it; maintains he is not a comedian, comic, or wit, but "a clown"; his father, who died two months before he was born, was a circus clown, he himself was clowning in burlesque by the time he was 17, and in later years his paintings of clowns—once only a hobby—have sold for up to $40,000 apiece; to support Red and his two brothers, their mother worked as a vaudeville-house charwoman; at 10 he did a song-and-dance routine on the streets and at 12, left home to join a traveling medicine show; says, "I was never an amateur. I got pennies for dancing, and when I joined the medicine show I got ten bucks a week"; during his hard-scrabble years, was in dance marathons, tent shows, minstrels, the Hagenback–Wallace Circus (as a clown), and vaudeville; compensating for the schooling he never had, he later acquired a high school diploma via tutoring and became a dedicated student of the life and times of Lincoln; in '31 he met and married Edna Stilwell, a 15-year-old usher at a Kansas City burlesque house in which he was playing; always called her "Mummy," and she became his business manager, remaining so long after their divorce in '43; billed Richard "Red" Skelton, he made his movie debut in '38 in Ginger Rogers' *Having Wonderful Time*, playing a comic character named "Itchy"; began his 13-year contract at MGM in '40 with a very minor role in Robert Taylor's *Flight Command*; also had secondary roles in two "Dr. Kildare" movies before breaking through to stardom in 1941's *Whistling in the Dark*; concurrent with his stint at Metro, had a vastly successful radio program (and, in '51, segued from it to "The Red Skelton Show" on TV, which ranked high in the Nielsens for exactly two decades); in the army 1943–45, and assigned to Special Services, he appeared in some 3,800 shows on troop carriers and hospital ships crossing the Atlantic and Mediterranean; went in and was discharged as a private; in '45, was married to Georgia Davis, a titian-haired model; referred to one another as "Big Red" and "Little Red" and exchanged Valentines on each of the first 14 days of February; children: daughter Valentina and son Richard Freeman, who died in '58, at 9, after a prolonged battle with leukemia (the year before, his parents took him on a month-long tour of Europe to show him sights he would not live to see otherwise); a friend, writer Bill Davidson, has said: "For four years after Richard died, Skelton kept the boy's room exactly as he had left it, with his toys scattered around. He used to go into the room and sit there alone for hours at a time"; after his son's death, the comedian, long a heavy drinker, became a teetotaler—and his wife drifted into the oblivion of pills and alcohol; in '71, following a long separation, Skelton filed for divorce; two years later, he married famed cinematographer Gregg Toland's daughter, Lothian; on May 10, 1976, on the 18th anniversary of their son's death, Skelton's ex-wife committed suicide; growing older, and still occasionally active, the star has spoken of his admiration for fellow comic George Burns, saying, "His humor is about age. We all laugh, but we lie when we do."

MOVIE HIGHLIGHTS: *Lady Be Good, Dr. Kildare's Wedding Day, Whistling in Dixie, Ship Ahoy, Maisie Gets Her Man, Panama Hattie, Du Barry*

Was a Lady, Thousands Cheer, I Dood It, Whistling in Brooklyn, Bathing Beauty, Ziegfeld Follies, The Show-Off, Merton of the Movies, A Southern Yankee, The Fuller Brush Man, Neptune's Daughter, The Yellow Cab Man, Three Little Words, Watch the Birdie, Excuse My Dust, Texas Carnival, The Clown.

Alexis Smith

(b. Margaret Alexis Fitzsimmons Smith, June 8, 1921, Penticton, B.C., Canada) Between '40 and '50 Warner Bros. repeatedly cast this Junoesque (5'9") blonde beauty with blue-green eyes as an "Ice Princess," and, often as not, as a glacial sophisticate years older than she actually was; because of her height (and his) was regularly seen opposite Errol Flynn—in 1941's *Dive Bomber* (first romantic lead but a minor role), *Gentleman Jim, San Antonio*, etc.; fans may have fonder memories of her career than she; has remarked: "So many of the films were not very good. And I always got the roles everyone else—Bette Davis, Ida Lupino, Ann Sheridan—turned down"; also says of her early years in movies: "It was awful, really, for actors of stature like Fredric March [they co-starred in *The Adventures of Mark Twain*] to be stuck with some starlet in a leopard bathing suit"—but only one actor, Sydney Greenstreet, ever complained; the only child of a Canadian mother and a Scottish father (a food products company exec)—to whom she always remained devoted—she grew up in Los Angeles after age 5; made her professional stage debut at 13 with a ballet troupe in a Hollywood Bowl production of *Carmen*; attended Hollywood High (with Lana Turner and Marge Champion) and, in her senior year, choreographed and danced in *The Red Mill*— and decided to become an actress: was next a drama major for two years at Los Angeles City College; movie agent Vic Orsatti saw her in her final show there, *The Night of January 16th*, and arranged a Warners screen test; signed a $50-a-week contract, posed for cheesecake, was publicized as "The Dynamite Girl," and was seen, but not heard, in Miriam Hopkins' *The Lady with Red Hair* and Eve Arden's *She Couldn't Say No*; spoke her first dialogue—one line—in *Flight from Destiny*, starring Geraldine Fitzgerald; first major lead was in a '41 B picture, *Steel Against the Sky*, opposite a handsome newcomer named Craig Stevens (real name: Gail Hughes Shickles Jr.); they had a church wedding in '44 after he'd completed a three-year stint in the Army Air Force; hoped for a large family but never had children; bigtime fame eluded him until more than a decade later, when he starred on TV in "Peter Gunn"; his movie career flagged as hers surged forward and she co-starred with Cary

Grant in *Night and Day*, Bogart in *The Two Mrs. Carrolls*, etc.; Craig Stevens has said, "In the early '50s we grew apart. She was in London making a movie, I was in New York trying to get a stage career started. We were separated a whole year. What brought us together again—no thanks to 'friends,' who took sides—was our own discovery of how much we meant to each other, how much we were one"; shoring up their marriage—which has endured—they began acting on stage together in stock, in comedies *(Cactus Flower, Any Wednesday)* and musicals *(Plain and Fancy)*; after free-lancing at other studios, the actress returned to Warners in '59 for *The Young Philadelphians* (her favorite role), then was not seen on screen again until *Once Is Not Enough* in '75; in the meantime, in '71, fulfilling a lifelong ambition, she starred on Broadway in a musical, *Follies*, a smash hit; "Alexis Smith," said one critic, "is the living, dancing refutation of F. Scott Fitzgerald's axiom that there are no second acts in American lives. At 49 she is in the best second act of her life"; won the New York Drama Critics Award and a Tony, and, on stage and in movies, is still going strong.

MOVIE HIGHLIGHTS: *The Constant Nymph, The Animal Kingdom, The Doughgirls, The Horn Blows at Midnight, Rhapsody in Blue, Conflict, One More Tomorrow, Of Human Bondage, Stallion Road, The Woman in White, The Decision of Christopher Blake, Whiplash, South of St. Louis, Any Number Can Play, Montana, Here Comes the Groom, Split Second, The Sleeping Tiger, Beau James, This Happy Feeling.*

Charles Starrett

(b. Charles Starrett, March 28, 1904, Athol, Mass.) There were many "Hollywoods" once; the people who made Bs or serials, for instance, mainly knew only other people who worked in the same area; it's entirely possible that Hollywoodians living on the manicured lawns of Beverly Hills never even knew this star existed; millions of small-town moviegoers, though, knew Charles Starrett, hard-riding, two-fisted cowboy, to be one of the handsomest heroes on the screen; for 17 continuous contract years at Columbia (1935–52), he turned out thrill-a-minute Westerns—a total of 115 quick-on-the-draw Saturday afternoon specials; except for one year ('43)—when he was inexplicably omitted, though he starred in nine that season—he was among the top ten of Western moneymakers from '37 through '52; after *The Kid from Broken Gun* that year, when only 48, he hung up his spurs and shootin' irons; had been most popular as "The Durango Kid," the mysterious masked rider he played countless times after first portraying him in a 1940 movie of that title; writers of Starrett's movies, incidentally, were warned to avoid the letter "r" in scripts (as in "wrangler" and "horse") for, with the speech of a New England gentleman, he was never able to "Westernize" that particular sound; unlike many Western heroes, for the first few years he usually had the same "villain" to beat (a hulking brute of an actor named Dick Curtis), the same heroine to woo (the beautiful Iris Meredith, whose "father" was invariably Edward Le Saint), and he was nearly always called "Steve"; born to wealth (the son of the founder of the Starrett Precision Tool Co.), he announced his intention to become an actor at 9; ran off at 13 and joined a troupe of actors but was brought back and installed in military school (where he learned his horsemanship); at Dartmouth, where he was a gridiron hero, he acted in school plays; made his movie "debut" on campus in '25, when he and some of his football teammates were picked to be extras in Richard Dix's *The Quarterback*, made at Dartmouth; winning his B.S. in '25, he toured for two years with the Stewart Walker Stock Co., made his Broadway debut in '27 in *Courage*, and, two years later, was appearing in *Claire Adams* when spotted by movie scouts; arrived in Hollywood with a wife (whom he kept), the former Mary McKinnon (married in '27), and their twin sons (not identical), David and Charles; first Hollywood movie: *Fast and Loose* ('30); played romantic roles only, in 38 features, over the next six years—in *Our Betters, The Mask of Fu Manchu, Sweetheart of Sigma Chi*, etc.; one of the founders of the Screen Actors Guild, he is the holder of the lifetime SAG membership card #10; replacing Tim McCoy, who'd left Columbia, he first donned chaps and a ten-gallon hat in 1935's *Gallant Defender* (in which there was a bit player named Leonard Slye, who became more famous later as Roy Rogers); riding off into the sunset—to early retirement at Laguna—he was a very rich man.

MOVIE HIGHLIGHTS: *Silver Streak, The Return of Casey Jones, Three on a Honeymoon, So Red the Rose, Two-Gun Law, Call of the Rockies, West of Cheyenne, South of Arizona, Western Caravans, The Man from Sundown, Riders of Black River, Outlaws of the Panhandle, Down Rio Grande Way, Cyclone Prairie Rangers, Phantom Valley.*

Linda Stirling

(b. Louise Schultz, Oct. 11, 1923, Long Beach, Calif.) Fleet as a gazelle, in a sexy short tiger skin with matching cap and calf-length boots, this long-limbed

(5'7"), hazel-eyed brunette raced her way to stardom as the serial queen of the '40s; the 12-episode thriller turning the trick for her: 1944's *The Tiger Woman*; had never faced a movie camera before: recalls her skimpy costume with shivers ("I would arrive at the location 'jungle' at 4 A.M. and find the crew sweeping the ground to remove the frost"); also says, "I thought I had signed a contract to *act* in a movie. Instead, I learned by the second day of filming that I'd signed up for an endurance contest"; five more chapter-plays followed before she left the screen in '47: *Zorro's Black Whip*, *Manhunt of Mystery Island*, *The Purple Monster Strikes*, *The Crimson Ghost*, *Jesse James Rides Again*; "Her reign," a critic said later, "was one of hard riding, accurate shooting, and a thousand thrills, some of them for the big boys as well as the small ones"; some of her daredevil stunts were done by a double—usually a man—but she also experienced her perilous moments; barely escaped a certain-death fall in one serial and came close to drowning, thanks to her hands' being tied, in a *Purple Monster Strikes* ocean sequence filmed off San Clemente; between serials she starred in Bs and was the exceptionally beautiful heroine of Western heroes Allan Lane and "Wild" Bill Elliott; had planned a quite different future as an actress; performed with her hometown's Long Beach Players during high school days; moved to Hollywood and became a student at the Ben Bard Playhouse; considering the career she soon had, it's interesting to note that Bard was the widower of Ruth Roland, star of the silent cliff-hangers; continued her dramatic studies with Maria Ouspenskaya and paid for lessons by working as a photographer's model; her picture on a magazine cover led to a Republic contract; late in '46, shortly before quitting movies, she became—and remained—the wife of Sloan Nibley, scriptwriter of top-grade Westerns (*Springfield Rifle*, *Carson City*, etc.); two sons: Chris and Tim; continued for a decade on TV, as a guest star ("Wyatt Earp," "Mr. District Attorney," etc.) and as a panelist on "20 Questions"; next took a few college courses, discovered she was "hooked," and, as this "whole new world opened up," she "began turning down acting jobs so that I wouldn't miss a class"; became a full-time student at UCLA, where in '64, making Phi Beta Kappa, she received her B.A.; went on to get her master's degree; in '65, began what proved to be a long and highly rewarding career as an associate professor of English and drama—Shakespeare included, naturally—at Glendale College in Glendale, Calif.; has said, "No one could have been more surprised than I. It was stranger than I can describe to find myself in front of a class, especially the first year or so. Right in the middle of a sentence I'd find myself thinking, What am I doing here? How did I get here? And, even though I've been teaching now for years, there are still moments when I think I must be playing a 'teacher' part in a movie."

MOVIE HIGHLIGHTS: *San Antonio Kid, Vigilantes of Dodge City, The Cherokee Flash, Sheriff of Sundown, Santa Fe Saddlemates, The Topeka Terror, Wagon Wheels Westward, D-Day on Mars, Cyclostrode-X, The Invisible Informer, The Mysterious Mr. Valentine, The Madonna's Secret, Rio Grande Raiders, The Pretender.*

Gale Storm

(b. Josephine Owaissa Cottle, April 5, 1922, Bloomington, Texas) Television viewers know the bubbly brunette best for her TV series, "My Little Margie" (1952–55) and "Oh, Susanna" (1956–60); movie fans, though, have fond recollections of her in dozens of B pictures of the '40s—dramas, Westerns, musicals—in which she usually was cast in girl-next-door roles; they even knew that her middle name, Owaissa, was Indian for "bluebird" (but none of her ancestors were Indian); was the youngest of five, and her father, who worked in a pottery factory, died when she was 13 months old; her mother, moving the family to Houston shortly afterward, worked as a seamstress and later married a widower who added his three children to the brood; at San Jacinto High, Gale played leads in many shows and won a "best actress" prize in an interscholastic drama contest; was 17 and a high school senior when teachers insisted she enter Jesse L. Lasky's "Gateway to Hollywood" radio competition, a nationwide program designed to discover new dramatic talent for movies; two names had been chosen in advance to bestow upon the winners—the girl would be "Gale Storm" and the boy "Terry Belmont," and each would receive a "seven-year contract" at RKO (no mention being made of options); her early philosophy—"Don't plan anything and everything will happen for you"—soon proved accurate; she and a would-be actor from Indiana, Lee Bonnell, were among the three finalists of each sex; "It really was love at first sight," she recalls, after seeing him in a rehearsal hall. "It popped into my head that here was the boy I was going to marry"; won their new names—and $125-a-week contracts—on Sunday evening, Dec. 31, 1939; at the studio, where she finished high school, she had a minor role in *Tom Brown's School Days* and a lead in *One Crowded Night* (in which she was outfitted in shorts once worn on screen by Ginger Rogers, which did not prove lucky); RKO dropped her after six months; "Terry Belmont"—quickly ditching the phony name for his real one—continued under contract (in *Parachute Battalion*, *Lady Scarface*, etc.) through '47; they married ("forever") in '41 and eventually had four children: Phillip, Peter, Paul, and Susanna; after appearing in Roy Rogers Westerns (*Red River Valley*, etc.), Gale began a years-long contract at Monogram (starting at $300 a week) with 1942's *Rhythm Parade*; first big hit there: *Where Are Your Children?* ('44), which, made for pennies, grossed over a million; with other successes came a promotion to $50,000 a year; meanwhile, Lee Bonnell quit acting and went into the insurance business, becoming such a winner that he soon occupied the penthouse of Massachusetts Mutual's office in Sherman Oaks; leaving movies after 1952's *Woman of the North Country*, the actress became vastly more popular in television, later starring in summer stock in many shows (*South Pacific, The Unsinkable Molly Brown*, etc.); despite success, a solid family, and church life (is devoutly Methodist), she became an alcoholic—as she revealed in her autobiography, *I Ain't Down Yet* ('81); "I started to drink in the early 1960s . . . and I started to drink too much in the early 1970s," she admits; sought a solution to her problem with counseling, AA, private doctors, even a stay in a psychiatric ward; victory over her addiction came in '79 via the "calculatedly grim treatment of aversion therapy" at Raleigh Hills Hospital in California, an alcoholic treatment center that is one of the facilities of Advanced Health Systems—for which she later became a dedicated volunteer spokesperson.

MOVIE HIGHLIGHTS: *Saddlemates, City of Missing Girls, Foreign Agent, Lure of the Islands, The Man from Cheyenne, Campus Rhythm, Revenge of the Zombies, The Right to Love, Forever Yours, Sunbonnet Sue, G.I. Honeymoon, Swing Parade of 1946, It Happened on Fifth Avenue, The Tenderfoot, The Dude Goes West, Stampede, The Kid from Texas, Underworld Story, Between Midnight and Dawn.*

Elizabeth Taylor

(b. Elizabeth Rosemond Taylor, Feb. 27, 1932, London, England) Gossip columns, for decades, would have been duller without this violet-eyed star whose life—more than that of any other—has been lived under a spotlight at center stage; being born in London gave her dual American-English citizenship, both parents being American; father Francis, from Indiana, was an art dealer; Kansas-born mother, Sara Warmbraten, was an ingenue known as Sara Sothern in four Broadway shows (*Mama Loves Papa*, etc.) in the '20s; the threat of war in England in '39 caused the family to flee to Beverly Hills; made her movie debut at 9 as a bratty kid—bit part—in a B comedy at Universal starring Hugh Herbert, *There's One Born Every Minute*; studio dropped her option ("This kid has nothing. Her eyes are too old"); was signed by MGM in '43 and worked first with boy actor Roddy McDowall (who, like many later co-stars, became a lifelong friend) in *Lassie Come Home*; at the studio for 15 years, she grew up on screen under the eyes of an ever-growing public—from spunky kid *(National Velvet)*, to debutante *(Cynthia)*, to romantic lead *(Conspirator*, with Robert Taylor, at 17), to newlywed *(Father of the Bride)*, to superstar *(Ivanhoe)*; was no pushover, even as a child—when Louis B. Mayer once insulted her mother in her presence, she yelled at the most powerful man in Hollywood: "Don't you dare speak to my mother like that! You and your studio can both go to hell!"; vocabulary became even more colorful with age; swore she'd never enter Mayer's office again and never did; began hitting the columns in her teens via fleeting romances with Peter Lawford, actor Marshall Thompson, and singer Vic Damone, and soon-broken engagements to Army football hero Glenn Davis and wealthy William Pawley Jr.; for three years in a row was nominated for the Best Actress Oscar *(Raintree County, Cat on a Hot Tin Roof, Suddenly Last Summer)*—and lost; won the following year ('60) for the movie she likes least, *Butterfield 8*; "The only reason I got the Oscar was that I had come within a breath of dying. . . . It was a sympathy vote," she has said, referring to a near-fatal siege of pneumonia in a London hospital when only a tracheotomy saved her life, as newspapers everywhere had her obituary prepared and ready to run; was just one of her more than 70 stays in hospitals—all making headlines; even bigger news was generated by her many marriages, divorces, and the dramatic events surrounding them; husband #1 (1949–51) was hotel heir Nicky Hilton (gave her a Cadillac convertible, a $15,000 engagement ring, a white mink stole, 100 shares of Hilton Hotel stock—and a miserable few weeks before she left him); #2 (1952–57) was English star Michael Wilding (bought herself a huge sapphire-and-diamonds engagement ring; he gave her two sons, Michael Jr. and Christopher, and, finally, a "quickie" Mexican divorce to wed her next); #3 (1957–58) was Broadway-movie producer Mike Todd (saying "Thirty carats would be vulgar," he gave her a 29.7-carat diamond costing $92,000, a daughter, Liza, born prematurely, over whom doctors worked 14 minutes before she breathed, and left her a widow when he perished in a plane crash); #4 (1959–64) was singer Eddie Fisher (the best man at her wedding to Todd, he gave her an ice-cube-sized diamond ring and a 40-carat diamond-studded bracelet—"and that was just for starters"—and a rough time when she wanted a divorce to marry his successor, with whom she fell in love while making *Cleopatra*); #5 (1964–74) was Richard Burton (lavished jewels on her—the 33-carat Krupp diamond, the 69-carat Cartier diamond, valued at $1,050,000, and the lustrous Peregrina pearl that King Philip II of Spain gave Mary Tudor in 1554; volatile lovers, they lived like Arabian royalty with, at

206

one point, 25 full-time employees at various far-flung places—servants, body-guards, a helicopter pilot, and a yacht crew; made eight movies together); #6 (1975–76) was also Richard Burton (June of '76 marked an historic event—*he* divorced *her*, the first man known to walk out on her); #7 (1976–81) was U.S. Senator John Warner of Virginia (a millionaire whom, reportedly, she often called "cheap," he designed for her a red-white-and-blue engagement ring with one small ruby and one small diamond); in '81 she made a triumphant debut on Broadway in *The Little Foxes*, following up two years later with *Private Lives*—co-starring with "double ex" Richard Burton; starred at 21 in a movie titled *The Girl Who Had Everything*, and it would seem that, in time, she did have.

MOVIE HIGHLIGHTS: *The White Cliffs of Dover, Jane Eyre, Life with Father, A Date with Judy, Julia Misbehaves, Little Women, Father's Little Dividend, A Place in the Sun, Rhapsody, Elephant Walk, Beau Brummel, The Last Time I Saw Paris, Giant, The V.I.P.s, The Sandpiper, Who's Afraid of Virginia Woolf?* (won her second Best Actress Oscar), *The Taming of the Shrew, Reflections in a Golden Eye, Secret Ceremony, Under Milk Wood, The Mirror Crack'd.*

Gene Tierney

(b. Gene Eliza Taylor Tierney, Nov. 20, 1920, Brooklyn, N.Y.) At 20th Century–Fox in the '40s, this green-eyed beauty was the distaff version of Tyrone Power (with whom she often co-starred)—the "class act" of the lot, the femme star given first consideration when any grade-A melodrama was being cast; there were, however, some strange early roles—the Polynesian in *Son of Fury*, the Arabian in *Sundown*, the unwashed, barefooted Ellie May in *Tobacco Road*; soon settled in as the young American woman of breeding; her unusual "boy's name," publicists were obliged to explain, was given her in memory of her mother's only brother, who had died in his teens; though nominated for the Best Actress Oscar as the malevolent socialite in *Leave Her to Heaven*, the haunting title character in *Laura* was by far her most famous role; that time she was second choice (Jennifer Jones, whom the studio would have had to borrow from Selznick, had turned it down), and her own reaction was, "Who wants to play a painting?"; had to be persuaded to do the role; stardom that ensued was reassurance to this stockbroker's daughter that aban-doning the life of a debutante to act—after being educated at the best private schools in the U.S. and Switzerland—had been the proper choice; took three tries to get her career properly launched; at 17 was a visitor at Warner Bros. when a studio talent scout induced her to make a test; refused to sign a "stock" contract at $150 a week when she learned she was being offered triple the usual newcomer's salary because of the publicity value of her society background; totally without dramatic training, she landed a small role on Broadway in *Mrs. O'Brien Entertains*, since she looked Irish (which she is) and could manage a brogue; though the play flopped, Columbia took her to Hollywood, tested her (a scene from Ginger Rogers' *The Primrose Path*), put her under contract, and kept her idle for six months; asking out, she returned to the New York stage for flop #2, *Ring Two*, before, at 19, scoring a hit in *The Male Animal*; signed a Fox contract with clauses inserted that her name and looks (including slightly protruding teeth) could not be changed, and finally, the deal would be void if the studio did not put her to work within 30 days; was playing the feminine lead opposite Henry Fonda in *The Return of Frank James* before she'd been in Hollywood two weeks; remained a star at the studio for 15 years; to protect her earnings at the start of her career, her father set up a family corporation; was not quite 21 when she eloped with designer Oleg Cassini, long before he became famous, and her father made ugly headlines by suing her for breach of contract ("a tremendous disillusionment," she said); her first daughter, Daria, was born deaf, blind, and hopelessly retarded; filed for divorce from Cassini in '47, but they reconciled and had another daughter, Christina; were finally divorced in '52; courted by both Howard Hughes and the young John F. Kennedy, the star next was involved in a globe-trotting romance with Prince Aly Khan; suffered a total nervous breakdown when that affair terminated abruptly; has said, "I was ill when I made *Black Widow* and *The Egyptian*. And when I made *The Left Hand of God* ['55], I was very sick, indeed. Curiously enough, my doctors, looking at these movies, detected no signs of illness"; was at Menninger's and other clinics, see-sawing between advances and severe setbacks (including a suicide attempt) until, after years of treatment, was pronounced sufficiently recovered to resume a normal life; worked in a few movies later but always in nontaxing cameo roles; admitting that she still must combat depression, she has said, "My mental illness is something I have to live with. It has been like a door opening and closing"; making her home in Houston, Texas, she was happily married from '60 until his death in '81 to wealthy W. Howard Lee (once wed to Hedy Lamarr); published a book about her life, *Self-Portrait*, written with Mickey Herskowitz, in '79.

MOVIE HIGHLIGHTS: *Hudson's Bay, Belle Starr, The Shanghai Gesture, Rings on Her Fingers, China Girl, Thunder Birds, Heaven Can Wait, A Bell for Adano, Dragonwyck, The Razor's Edge, The Ghost and Mrs. Muir, The Iron Curtain, That Wonderful Urge, Whirlpool, Night and the City, Where the Sidewalk Ends, The Mating Season, On the Riviera, Close to My Heart, The Secret of Convict Lake, Plymouth Adventure, Never Let Me Go.*

Sidney Toler

(b. Sidney Toler, April 28, 1874, Warrensburg, Mo.; d. Feb. 12, 1947) Being no more Chinese than Swedish-born Warner Oland was, this American actor—of Scottish descent—succeeded him as the screen's Charlie Chan; played the famous sleuth more times than any other star—in 22 films (11 at 20th Century–Fox and, later, another 11 at Monogram) vs. the 16 in which Oland appeared (all at Fox); took over the part in '38, following Oland's death, starting with *Charlie Chan in Honolulu*; won the role against stiff competition from Noah Beery and Leo Carrillo, both of whom tested; played it—as his predecessor had done—with a minimum of makeup; his eyes had a natural slant so all that was necessary to create the character's look was to paste on a moustache and that tiny tuft of hair beneath the lower lip; directors complained that he was a less engaging actor than Oland and that his age (was 64 when he began playing the role) made him a less vital figure; they also carped that his excessive drinking resulted in his being the screen's most somnolent Charlie Chan; still, most aficionados of the series would agree that at least three of his entries rank among the best of all those done at Fox: *Charlie Chan at Treasure Island, Charlie Chan in Panama*, and *Charlie Chan at the Wax Museum*; before assuming the role, had never before, on stage or screen, portrayed an Oriental; in his debut movie, Ruth Chatterton's *Madam X* ('29), he'd played an Englishman, as he did in numerous films of the '30s; was so versatile, though, that in Hepburn's *Spitfire*, he was a hillbilly, and in Crawford's *Gorgeous Hussy*, he portrayed Daniel Webster; a graduate of the University of Kansas, he was a stage actor for decades before entering movies; in the '20s, starred on Broadway for famed producer-director David Belasco (*Deburau, The Dove, Lulu Belle*, etc.); he wrote numerous Broadway plays, too, including *Golden Days, The Exile*, and *Ritzy*, the last of which he also directed; in '43, after Fox dropped the Chan series and before Monogram picked it up in '44, he worked at Universal; there he played Chinese roles in Maria Montez' *White Savage* and *The Adventures of Smilin' Jack* serial—and in Loretta Young's *A Night to Remember*, was a New York detective, Inspector Hankins; was married to supporting actress Viva Tattersall.

MOVIE HIGHLIGHTS: *The Phantom President, Blonde Venus, Tom Brown of Culver, King of the Jungle, Call of the Wild, The Daring Young Man, Our Relations, Quality Street, If I Were King, Gold Is Where You Find It, Wide Open Faces, Charlie Chan in Reno, Charlie Chan in the City of Darkness, King of Chinatown, Charlie Chan's Murder Cruise, Murder over New York, Dead Men Tell, Charlie Chan in Rio, Castle in the Desert, Charlie Chan in the Secret Service, The Jade Mask.*

Sonny Tufts

(b. Bowen Charleton Tufts III, July 16, 1911, Boston, Mass.; d. June 5, 1970) Like some overaged, oversized high school football hero, this blond galoot bumbled his way into pictures and had his season in the sun at Paramount—a season that lasted five years—before he fell into Bs elsewhere; femmes favored his rugged, often bared torso and goofy don't-give-a-damn charm; males found him to be "one of the guys"; "Sonny" was his nickname from childhood; was one of the few Boston Brahmins to become an actor; one early forebear founded Tufts College, and many ancestors, including his father, were pillars of Boston's merchant and banking communities; since Harvard was a family tradition, he went to Yale—played football (tackle), acted, sang in the glee club, and got his degree in anthropology; receiving no help from his family, he went into show business after leading his own band during school vacations; sang, as Bowen Charleton, in the chorus of Broadway musicals *(Who's Who, Sing for Your Supper)*, while selling refrigerators on the side; later was a solo attraction—doing humorous musical sketches—in nightclubs in New York (The Beachcomber) and Palm Beach, Fla. (The White Hall); convinced he should be in movies, millionaire pal Alexis Thompson signed him to a personal contract, paid his way to Hollywood, gave him a salary until he got started, and provided an introduction to an agent—in exchange for 50 percent of his first two years' salary; arrived in California in '43 with his wife, dancer Barbara Dare (were married from '38 to '53, when they divorced); for his screen test (with beautiful Helen Walker), Paramount handed him a sheet of dialogue ("I clowned it up good") that he learned later was one of Boyer's big romantic scenes from *Love Affair*; "He's either the lousiest actor or funniest guy I've ever seen," said director Mark Sandrich, assigning him the role of Kansas, a "good ol' boy" G.I., in *So Proudly We Hail*; love scenes were with Paulette Goddard, "the most fascinating woman I met in Hollywood. She knew all the answers but had a little-girl manner about her that was wonderful. I was so green about movie acting and

210

asked so many questions that she put a sign on her dressing room door: Information Bureau"; was often cast in military roles, but physical disabilities—cracked pelvis, broken kneecaps, enlarged heart—kept him out of the service; movie success ended family objections to his choice of career; boasted that he was "not a conventional person"—and also of his fondness for alcohol, which eventually brought several arrests for drunkenness and made producers leery of hiring him; ended his career playing paunchy, smiling villains.

MOVIE HIGHLIGHTS: *Government Girl, In the Meantime, Darling, Here Come the Waves, I Love a Soldier, Bring on the Girls, Duffy's Tavern, Miss Susie Slagle's, The Virginian, The Well-Groomed Bride, Swell Guy, Easy Come, Easy Go, Blaze of Noon, Cross My Heart, Untamed Breed, Easy Living, The Crooked Way, Run for the Hills, No Escape, Glory at Sea (aka The Gift Horse), City on the Hunt, The Seven Year Itch, Come Next Spring, The Parson and the Outlaw.*

Lana Turner

(b. Julia Jean Mildred Frances Turner, Feb. 8, 1921, Wallace, Idaho) Gossip column item from 1946: "Howard Hughes walked into a nightclub with Ava Gardner, his current flame, clinging to his arm. A few minutes later in came Frank Sinatra and Lana Turner, the girl Howard almost married a few months ago. The natives got a big chuckle when Frank and Howard exchanged partners for a few dances"; Sinatra eventually married Ava, of course; as for Lana, earlier and later, she "exchanged partners" with great regularity ("If you want a blueprint, here it is: Lose one love, snap right back and catch another; I've done it again and again"); marital record: seven husbands, eight marriages, one annulment, seven divorces; husbands: #1 (1940–41) was bandleader Artie Shaw (wanted her to dress simply, wear no makeup, and read books—which he "pushed at me so fast that I couldn't have kept up if I had been working for an advanced degree"); #2 (1942–44) was Steve Crane (she had the marriage annulled after learning that his prior divorce wasn't final; remarried in '43, five months before the birth of their daughter, Cheryl; he, said she, "liked to gamble and began borrowing money from me to gamble with"; divorced in '44); #3 (1948–52) was millionaire Bob Topping (also a heavy gambler, he was an alcoholic who became violent when drunk; she suffered two miscarriages and later slit her wrists in her only recorded suicide attempt); #4 (1953–57) was Lex Barker (was reportedly unfaithful to her; she had another miscarriage); #5 (1960–62) was business tycoon Fred May (she has claimed her lack of punctuality was their big problem— "Finally, my taut nerves snapped, and we had a bitter quarrel. . . . Fred left the house, and I impulsively went to Juarez to get a divorce"); #6 (1965–67) was Robert P. Eaton (was good-looking, ten years younger, and had producing ambitions, so she "rented a handsome suite of 'production' offices" and "arranged a monthly allowance for him," but the "parties" he hosted while she was out of town broke up the marriage; he later wrote a sexy, successful novel, *The Body Brokers*, about a famous beauty rather like his ex); #7 (1969) was hypnotist Ronald Dante (he deserted her soon after the marriage ceremony and—the first husband to do so—sued her for divorce); in '81 her autobiography was published, *Lana Turner: The Lady, The Legend, The Truth*, and she said then, "I've been celibate by choice since 1969"; her first love and first Hollywood fiancé had been handsome attorney Greg Bautzer, until Joan Crawford came between them—but it was Bautzer who arranged her divorces from Shaw, Crane, and Topping; among the many other men between marriages: Mickey Rooney, Robert Hutton, Turhan Bey, Don "Red" Barry, Tony Martin, Victor Mature, Fernando Lamas, Tyrone Power ("I have loved other men in my life, but Tyrone was special. He was the one who broke my heart")—and underworld figure Johnny Stompanato; sleekly handsome, and "possibly insane," Stompanato brutalized her, beat her, threatened to scar and kill her; in 1958, at the height of one of his rampages, her daughter, Cheryl, killed him with a butcher knife; after one of the most headlined trials of the era, the jury brought in a verdict of "justifiable homicide"; a few months before the tragedy, the star was nominated for the Best Actress Oscar for *Peyton Place*; many predicted her career was ended; instead, in '59, she starred in *Imitation of Life*, which proved a success of such proportions that many others followed; her father was a bootlegger and gambler who moved the family to Stockton, Calif., when she was 7 and was murdered when she was 9; she and her mother, a beautician, lived next in San Francisco and moved to Los Angeles in '36; one month later, while attending Hollywood High, she skipped a class and went to a malt shop (not Schwab's Drug Store, publicity to the contrary) across Sunset Boulevard from the school; was seen there by Billy Wilkerson, publisher of *The Hollywood Reporter*, whose office was nearby; her full-blown, red-haired beauty so impressed Wilkerson that he arranged an introduction to an agent; Fox Studios rejected the 15-year-old, but Warner Bros. director Mervyn LeRoy put her under personal contract at $50 a week; after a bit in *A Star Is Born*, the studio gave her a featured role, a too-tight sweater (no bra), and a long, bouncing, on-camera walk in a movie most appropriately titled *They Won't Forget*; in the eventful decades that followed, no movie fan in the world was likely, even for a brief while, to forget this star.

MOVIE HIGHLIGHTS: *Love Finds Andy Hardy, Dramatic School, Calling Dr. Kildare, These Glamour Girls, Dancing Coed, Two Girls on Broadway, Ziegfeld Girl, Dr. Jekyll and Mr. Hyde, Johnny Eager, Honky Tonk, Somewhere I'll Find You, Slightly Dangerous, Marriage Is a Private Affair, Keep Your Powder Dry, Weekend at the Waldorf, The Postman Always Rings Twice, Green Dolphin Street, Cass Timberlane, The Merry Widow, The Bad and the Beautiful, Latin Lovers.*

Conrad Veidt

(b. Conrad Veidt, Jan. 22, 1893, Berlin, Germany; d. April 3, 1943) A glorious actor, lean as a greyhound, with a magnificently sculpted face, he had two careers in Hollywood; the first (1927–28 silents) was of little consequence *(The Beloved Rogue, A Man's Past, Erik the Great, The Man Who Laughs)*; the second was quite something else—started in '39 with *The Thief of Bagdad* (his hypnotic, deep-set blue eyes smoldering for the first time in Technicolor) and crested with *Casablanca*, in which he was suavely sinister Major Strasser; specialized at playing dangerous, often sadistic men, but friends, who called him Connie, vouched that off camera he was a man "with the sterling qualities of sincerity, kindness and never failing courtesy"; besides terming himself "a great lover of *all* women," he was a lover of the arts and of humanity; once said, "To me, the most beautiful thing in all California is the Hollywood Bowl. I have never seen an audience like that—30,000 people listening to music under the stars, so quiet, so *one*. I like to think them a symbol that one day there may be that oneness for all mankind"; was also a lifelong student of the occult and often spoke to intimates of "the strange cabals I have kept with unseen and unknown powers as I have tried to find the solution to The Forbidden Mystery"; was superstitious in the extreme about the number 17, which, he said, "has cropped up uncannily throughout my life"; was 17 when—over family objections ("Actors are gypsies," said his father)—he acted for the first time; made his first stage success *(Sea Battle)* and his first movies *(Das Rastel von Bangalore, Der Spion, etc.)* in 1917; on his first voyage to America he had Cabin 17 (and 17 was on his ticket); his earliest house number in Beverly Hills was 817, and 17 years later when, again in Hollywood, he bought a house there, the number was 617 (on the same Camden Drive and entirely by coincidence as his latest wife, who found the house, had no knowledge he'd ever lived on the street); had studied for the stage under Max Reinhardt in Germany, where he won a vast following in scores of silents and early talkies; his first notable success, *The Cabinet of Dr. Caligari* ('19), was followed by *Nju, Der Januskopf (The Two-Faced Man), Die Wachsfigurencabinett (Waxworks), Orlacs Hande (The Hands of Orlac), Der Student von Prag (The Man Who Cheated Life), Congress Dances,* etc.; with the rise of Hitler, he settled in England and was starred there—in alternately villainous and valiant roles—in many films of the '30s (*Rome Express, I Was a Spy, The Passing of the Third Floor Back,* etc.); was married three times—to music hall artiste Gussy Hall (by whom he had a daughter, Viola), Felicitas Radke of Austria, and Lily Barter; said of himself: "I am a religious man. I believe in prayer. I believe we all should pray more, because when we pray, we always pray for something—*good.*"

MOVIE HIGHLIGHTS: *The Wandering Jew, Bella Donna, Rasputin, King of the Damned, Under the Red Robe, Dark Journey, Alex, The Spy in Black* (aka *U-Boat 29*), *Blackout* (aka *Contraband*), *Escape, A Woman's Face, The Men in Her Life, Whistling in the Dark, Nazi Agent, All through the Night, Above Suspicion.*

Vera-Ellen

(b. Vera-Ellen Westmeyer Rohe, Feb. 16, 1920, Cincinnati, Ohio; d. Aug. 30, 1981) Sunny-faced dance star—with reddish-blonde hair, a bouncy ponytail, and pencil-slim legs—who was discovered on Broadway by Sam Goldwyn in the '43 revival of *A Connecticut Yankee;* "She has a refreshingly different personality," said the producer. "She is radiant, buoyant, wholesome energetic and ambitious, and all these qualities come out to you as you watch her on the screen"; was known to be a perfectionist and a nonstop worker; recalls a friend, Hollywood reporter Army Archerd, "When filming the classic 'Slaughter on Tenth Avenue' number [in *Words and Music*], she had to be packed in ice at day's end and it was not uncommon for her to continue working with bleeding feet"; most famous role: Miss Turnstiles, the Subway Cinderella, in *On the Town;* after it, one critic wrote: "Vera-Ellen, like Ginger Rogers, somehow appeals to the heart as well as to one's judgment of technical excellence"; Gene Kelly, her co-star in the movie, said in praise of her: "She acts a dance number as well as she dances it"; her acting itself was marked by overly precise diction, suggesting that other languages besides English were spoken in the home in which, an only child, she grew up; was of

Swedish-German parentage, her father being a piano salesman; was given a hyphenated name because her mother "had a dream and saw that name in lights"; a frail child, she was given dance lessons at her hometown's Hessler Studios to build up her body; first danced in public at 13, on a floating stage at the Chicago World's Fair; next was a winner on *"Major Bowes' Amateur Hour"* on radio, a Rockette, a chorus dancer at Billy Rose's Casa Mañana Club in New York (he gave her a specialty when she informed him she was capable of something better than high kicks and the time step); starting in '39 was in a series of Broadway musicals: *Very Warm for May* (roomed with June Allyson), *Higher and Higher* (infatuated stagehands presented her a sugar cube with message attached: "Stay as sweet as you are"—which she did), *Panama Hattie, By Jupiter*; did not "play the game" in Hollywood—refused all studio-arranged publicity "dates"; first marriage, to dancer (then a flying lieutenant) Robert Hightower, ended in divorce in '46 after one year; was engaged for a while to Rock Hudson, who has said, "I wanted to marry Vera-Ellen, my first glamour date in Hollywood. We didn't because of my objections to a two-career mating"; her second husband (1954-66) was oil millionaire Victor Rothschild; their only child, a daughter, was born in March '63 and died two months later; became a recluse, living in a mansion in the Hollywood Hills, and was not photographed in public during the last decade of her life; invited to attend the premiere of *That's Entertainment*, in which her dance scenes were prominently featured, she begged off: "I've changed so much—I don't want to disappoint my fans"; long afflicted with arthritis, high blood pressure, and anorexia, she died of cancer; 150 friends attended her memorial service, but only one was a former co-star, Cesar Romero, who was with her in *Carnival in Costa Rica*.

MOVIE HIGHLIGHTS: *Wonder Man, The Kid from Brooklyn, Three Little Girls in Blue, Carnival in Costa Rica, Words and Music, Love Happy, On the Town, Three Little Words, Happy Go Lovely, The Belle of New York, Call Me Madam, The Big Leaguer, White Christmas, Let's Be Happy.*

Robert Walker

(b. Robert Hudson Walker, Oct. 13, 1918, Salt Lake City, Utah; d. Aug. 28, 1951) No star was more gifted than this lanky curlyhead at portraying shy, wistful, bewildered youths; a screen test in New York won him just such a role, that of a doomed young sailor in 1943's *Bataan*, and his career as an MGM star got off like a jet fighter plane; conveniently forgotten by studio publicists was that, a bit earlier, he'd played minor roles in Ann Sheridan's *Winter Carnival*, a Jack Randall Western at Monogram, *Pioneer Days*, and even a couple of Lana Turner movies at MGM itself (*Dancing Coed* and *These Glamour Girls*); two years into his starring career at Metro, where his "little boy" charm was repeatedly utilized, he was earning $2,500 a week, with a no-options seven-year contract guaranteeing a raise each year of $1,000 a week; on the screen, his large, soulful eyes seemed to brim with sympathy for mankind—the effect, in the main, being due to his inability to focus properly without glasses; though his fame took a great leap when he was cast in *See Here, Private Hargrove* (and its sequel), he came to hate the fictional gawky, always-in-a-jam enlisted man, so eager was he to play more versatile roles, which he finally did; the youngest of four sons of a newspaper editor (*The Deseret News*), and an incorrigible runaway and school truant, he was sent to the San Diego Military & Naval Academy to "learn discipline"; there he was most noted for his acne (the scars usually being evident later on the screen) and his playing of the drums; after a dramatic course at the academy, decided, at 16, to become an actor; attended the Pasadena Playhouse on a scholarship until a wealthy aunt volunteered to pay for him to study at the American Academy of Dramatic Arts in New York; fell in love with and married (in '39) a fellow student named Phyllis Isley, who would become famous as Jennifer Jones; they lived in a one-room, $16-a-month tenement, acted together in a stock company at Greenwich Village's Cherry Lane Theater (at 50¢ a performance), did a stint with another stock company in Tulsa, her hometown, returned to New York where she modeled and he acted in radio soap operas, and had two sons, Robert Jr. and Michael (both later acted in movies); marriage dissolved and ended in divorce in Hollywood in '45— after a long separation—after both became stars and she fell in love with producer David O. Selznick, who had discovered her; following the breakup, MGM studio chief Dore Schary has said, "Bob began drinking and asserting his vigor and masculinity by going into bars and brawling with men who were bigger and hit harder"; Walker was repeatedly arrested for drunkenness, and studio publicists confided that he'd become "the most difficult and cantankerous actor" they'd ever had to work with; at Dore Schary's insistence, he reluctantly submitted to treatment at the Menninger Clinic; was helped by his 11-month stay there, and by later sessions with a Beverly Hills psychiatrist, but his alcoholism and emotional problems were never to be conquered; after dating such movieland beauties as Marie Windsor, Gloria Lloyd, and Shirley Patterson, he was married, on July 8, 1948, to Barbara Ford, daughter of famed director John Ford; she left him after five weeks and, three months later, was granted an annulment—amid reports he had physically assaulted her; John Wayne and Ward Bond, friends of John Ford who had known his daughter from childhood, were among the actors who had to be restrained from beating up Robert Walker; on the last night of his life, intoxicated and violent, he was given a medically administered shot of sodium pentothal, and respiratory arrest followed; all major scenes of his final movie, *My Son John* (in which he played a Communist of despicable character), had been completed, but a double, filmed from the back, was employed for a few transitional shots.

MOVIE HIGHLIGHTS: *Madame Curie, Since You Went Away, Thirty Seconds over Tokyo, What Next, Corporal Hargrove?, The Clock, Her Highness and the Bellboy, The Sailor Takes a Wife, Till the Clouds Roll By, The Beginning or the End?, Sea of Grass, Song of Love, One Touch of Venus, Please Believe Me, The Skipper Surprised His Wife, Vengeance Valley, Strangers on a Train.*

John Wayne

(b. Marion Michael Morrison, May 26, 1907, Winterset, Iowa; d. June 11, 1979) When, after a decade in B Westerns, he became a star in 1939's *Stagecoach*, the screen was filled with heroes—Gable, Flynn, Cooper, Power, Taylor et al.; no one could have predicted that he would outlast them all, become richer than any of them, be nominated for a Best Actor Oscar for *Sands of Iwo Jima*, win one for *True Grit*, and evolve into a national institution; secret of his phenomenal popularity, as one writer put it, was that he was "a man of impregnable virility and the embodiment of simplistic, laconic virtues, packaged in a well-built 6-foot-4-inch, 225-pound frame. When he shambled into view, one could sense the arrival of coiled vigor awaiting only provocation to be sprung"; except for 1958, when in a trio of duds, he was among the Box-Office Top Ten every year from '49 through '74—and was #1 in '50, '51, '54, and '71; in brief, he was the biggest box-office attraction in motion picture history; made 156 movies, the last being 1976's *The Shootist*, which grossed $700 million (a record); born to a Scots father (a druggist) and an Irish mother, he, the elder of two sons, was 6 when the family moved to Glendale, Calif.; father gave him a three-rule philosophy he followed throughout his life: Always keep your word, a gentleman never insults anyone unintentionally, and, don't look for trouble; an honors student in high school, he attended USC for three years on a football scholarship and expected to become a U.S. Navy officer; was 21 when Tom Mix, a football fan, got him a

$35-a-week summer job as a prop man at Fox Studios, and he never went back to school; director John Ford saw him on the lot and gave him a small part in *Mother Machree*, saying later, "I liked the way he walked"; little known fact revealed by veteran stuntman and lifelong friend Yakima Canutt: "One day I turned around and noticed he was following me, and I said, 'What the hell are you following me for?' And he said, 'I'm trying to copy that damn walk of yours.' Well, he never got my walk, but he got a better one"; used two different screen names at the start—Michael Burn and Duke Morrison ("Duke" was the name of a dog he owned as a kid, and he got stuck with it as his own nickname); in '30 director Raoul Walsh gave him a starring role in a major Western, *The Big Trail*, and studio chief Winfield Sheehan tagged him "John Wayne"; said *Photoplay*'s critic: "John Wayne, newcomer, moves right into the star class"; didn't stay—slipped quickly into Bs and "quickie" cowboy flicks until John Ford starred him as The Ringo Kid in *Stagecoach*; made 12 later pictures for the director (*The Long Voyage Home*, *Fort Apache*, etc.) and, even when the biggest star of all, deferred to the older man like a schoolboy; typecast in heroic roles, he yearned for more versatile assignments until a friend, character actress Olive Carey, set him straight: "The American public doesn't want to see you any other way. So wake up, Duke! Be what they want you to be"; his personal heroes, incidentally, were John Ford, General Douglas MacArthur, and Winston Churchill; several femme stars (Marlene Dietrich, Claire Trevor, Marie Windsor, and Vera Miles) appeared with him three or more times, and numerous others twice, but the record-holder was Maureen O'Hara; were in five films together: *Rio Grande*, *The Quiet Man*, *The Wings of Eagles*, *McLintock!*, *Big Jake*; later, in retirement, she said: "He's a good and great friend. Any time I've needed him, all I ever had to do was just pick up the phone"; also said, "Many people don't realize it, but he's very sentimental. He gets tears in his eyes at the drop of a hat. Play soft music and off he goes. I've seen him cry plenty of times"; explaining what shaped him into the man he was, Katharine Hepburn, his *Rooster Cogburn* co-star, observed: "He was surrounded in his early years in the motion picture business by people like himself. Self-made. Hard-working. Independent. Of the style of men who blazed the trails across our country. People who were willing to live or die entirely on their own judgment"; consistent in his choice of wives, he was married three times—always to beautiful, brunette Latin types; first wife (1933–45) was Josephine Saenz, daughter of the Panamanian consul in Los Angeles, by whom he had two sons and two daughters (Michael, Patrick, Toni, and Melinda); wife #2 (1946–53) was Mexican actress Esperanza "Chata" Baur; a tempestuous union, it erupted in torrid headlines (she accused him of having affairs with Marlene Dietrich and Gail Russell, and he made countercharges) and ended in a bitter divorce; he regarded this as the one bleak, undignified chapter in his life; was married from '54 on (though they were estranged in later years) to Pilar Palette, of Peru, by whom he had two daughters and a son (Aissa, Marisa Carmela, and John Ethan); eventually was the grandfather of 22; in '64 he lost his left lung to cancer, in '78 he underwent open heart surgery, and early in '79, when it was discovered that cancer had recurred, both his stomach and gall bladder were removed; after visiting him at his bedside, President Jimmy Carter said: "He extends through me to the people of our country his thanks. . . . He knows he has their best wishes and covets their prayers"; his self-chosen epitaph was "Feo, fuerte y formal," which translates, "He was ugly, was strong, and had dignity."

MOVIE HIGHLIGHTS: *Allegheny Uprising, The Dark Command, Seven Sinners, Shepherd of the Hills, Reap the Wild Wind, The Spoilers, Flying Tigers, Pittsburgh, Reunion in France, The Fighting Seabees, Back to Bataan, Flame of the Barbary Coast, They Were Expendable, Red River, Three God-fathers, Wake of the Red Witch, She Wore a Yellow Ribbon, Island in the Sky, The High and the Mighty, The Searchers, The Horse Soldiers, Rio Bravo, The Man Who Shot Liberty Valance.*

Clifton Webb

(b. Webb Parmalee Hornbeck, Nov. 19, 1889, Indianapolis, Ind.; d. Oct. 13, 1966) 20th Century–Fox's viper-tongued character star, who began his career at the studio in '44 as the foppish critic Waldo Lydecker in *Laura*, set something of a record for cultivated nastiness, and was nominated for a Best Supporting Oscar; said he of the character: "He was an original—a species of adder turned out impeccably by Sulka and Charvet"; was nominated again two years later, in the same category, for *The Razor's Edge*, and, two years after that, was up for the Best Actor Oscar for *Sitting Pretty*; playing the acerbic, old-maidish baby-sitter, Mr. Belvedere, in the latter, and dumping a bowl of oatmeal on a wailing infant's head, won him a vast fan following—and the same starring role in two sequels; it was the studio's inspiration to cast him repeatedly with youngsters, even in *Cheaper by the Dozen*, as the stern but loving parent of 12; this was incongruous, as he was a confirmed bachelor (lived all his life with his party-loving mother) and an avowed homosexual, and had no particular affection for children; even he found it a bit perplexing; in his first two movies in the '40s, *Laura* and *The Dark Corner*, he'd played killers, yet when he was later offered the role of a murderer in a British film, the studio would not permit him to do it; "They told me," he reported, "that to play a murderer again I would be committing professional suicide. 'Don't you know,' they said, *that you are now America's sweetheart?* "; was in show business his entire life; trained in dancing schools from early childhood, he was taken by his mother to New York, where, at 7, he went on the stage; by 17, was singing leading roles in *Madame Butterfly* and *La Boheme* with the Aborn Opera Company; during WWI, he was teamed with Bonnie Glass in a sophisticated dance act that achieved a fame comparable to that of Vernon and Irene Castle; in the '20s and '30s, dapper in tie and tails, he starred on New York and London stages in such musical comedies as *Sunny, Treasure Girl,* and *As Thousands Cheer;* was on screen in several silents of the '20s: Ina Claire's *Polly with a Past,* Richard Barthelmess' *New Toys,* and Barbara La Marr's *The Heart of a Siren* ("Clifton Webb contributes some clever comedy," said *Photoplay's* critic); 20th Century–Fox later snagged him from the stage after he'd succeeded Monty Woolley as the cantankerous Sheridan Whiteside in *The Man Who Came to Dinner;* ever sartorially elegant, he was famous as a creator as well as a model of male fashion; was credited with introducing to America such innovations as the white mess jacket and sack-cloth slacks, which became a national fad; arrived in Hollywood with six trunks of clothes, had a wardrobe of 100 suits (even more, reputedly, than Adolphe Menjou), and in '45, was named among the ten best-dressed men in the world; his dinner parties were famous—especially the one to which he invited both Louella Parsons and Hedda Hopper, rival gossip columnists and bitter enemies, and seated them side-by-side; to everyone's surprise, they behaved like angels; a realist, and a hedonist, he said, "I love Hollywood. I love everything about it, especially the opportunity to make more and more films, and the chance to make more and more money. I *love* money. Furthermore, I *need* money, and I will do positively anything to get it."

MOVIE HIGHLIGHTS: *Mr. Belvedere Goes to College, For Heaven's Sake, Mr. Belvedere Rings the Bell, Elopement, Dreamboat, Stars and Stripes Forever, Titanic, Mr. Scoutmaster, Three Coins in the Fountain, Woman's World, The Man Who Never Was, Boy on a Dolphin, The Remarkable Mr. Pennypacker, Holiday for Lovers, Satan Never Sleeps.*

Orson Welles

(b. George Orson Welles, May 6, 1915, Kenosha, Wis.) At 25, the "boy wonder" of Broadway and radio anchored at RKO, where he produced, directed, co-wrote, and starred in *Citizen Kane*, which newspaper king William Randolph Hearst tried unsuccessfully to suppress (the story, he felt, followed too closely, and too critically, his own life); a cult film at first (as many theaters feared to screen it), it became an acknowledged classic, and in '72, in a poll of international critics, was chosen as the greatest film of all time; nominated for a Best Actor Oscar, Welles (and coscriptwriter Herman Mankiewicz) won the Academy Award for the best screenplay of 1941; wrote, produced, and directed (but did not appear in) his next, *The Magnificent Ambersons*, which almost matched *Citizen Kane*'s quality; few of his later behind-the-screen efforts even came close, but there were many stunning stints as an actor (*The Third Man, Tomorrow Is Forever, The Stranger*, etc.); his keen sense of creation and utter disregard for the established order of things may have been inherited from his father, a wealthy inventor and manufacturer (and also a cool gambling man who once broke the bank at Monte Carlo); sensitivity, artistic perception, and talent for scoring bullseyes surely came from his mother, a concert pianist and champion rifle shot; an authentic genius, he read at 2, played the violin at 4 for Stravinsky and Ravel (friends of his mother's), recited *King Lear* at 7; first performed in public at 9, playing Peter Rabbit at Marshall Field's department store in Chicago; made his professional stage debut at 16 at the Gate Theater in Dublin, Ireland, portraying the Duke of Wurtemburg in *Jew Suss*; started on the stage in America at 18 when playwright-novelist Thornton Wilder gave him a letter of introduction to critic Alexander Woollcott, who took him to Katharine Cornell, who gave him supporting roles in plays in which she toured (*The Barretts of Wimpole Street, Candida*, etc.); made his Broadway debut with Cornell a few weeks after his 19th birthday in *Romeo and Juliet* (as both Chorus and Tybalt); soon established his own famous Mercury Theater Players, which left its mark on Broadway and even more so on radio; on CBS on Sunday evening, Oct. 30, 1938, he presented a drama, "War of the Worlds," that panicked the country (and provoked a number of suicides) with its too-convincing depiction of an "invasion" of Martians; a wizard in other, unexpected areas, he performed as a magician (taught by Houdini) at the California State Fair in '41; during WWII, entertained military troops with his Merlinesque feats, including the "sawing in half" of Marlene Dietrich, his romantic interest at the time; has edited books (*Everybody's Shakespeare*) and written a novel, *Mr. Arkadin*, which he later made into a movie in which he starred; little-known fact: President Franklin D. Roosevelt (a personal friend) once urged him—though he declined—to run for senator from Wisconsin; Joseph McCarthy won that election and soon had the nation in a frenzy with his Communist "witch hunts" ("If I had run and beaten him, a whole decade of American politics would have been different"); has been married three times; wife #1 (1934–40) was stage actress Virginia Nicholson (daughter: Christopher); #2 (1943–47) was Rita Hayworth, whom he lured away from Victor Mature (daughter: Rebecca); #3 (since '56) was La Comtesse di Girafalco, who, as Paola Mori, acted in Italian films and in his *Mr. Arkadin* (daughter: Beatrice); in '70, received a special Oscar "for superlative artistry and versatility in the creation of motion pictures."

MOVIE HIGHLIGHTS: *Journey into Fear, Jane Eyre, The Lady from Shanghai, Macbeth, Prince of Foxes, The Black Rose, Othello, Moby Dick, The Long Hot Summer, Touch of Evil, The Roots of Heaven, Compulsion, David and Goliath, The Trial, The V.I.P.s, A Man for All Seasons, Is Paris Burning?, Casino Royale, The Sailor from Gibraltar, I'll Never Forget What's 'is Name, House of Cards, Oedipus, Catch-22, Treasure Island, Voyage of the Damned, Fake.*

Richard Widmark

(b. Richard Weedt Widmark, Dec. 26, 1914, Sunrise, Minn.) In '47, as psychopathic killer Tommy Udo in *Kiss of Death*, he giggled maniacally as he pushed an old lady in a wheelchair (Mildred Dunnock) down a flight of stairs, and a star was born; was nominated for the Best Supporting Oscar; marked a strange movie debut for an actor who, on Broadway, had played nothing but romantic leads; the word "Kiss" was lucky for him—two of his biggest stage hits had been *Kiss and Tell* (his debut, in '43) and *Kiss Them for Me*; was on screen as a psychotic again in *Road House*, as a criminal gang leader in *The Street with No Name*, and as a Western villain in *Yellow Sky*; in '49, though, broke out as a two-fisted good-guy in *Down to the Sea in Ships* and got his first screen kiss, from Linda Darnell, in *Slattery's Hurricane*; starred heroically, or played strong dramatic leads, for 20th Century–Fox through '54, after which he free-lanced; background was apple-pie wholesome; was the elder of two sons of a general sales manager for a national outdoor advertising firm; lived with his family in Sioux Falls, S.D., between the ages of 1 and 12; next was in Princeton, Ill., where he attended high school and began acting in plays; fell in love with movies as a kid and remains fascinated enough with the silent era to collect stacks of old movie magazines from that period; graduated from Lake Forest (Ill.) College; was president of the senior class and of the Iron Key honorary fraternity, a football letter man (played end), captain of the debating team, and a member of Phi Pi Epsilon; then for two years, was the $50-a-week assistant to the head of the drama department at Lake Forest before going to New York; there he first acted on radio ("Inner Sanctum," "Cavalcade," "The Shadow," etc.); since '42, has been married to Jean Hazlewood, a fellow student at Lake Forest who also taught there after graduation and in later years was a screenwriter; one child: Anne Heath (grew up to marry legendary pitcher Sandy Koufax); director Henry Hathaway tested him for *Kiss of Death* and thought him "too clean-cut"; studio chief Darryl F. Zanuck, however, saw the test and, fascinated by his homicidal glee, gave him the role and a sinister hairpiece (to lower his forehead); across the nation, fraternities—ten in all—immediately formed Tommy Udo fan clubs—stressing male superiority; always studiously avoided personal publicity and has never once appeared on a TV talk show, arguing, "As Humphrey Bogart said, the only thing you owe your public is to do a good job"; asked once if he regretted having done any of his films, even such bombs as *My Pal Gus*, he grinned and said, "Not really. I look upon my whole career as having been terribly lucky"; personal favorite of his movies: *Panic in the Streets*; still averages at least one picture a year but prefers to take it easy on his Hidden Valley ranch in California or his farm in Connecticut, saying, "I'm really just a farmer at heart."

MOVIE HIGHLIGHTS: *Night and the City, No Way Out, The Halls of Montezuma, The Frogmen, Red Skies of Montana, Don't Bother to Knock, Destination Gobi, Take the High Ground, Pickup on South Street, Hell and High Water, Broken Lance, Garden of Evil, The Cobweb, Run for the Sun, The Last Wagon, Time Limit, Tunnel of Love, Two Rode Together, Judgment at Nuremberg, Cheyenne Autumn, Madigan, Murder on the Orient Express, Coma, Who Dares Wins.*

Cornel Wilde

(b. Cornel Louis Wilde, Oct. 13, 1915, New York, N.Y.) This muscular star's year to remember will always be 1945, for it was then that, romantically and elegantly costumed, he played the consumptive Chopin in *A Song to Remember* (copping his only Best Actor Oscar nomination) and became *the* screen heartthrob of the moment; had been in movies for five years earlier, and was in many great hits later, but fans recall most fondly the time when he sat down to a piano, and the "Grand Polonaise" poured forth (provided on the soundtrack by Jose Iturbi); had to test three times for the part, as Columbia Studios chief Harry Cohn deemed him "too healthy" to play the frail musical genius; next was a popular swashbuckler with boundless energy and flashing sabers, in silken shirts slashed to the belt buckle to reveal a Charles Atlas chest; his swordsmanship was no accident; had studied fencing as a youth in Budapest, was on America's Olympic fencing team in '36 (declined the chance to go to Germany with it as a stage opportunity came along simultaneously), and in '40, won his big break in the theater as Tybalt in *Romeo and Juliet*, starring Laurence Olivier and Vivien Leigh, because of his fencing expertise and acting ability; had been on Broadway in five previous shows, starting in '33 with *They All Came to Moscow*, followed by *Moon over Mulberry Street*, *Daughters of Atreus*, etc.; arrived in Hollywood (on borrowed funds) with the wife he'd married in '37, actress Patricia Knight; had one child: Wendy; early movie stints were not promising; signed first by Warner Bros., he began with a bit in '40 in Miriam Hopkins' *The Lady with Red Hair*; next came villainous roles in several films, including Bogart's *High Sierra* (as the Mexican hotel clerk) and Dennis Morgan's *Kisses for Breakfast*; began his seven-year contract at 20th Century–Fox as the lead in a B, *The Perfect Snob* (replaced John Shelton on one day's notice when that actor became ill), followed by an A, *Life Begins at 8:30* (replaced Shepperd Strudwick—same situation); loaned to Columbia for three (*A Song to Remember*, *A Thousand and One Nights*, *The Bandit of Sherwood Forest*), he returned to his home studio a major star; in '51, two days after being divorced by Patricia Knight, was married to Jean Wallace, former wife of Franchot Tone, by whom he eventually had two sons and a daughter; formed his own company, Theodora Productions, and, with Wallace as his recurring leading lady (in *The Big Combo*, *Lancelot and Guinevere*, etc.), produced, directed, and starred in numerous films; one critic observed that many of them dealt with the "survival of the individual man"; agreeing, the star said he became "painfully aware of survival as a personal necessity" when young; though born in New York, his earliest years were spent in Europe; his father, a native of Hungary, was recalled during WWI for duty as a captain in the Austro-Hungarian army, taking his family with him; shell shocked at the front, he was put in charge of a Hungarian prison camp; after several years back in America, the family once more returned for a while to Budapest, where the future star studied art and fencing; had completed Townsend Harris High School in Manhattan (doing a four-year course in three) and entered Columbia University, expecting to study medicine, when a recurrence of shell shock forced his father to stop working; held many odd jobs: sales clerk at Macy's, ad salesman for a French newspaper (being fluent in French as well as German and Russian), pharmacy clerk, etc.; studied acting (on a full scholarship, as he was penniless) at the Theodora Irving Dramatic School, acted in summer stock, and then on Broadway; penned a magazine article when a brand new star in which he

publicly thanked all those who had given him an assist on his road to fame—
and it was a long list.

MOVIE HIGHLIGHTS: *Wintertime, Guest in the House, Leave Her to Heaven, Centennial Summer, Forever Amber, The Homestretch, It Had to Be You, Road House, The Walls of Jericho, Two Flags West, The Greatest Show on Earth, At Sword's Point, The Treasure of the Golden Condor, Saadia, Woman's World, The Scarlet Coat, Storm Fear, Star of India, Omar Khayyam, The Naked Prey, Beach Red, The Raging Sea.*

Esther Williams

(b. Esther Williams, Aug. 8, 1921, Los Angeles, Calif.) "Wet she's a star, dry she ain't," said comedienne Fanny Brice in an oft-quoted observation of hers; gloriously "wet," diving into fiery pools from sky-high trapezes rigged by Busby Berkeley, the Junoesque swimmer, a blessing to Technicolor, produced waves of golden shekels for MGM and languidly breaststroked her way into the Box-Office Top Ten in '49 and '50; having no illusions about herself as an actress, she said: "The only time I really relax when watching one of my own pictures is when I'm in a water scene. I thoroughly enjoyed seeing myself in *Ziegfeld Follies*, because I didn't say a word"; remarked at the height of her popularity, "Winning the National Swimming Meet was a greater thrill than getting a film contract because I worked so hard for the swimming title, while I only fell into pictures"; was set to compete in the '40 Olympics when war broke out in Europe and they were cancelled; turned professional, went to work for Billy Rose (Fanny Brice's ex, by the way) as the star of his Aquacade at the San Francisco World's Fair, and had to learn to swim all over again— "showbiz style" instead of competitively; next worked as a sales clerk and model at Magnin's in Los Angeles, was married (1940–44) to Dr. Leonard Kovner, and turned down repeated offers from MGM before signing a contract there; until she married, she had always lived—the youngest of five—in the same house in which she was born; husband opposed her going into movies; also her Aquacade experience had soured her on show business ("The backstage life, with its pettiness and gossip, was not pleasant; Billy Rose was almost responsible for my not being in pictures, *ever*"); MGM brought her along slowly, gave her a year's coaching and minor roles in *Andy Hardy's Double Life* and *A Guy Named Joe*, before presenting her as a full-fledged star—doing for a swimsuit what Lana Turner did for a sweater—in 1944's *Bathing Beauty*; was such an immediate sensation that, said one critic, "Her splash is worth as much to MGM as Gable's profile or Sinatra's voice"; Metro accountants groaned when her second marriage (1945–57), to radio announcer Ben Gage, resulted in three children (Benjamin, Kimball, and Susan), causing her to take time out for motherhood when she could have been making more millions for the studio; was a Metro luminary of the first rank for exactly 14 years; had two failures as a dramatic actress later at Universal *(The Unguarded Moment, Raw Wind in Eden)*, followed by two other flops elsewhere in '61, *The Big Show* and *The Magic Fountain*, after which she retired; swimming alongside her in one of her final Technicolor spectaculars at MGM, *Dangerous When Wet* ('53), was Fernando Lamas; long after her divorce from Ben Gage, she and Lamas were married twice—in a civil ceremony in Europe in '67, followed by another wedding two years later at the Founders' Church of Religious Science in California; remained happily together until his death in '82; later she revealed they'd had an unorthodox domestic arrangement—two separate households; in Bel Air, she lived with the actor, and in nearby Mandeville Canyon, she lived with her children—as Lamas felt that their marriage would not survive if the children moved in with them; describing her husband as "a really good, terrific, exciting man," she said: "It was hard for him to accept that I had had children with another man, with his Latin feelings about things. And the children didn't want to put up with somebody from another culture, either. So we actually solved an untenable problem in a tenable way."

MOVIE HIGHLIGHTS: *Thrill of a Romance, The Hoodlum Saint, Easy to Wed, This Time for Keeps, Fiesta, On an Island with You, Take Me Out to the Ballgame, Neptune's Daughter, Pagan Love Song, Duchess of Idaho, Texas Carnival, Skirts Ahoy!, Million Dollar Mermaid, Easy to Love, Jupiter's Darling.*

Marie Wilson

(b. Kathleen Elizabeth White, Aug. 19, 1916, Anaheim, Calif.; d. Nov. 23, 1972) Long before Marilyn Monroe, she was Hollywood's funniest, most beautiful, most lovable "dumb blonde"—but what she was, actually, was one of the world's most childlike innocents; her malapropisms were hilarious on screen and, being spontaneous and unintended, perhaps even more so off; once when a visiting theater-chain owner was introduced, she declined to shake hands, saying sweetly she didn't want to contaminate him as she was suffering from a "social disease"; to her irate studio bosses, she later calmly explained she had a bad cold—"I caught it at a social event, and a cold *is* a disease, isn't it?"; visually, she was like a black-eyed susan, with a shock of white-gold hair and the longest, blackest eyelashes—her own—mankind has ever seen; her shape, too, was a knockout: 39–21–36; show business was her goal from childhood—and her career would soar, plummet, then fly again; after attending private schools in Hollywood (Miss Page's and the Hollywood Comnock School for Girls), she acted on local stages (in *Call Me Neighbor*, *The King's Pleasure*, etc.) and did walk-ons in movies *(Babes in Toyland, My Girl Sally)*; was clerking in a Hollywood five-and-dime when a Warner Bros. scout discovered her and placed her under contract in '35; played scatter-brained bits in many: *Slide, Kelly, Slide, Satan Met a Lady, China Clipper*, etc.; got her big break in '38 when the studio starred her with Cagney in *Boy Meets Girl*; in his book *Those Crazy Wonderful Years When We Ran Warner Bros.* (about his experiences then as a studio messenger), screenwriter Stuart Jerome related: "It was during the filming of *Boy Meets Girl* that she casually made a remark . . . that epitomized her ingenuousness. In a scene with Jimmy Cagney in which she sat on his lap, he kept fluffing his two lines. . . . It took a dozen takes before he got it right. Afterwards, Wilson said to her makeup woman, 'Sitting on Jimmy's lap was like being on top of a flagpole.' She honestly had no idea why the woman suddenly broke up"; starring career, that time, was short-lived; was soon back to providing the brighter (but daffier) moments in movies headlining others; had a long marriage, which ended in divorce, to actor Allan Nixon; between '42 and '45, while continuing in movies, she starred on stage at the El Capitan Theater in *Ken Murray's Blackouts*, becoming famous for never missing a performance; was a huge drawing card as the comedian's pneumatic stooge, in eye-filling skimpy costumes while so-innocently delivering off-color nonsequiturs—and hundreds of thousands of G.I.s would recall *Blackouts* (and Marie Wilson) as the highlight of their Hollywood visit; sidelight: was still in *Blackouts* when Ken Murray auditioned a prospective understudy for her, a teen-aged beauty named Norma Jean Baker, eventually known as Marilyn Monroe, and turned her down—only because she lacked the measurements to fill his femme star's costumes; became famous on radio in '47 in the title role of "My Friend Irma," playing the world's most endearingly kooky secretary; starred as the character in two moneymaking movies in '49 and '50: *My Friend Irma* and *My Friend Irma Goes West* (in which Martin & Lewis were introduced as supporting comics); only increased her fame when "My Friend Irma" became a hit TV series in '52—but her later movie career amounted to little; from '51 on, was married to producer Bob Fallon (real name: Friedman), with whom she adopted a son, Gregson.

MOVIE HIGHLIGHTS: *Melody for Two, Public Wedding, Broadway Musketeers, Fools for Scandal, Should Husbands Work?, Virginia, Flying Blind, Rookie Parade, Broadway, Harvard, Here I Come, She's in the Army, Shine On, Harvest Moon, You Can't Ration Love, Music for Millions, No Leave, No Love, Young Widcw, Fabulous Joe, Linda Be Good, The Private Affairs of Bel Ami, Never Wave at a WAC, Marry Me Again, Mr. Hobbs Takes a Vacation.*

Shelley Winters

(b. Shirley Schrift, Aug. 18, 1922, St. Louis, Mo.) Women sighed with envy—and males merely sighed—at WWII pinups of this blonde bombshell in bathing suits, standing on anticipatory tiptoe in platform wedgies; a blimpish character actress she was not; put in five years at a bit player, the first three as a Columbia "cutie" (in *Cover Girl, Tonight and Every Night*, etc.) and posing for cheesecake before everything changed in '48; that year she portrayed the sexy waitress–victim of Ronald Colman in *A Double Life* and made her mark as an actress of note; Universal accidentally changed her name from "Winter" (mother's maiden name, which sne'd used till then) to "Winters," but what happened in later years was no accident: a Best Actress Oscar nomination for *A Place in the Sun*, two Academy Awards as Best Support (for *The Diary of Anne Frank* and *A Patch of Blue*), and another Supporting Actress nomination for *The Poseidon Adventure*; period as a glamour star lasted a decade; in '59 she had to gain 25 pounds for a mother role—her first—in *Anne Frank* ("My metabolism has never been the same, but it was worth it"); columnist Sidney Skolsky once said, "Shelley Winters invented herself," and he came close to the mark; "I can't remember a time when I didn't want to be an actress," says this daughter of a Jewish tailor's cutter from Austria, and an American-born mother who once sang in the chorus of the St. Louis Municipal Opera; began singing in amateur shows at 3; was 11 (and, she has said, "a violent tomboy") when her family moved to Brooklyn, where she acquired an accent difficult to shake off; "I lived at the movies; I saw my favorite star, Ronald Colman, fifty times in *Lost Horizon* alone"; following high school, worked as a model in Manhattan's garment district, did summer stock, became a chorus girl at La Conga nightclub, and, renaming herself "Shelley" (for her favorite poet), landed bits on Broadway (*Rio Rita*) and in touring musicals (*Meet the People*); a singing-dancing supporting role on stage in *Rosalinda* won her a $150-a-week starlet's contract at Columbia; received no billing when making her screen debut as a secretary in Rosalind Russell's

What a Woman!, but in her second, *Sailor's Holiday*, a B starring Arthur Lake, was billed fourth; when Columbia dropped her option, did not work in movies for more than a year while failing screen tests at Warner Bros., 20th Century–Fox, and MGM—all being studios at which she eventually played starring roles; once said, "I owe my success to men"; cited on the list: her father who, though opposed to her becoming an actress, paid for her drama classes at The New Theatre School; Michael Gordon, then an instructor at the school, who "was the first person to give me the brand of self-confidence an actress must have," and, later, as the producer of *A Double Life*, referred her to director George Cukor, who cast her, "patiently coached me through it," and set her on the road to fame; director Chester Erskine, who "not only gave me my first chance on Broadway, but later my first starring opportunity in the movies" *(Take One False Step)*; and Ronald Colman ("I was so frightened at meeting him I couldn't function but, gallantly, he put me at ease and lived up to all my expectations"); reportedly engaged to Farley Granger during her glamorous heyday, she had romantic affairs, she has confessed, with many famous stars—Burt Lancaster, William Holden, Marlon Brando, John Ireland, etc.; was married and divorced three times; husband #1 (1943–48) was salesman Mack Paul Meyer; #2 (1952–54) was Italian star Vittorio Gassman (daughter: Victoria); #3 (1957–60) was actor Anthony Franciosa; in '80, published *Shelley*, her self-written, frank, and breezy autobiography (in which, for some reason, her first spouse was referred to as "Paul Miller"), which became a best seller; concluded the book with: "To Be Continued, I Hope . . . "

MOVIE HIGHLIGHTS: *Knickerbocker Holiday, The Gangster, Larceny, Cry of the City, Johnny Stool-Pigeon, The Great Gatsby, South Sea Sinner, Winchester '73, Frenchie, He Ran All the Way, Behave Yourself, The Raging Tide, Meet Danny Wilson, Phone Call from a Stranger, My Man and I, Tennessee Champ, Saskatchewan, Executive Suite, Playgirl, I Am a Camera, The Night of the Hunter, The Big Knife, Odds Against Tomorrow, Lolita.*

Natalie Wood

(b. Natasha Gurdin, July 20, 1938, San Francisco, Calif.; d. Nov. 29, 1981) To many fans, following her from afar through the decades, her life was a fairy tale, and in certain respects it actually was; went from Mary Janes to minks and memorable movies that brought her three Academy Award nominations: *Rebel Without a Cause* (nominated as Best Support), *Splendor in the Grass*, and *Love with the Proper Stranger* (was in the running for Best Actress for both); finally came million-dollar salaries; at the time of her death (drowned off Catalina Island), she had been in movies 38 years; was one child who became a star not only because she was bright and appealing, but also a born, bona fide actress; was 5 when director Irving Pichel, filming *Happy Land* in Santa Rosa, Calif., her hometown, picked her to do a bit as a youngster who, after dropping an ice cream cone, could cry on cue; Pichel sent for her two years later to play Orson Welles' adopted daughter in *Tomorrow Is Forever*; portrayed a German child and bowled critics over with her pitch-perfect accent; said Welles, "She was so good, she frightened me"; languages came easily as both parents were Russian immigrants, and Russian was spoken in the home as often as English; early, and always, her enormous brown eyes overshadowed every other feature of her expressive face; was 8 when, as the sophisticated city child who learned to believe in Santa Claus, she starred in a classic, *Miracle on 34th Street*; at 9, was chosen "most talented juvenile in America"; said then and later, "I just love to act; to me the best part is when the cameras roll"; was on screen every year, without a break, from '46 to '63; had made an easy transition from juvenile to leading lady at 17, when she played a hot-blooded young temptress opposite James Dean in *Rebel Without a Cause*; said: "*Rebel* was the picture that really did it for me; I had reached the age when I would either become a former child actress or go on as a young adult"; starred in her two favorite films, *West Side Story* and *Splendor in the Grass*, in the same year ('61), and followed them with *Gypsy* and brief retirement; returning after that one-year sabbatical, she starred in many other films; was 10 when she spotted 19-year-old newcomer Robert Wagner on the 20th Century–Fox lot and informed her mother, "I'm going to marry him," and she did—twice; they were married first in '57; co-starred in one movie while wed, *All the Fine Young Cannibals*; her off-screen romance with Warren Beatty, her *Splendor in the Grass* leading man, allegedly contributed to their divorce in '62; later (1970–71), was married to British producer Richard Gregson, by whom she had a daughter, Natasha, before she and Wagner rewed in '72 and also had a daughter, Courtney; before and between marriages, the petite (5', 98 lbs.) charmer found many famous men susceptible to her charms, from Elvis Presley to Soviet poet Yevgeny Yevtushenko; meeting her at a Hollywood party, the impassioned Siberian declared: "Now that I have seen your beauty, I could believe in God"; when, fielding his advances, she informed him in fluent Russian that she already had an escort for the evening, the crestfallen poet retired to a corner and burst into tears; on screen and off, always wore a heavy gold bracelet on her left hand, causing fans to conclude it was something of a trademark, but it was more—a broken wrist when young failed to heal properly, leaving a large knot, and her bracelet served to camouflage this; as an adult, she said: "When I review my life, I have no regrets. Maybe I didn't have a real childhood or a sufficient, well-rounded education. But I wouldn't change a thing if I had to do it over."

MOVIE HIGHLIGHTS: *The Bride Wore Boots, The Ghost and Mrs. Muir, Driftwood, Chicken Every Sunday, Father Was a Fullback, Our Very Own, The Green Promise, No Sad Songs for Me, Never a Dull Moment, The Blue Veil, The Star, Just for You, One Desire, A Cry in the Night, The Searchers, The Girl He Left Behind, Kings Go Forth, Marjorie Morningstar, Sex and the Single Girl, The Great Race, Inside Daisy Clover, Bob & Carol & Ted & Alice, This Property Is Condemned, Meteor, Brainstorm.*

Monty Woolley

(b. Edgar Montillion Woolley, Aug. 17, 1888, New York, N.Y.; d. May 6, 1963) On a day in '38, when MGM was dunking a little-known character actor in a pool for a comedy sequence in Lana Turner's *Dancing Coed*, Orson Welles was in New York rejecting the lead in a sure-fire hit play "because I knew I'd be stuck in it for five years"; the call went out for Monty Woolley, and *The Man Who Came to Dinner* became the bearded one's overnight transport to fame; for 738 performances, he regaled audiences as Sheridan Whiteside, the crotchety critic who, as the guest of a Midwestern family while on a speaking tour, breaks his hip and creates havoc in the household during his weeks of recovery; found movie stardom in the same part, opposite Bette Davis—after the studio tested John Barrymore, Fredric March, and Cary Grant; had been in Hollywood earlier for a dozen forgettable roles; made his debut, rather ignominiously, in *Nothing Sacred*; was originally cast as the blustery "Dr. Eggelhoffer," who exposes "radium-poisoning victim" Carole Lombard as a fraud; the director pulled a switch—gave Sig Rumann the part and demoted Woolley to being one of his assistants, without a line of dialogue; returned to New York, made his acting debut on Broadway at 48 in *On Your Toes*, and won an MGM contract; acted—all but invisibly— in *Lord Jeff, Young Dr. Kildare*, etc., playing ambassadors and dukes; after *The Man Who Came to Dinner*, went back to Hollywood as a star—bluff, bristling, and bearded; loved his beard—grew it in '27 after meeting his idol, George Bernard Shaw; "I am always mistaken for a Grand Duke or a Supreme Court Justice," he said. "My beard gets me the best service in the world. Waiters scurry at the wag of my whiskers. I am listened to with reverence.

231

Everywhere, people stand aside to let a Great Man pass. Best of all, I never have to shave"; a rampant individualist, he always lived alone in hotels or rented apartments ("I love loneliness"), lunched alone at the studio, dined alone of an evening at Mike Romanoff's ("and if anyone speaks to me, I bark!"), and raced about Hollywood alone in a red convertible with the top down; independently wealthy (his father owned many famous hotels, including Manhattan's Hotel Bristol, where he was born), he said: "I own no objects of any kind. I *want* no object of any kind—neither a watch, nor a what-not, nor a wife. I don't own anything except what I must, of necessity, wear" (and he wore only the best); came close to owning an Oscar—was nominated as Best Actor for *The Pied Piper* and as Best Support for *Since You Went Away*; idiosyncrasies aside, co-stars doted on him—was "Monty" to most, "The Beard" to some, and to Ann Sheridan, "Mr. Wool-Puss"; had gone from the groves of Academe to the theater; got his B.A. at Yale, his Ph.D. at Harvard, and returned to Yale for 12 years as professor of drama; among his celebrated students: poet Stephen Vincent Benet and novelist-playwright Thornton Wilder; was an upperclassman at Yale (and described as a "bitter, witty, unattractive young extrovert") when Cole Porter entered the school and became his protégé and lifelong crony; in the late '20s, directed two of the composer's Broadway hits: *Fifty Million Frenchmen* and *The New Yorkers*; is credited with aiding the composition of Porter's "It's De-Lovely"; the sight of the sun rising over Rio harbor caused the composer to murmur, "It's delightful," his wife to add, "It's delicious," and Woolley to chime in, "It's de-lovely"; naturally, he portrayed himself when Cary Grant played Cole Porter in *Night and Day*; held mixed feelings about the movie capital; said, "The most devastating and, at the same time, the most compelling thing about Hollywood is the way you are kept on a string and held dangling, with that Bucket of Gold there at the string's end"; found his "bucket of gold" when 20th Century–Fox stole him from Warners and made him the most lovable grouch of the '40s.

MOVIE HIGHLIGHTS: *Girl of the Golden West, Three Comrades, Man about Town, Life Begins at 8:30, Holy Matrimony, Irish Eyes Are Smiling, Molly and Me, The Bishop's Wife, Miss Tatlock's Millions, As Young As You Feel, Kismet.*

Teresa Wright

(b. Muriel Teresa Wright, Oct. 27, 1918, New York, N.Y.) Smiling-through-tears was the expected performance from this wistful star; early in her career, when her earnest, clean-scrubbed young face appeared on screen, it was a foregone conclusion that someone was sure to die—either herself (*Mrs. Miniver*), a beloved father (Herbert Marshall in *The Little Foxes*), an adored and adoring husband (Gary Cooper, as Lou Gehrig, in *The Pride of the Yankees*), or a favorite uncle (Joseph Cotten in *Shadow of a Doubt*); set two Academy Award records in '42: was nominated as both Best Actress (*The Pride of the Yankees*; lost) and Best Support (*Mrs. Miniver*; won), and had been nominated the year before as Best Support for *The Little Foxes*, her debut, making her the only actress ever to be Oscar-nominated for each of her first three films; reared by various relatives after her father (an insurance salesman) and mother divorced, she was in boarding school in Maplewood, N.J., when she decided to act; after experience in summer stock, understudied Dorothy McGuire in *Our Town* on Broadway; became a "name" when she won the ingenue role of Mary in the greatly successful *Life with Father* and was discovered by Hollywood's Sam Goldwyn; during her seven years as a Goldwyn star, she and the producer had a friendly but sometimes fractious relationship; an intelligent beauty who knew her own mind, she refused—firmly but quietly—to pose for "leg art," go to nightclubs on "arranged" dates, or to do publicity photographs in pinafores "whipping up a cake"; explained: "I don't *put* cakes into ovens. I *act* Why should an actress pretend to be occupied with kitchen chores when everyone knows she's never in one?"; married writer Niven Busch in '42, and when she became pregnant with the first of their two children, Niven Terrence (followed by Mary Kelly), Sam Goldwyn was irate, as it meant shelving a movie he'd planned for her; to an associate, he shrieked in his high-pitched voice: "Niven Busch ——— me. He got Teresa pregnant, and he did it deliberately because I fired him so I won't be able to make the picture with his wife. He——— me!"; the colleague calmly corrected him: "You've got it wrong. You're not the one he ——— "; years later, when doing makeup tests for *Enchantment*, Goldwyn insisted that Wright wear more lip rouge than she thought right for the character; the producer's "quiet rebel" went to Makeup, drew a wide streak from one ear lobe to the other, added another blob between her nose and chin, and had herself photographed; Goldwyn surveyed the result and, amused, sent for her; "I have on my desk," he said, mildly, "a picture of a very angry girl"; once more, without raising her voice, she won; "I'm not so soft," says the actress who specialized in playing gentle women. "Determined is the nice word for it, but *stubborn* is more accurate"; has said that Goldwyn finally dropped her "because I wouldn't go out on those dumb publicity tours"; divorced from Niven Busch in '52, she later returned to New York to live and work; movie career had taken a nose dive when, as a free lance, she accepted a minimal wage of $25,000 to act with Brando in *The Men*; once told columnist Rex Reed, "From then on, that's what my salary was listed as in Hollywood . . . and after that I never got the quality films again"; one outstanding exception: 1953's *The Actress* with Spencer Tracy (though segueing into mother roles—played Jean Simmons' in that—did diminish her as a star); in '59, married *Tea and Sympathy* playwright Robert Anderson; he published a largely autobiographical novel, *After*, in '73, based closely on his relationship with his first wife, who died of cancer, and dedicated it: "For Teresa"; divorced since '75, the star lives alone, acts mainly on stage in New York and in regional theaters, and says, "I don't miss anything about the Hollywood years."

MOVIE HIGHLIGHTS: *Casanova Brown, The Best Years of Our Lives, Pursued, The Trouble with Women, The Imperfect Lady, The Capture, Something to Live For, California Conquest, The Steel Trap, Count the Hours, Track of the Cat, The Search for Bridey Murphy, Escapade in Japan, The Restless Years, The Happy Ending, Hail, Hero! Roseland, Somewhere in Time.*

Jane Wyman

(b. Sarah Jane Fulks, Jan. 4, 1914, St. Joseph, Mo.) Two oil portraits of the star hang in her home—one shows her in a glamorous pose, the other as "Ma Baxter," the strong countrywoman she portrayed in *The Yearling* (the first picture for which she was Oscar-nominated as Best Actress); both were gifts from Ronald Reagan, then her husband; Reagan was her third; when young, she had been briefly married to a man whose name she never revealed publicly, and then, 1937–38, to millionaire dress manufacturer Myron Futterman; she and Reagan, who played sweethearts in *Brother Rat* and other movies later, were married in '40, had a daughter, Maureen (born on Wyman's 27th birthday), adopted a son, Michael, and divorced in '48; has said in recent years of the star-turned-president: "We're very good friends and I just adore him"—but she'd rather not talk about him, insisting it would be in "bad taste"; was married twice more, in '52 and '61, to the same man, studio music director Fred Karger, both marriages ending in divorce; made 74 movies, won the Best Actress Oscar for *Johnny Belinda* ('48), and was later nominated in the same category for *The Blue Veil* and *Magnificent Obsession*: her last film to date was 1968's *How to Commit Marriage*, in which she co-starred with Bob Hope; was pointed toward stardom from childhood by her stagestruck

German-born mother (her father was chief of detectives in St. Joseph); "I was one of those little curly-headed kids, with a button nose, and my mother thought I was destined for the movies. After all, if Jackie Coogan and Baby Peggy could do it, why not her little Sarah Jane?"; at 8, was flatly rejected by silent-movie producers, so it was back to Missouri and more ballet classes; was 15 when the family moved to California; her father, an older man, was especially hard hit by the Depression, and they "lost everything"; she has said: "I got into show business out of necessity. Overnight I was thrust from my safe little book-world into the world of job hunting. And I did the only thing I knew how to do—I danced"; movie choreographer LeRoy Prinz, son of her hometown dancing teacher, helped her get chorus jobs in *The Kid from Spain, King of Burlesque*, etc.; performing in public made her "quake with fear," she says, until she made the discovery that "the perfect shield for shyness is a bold exterior. I covered up my inner fears by becoming the cockiest kid in town—talking the loudest, laughing the longest, wearing the most garish make-up"; dying her raven-black hair and becoming a platinum blonde completed her newly manufactured image as a sharp-tongued, smart little cookie; between movie chorus jobs, was a radio singer ("Jane Durrell") on stations in New Orleans, Detroit, Chicago, etc.; character actor William Demarest, then also a Hollywood agent, spotted her at the Brown Derby, signed her as a client, got her a bit in *My Man Godfrey*, and then a stock contract at Warners; was given her new screen name by publicists at this studio, where she was under contract from '36 into the '50s; zeal to win was such that, filling out an early publicity questionnaire, she declared her ambition was "not to be just an actress but *the* actress at the studio"; became that finally, in successes like *The Glass Menagerie* and *Stage Fright*, after years of typecasting as a wisecracking blonde in *The King and the Chorus Girl, The Singing Marine*, etc.; personality change began when veteran actor Frank McHugh took her aside and, like a Dutch uncle, said, "There are two kinds of people in Hollywood. There are the 'closed people,' the careful ones who keep others at a distance, and they are seldom happy people. Then there are the 'open people,' who reach out and embrace the world—and they get back a lot of joy"; Ronald Reagan, reportedly, influenced her even more in this personal transformation; acknowledging this, she said in the '40s, "He was such a sunny person; I had never felt free to talk to anyone before I met Ronnie"; who could have predicted that the reborn "nice" Jane Wyman would achieve the greatest fame of her life, long after pronouncing herself "retired," on the hit television series "Falcon Crest," playing the nasty Angela Channing?

MOVIE HIGHLIGHTS: *Fools for Scandal, Torchy Plays with Dynamite, Tail Spin, Brother Rat and a Baby, My Love Came Back, Tugboat Annie Sails Again, Footlight Serenade, Princess O'Rourke, The Doughgirls, Make Your Own Bed, The Lost Weekend, Night and Day, One More Tomorrow, Magic Town, Cheyenne, Kiss in the Dark, Three Guys Named Mike, Here Comes the Groom, Just for You, So Big, Let's Do It Again, The Story of Will Rogers, All That Heaven Allows.*

Gig Young

(b. Byron Ellsworth Barr, Nov. 4, 1913, St. Cloud, Minn.; d. Oct. 19, 1978) No Academy Award winner ever had a stranger fate than this blithe-spirited, handsome man who won the Best Supporting Oscar as the oily dance marathon promoter in *They Shoot Horses, Don't They?* (had been nominated earlier in the same category for *Come Fill the Cup* and *Teacher's Pet*); making his final movie in Hong Kong, prophetically titled *The Game of Death*, he fell in love with and married German actress Kim Schmidt, 31, who played opposite him; she was his fifth wife; he'd been married previously, as a struggling actor, to Pasadena Playhouse actress Sheila Stapler, then, as a Warner Bros. newcomer, to much-older studio drama coach Sophie Rosenstein (was beside her when she died of cancer in '52), and finally, as a star, to actress Elizabeth Montgomery and Hollywood realtor Elaine Whitman (made him a first-time father, of Jennifer), both of whom divorced him; the latter, still known professionally as Elaine Young, once described Young as a "Jekyll-and-Hyde" personality, particularly when he was under the influence of alcohol; also said in her book, *Beverly Hills Confidential*, that his "snaky, corrupt" Oscar-winning character in *They Shoot Horses* was one "whose scars sometimes struck me as being so true to life it was as if he were playing a part of himself"; married Kim Schmidt on Sept. 27, 1978; three weeks later, according to police reports, he killed her and then committed suicide with the same .38 revolver; ex-wife Elaine is among those who remain convinced that Schmidt's death was accidental because "I know beyond a shadow of a doubt that sober he could not have perpetrated such a crime"; to Hollywood friends, Young was a man of vast charm, with a ready wry wit and a sense of humor that allowed him, often, to sign his personal letters "Gigham Young"; he began his movie career under his own name, in '40, with a bit part in a B picture at lowly PRC, *Misbehaving Husbands*; played many other minor roles as Byron Barr during his first two years at Warners (in *Dive Bomber, They Died with Their Boots On*; in '42, the studio gave him a new name, Bryant

Fleming, and a romantic lead with Stanwyck as a character named "Gig Young" in *The Gay Sisters*; when all the preview cards raved about "Gig Young," Warners redid the screen credits to read "Introducing Gig Young"; was finally famous at 29; had finished high school in Washington, D.C., where his father, once a cannery owner in Minnesota, was a government official; family refused to help when he chose to become an actor, so he studied tap and ballroom dancing at night, along with dramatics, while working as an auto salesroom handyman, then became a dance instructor; hitching his way to Hollywood, he built sets at a little theater in exchange for dramatic lessons while holding the usual odd jobs: hotel night clerk, gas station attendant, nightclub waiter; was a car-hop at a drive-in while attending the Pasadena Playhouse—on a scholarship—along with Victor Mature, Laird Cregar, and Helmut Dantine; camouflaging his Nordic features with makeup, Young made his professional stage debut in Los Angeles as Abie, the Jewish lad, in *Abie's Irish Rose*, and the many movie bits followed, leading to stardom; his career was interrupted for four years (1942–46) after he enlisted in the Navy; served as a pharmacist's mate 3rd class and saw action in the Salomons, New Guinea, and the Philippines; returned to Hollywood and resumed his career without a hitch, co-starring with Errol Flynn in *Escape Me Never*; later, continuing in movies, he became one of Broadway's most popular romantic comedy leads, starring in such hits as *Oh Men! Oh Women!*, *Under the Yum-Yum Tree*, and *There's a Girl in My Soup*.

MOVIE HIGHLIGHTS: *Captains of the Clouds, Air Force, Old Acquaintance, The Woman in White, Wake of the Red Witch, The Three Musketeers, Lust for Gold, Tell It to the Judge, Hunt the Man Down, Only the Valiant, Too Young to Kiss, You for Me, The Girl Who Had Everything, Arena, Torch Song, Young at Heart, The Desperate Hours, Desk Set, The Tunnel of Love, Ask Any Girl, That Touch of Mink, Lovers and Other Strangers.*

INDEX